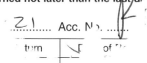

By the same author

Roald Dahl: A Biography
Romancing: The Life and Work of Henry Green

Editor

The Letters of John Wilmot, Earl of Rochester
Spirit of Wit: Reconsiderations of Rochester
The Lantern-Bearers: Essays by Robert Louis Stevenson

with Bridget Bennet

Grub Street and the Ivory Tower: Literary Journalism and Literary
Scholarship from Fielding to the Internet

V. S. PRITCHETT
A WORKING LIFE

Jeremy Treglown

Chatto & Windus
LONDON

Published by Chatto & Windus 2004

2 4 6 8 10 9 7 5 3 1

First published in Great Britain in 2004 by
Chatto & Windus
Random House, 20 Vauxhall Bridge Road,
London SW1V 2SA

Random House Australia (Pty) Limited
20 Alfred Street, Milsons Point, Sydney,
New South Wales 2061, Australia

Random House New Zealand Limited
18 Poland Road, Glenfield,
Auckland 10, New Zealand

Random House (Pty) Limited
Endulini, 5A Jubilee Road, Parktown 2193, South Africa

The Random House Group Limited Reg. No. 954009
www.randomhouse.co.uk

A CIP catalogue record for this book
is available from the British Library

ISBN 0 7011 7322 X

Papers used by Random House are natural,
recyclable products made from wood grown in sustainable forests;
the manufacturing processes conform to the environmental
regulations of the country of origin

Typeset by SX Composing DTP, Rayleigh, Essex
Printed and bound in Great Britain by
Clays Ltd, St Ives Plc

Contents

List of Illustrations

The author and publishers are grateful to the following for providing illustrations and granting their permission to reproduce them: A. Alvarez 19; Josephine Bryant 16, 24, 25, 26, 32; Chatto & Windus 18, 20, 34; Evelyn Hofer 26; Venetia Kay 9; Barbara Kerr 21; Elizabeth Paterson 32; Oliver Pritchett 1, 4, 5, 6, 7, 8, 10, 36; Clara Vulliamy 33.

Acknowledgements

This book was first suggested in 1989. V. S. Pritchett's health was then beginning to fail, and he and his wife understandably put the idea off. It was revived ten years later, after Pritchett's death, and the family couldn't have been more helpful. In her last illness, Lady Pritchett sent me messages of encouragement, urging me to write quickly 'so that I can read it'. I'm sorry not to have been quick enough. The nonagenarian Gordon Pritchett told me almost as much about his elder brother through his energetic personality as through his many stories. (When I arrived at his house for our second interview, he greeted me by singing and reciting favourite music-hall pieces of their mother's, at length and from memory.) Pritchett's daughter Josephine Bryant, and his son and literary executor Oliver Pritchett, talked to me frankly and at length, lent me letters and photographs, patiently answered my frequent queries and read drafts, without ever hinting at any direction the book might or might not have taken.

Apart from the immediate family, I was helped by talking to two of Dorothy Pritchett's sisters, Jean Davies and Edith Webb, and to three members of the family of Pritchett's first wife, Evelyn Maxwell (née Vigors): her son, Nicholas Maxwell; one of her daughters, Venetia Kay; and her sister's son, David Willison. Justin Murphy, Caspar Murphy, Matthew Pritchett and Georgia Pritchett talked to me vividly about their grandfather. Many of his surviving friends also gave me interviews. Like members of the family, some saw me more than once, and/or subsequently read drafts of parts of the book. For reasons that will become clear, I am particularly grateful to Barbara Kerr. I also thank A. Alvarez, Arthur Crook and Juliet Wrightson, Nell Dunn, Jason Epstein, Jocelyn Herbert, Evelyn Hofer, Elizabeth Jane Howard, Paul Johnson, Francis King, Naomi Lewis, Peter Matson, Derwent May, Elizabeth Paterson, Frances Partridge, Serena Rothschild, Claire Tomalin and Peter Vansittart. Numerous other people who knew Pritchett, or had information or suggestions about the project, took trouble to help. Their names appear in the Further Acknowledgements on pp. 252–4

Amanda Smyth and Ann Totterdell undertook research into

hundreds of fugitive pieces by and about Pritchett. Roy Foster was a constant source of encouragement and advice, and commented helpfully on a draft of chapter 2. Pritchett's last British agent, Michael Sissons, has given the project his support ever since it was first mooted. I also thank my own agents, Deborah Rogers in London and Amanda Urban in New York, and my editors, Jenny Uglow at Chatto & Windus, and Susanna Porter at Random House (USA) and indexer, Douglas Matthews.

Individuals apart, the main sources of information about Pritchett are the voluminous papers which he and his relatives and friends accumulated over more than seventy years: letters, journals, notebooks, drafts of books and stories, drafts even of reviews. It won't surprise anyone with an interest in the manuscripts of important British writers that most, though not all, of Pritchett's papers are split roughly equally between two great American archives: the Harry Ransom Humanities Research Center at the University of Texas and the Berg Collection at the New York Public Library. The Berg's holdings alone consist of fifty-six boxes of manuscripts, typescripts and proofs, plus several as yet uncatalogued boxes thickly packed with cuttings of Pritchett's journalistic work. Among the documents divided between the two libraries are forty-four notebooks, their contents ranging from scraps of overheard talk to near-complete narratives. In addition, substantial amounts of relevant material are stored in the archives of Pritchett's publishers and literary agents on both sides of the Atlantic, of the BBC, of magazines for which he wrote, especially the *New Statesman* and *The New Yorker*, in a variety of other collections (for example, at Princeton University and in the British Library), and also in private hands. Further details are given in the Notes and in the section on References on pp. 255–8.

I couldn't have worked through these materials in the time available without the generosity of four institutions. The Leverhulme Trust gave me a Senior Research Fellowship, freeing me from my duties at the University of Warwick for two years, and providing financial help with travel and research assistance. The University, and in particular Peter Mack and other colleagues in my department there, were as supportive as ever. The Ransom Center at Austin made me a Mellon Fellow in the autumn of 2001. Finally, the Dorothy and Lewis B. Cullman Center for Scholars and Writers at the New York Public Library awarded me its Margaret and Herman Sokol Fellowship in 2002–3. I thank Mrs Sokol and Mr and Mrs Cullman for their kindness and hospitality. It was a happy privilege to work day by day in the company of the other Fellows in my year and of the Center's then Director, Peter Gay. They gave me an inkling of what Pritchett experienced at the Residencia de Estudiantes in Madrid in the early 1920s, among writers of 'conscience and sensibility', all of them following 'some private footpath of the mind'.

My biggest debt of gratitude, though, as always, is to my wife, Holly.

JT, January 2004

I

Material

'What a price one pays for one's material,' V. S. Pritchett wrote to his best friend and fellow author Gerald Brenan, in the mid 1940s. Pritchett and his wife had just had their respective parents to stay. 'My father and Dorothy's mother are a pair of very low comedy characters and they devastate us. Dorothy's mother is raucous, ill bred & suspicious, my father is vulgar, hypocritical and never stops talking. It was awful.'[1]

He was joking, but he meant what he said about material, particularly in the case of his father. 'He is so *vulgar* so boring, so destructive,' he said on another occasion. 'I must write about him quickly, turn him into cash.'[2] He didn't need to remind himself. Cash was important. Pritchett was a serious imaginative artist but first and foremost he was a professional writer, one who took intense pride in managing to support himself as that. His father, the spendthrift mythomaniac and spiritual confidence trickster Walter Sawdon Pritchett, in one guise or another provided some of Victor Sawdon Pritchett's best material.

There was plenty more. V. S. Pritchett watched and listened to people with the absorption of a psychologist, the opportunism of a collector, the unconditional affection of a man to whom other humans were his sole religion. In the mid 1980s, which were also his own eighties (he was born in 1900), he told an interviewer,

The human race is almost mythological: it's a perpetuator of myths. I have no religious interests, except for the fact that religion is psychologically and historically very interesting. . . . I think that life contains its meaning unaided. I should like to think that a writer just celebrates being alive. I shall be sorry to die, but the notion of seeing life celebrated from day to day is so wonderful that I can't see the point of believing anything else.[3]

The novelist Peter Vansittart recalled how even a private conversation with the erstwhile docklands clerk and adventurous traveller was like being in a crowd:

> he seemed never far from the leather-works, the Spanish bar, Irish cabin, Corsican doss-house . . . Something about him invited confidences from shepherds, weekend Home Guards, colonels' daughters, suburban misfits on a spree, dockside boozers, aunts' lovers, sailors, malevolent or puzzled loners . . .[4]

To Martin Amis, one of the things that distinguished the older writer's fiction was that he 'went into ordinary people and showed us that they weren't ordinary. . . . [He] came away with their genius in all senses.' However far Pritchett had moved from his social origins, 'He didn't gentrify his imagination an iota. . . . Almost frighteningly intimate, he possesses his characters, he knows almost everything about them in a way that startles me when I look at him.'[5]

Pritchett was a small man with big appetites and energies. He was no glutton, but everyone who knew him well mentions his relish for good food and drink, and comfortable surroundings. In his happiest years, which were many, he and his wife Dorothy took a Lawrentian – sometimes even a Rabelaisian – zest not only in their sex life together, but in writing to each other about it. There's something of this interplay between hunger and connoisseurship in how he found material in everyone he met, everything he saw them doing or overheard them saying. They were used in the travel writing, which was always an important component of his huge output, including his first book, *Marching Spain* (1928). They went into his novels (to be a novelist was his main early ambition and at least one of the results, *Mr Beluncle*, ranks with any novel of the mid century). They went, too, into the more than a hundred short stories which have seemed to other writers, from Eudora Welty to A. S. Byatt and William Trevor to John Updike, among the most original of their time, or of any time. A dozen of these stories, involving characters and situations closely based on Pritchett's early life, were in effect drafts for sections of the two books which made him most famous and which will certainly last: his memoirs *A Cab at the Door* (1968) and *Midnight Oil* (1971). These portraits of the artist are also portraits of an age, a country, above all a class: the 'lower middle' class. As Pritchett's career was to illustrate, in terms of creative potential that social group was the strongest – the hungriest – as well as the largest in the fluid England of the twentieth century.

Even Pritchett's literary essays are not only humane but human. He approached books as he approached people: with sympathetic and respectful curiosity, and with undoctrinaire discrimination. He was easily amused and, though not easily pleased, keen to be. In his time, he was the most influential 'man of letters' in the English-speaking world, though he disliked the term (he preferred 'writer'). He is as vivid, sharp and funny a critic as Virginia Woolf, but he responded to a much wider range of writing than she did, both old and new. The reactions he recorded in his many thousands of reviews, radio talks and lectures are still alive because, like his fiction, they are so sharply impressionistic. Despite, or rather because of, his relative lack of formal education – he left school before he was sixteen – he had read more than anyone else, while never losing touch with the environment he had come from.

The fact that it's often hard to draw a line between Pritchett's work in different forms, not least between fiction and non-fiction, points to the sheer range of his achievement. The career of this great fiction writer, autobiographer, travel writer, critic – and also, though not yet published as such, letter writer and diarist – spanned his century. He played a crucial part in the continuing growth of traditional literary forms during modernism and postmodernism, building as he did on the techniques of nineteenth-century fiction. At the same time he carried on the supposedly fast-disappearing profession of a freelance critic, becoming an important broker in the literary exchanges between Britain, Continental Europe and the United States. In some of his responses to his social and educational formation, he both exemplified and helped to form his period. He has devoted fans everywhere in the English-speaking world, and of every age. Even so, if you mention the name V. S. Pritchett today, you have to be careful to distinguish him from V. S. Naipaul, or Terry Pratchett.

Pritchett would have been disappointed if he had known how his fame would decline in the years immediately following his death, but he wouldn't have been surprised or dismayed. Some of his best work was driven by his generous eagerness to show why this or that forgotten writer should still be read. Besides, if he saw the human race as 'mythological', one of his myths of himself was that he was uninteresting. 'Nothing continues to happen to me,' he wrote in his early fifties. He was daunted by having just heard the English novelist

Rosamond Lehmann and the American publisher Blanche Knopf discussing possibilities for Lehmann's next book. When Lehmann said, 'I might write about George Eliot,' Knopf replied, 'Why, did anything happen to her? Is there any colour in her life?'[6]

It was an absurd question, not least because Eliot, like Pritchett, devoted so much of her career to showing that every human life is interesting. But in any case, Pritchett's modesty shouldn't be taken at face value. At the time when he claimed that nothing happened to him, he was actually going through a crisis in his personal life – one which is recorded in painful detail in his letters and notebooks. The disavowal was the equivalent of a physical gesture he had, a distinctly Edwardian one, of pulling his chin wryly and a little sideways into the folds of his neck. It was a sign which combined affability, reassurance, mild self-scepticism. It was also comic, turning his face into a convulsion of malleable flesh. What would it become next? Would it disappear into his shoulders? And the movement had the effect of emphasising his lips: what they were saying, how they were saying it, even what they didn't say (Pritchett sometimes seemed to use his mouth for listening). Meanwhile, though, the gentle pantomime distracted attention from the alertness of his quizzical gaze. Because one of its motives, conscious or not, was to allow him to watch better. Self-effacement was among Pritchett's professional tools as a writer, as well as part of his personal magnetism.

Both contributed to the impression he gave of unusual happiness. Over all, and in the end, V. S. Pritchett does seem to have been happier than most people. Yet the qualities that were often seen as happy in him – especially his zest and energy and humour, his innocent appetites – were, like his writing, far from simple in effect.

His emphasis on myth is important because, given how much of him went into his writing, the man has to be seen to some extent through his versions of himself. Myths are cumulative and progressive, and this was how Pritchett's repeated explorations of his family and upbringing worked. He was a performer, an anecdotalist, always improving and adding to his repertoire of self-revelation. His friend the diarist Frances Partridge said, 'he was a bit of an actor, a great raconteur. . . . I see VSP always – when he was telling a story – acting movements, rather crouching ones, slightly grotesque. He wasn't a natural man. . . . I sometimes think he was an actor manqué and would have been a good comic.'

So the showman in Walter Sawdon Pritchett lived on in his gifted son. In his seventies, 'VSP', as he was always known, even gave readings from Dickens to audiences in America.[7] This aspect of his personality sometimes bothered the writer, because he knew too well that performance could dispense with truth. He often pondered the negotiations between the two in autobiography and came to believe that in writing about himself, there was 'no absolute truth': 'You write twenty pages and then you stop. Why is it that you are bewildered? Why do you have the sensation of being in a rowing boat in the middle of the ocean and have [sic] lost your oars? Who is this "I", you wonder; which of my many selves is writing?'[8] He concluded that, 'like my story telling mother, I was an inventive person. I was one of those . . . who invents himself and had not much capacity for self-analysis.' In a BBC radio interview, he made the same point more strongly. 'I inherit from my mother a tendency to turn everything that happens into a story and the story is a kind of lie, really. . . .'[9] Perhaps he was thinking of the fact that in *A Cab at the Door* and *Midnight Oil* he gives two completely different versions of his father's last words, neither of them – as was pointed out to him by his younger brother Gordon (in whose arms Walter died) – at first hand.[10]

To tell Pritchett's unexpectedly complex story, then, it helps to start with the story of the stories he told about it. They took various forms. His parents' marriage, for example, was an obsessive theme not only of his published work but of his conversation and letters, especially his long, vivid, unguarded correspondence with Gerald Brenan. 'I went to see my parents yesterday,' he wrote in September 1950:

In a little dark suburban room piled up with new books, hundreds of them, that have never been read, newly bound volumes of Christian Science publications, and so crowded with sofas, armchairs, desks & tables that one can hardly walk across it, sit my father & mother. She is white and skeletal, nervous and alert and the whole time she gazes at her husband with a hypnotised look of fear, desperation and hopelessness. He, spread in an armchair with his fat hands twiddling continuously on a spherical stomach, smiles continuously as he continuously talks about house property and what he said to the butcher. . . . My mother often opens her mouth to say a word, and a look of hatred comes over his face, a hatred all the more terrible because it is now mechanical and automatic. . . . The horrible notion of 'one flesh' and the fight to be the tongue of it.[11]

Like Pritchett's fictional characters, they are vividly, almost grotesquely present: that battling tongue could be a character in a Samuel Beckett play. But no one else who knew Walter and Beatrice seems to have thought of them in quite this way. This was partly a matter of family secrets. Victor's son Oliver, for example, was to be astonished by the stories of scams and bankruptcy his father wrote about Walter, who had impressed Oliver as 'absolutely the epitome of virtue and uprightness'. By this, Oliver wasn't, of course, implying that Victor's version wasn't true. Yet – if only in emphasis and degree – there was a subjective element in it. Oliver's sister Josephine remembered her Pritchett grandparents as much more ordinary than in her father's versions. The idea that Beatrice was downtrodden, so vehement in Victor's many accounts of her, didn't fit Josephine's recollection: 'No, I remember her as being a sweet, funny old lady who liked to laugh.' And Victor's younger brother Gordon felt strongly that the writer had exaggerated their mother's vulnerability and, with it, their father's faults.

To everyone, though, there was something magnificent about Walter's charlatanism. As Gordon recalled him,

> He was an impressive figure. He had all his clothes made in Savile Row, but I don't think he paid for many of them. He would produce a soft leather case with a real gold rim all round it. Inside would be an engraved card: 'Sawdon Pritchett' and, underneath, 'The Athenaeum'. He would walk in anywhere and say, 'Well, I'd like four of those. Send me the account. Here's my card.'

(The Athenaeum, needless to say, has no record of Sawdon Pritchett among its past members.) Gordon also remembered his father showing him a little book entitled *How To Avoid Payment of Debt*: 'He said it had belonged to his father but I don't believe a word of it.' Gordon was ninety-two years old when he told this story, and he had his own share of the family's appetite for myth making,[12] but there was nothing wrong with his memory. The useful pamphlet, *How To Avoid Payment of Debt. By a Solicitor* was published in 1901. The first of Walter's bankruptcies was filed in that year.

Victor was then one year old. To the lower middle class, so desperate to be more middle than lower, bankruptcy was a stain – one which, intensified by the fear that it would happen again, spread through Victor's early years. In some ways it was to colour his whole life. Though it was a nightmare and could lead the boy to feel suicidal, it was also a stimulus. For most of his long career, Victor was driven by the need to find intellectual and artistic scope without forfeiting financial security. But, as he recognised when he came to write about another financial fantasist, Honoré de Balzac, the storytelling ways by which he himself earned his living derived something from Walter's inventiveness about money.

On both sides, the family was socially very mixed. Victor's paternal grandfather was a Congregationalist minister in Yorkshire. In addition to Walter, the minister had another son, Edward, who, according to Victor, was a still blacker sheep. The details are muted in the published version of *A Cab at the Door*, but an early draft mentions 'horrifying rumours of drunkenness, police, prostitutes – the usual tale of a clergyman's son'.[13] In Pritchett's 1951 novel, *Mr Beluncle*, there is a loose-living and hard-drinking aunt who is a fictional version of Edward. But perhaps the fiction didn't start here. Already, we have to be on our guard. Edward, as a previously unknown cousin of Victor's told him after reading *A Cab at the Door*, emigrated to Canada, where he lived perfectly respectably and brought up a large family.[14]

Victor's maternal grandfather, meanwhile, had been a stable-boy and then a coachman, his grandmother a barmaid. Their volatile daughter Beatrice, Victor's mother, became a shop assistant in Kentish Town, north London, which is where she met Walter. One of Beatrice's sisters, by contrast, eventually married into a well-off family in Suffolk. When Victor was born, his parents were living near this sister in Ipswich, where Walter briefly had an ailing business as a newsagent and stationer. The rich relations were at the top of the hill, in the desirable recent Victorian development of Warrington Road. Walter, Beatrice and the baby lived above a shop in St Nicholas Street, a dilapidated part of the medieval town down by the docks, just along the road from an old Unitarian meeting house. One side of Victor's birthplace looked over the wonkily gabled street towards middle England; the other side towards the port and Continental Europe.

The combination of Walter's financial undependability and Beatrice's emotional fragility meant that the steadier of the couple's relations often, directly or indirectly, took charge of the young family. When they were small, Victor and one of his brothers, Cyril, lived for some time with Walter's parents in Yorkshire. William Pritchett, Walter's father, had struggled out of the working class – his father had been a North Sea trawlerman – to become a minister, first in Ripon[15] and then in the solid market town of Sedbergh, just south of the Lake District. It was in Sedbergh that Victor went to the first of his many schools, walking the steep short distance up Joss Lane behind his grandparents' square little manse, its walled garden opening on to a busy cattle market beyond the self-important Victorian stone chapel. From the school, now a shop, you can see over the roofs of the town – and also over the roofs of the exclusive 'public' school by which it is still dominated – to wild moorland and fells all around.

A little later, again in retreat from Walter's creditors, Beatrice took her children back to Ipswich for about a year, where they went to another primary school and began to find out not only about social divisions but about social mobility. Their aunt's in-laws, they learned, had prospered in shoemaking and had bought land at Felixstowe which, when the town became a resort, they developed lucratively, building a waterworks and a hotel as well as several houses. There was a lesson for the children here, about how people could use enterprise and ambition more shrewdly than Walter.

All Victor's siblings eventually did well. Cyril became a successful buyer of materials for women's clothes and, later, a farmer. There was a touch of their father's grandiosity about him – at one point he employed a valet at his flat in Lower Regent Street – but he paid his dues, metaphorically as well as literally. In the Second World War, despite his age and the fact that farming was a 'reserved occupation', Cyril enlisted in the Royal Navy, served as a gun loader on a destroyer accompanying Russian convoys, was commissioned and ended up as liaison officer on the French battleship *Richelieu*. His hobbies included binding books in leather, among them his brother's. ('It is his passion,' Victor grumbled, half pleased. 'It is his ambition to supply me with Prize-Giving copies of all my works.')[16] The boys' forthright, artistic sister Kathleen, a skilful ceramicist, married a printer at the Bank of England.[17] Gordon, after a period spent, like his brothers, in Walter's immediate thrall, and with the interruption of wartime service as a tank driver, made a successful independent career in the clothes trade. He bought and sold shops, sang enthusiastically in the church choir, and retired in comfort to a sizeable house and garden in Sudbury, Suffolk.

Victor's aspirations were more intense and far-reaching, but all four of Walter's children were determined from an early age not to live from hand to mouth. If the fastidious Cyril had ever gone to the Public Record Office to look up Walter's bankruptcy records, the book restorer in him, as well as the embarrassed son, would have been horrified. When the heavy volumes are taken out of their boxes, their dry leather bindings crumble like biscuit, leaving the reader literally red-handed. But the names inked in black on vellum will stay for ever: army officers, butchers, coal merchants, confectioners, drapers, engineers, florists, 'gentlemen' and 'gentlewomen', grocers, hosiers, jewellers, journalists, plumbers, publicans, shoemakers, solicitors, spinners, tailors, tobacconists, veterinary surgeons: a ledger of failed hopes and of fear. Of astounding buoyancy, too, at least in one case. In 1901, the 840th listed as having succumbed to his creditors was Walter Sawdon Pritchett, of Woodford, Essex, 'late Ipswich Stationer'. He was twenty-four.

For Walter this was just the beginning, a rite of passage. He never went back to newspapers and stationery but, with dauntless optimism and charm, turned to other enterprises, from women's clothes and accessories to, in the First World War, aircraft design ('he knew nothing about aeroplanes,' Gordon recalled), from art needlework to property speculation to faith healing.

All of Walter's schemes depended on faith, one way or another. They made a no less vivid impression on the other children than on Victor. Gordon recalled how in the late 1920s, Walter was making

> things like Magyar sashes, tea-cosies, expensive things for ladies to keep their handkerchieves in – there had been a big trade in that up to the '14–18 War but after that, of course, it was dead as a doornail because women didn't lead that sort of life. So his trade went down and down and down and he borrowed more and more and more.

Immediately after the First World War, there was an amnesty for undischarged bankrupts. Walter always found just enough people, usually fellow members of his Christian Science congregation, who could be persuaded to invest in him, to work for him, to buy from him – though never as many as he expected. He was a big man, eventually seventeen or eighteen stone, elegantly dressed, light in his hand-made shoes,[18] forceful and persistent: a formidable figure from anyone's perspective, let alone that of a sensitive, emulous son. In old age, undaunted by the dubious fame he had acquired through Victor's writing, Walter would visit the more upmarket bookshops such as Bumpus's in Oxford Street, and engineer a conversation with one of the staff in which his connection to the famous author would be let slip and judicious enquiries would be made about the state of his son's sales. Meanwhile, his own career as a bankrupt went from strength to strength. Even when he was in his seventies, Walter's bank had to foreclose on him when he failed to find tenants for the flats into which he had converted the former family home in Bromley.

Houses were among Walter's main passions: one which Victor, despite his resistance, obliquely inherited. Very often in V. S. Pritchett's work, people are defined in relation to the houses they aspire to, buy, live in, lose. English suburban villas of the kinds that were still going up in every London suburb, with their mix of uniformity and self-differentiation – gables, gargoyles, castellations, balustrades, pillars, cornices, mythological statuary over elaborate porches, as well as disproportionately significant-seeming differences of height, width, shape of garden – all this meant as much to Pritchett as to his younger contemporary John Betjeman. He had to learn early on how to tell one house from another. Following the family's moves on a map is like doing one of those puzzles where you connect dots to make a picture, drawing lines up and down and in and out – except that in this case no picture emerges, just frequent movement to every point of the London compass. *A Cab at the Door* has that title not because cabs were his parents' usual means of transport (though Walter, left to himself, had a taste for it), but because his father was so often in flight from creditors:

> And then – the magic of the man! – without warning we would . . . get up one morning to find my mother in her fawn rain-coat (her only coat), and hat . . . A cabby and his horse would be coughing together outside the house and the next thing we knew we were driving to an underground station and to a new house in a new part of London, to the smell of new paint, new mice dirts, new cupboards, and to race out into a new garden to see if there were any trees and start, in our fashion, to wreck the garden and make it the byword of the neighbourhood. . . .

It was, Victor says a shade too neatly, the beginning of his love of 'change, journeys and new places'. After Ipswich, the family moved to Woodford in Essex, out to Derby, back to Woodford, then to Palmers Green in north-west London, to Balham in the southern suburbs, west to Uxbridge, Acton, Ealing and Hammersmith, south again to

Camberwell Green, then once more to Ipswich, before arriving at the nearest Beatrice and the children found to stability, in the respectable, semi-rural south-eastern commuter regions of Dulwich and Bromley.

It's not surprising that, like other rogue fathers of writers, Walter became his son's obsession, even his muse. Victor worked and reworked him, comically, bitterly and as a warning. Walter warned not only that imagination can get out of hand, but that charming, forceful men can harm those closest to them. In all this, Victor's views of his father – which changed as his own life changed – differed in some respects from those of others, not only because he was so imaginative, but because it was sometimes his fears of himself, as much as of his father, that had come to absorb him.

In the development of Pritchett's lifelong preoccupation with auto-biography, as with much else in his life, a crucial year was 1935. True, his family upbringing and day-to-day experiences had from the start been pervasive elements in his work. The first story he published, when he was twenty-one, fictionalises a suburban weekend at home with his parents and siblings, and the arrival of a newcomer, Curly, a boyfriend of the narrator's sister. (Curly dares to sit in their father's chair, which anticipates other aspects of the boy's revolutionary impact: the family collectively start to go to bed later on Saturday evenings and forget about going to church the next day.) 'Cyrano of the Gasworks' appeared in the *Westminster Gazette* on 19 August 1922, the year after Victor left home to live in Paris. Fiction writers credited by name in the magazine that summer included E. Nesbit, Aldous Huxley and Richard Hughes, but Pritchett's story was simply initialled 'VSP'. The abbreviation stuck.[19]

Two weeks earlier, according to a ledger which he kept meticulously from then until 1935,[20] Pritchett had submitted a piece to the *Christian Science Monitor* for the first time. It was about a walking trip undertaken partly in homage to Robert Louis Stevenson ('RLS'), south of Paris from Melun to Orléans by way of Fontainebleau.[21] By the time it appeared, Pritchett had already had several other pieces published in the *Monitor*: light articles about his travels, his landlady, old school friends. In February 1923, two months after his twenty-second birthday, he became the paper's correspondent in Ireland and his career as a professional writer was under way. In France, Ireland, Spain, the USA, Canada and elsewhere, he wrote about whatever he was experiencing: the journalism is a serial autobiography. Simultaneously, in his other writing he turned it all into fiction. Although 'Cyrano of the Gasworks' was his first published story, Victor later often spoke of a different start, when an episode he watched and heard in an oyster bar in Dublin went straight on to paper as 'Fishy'.[22]

Not until 1935, though, when he was at the traditional mid point of any life, did Pritchett try to give a sense of the entirety of his early years, and of where and how 'the vocation as a writer . . . came to me'. He had been asked to contribute to a collection of autobiographical pieces by various authors, among them A. J. Cronin, Wyndham Lewis and V. Sackville-West, called *Beginnings*. The result was a maquette for the much later *A Cab at the Door* and is an absorbing, as well as very funny, summary of how he saw himself.

In *Beginnings*, Pritchett economically describes his forebears: a cheerful, storytelling great-uncle who had been a fishmonger; his father and clergyman grandfather, 'men of egotistical and romantic nature, who loved words' and whose religious feelings had a big effect on his imagination.[23] He touches on the lack of good books in his parents' household and his education at a 'board school', where he was first encouraged to write. He mentions how Spain made an early impression on him when he read an article about the Alhambra in the *Children's Encyclopaedia*. He wrote a narrative poem set there, which he took to school. ('I . . . lingered near the master, hoping for the word "genius" to come from him. He seemed to avoid me.')[24] His ambition was to be a poet: he prayed that he might become Poet Laureate, or 'Poet Lawrence', as he later described having misread the title, by the time he was twenty-one. He also fantasised about being one of the Lake Poets, a more difficult dream to sustain in Dulwich than in Sedbergh, but one facilitated by the modest boating lake in the local park. His father learned of his literary ambitions and derided them. Poets were dirty, the fastidious man said, and dirty men always got the sack. The boy was discouraged, but not for long. On Walter's advice, he read Marie Corelli's bestseller *The Master Christian*[25] and his fantasies changed direction: 'for many months one winter I wished to be a blind organist in a church that caught fire, and to rescue a beautiful woman from the flames. I set to work upon a novel.'[26] Walter continued the attack on his son's writing and also on his addiction to a boys' comic, the *Magnet* (soon to be canonised by George Orwell), some copies of which Walter threw into the fire. Once again, though, even while trying to thwart him, Victor's father showed him a way forward: 'Now, what about John Ruskin – there's a fine man for you.'

Few writers have been more fair-minded than V. S. Pritchett. Even when describing discouragement and humiliation, he can't help revealing their opposites. Born and brought up in south-east London, Ruskin was a local hero there. With his sense of the intrinsic value of work, and his secular gospel that art could transform anyone who submitted to it, he was a turning point for Victor. Soon, the boy was reading Francis Bacon, Balzac, Chateaubriand.

He was good at foreign languages and, once he got to Alleyn's School in Dulwich, he had a chance to develop the skill. But a more intimate influence was his mother. In the eyes of the self-absorbed teenager, his father's scornful domineering was directed more or less equally at Victor and her. As a child, Victor was more like his mother than his brothers were – very short in height, animated, emotionally labile – and they had other things in common. In particular, they often sang together, Beatrice playing the piano: 'Bless This House', 'Shipmates o' Mine', 'Come to the Fair', 'My Ain Folk'.[27] No one knew how she had learned to read music, but she could. All the children enjoyed these sing-songs but (though he doesn't say this in his memoirs) it was mainly with Victor that Beatrice performed. Just as Victor sang to the same music sheet as his mother, so, when the First World War added external dangers to a vulnerability already heightened by her husband's spendthriftness and absences, the son entered into her fears, not least of air raids. Although the word 'material' wasn't yet in his vocabulary, it occurred to him that he could use this sympathy in a school writing exercise: 'why not write as if I were a woman and very afraid?'[28]

The article in *Beginnings* stops at one of Pritchett's significant starting points: his leaving home for France. In the three and a half decades which separate this piece from *A Cab at the Door*, he worked over the same material in many different forms, including his novels *Nothing Like Leather* – published, like *Beginnings*, in 1935 – and the later *Mr Beluncle*.

Pritchett's first job, when he was sixteen, was sorting skins in the docks at Bermondsey. 'There's nothing like leather,' adults would say to the unimpressed boy, by way of encouragement. The opening pages of *Nothing Like Leather* are Zolaesque in the detail and resentful ferocity with which Pritchett recalls his feelings about what seemed at the time to be his fate: 'Lives are being consumed . . . as well as coal; lives are being treated, soaked, tanned, dressed and worn out. Take a man, skin him, put the skin into the soak of work and watch the rest of him flutter away in the black flag of smoke.'[29] The narrative is often as closely textured as a short story, but its scope is that of a nineteenth-century family saga.* It's also at some points a prose-poem about the lives of working people – one which shows the influence not only of Zola, and also Balzac, but of D.H.Lawrence.

Mr Beluncle is more nuanced and much funnier. Although the most overtly autobiographical of Pritchett's novels, it is also the one which works best in its own right and, for that reason, it needs to be treated separately. From the point of view of the persistent, multifarious development of Pritchett's thinking about himself and his family, its interest lies partly in the fact that it took him more than a decade to write. It was his last novel and, although it wasn't intended as that, he acknowledged after completing it in 1950 that if he wrote another, he would be 'bound to slip into something autobiographical'.[30] Between then and the publication, twenty years later, of *A Cab at the Door* and *Midnight Oil*, Pritchett drew again and again on his own experiences, including in studies of countries and cities which had meant a lot to him: Spain, London, New York, Dublin.[31] The process was one of long gestation, carried on not only in his published work, but in his copious notebooks and correspondence.

The earliest letters of Victor's which survive were written to his younger brother, Gordon, starting in 1918 and continuing through the 1920s.[32] Victor's anger at Walter's inadequacy and at the mistakes that had been made in his own upbringing was so strong that from early on his protectiveness towards his siblings, and particularly to Gordon – eight years his junior – earned him another nickname, 'Uncle Vic'. Mixed with Uncle Vic's relief at escaping from home to Paris was increasing anxiety about having left Gordon to his fate.

*The ambition and greed which, after his marriage, increasingly dominate Mathew Burkle (who in the book's earliest drafts was called Horatio Beluncle) are clearly based on Walter Pritchett, though several of his experiences were Victor's own. The book is an early attempt to settle scores with Walter, not least through its sympathetic attention to the women in Burkle's life. Among these are his downtrodden wife, Dorothy, and her rival Henrietta Petworth, whose father owns the tannery where Mathew works and who makes Mathew – with whom (like Walter and his own business partner) she has an on-off *amitié amoureuse* – a partner in the company. Henrietta is for a time a suffragette and the portrait of her, though patchy and sometimes improbably plotted, is one of Pritchett's several explorations of the predicament of an emancipated unmarried woman – intelligent, vulnerable and in various ways ill used by men. The final section, in which Dorothy gains strength from her children and Henrietta brings a new man into the business, is called 'The Rise of the Women', but it is really about the sinking of Mathew. Literally so. He misses his footing and falls into the tannery pit, as Victor had once done; but, unlike Victor, he drowns.

To begin with, his letters to the boy are jaunty and descriptive. Some are in verse doggerel, several are illustrated with cartoon sketches – at this stage, Victor half wondered whether he might be an artist as much as a writer, and his rapid drawings are full of life – and there's nonsense aimed at the twelve-year-old's enthusiasms, especially for animals. In one, the affectionate Victor builds a nonsense fantasy around a pet shop on the Ile de la Cité which he passed every day, with its 'snakes and ladders, an occasional ludo, three llamas, and a large snapdragon . . . also peahens & peanuts & pease puddings'.[33] He parodies school slang – 'Oh youngest of the Beans, In fact the greenest of the haricots blossoming . . . How does the world treat thee & has your house won the football cup?'[34] – and also the material of school lessons: 'Gordanus These presents:– Whereas I the undersigned and over fed acknowledge receipt of a piece of paper

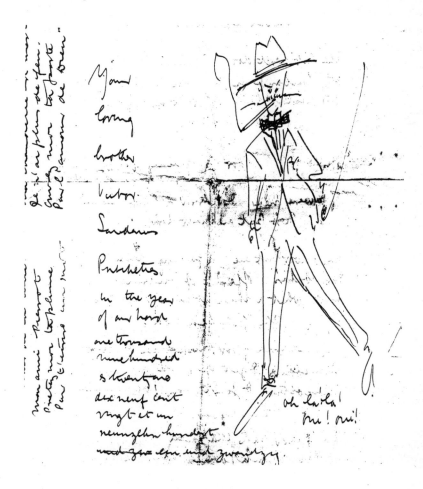

covered in ink marks, alleged to be a letter . . .'[35] There is news about what he's doing: growing a moustache, working as a travelling salesman ('I've been trying to persuade people that gum & glue are the only decent things on earth, but few believe it'), going for long hikes in the countryside and meeting French people of all kinds. The element of fantasy in his new life is clear from a postcard which he sent Gordon from Orléans, signed 'your gipsy brother'.[36]

Around 1925, though, the tone changes. Gordon was now sixteen, the age at which Victor had been forced by Walter (who was in turn under pressure about this from his own father) to leave school. But Gordon, who had followed Victor to Alleyn's, actually wanted to leave, and 'there was no one in the family to talk to, other than VSP'. Gordon was bored and had fallen in love with a girl called Mary Lockwood whom he thought he wanted to marry. He had noticed, too, that, whatever Victor's own feelings about it, going out to work at that age hadn't done him much harm (a view which Victor himself also eventually came to, though he was always ambivalent about it).

Gordon's plan was to become a postman. His brother's response was instant and fierce:

why the blazes you immediately want to leave school at the moment when your scholastic career is looking up I'm damned if I can see. I spend quite a lot of time vainly regretting that I was not able to continue my education. You dont even know what you want to do. You must have some special bent. Why don't you thrash it out with your form master and housemaster. 'The City' absorbs thousands of young fellows like you every year, puts unaccustomed money in their pockets for a few years; & then wears them down to its ruts & routine. Why not stay, have a shot for an exhibition, or at least get an extra year which may be the making of you.*[37]

Victor was in New York by the time he wrote this, and was in a position to compare English attitudes to education with what he had seen of American ones, for Gordon's benefit.

American youths, they sweat at school. They strive for education. They even go as waiters in hotels to pay their way to the universities.

---

*Pritchett was casual about punctuation, and so were several of his correspondents. I have reproduced what they wrote, e.g. 'dont', with few corrective '[sic]'s.

They are not doing it for fun. It's the most necessary thing there is . . . No one at home takes me seriously about this. They will say 'Education doesn't matter. You must work your way through.' That's all nonsense.

But the main element is his deep resentment at the obstacles he believed he himself was meeting: 'the man of education starts at a premium every time. I know I'm right about this.'

Gordon let himself be persuaded to stay on at school until he was eighteen, though he didn't go to university. But was Victor as right as he thought he was about his own disadvantages? Certainly, like several other English authors of the mid century, Laurie Lee and Patrick Leigh Fermor among them, he got crucial elements of his education less from teachers than from travelling and from his own reading. But although he changed schools often, their standards were in fact high. He himself acknowledged that the teaching at one of his 'board' (i.e., state) schools, Rosendale Road School in Dulwich, was imaginative and stimulating. And at thirteen he went to Alleyn's, then as now among the best of the ancient English grammar schools. Embarrassed by feeling an outsider, oppressed by some of the more pedantic masters, he nonetheless had an excellent formal grounding there, especially in modern languages, which were to be of far more use to him than the Greek and Latin of his more expensively educated contemporaries.[38] (Not that Alleyn's cost nothing; Walter's business partner and, it seems, platonic mistress, 'Miss H', paid the fees.)

Reading Pritchett's memoirs at a time when more than a third of British eighteen-year-olds go on to some form of higher education, it's worth remembering that compulsory schooling beyond even the age of eleven was to his parents a novelty, one which had been introduced in his own lifetime, in 1902. Historically and by the standards of his family background – though not, of course, of his aspirations – going to Alleyn's was an exceptional privilege. Even his having to leave just before he was sixteen, though to him a lasting grievance, was far from unusual. At the time, out of every hundred British children, fewer than sixteen stayed on to that age; less than four beyond it. Only one or two per cent continued into higher education.[39] If Pritchett was excluded, so, too, were most of his contemporaries and many of them felt as passionately about it as he did. The pages of *John o'London's Weekly*, a magazine for aspiring writers in which he was later published, were stuffed with ads for part-time study and correspondence courses, aimed at this market. 'U can have a college training . . . for a few shillings monthly' promised Bennett College, Sheffield; 'Do *your* words hit the bull's eye?' asked the proprietors of the Kleiser New Course in Practical English and Mental Efficiency, 'or do they miss the mark and fall weakly aside, causing you loss and embarrassment?' Some of Pritchett's later success, in fact, has to be attributed to the number of readers who identified with, and found hope in, his life story.

Pritchett often admitted later that he had been lucky not to end up on the middle-class treadmill, which he suspected would have led to his becoming a schoolteacher: 'I had had a narrow escape.'[40] He also came to think that many of his contemporaries who had been to boarding schools suffered from being fixated on that period in their lives. But the myth of deprivation – Dickensian except in the good humour with which he treats it – remained important to him; indeed, was as much of a fixation as anything written about by the boarding-school memoirists.

Alleyn's was not a bad place for a budding writer. Ever since its founding by the Elizabethan actor after whom it was named (Marlowe's leading man and a son-in-law of John Donne), the school had nourished a strong arts tradition. When Pritchett was there, the future novelist C. S. Forester was among the senior pupils. Through what the curriculum required, as well as his own enthusiasms, Victor read a lot, and not shallowly. For the rest of his life he kept the copy of William Aldis Wright's 1880 edition of Bacon's *Advancement of Learning*, a set text which he bought second-hand when he was fourteen and which he annotated alongside the comments of its previous owner.[41] However deep his regrets about his schooling, he must have taken comfort in Bacon's criticisms of 'distempers of learning' such as affectation, excessive systematisation, narrowness and over-intellectualisation, 'a kind of adoration of the mind and understanding of man; by means whereof, men have withdrawn themselves too much from the contemplation of nature, and the observations of experience, and have tumbled up and down in their own reason and conceits. . . .' Bacon would have approved of Pritchett's career, with its strong basis in practical experience.

Even while Pritchett was still at school, of course, much of that experience happened outside the classroom. *A Cab at the Door* is the mainly suburban counterpart of Laurie Lee's bucolic *Cider with Rosie* (1959). Both trace early twentieth-century English childhoods rooted in place and flowering into an intense pre-adolescent sexuality. Later, at a sage, married twenty-four, while sceptical of Gordon's being in love at sixteen, Victor admitted that he 'also was, and have been tons of times with many, many women, they are all so adorable. Some I was in love with for a long time, quite deeply in love too & wanted to marry them. I am young enough still to be in love with my own wife, but I'm damn glad I didn't marry the first woman I fell in love with. . . .'[42]

That first wife, as we'll see, was one of the few people whom Pritchett didn't bring to life in his own memoirs, but his books are otherwise full of nostalgia for the diffuse sexual longings of childhood. There's the tall, voluptuous schoolgirl Else, for example, with her 'wide warm mouth' and her rumoured affairs with the teachers – Else, who steps imperiously out of a rowing boat in the middle of the lake in Dulwich Park and wades to join Victor on the bank, whose skirt Victor helps to dry and who asks him to show her his poems. In the ruminative intensity of his autobiographies, their mix of tenderness and comedy, and the stealthy revelation of the narrator through his observation of and feelings about other people, Pritchett is an English Proust – but because of the obvious differences between the two writers' social worlds, this hasn't generally been said. He wrote so evocatively about Else that a reader was prompted to send him a photograph of her, half a century after they had both known her. Her full name was Eileen Stulchen and, in a prosaic ending which could have come out of one of Pritchett's fictions, it transpired that she had grown up to marry a local builder who became a successful developer.[43]

The architectural surroundings of romances like this were for the most part Victorian and Edwardian – in a word, new. Victor was named after Queen Victoria, who was still alive when he was born. His childhood world – those hansom cabs – can seem so remote to modern readers that one easily forgets that it was not only contemporary to him, but lacking in much of the visible history to which he later responded, and which his upbringing had made him long for: that 'growing piety towards the London past' which was eventually stimulated, he says, by visits to lunchtime organ recitals at the medieval City church of St Bartholomew's, Smithfield ('The one real church, for me'), when he was working in the leather trade.[44] Until then, his was the age and the suburban environment of the new man, of H. G. Wells's Kipps and Mr Polly, of people who, in the upper-class phrase of the time, came from nowhere. His father's eager if ill-judged self-identification with modernity in its commercial, entrepreneurial aspects was one of the things Victor was rebelling against. When he broke free for Paris, it was not – as for many other artists who made similar journeys around the same time – to find the modern, but to escape it.

One of Walter's modernisms was Christian Science. Every week, Victor and his siblings walked to church with their father in his opulent Sunday best, and imbibed Mary Baker Eddy's hotchpotch of late nineteenth-century beliefs: a counter-rational late Transcendentalism not unconnected to the rise of Spiritualism, but firmly balanced by optimistic worldliness. As the historian Bryan R. Wilson has put it in his study of new religions in early twentieth-century Britain, the real concern of the creed – which had been founded in Boston, Massachusetts, but had spread quickly through North America and across the Atlantic – was 'reassurance about this world, rather than promises about the next'.[45] Christian Science is best known for its views on illness, but it also deals with 'other sorts of problems – business, unemployment . . . anxiety of every kind'. It does this partly through the notion of 'defensive work' – what a sceptical outsider would call putting your head in the sand. But if the adherents of Christian Science were encouraged by Jesus's admonition that they should take no thought for the morrow, they were also urged to take plenty of thought for their fellow votaries. As with most young religions, there was a freemasonry in its activities. This helped its rapid expansion in the fast-growing English suburbs which were the Pritchetts' home ground. No other sect showed such a rise. While Congregationalism, for example – Walter's father's church – was static, the more self-indulgent organisation to which the expansive Walter belonged grew twenty-fold between 1902 and 1940.[46]

Victor soon rejected Christian Science, along with all metaphysics, but his autobiographies don't disguise either the extent to which he went along with it as a teenager, or its usefulness to his early writing. It provided him with material (one of his best-known stories, 'The Saint', came out of his disenchantment with the faith). More important, it gave him an immediate professional entrée as a writer, in the pages of the *Christian Science Monitor*.

The *Monitor* was a daily newspaper run, ultimately, by the First Church of Christ, Scientist in Boston, Mass. But the church gave it a good deal of freedom, and the paper's international organisation and, even more, its readership gradually extended far beyond the Christian Science movement. In 1922 a new editor, Willis J. Abbot, took over, shaking up the editorial staff, appointing a new head of the European

Bureau and putting a bohemian Yorkshireman, Sisley Huddleston (formerly of *The Times* and the *Westminster Gazette*), in charge of the Paris office. Among the changes were an increase in the number of light essays and columns, which Abbot brought together in a section called 'Home Forum'.[47] 'VSP' was among the first new bylines to appear in his pages. The *Monitor* was the only paper which published Pritchett regularly in his twenties. In its columns, he began to find his literary voice – at first, rather *too* literary a one – and, with it, much of his personality. The paper's editorial mix of intelligent factual reporting with upbeat conservative apoliticality – what Bryan Wilson calls an ethos of 'contentment with the established order of political and economic arrangements'[48] – was not always good for his work, either at the time or later. But by tying him in to the support systems and professional contacts of Christian Science, Walter Pritchett proved once again to be more of a help to his son's writing than was clear to either of them. In this as in other respects, the Oedipal drama of Victor's memoirs has to be interpreted with caution.

The same is true of Pritchett's account of his early environment as a cultural desert. Not only did his schools and his religion help him a great deal, but so, too, did some of his personal relationships. There's a telling reminder of this in a letter he sent in his sixties to a dilettante writer friend, James Stern, whom he was trying to console for his small output. Pritchett told Stern a story he would soon put into *A Cab at the Door*, about an Ipswich cousin, Hilda, who, on learning that he wanted to be a writer, inscribed a volume of Victor Hugo's poems for him with Alfred de Vigny's words '*Seul le silence est grand; tout le reste est faiblesse*' (Only silence is grand; everything else is feeble).[49] As Pritchett tells it, the joke is at the expense of his own overproductiveness, as well as Hugo's. What's most interesting about it, though, is the glimpse of an area of the young Pritchett's life in which so literate a cousin existed. Rereading *A Cab at the Door* in this light, one is struck by the number of other cultivated people whom he not only came into early contact with, but who actively looked out for him: the neighbouring Carters with their enthusiasm for Thucydides; the Racine-loving Mrs O'Dwyer, who tried to get Beatrice Pritchett to share her interests ('Mrs Preech, vy don't you educate yourself. Give up the vashing. I'm reading a book, vat are you doing? Read. Improve your mind.');[50] the art teacher who gave Victor eight volumes of Ruskin as a prize; the many book lovers whom he met at work; the exuberant and talented French pianist in Bromley who became a close friend in his late teens.

None of this is to suggest that Pritchett falsified his background. While his voluminous letters, journals, notebooks and other unpublished materials make one's sense of his early life richer, suggesting as they do that it offered stimuli and opportunities of kinds not generally associated with him (least of all by himself), much of the basic information is to be found, if only between the lines, in his published writings. Just as his fiction drew heavily on the material of his life, so his life writing employed some of the devices of fiction. The memoirs contain pages of comic dialogue that could go straight into a story, even a play. At first, most of the attention is on people other than Victor. The drama only gradually becomes his own. The autobiographer is too much of an artist not to realise that a transition has to occur. By way of achieving it, in the closing pages of A Cab at the Door he reflects movingly on the problem, for his siblings as well as himself, of coming to a settled and fair understanding of Walter.

There have been hints of this earlier. He describes how the intelligent Hilda found Victor's teenaged attitude to his father no more than a rather clichéd invention, 'as if I were suffering from a well-known illness'. 'He is a dear jolly man,' Hilda says. 'You're lucky to have such a father. I adore him.'[51] It's after this change of gear that Pritchett turns to the scene in which, 'moved because I could see he was moved', son says goodbye to father at Victoria Station. The book's first words are collective, in the first person plural: 'In our family, as far as we are concerned . . .' But at the end, in perfect equilibrium with that opening, the narrator is emphatically alone: 'I became a foreigner. For myself that is what a writer is – a man living on the other side of a frontier.'

There is a change in the writing of the next volume, Midnight Oil, but many aspects continue. Both books are memorable for the Dickensian vividness with which they describe objects in relation to people (Victor's rich uncle's clock 'like a temple' on the mantelpiece); for their evocation of the ordinary life of home and street – food, quarrels, games, mischief: shredding calico window blinds to smoke in a pipe; above all for the frankness of their recall: the fact, for example, that the First World War seemed a liberation to the teenaged Victor. In all this, he puts things down as if they had just happened for the first time, apparently without literary artifice or improving idealism. A good deal of contrivance was actually involved. But the aim was to make it new: an ancient ambition, though one which, at the time he was describing, was made to seem distinctively modern by a conjuring trick of Ezra Pound's.

It would be hard to think of two writers more dissimilar than Pritchett and Pound. Yet in one of those coincidences which frustrate cultural historians in their attempts at pattern making, the avant-garde experimental poet and literary activist was in London throughout Pritchett's adolescence, publishing busily. Pound arrived in Paris with James Joyce in 1920, only a year before Pritchett. As Pritchett later confessed, or half boasted, he was oblivious that Paris was the centre of international modernism, not only when he moved into the avenue de Bourdonnais in May 1921 but throughout his time in France. There's nothing whimsical about this. Part of his importance as a writer lies in how much he valued and exploited the traditions of realist prose fiction and, through his criticism, encouraged others to do the same. It became a matter of deliberate choice, but he was plain about the fact that it began in ignorance: 'When I read memoirs of the Paris of the Steins, Sylvia Beach, Joyce, Hemingway, and Scott Fitzgerald, I am cast down. I was there. I may have passed them in the street; I had simply never heard of them. . . . I had really carried my isolation in England with me.'[52] He also said that if he had known that he was living 'at the centre of a literary revolution', the fact would have angered him. What were the Dadaist Tristan Tzara and other cultural radicals doing, 'smashing up a culture', just when serious strivers like Pritchett were trying to learn about it in the first place?

The reference to revolution draws attention to another absence in his accounts of those years: politics. Pritchett's two-year stay in France coincided with the growing public realisation that the Versailles Treaty wasn't, and couldn't be, a success.[53] German debts were piling up, as they had been bound to do, and soon the French, in an attempt to call in their share, took over the German industrial area of the Ruhr. Since this was the final blow to the collapsing German economy, the benefits to France were short-term. In the immediate, though, France was enabled to continue its extraordinarily successful programme of reconstruction, especially in the devastated areas of the north, where – as many visitors described, among them Maynard Keynes in *The Economic Consequences of the Peace* – towns stood in ruins and much of the farmland was still poisoned.[54] None of this – none of the ghosts of men who had died in France before reaching even Pritchett's tender age, no glimmer of another coming war – figures in his writing in the *Christian Science Monitor* so soon after the First World War had ended. The landscapes through which the dazed young romantic travelled are described as though nothing had touched them since Stevenson wandered there forty-odd years earlier. The sunlight and shadows chasing each other across the fields of Pithiviers 'like flying battalions' are a purely literary simile and, when Pritchett looks out over the sea from the Normandy coast, the naval commanders he recalls – Benbow, Collingwood, Raleigh, Drake – come from history books, not the recent past.[55]

This escapism suited editorial policy. As Pritchett was to explain later, 'Americans in 1920 loved the picturesque. I began to get the suspicion that I was hired to leave half of life out.'[56] But he loved the picturesque himself, too, at this stage and in private he treated politics – if at all – as a joke. 'I am at present spending most of my time in convincing gesticulating frenchmen that I am *not* Mr Lloyd George,' he told Gordon in Wodehousean vein in May 1922, 'nor will I be responsible for his doings. I thought one old bean was going to throw a cask of petrol at me – politics are so dangerous.'[57]

So, too, with sex, though here, for this period, we have no information outside Pritchett's published work. *Midnight Oil* is particularly truthful seeming about his relationships with girls, conveying his inexperience, and then such experiences as he had, in all their intensity and muddle, and with few signs of comic exaggeration – though some of these episodes are very funny, such as the one where, too embarrassed to ask clearly for condoms, he discovers at the crucial moment that he has bought liver pills. Such scenes are also tender and erotic, both in their near-non-description of the sexual act when it occurs and in their frankness when it doesn't. But even Pritchett's use of the inexplicit can become a tool of fiction, for example, in the way he gives new names to many of the people he writes about.

At one level, a simple scruple seems to have been involved. Members of his family and public figures were too readily identifiable to be encoded. Private individuals, on the other hand, were entitled to keep their privacy. Why should the mere fact of Pritchett's having known them give him licence to reveal anything about them, however prosaic and undamaging? This was an honourable principle and one more common in his time than now. But it also had the advantage of freeing him imaginatively. There is a continuum between the factual characterisation and the fictional, and he is too artful not to admit to it, at certain points and in certain ways. *Midnight Oil* alerts the reader to, and yet still depends on, various exaggerations, such as that Victor broke away from England – broke 'with his family and with everything and everyone he knew' – against his father's will.[58] Gordon was to stress that this wasn't the whole story. Their brother Cyril had already gone to France, to work in the silk trade in Lyon. The move was much easier for Victor than it would have been if he had been the first to leave, and he saw quite a bit of Cyril in France. Besides, Walter actually helped him in various ways, not least by supplying him with a characteristically opulent pair of big leather suitcases.

This isn't the impression readers take away from the memoirs. Again, the essential facts are there: about Cyril, about his father's generosity. They are there, yet they are almost ostentatiously buried, as in a belated parenthesis where Victor mentions, '(I ought to have said that [Walter] had paid for my typewriter.)'[59] We are reminded – Pritchett himself reminds us – that the story could have been told quite differently. It could have emphasised Cyril's daring, rather than Victor's. It could have begun with the gift of the typewriter.

The beginnings of these memoirs were, in fact, among the sections which Pritchett reworked most often. What seems to be the first surviving attempt at the opening of the then untitled *A Cab at the Door* reads, 'It is very difficult to say who I am or, accurately, anything very certain about the history of my family.'[60] This is the germ of the final version. (The published words are, 'In our family, as far as we are concerned, we were born and what happened before that is myth.') Whatever his uncertainties, though, they were forgotten in the next attempt, which could not have been more self-assuredly concrete or immediate: 'A hundred years ago, a young builder's labourer and disgraced soldier born in Hull & brought up in Bradford marries the youngest daughter of a village tailor in the East Riding. He has turned theology student . . .' Having written this, Pritchett then crossed out the bald words which follow 'marries the youngest daughter' and built up yet more convincing detail. The disgraced soldier, he temporarily added,

> turns up in the small moorland town of Kirbymoorside in the East Riding of Yorkshire. There he has a vision of God and respectability, turns theological student and while still at college and only 18 or 19, marries the pretty youngest daughter of a small tailor in the town. He is a father before the year is out of his training – which takes place in Nottingham – he learns his Greek, Latin and Hebrew on the Nottingham trams and keeps his family out of the small sums he earns as a lay preacher.

In yet another completely different version, he tried out what eventually became the starting point not of *A Cab at the Door* but of *Midnight Oil*: a reflection on his own position as he wrote, looking back from the vantage point of old age.

Most of Pritchett's writing went through several very different drafts in this way, not to speak of the layer on layer of reworking involved in certain sections (of which the examples just given are a much simplified summary). In the case of the autobiographies, something which stands out in the many kinds of alteration which he made is how much he played up his isolation. In *Midnight Oil*, for example, he relates a hike to Dieppe with his brother Cyril and a friend. But the other young men are much more present in the manuscripts than in the published version. In the latter, he concludes this episode by saying that it had taught him that 'to travel well, one must be alone'.[61] It is as if this discovery was one which, even while he was recalling it, affected the very processes of writing and rewriting.

Every writer needs isolation, and feels isolated: the job is inevitably solitary. But Pritchett needed the opposite, too: for companionship and also for material. Much of the Paris section of *Midnight Oil* consists of a series of character sketches, artfully linked as a narrative. There is 'Hotchkiss', aka Walter's Christian Scientist friend John Allwork, who looked after Victor on his arrival but was poorly rewarded when Walter didn't pay him a large sum which he owed him. There's the homosexual English *soi-disant* aristocrat who picks him up in a tearoom in the rue de Rivoli. There is 'Judy Lang', the aspiring actress who is travelling with her mother. Pritchett used this pair early on, in his 1930 novella, *The Spanish Virgin*, but in *Midnight Oil* he develops still further their, and his own, self-fictionalising aspects: 'By four o'clock that afternoon . . . we had told one another what is called "everything" about ourselves. It was in fact a meeting not of three people, but of six – ourselves and our fictions.'[62] Then there is 'Hester', the Danish girl, who creates her own jealous fictions about Victor, and with whom he has his débâcle with the liver pill condoms – an episode added (invented?) at a late stage in his writing of the book[63] – and also his first experience of sex. That outcome is artfully deferred by the introduction of yet another new figure in a new chapter – one which has the memorably funny opening words, by Proust out of Gogol, 'Now when I look back on the tragic figure of Mr Shaves I see he was not a born banker.'[64] Basil Shaves, again, is an actor, but one complicated by his appetite for embarrassing confessions, and enriched by the fact that he has a wife and children. It is against this family background that Pritchett sets his developing love affair with Hester.

The relationship, as Pritchett describes it, is among other things one of criticism, by his intelligent girlfriend, of the young writer's work. By now, he had published several articles for the *Monitor* and had been commissioned to write ten more. For the first time he could see what he was writing in terms of assured publication. Previously, he had always had to have a day job. In Paris, he had worked in a photography studio and then spent some time travelling as a glue salesman – a period which let him explore the city in much the same way as his years in the leather trade enabled him to explore London. At last, his only form of paid work was as a writer. Pritchett didn't record how much he was earning that way, but the effects on his confidence weren't directly related to the sums involved. He described his feelings later, though without noting a degree of resemblance to how money affected his father:

> I was a commissioned writer, not an amateur any longer. No more leather, photography, shellac and glue. . . . I looked into the windows of jewellers, hosiers, tailors, perfumeries; wealth seemed to coat me. I went to an expensive shop that sold luxurious stationery, tooled blotting pads and so on. I went in and ordered a hundred engraved visiting cards, taking care in choosing the print. Afterwards I went to the Café Weber and ordered a bock.
>
> Now my life as a professional writer . . . began.[65]

The temptations to please, as well as the sheer necessity, were considerable, and would continue to be. He gives Hester the credit of being the first person who pointed them out to him: 'Why do you exaggerate?' he has her ask; and again, 'That is superficial, isn't it? . . . Be careful. You will lose your integrity.'[66]

Early in 1923 the *Monitor* sent Pritchett to Ireland as a correspondent. In pursuit of a living for himself and, later, for his family, he couldn't always heed the kinds of question Hester asked, but he was always glad of people who put them to him. After 1935 his closest relationships – with his second wife, Dorothy, with Gerald Brenan and with a few powerful editors – all brought him something of this severity, along with the encouragement that most artists need above everything. So it seems probable that he found it, also, with the person who was most important to him between 1923 and the early 1930s, even though he subsequently had little to say about, or for, her. The professional writer, Pritchett says in *Midnight Oil*, 'finds he has written his life away and has become almost nothing'.[67] But no one in his life was to become more of a nothing to him than the first Mrs V. S. Pritchett.

2

Anglo-Irish Attitudes

In 1923, Evelyn Vigors was a junior reporter on the *Christian Science Monitor*, working from its newly established office in Dublin. The *Monitor*'s sales were going up fast, worldwide: between 1922 and 1928 they rose from around 2 million to 7 million. But the Dublin office wasn't a specially prepossessing place. There was a tailor's shop on the ground floor, on the corner of Dawson Street. A side door took you to a narrow staircase leading to the upper storeys, where the *Monitor* was. The building also housed a legal firm, a building society, some private tenants and a laundry. Still, it overlooked St Stephen's Green,[1] at the heart of the city – the heart, too, of the entire Irish Free State, which had been established the previous year. Around the corner, the new Irish Parliament met at Leinster House behind sandbags and barbed wire.

To a newcomer, Evelyn embodied both the new Ireland and the old. The new, in that she was 'anti-Establishment', and also in that she was working at all, neither of which would have been predicted from her background. She came from two long-established Anglo-Irish families of the just-superseded ruling class.[2] Her mother was a D'Arcy of Clifden Park, Connemara, on the west coast. The family claimed that it had come over with the Normans. A D'Arcy ancestor was a member of the Parliament convened at Dublin in 1640 by the ill-fated English Lord Lieutenant, Strafford, and this D'Arcy's son married a daughter of one of the Maids of Honour of Queen Henrietta Maria, wife of Charles I. They were part of a line of soldiers, colonial administrators and Church of Ireland clergy and, like most of their kind, they eventually lost their estates. In the early nineteenth century John D'Arcy had taken out big mortgages, on a dream of building up the harbour and town of Clifden. During the crop failures and famine of the mid century, his tenants were unable to pay their rents, local commerce collapsed, the hoped-for sea-borne traffic into Clifden never materialised, and John's heir was forced to sell almost everything to meet the accumulated debts.[3] But the family retained its big houses – Burgage and Borris, both in County Carlow, as well as Clifden Park – and, by comparison with most people on the west coast, was still very well off, if a little threadbare.

The match between Evelyn's mother, Anna-Louise Hyacinth D'Arcy, and her father, Philip Urban Walter Vigors, couldn't have been more symmetrical. The Vigorses were by then a predominantly military family. They, too, had come to Ireland centuries ago, supplying generation after generation of civil administrators, clergy and army officers, some of them staying put in Ireland, others heading for further-flung parts of the British Empire. A Vigors had been chaplain to Roger Boyle, first Earl of Orrery, at the time of his role in the British suppression of the Irish Rebellion of 1641. Three centuries later, Evelyn's paternal grandfather was a railway engineer in India, where he, too, helped to put down an anti-colonial insurrection. His son, Evelyn's father, fought in the South African ('Boer') War, was wounded twice when Ladysmith was besieged by the Boers in 1899, and was variously bemedalled and mentioned in despatches. Victor later sardonically described him in a notebook: 'The Major – the Meejor – knicker-bockers, rolled navy blue stockings, a small round frosted face, 5'2" high, shortest officer in Br. Army. . . . An invincible snob. Younger son . . . couldn't bear his wife.'

Repressive antecedents, then, and Evelyn's upbringing, as she later remembered it, was harsh and cold. Clever, alert to current psychological fashions, but constitutionally imperious, muddled and unhappy, she saw herself as rebelling against her background and boasted to Victor that she had once bitten her father's hand ('Very proud of this,' he later noted disenchantedly). But her mother and sister also broke out, in their different ways. Anna-Louise's modish Christian Science beliefs – which, like those of the very different Walter Pritchett, gave her child an entrée to the *Monitor* – exasperated her husband, leading to increasing tensions after his retirement. Once their children had grown up, they lived apart and Anna-Louise devoted herself to their young grandson, whose soldier father was abroad in Egypt and India with his wife, Molly, Evelyn's elder sister. This grandson, David Willison, eventually excelled in the family business, becoming a British general and, in the 1970s, head of Military Intelligence and Deputy Under-Secretary of State in the Ministry of Defence: a formidable role, not least in relation to Northern Ireland.[4]

Yet even he remembered his grandmother as 'not lively, and a bit heavy on the hand'.

David Willison's mother was a devoted army wife but, like her own mother, passionate about Christian Science: 'rabidly' so, as her son was to put it. In her late fifties, fatally ill, Molly was prevented by her creed from admitting to whatever her disease was, or allowing herself to be treated, and instead took herself off to the Mother Church of Christ Scientist in Boston, Massachusetts, where she died.[5]

Molly's sister Evelyn was much less religious, but still more impulsive. Dark, pretty, tiny (a little under five feet tall), very sensitive and intelligent, she was easily dissatisfied: not lacking in humour, but essentially melancholy and restless. For all her family's roots in Ireland, she had lived the peripatetic life of an army child, much of it near her father's regimental headquarters in Devon, and had been to finishing school in Paris. She wasn't really at home in Dublin, found her newspaper work frustrating and longed for some stimulus: perhaps a more creative-seeming career as an actress. When Victor Pritchett – animated, idealistic, funny, artistic and amorous – arrived at 13 St Stephen's Green from Paris in February 1923, she was twenty-four and he twenty-two.[6]

Pritchett's new job was ostensibly to cover the civil war. Then, as ever since, Irish Republicans rejected the partition of mainly Protestant northern Ireland from the Catholic south, which had been an essential element of the 1922 treaty establishing the Irish Free State. Tensions on this score were exacerbated by delays in implementing, and the eventual abandonment of, an earlier Home Rule treaty which had been provisionally settled in 1914 but put off by the First World War. In this agreement, partition was to have lasted for a fixed period only. By the time Pritchett arrived in Ireland, seven years had passed since the bloodily crushed Easter Rising of 1916, which had been followed by a no less bloody guerrilla war. Belfast as well as Dublin now had its own Parliament and the IRA was in revolt against the newly independent Irish government's acceptance of the situation.

Although he later downplayed his professional efforts, Pritchett covered the ground – literally. He travelled the length and breadth of the island, by train and by bus, on foot, even with a horse named Jemima, whose recalcitrance was a useful talking point in places where an English stranger might otherwise have been less welcome. Jemima also made good copy for the *Monitor*.[7] Pritchett went to political meetings, sat in the press gallery of the Dáil, conducted interviews.

Above all, he listened to anyone and everyone. From early February 1923, he was filing clear, confident copy on the intricacies of the situation as he found them. His initialled pieces were published alongside the editorials on the paper's back page: 'Republican Policy Condemned in Cork', 'Ireland – Old and New', 'In the Queen's County', 'Three Months in Ireland', 'Belfast in Transition'.[8]

Just as he subsequently forgot how hard he had worked, so he also tended in retrospect to simplify his earlier attitudes to Irish politics. As far as the north was concerned, he was unexceptional in loving the countryside and its people, while finding Belfast politically benighted and (apart from rare individuals such as the writer Forrest Reid) a cultural desert. In the south, though, he liked things exactly as they had been before independence: lackadaisical Ascendancy, impoverished peasantry and all. Unlike more inflammable commentators, especially in the *Morning Post*, he tended to treat the Troubles as something between a temporary nuisance and a joke. In this, he took his tone from many of the ordinary people he met. Travelling from Dublin to Cork within weeks of his arrival, he was delayed by a Republican action which blocked the line. He and the other passengers had to spend four hours in a small town sixty miles out of Dublin. Fortunately, it was lunchtime and the local innkeeper supplied them all well.

He knew all about our trouble, before we could start a conversation on our own account. He knew the line was blocked. He knew at what time it was blocked and how the Republicans did it. He knew so much that I half suspected him of having been present when the deed was done. But to look at, he hardly seemed the man to be out of bed at 3 in the morning tearing up railway lines.[9]

Having eaten and drunk, Pritchett and his fellow travellers resumed their journey, pausing again to change trains at Mallow, where the viaduct had been destroyed. 'My impression of the town is blurred. . . . I remember following a singing football team into a confusion of lights and faces.' After another hour's journey across the hills, they reached Cork, where 'The moon, its face all awry with the drollest of smiles, watched our stealthy progress'. 'Wandering through the streets of Cork,' he wrote the day after, 'it is difficult to see a very sad face. . . . There seem to be jokes on everyone's lips.'[10] Thus politics and war were charmed away.

Pritchett later came to believe that his reports from Ireland had been criticised for being too favourable to the Free State[11] but, at the time, he made no secret of his detachment. 'I have been looking all day for an excuse for not writing an article on Irish politics,' he typically confessed, in the summer of 1923, in a piece about 'An Irish Bookshop'.[12] The Republicanism of the more bookish people he met was, he said, 'that comparatively harmless intellectual type which, like university Socialism, is worked off easily in an hour or two . . . resembling the polite literary Bolshevism which finds poetically-reasoned expression among the clientèle of the Bomb Shop in Charing Cross Road'. Even at their worst, the Troubles were in his view the work of a 'noisy minority who . . . have fallen to the methods of the ordinary bandit', in furtherance of a 'bad cause'.[13] Once law and order had been established, the next ten years might see a series of elections by which 'the merely patriotic element will be ousted and replaced by men who have a stake in the country'. There were, Pritchett opined,

> two types of Irishman today. The one who will not easily forget old differences, a dweller in a melancholy and ineffectual past, perpetuating the old myth that an Irishman is never happy unless he is fighting; the other, one who sees the apathy and evils to be met, and is enthusiastic and practical enough to suggest remedies. I believe that in the new Ireland the world will be to him.

However good-hearted these views were, they were not shared by everyone – and even when they seemed to be, Pritchett was shrewd enough to recognise that what people said to a young English visitor was not necessarily what they said to each other. An expression he particularly enjoyed was 'Whatever you say yourself'. More expansively, one native told him, 'Och, ay, it's an awful country. Sure, every horse is one side or t'other. What the country wants . . . is an a-micable settlement. Why wouldn't they leave the people alone?'[14]

Despite his impression, though, many years after, that his views had been too pro-Republican to find favour with the *Monitor*, what he wrote for the paper suited its optimistic conservatism perfectly well, not least because it had the real merit of being based less on the activities and values of politicians than on what he heard and saw on his travels. Although he was expected to do the journalistic rounds, the *Monitor* was happy for him to continue mainly in the role he had developed in France, as a roving 'colour' writer. He later said that it was the journalist's job 'to interview everything',[15] and a notebook kept in these months contains scraps of overheard dialogue, soliloquies, passages of description.[16] Outbreaks of verbal doodling ('A blossoming of cumulus. In the fields of May . . . wild blossoming of mute cumulus . . . Clouds as grey as cherry blossom . . . the sky filled with blossoming boughs of cloud, boughs of cloud blossom laden . . .') are interspersed with sharp comments on the nature of Irish talk: 'Everyone is fine gentleman. Cunning knowing conversation. Always knowing what you're thinking.' And there are *objets trouvés* such as a newspaper cutting about an action for breach of promise brought by a farmer's daughter in her thirties, against a small farmer with whom her marriage had been arranged by matchmakers. (She won £60 damages.) The resulting articles for the *Monitor* were as likely to be about the wind and the rain,[17] or his struggles with his horse and cart on a journey he took with his brother Cyril, Evelyn and another girl,[18] as about gun-running. You sense a particular sympathy when he quotes a 'Mr Mulcahy of Blarney' saying (about Henry Irving's performance as Thomas à Beckett) ' 'Twas awful tragic. Oh yes, sure, it was awful tragic. I didn't like it much. I was never a lad for unhappy things.'[19]

Unhappy things there were in Ireland, though, and Pritchett, like Trollope before him,[20] was too good a writer not to respond to them, especially at the more fully contemplated level of some of his fiction (and also, much later, of his 1967 book *Dublin: A Portrait*). There are many overlaps between the stories he wrote in and about Ireland, and his lighter journalism. 'Fishy', for example, is a pleasantly whimsical piece about false intimacy and the gift of the gab.[21] But in 'The Two Brothers', written more than a decade after he left Ireland, he went much deeper. If, as he later suspected, the *Monitor* had hired him 'to leave half of life out',[22] this story and one or two others which he wrote about Ireland put it back in again.

'The Two Brothers' begins like a folk tale. One of the men has returned from abroad, where he has prospered; the other, weak and dependent, stayed at home. Even the landscape of the west coast, 'prostrating itself in rags before the Atlantic', echoes the latter's state, which is also, of course, the prostration of Ireland as a whole. The brothers set up house together in 'a grey, rambling place of two storeys with outhouses and stables all going to pieces. It was damp, leaky and neglected and barely furnished . . . the ribs of the roofless stable like a shining skeleton.'

Something more is involved, though, than rural poverty and

depopulation – more, even, than the contrast with Micky's trans-atlantic get-up-and-go. Charlie has had some kind of breakdown and Micky, in his clumsy way, wants to help him. After a day of drinking, he brings him home a dog, to which Charlie becomes devoted:

> Charlie drew courage from it as it loped along before him, sniffing at walls and standing stiff with ears cocked to see the sudden rise of a bird. Charlie talked to it in a low running murmur hardly made of words but easing to the mind. When it stopped, he would pass his clever hands over its velvety nose and glossy head, feeling the strange life ripple under the hair and obtaining a curious strength from the tumult.

As he gains confidence, so Charlie becomes less guarded about his unsureness. Partly as a result, the strains between the two men grow, rather than diminishing – intensified as they are, too, by Micky's restless energy, which attracts the dog and, both for that reason and for others as yet unclear, frightens Charlie. It begins to look as though Micky is actually not much help – as though he may in some way even be the cause of his sibling's frailty. Micky likes to shoot, he is quarrelsome. His behaviour reminds Charlie of the last time Micky came home, 'like a red lord out of hell in your uniform, pretending to be glad to see me'. Micky, we learn, having emigrated, spent the First World War in the British army and, on a period of leave in the middle of the war – at the height of the Troubles – came back to Ireland.

> In five minutes by a few reckless words in the drink shop and streets of the town he had ruined the equilibrium Charlie had tended for years. . . . Men were boycotted for having brothers in the British Army, they were threatened, they were even shot. In an hour a village as innocent-looking as a green-and-white place in a postcard had become a place of windows hollow-eyed with evil vigils. Within a month he had received the first note threatening his life.

The IRA subsequently spare Charlie. By the end of the story it is Micky who, indirectly, kills him. For all Micky's good intentions and generous impulses, the two men can't manage life together. As in a bad marriage – and, by the time he wrote the story, Pritchett knew what a bad marriage was – one of them can't leave and the other can't stay. In Micky's excitement at getting ready to depart, it is as if he has already gone. He forgets about his brother, gives away his dog, gets drunk with an ingratiating friend who tells him, 'Sure there's nothing you can do. Nothing at all.' At last Charlie is alone again, not only with his terrors but with a new knowledge that he has been abandoned and that nothing will get better now – himself least of all. Pritchett's uncharacteristically melodramatic (though, he believed, literally 'true')[23] ending leaves Charlie 'absorbed in the difficulty of cutting his throat'.

The story's politics, like everything else in it, are dense and subtle. No crude blame is attached to Micky, or to his having served with the British. He is the worse for the experience (among the factors contributing to tensions in Ireland was that many soldiers in the Black and Tans had been brutalised by their years in South Africa and in the trenches of northern France). But Micky joined the army because of the kind of man he is, just as Charlie has been bullied and abandoned in part because of the kind of man he is. Politics, Pritchett already saw, not only affect people, but are an extension of them. We aren't encouraged to admire Micky's schoolmaster friend, who sucks up to him, does nothing for Charlie and neglects his own wife. But that tragic-passive shrug of his – 'Sure there's nothing you can do' – is in a way the story's, too. And if we are not led to admire Micky, we come to understand him no less than Charlie, and to sympathise with the predicaments of both brothers and, through them, of the Irish more generally.

Pritchett wrote other far-reaching pieces set in Ireland, including a vivid article dealing with emigration from the point of view of a young girl, her unpreparedness for her new world thrown into relief by the fact that on the first leg of her journey, almost everyone she meets knows almost everyone else.[24] And in his 1929 novel, *Clare Drummer*, he had already tried to get into the mind of another member of the Black and Tans, but this time less successfully. Here, autobiography got in the way.

Captain David Tremble, recently retired from the British army, a veteran of the First World War and of 'the Irish rebellion', broke, self-dramatising, soliloquising, romantic, is in some respects, for all their differences, a version of Pritchett himself: not only can he quote Victor Hugo,[25] but much of the novel concerns his involvement with a family distinctly like the Vigorses. In *Clare Drummer* they are presented as a household of eccentrics out of Saki. Clare, partly based on Evelyn, is the daughter of a choleric, paranoid Anglo-Irish colonel and his intense wife, whose manipulativeness she has inherited. Much of the story –

which in early drafts began as Tremble's own narrative – concerns the romantic to-ings and fro-ings between Tremble, Clare, Clare's friend Julia, and the satirically named Oriel Enctrury, with whom Clare is in love. Tremble isn't at home in this world, with the girls' mixture of humiliating teases (they make him play a game in which he has to jump over the drawing-room furniture) and fabulation. Talking about her father, Clare begins to see in him possibilities 'as a character with which to dumbfound Tremble. The more she told the exact truth, the more the inflections of her voice, a timely casualness of manner, and studied deprecating pretences, transfigured the story by their lights so that it became a fiction.'

Not that Colonel Drummer, as more directly encountered by his daughter's admirer, lacks colour. 'This isn't your country,' he shouts crazily at Tremble. 'No! Nor mine! Neither. You know, eh! You know who it belongs to – Corner boys, murderers, eh? They don't want us! Betrayed, that's what it is, a betrayal. They'll crawl, creep on their knees for the English to come back, eh!' Although Pritchett later thought that he had been imperceptive at the time about the nature of colonialism and its decline,[26] the book is full of people whose lives have been deformed by Anglo-Irish attitudes and what they have brought about. In a tense episode not fully worked into the main action, Tremble, on a walking trip with Clare in countryside which he last saw on active service, spends the night at an inn where he shares a bedroom with two Irishmen. Feigning sleep, he hears them talk about an IRA action, at first comically thwarted but finally successful, at a house owned by the Enctrurys. Clare tells Oriel that she sympathises with the Republicans: 'They were only getting back some of the rack rents.' Oriel thinks this is mad. David keeps his counsel, perhaps because while he was in the army, he shot a local man.

Pritchett wasn't entirely in control of his material in his first novel, but there's some mimetic point in its irresolution. The over-aptly named Tremble is socially and emotionally shaky, particularly in his feelings about Clare. A torrid sexual encounter between the pair, in his room by the canal, ends in frustration. He feels that she has been playing with him and speculates about how this might affect a hypothetical future with her which the novel will not permit (the book ends with Clare leaving alone on the ferry to England), but which closely resembles how things actually turned out between Victor and Evelyn, at least as he perceived them: 'If he married her she would tantalise him to muteness with her theatrical passion, her inability to be angry even with his lust, her faintly mournful, tolerant consideration of it.'[27]

This was written four or five years after Victor and Evelyn first met.[28] Many years later still, in a section of *Midnight Oil* which he eventually cut just before publication, Pritchett gave a more prosaic account of their early relationship:

> Among my difficulties was that the Major, her father – a Ladysmith man – could not bear the sight of me. It was bad enough for him that his daughter insisted on earning her living; it was intolerable that she brought this 'nasty little London clerk' to his flat off Merrion Square where a large oil painting of Psyche, looking rather yellow and ill among a lot of greenery, looked down upon us. We mocked this heirloom, but, to tell the truth, I was impressed by it. A real oil painting; it was one up on the *Wedded* of my home. The Major was a correct and lonely man. . . . Being bumptious I was afraid of his puncturing manner. . . .
>
> Also, I was doing only moderately well in the touchy business of persuading the young woman out of friendship to thoughts of marriage.[29]

Why Victor wasn't doing better at persuading Evelyn, or even why he so much wanted to persuade her in the first place, are never explained. Even the fullest drafts of *Midnight Oil* are conspicuously short on detail about his first marriage. Sheer sexual impatience may have been an element. It's hard to exaggerate the impact on people's relationships in those days (and especially in Ireland) of moral codes which would now, at least in the West, seem deeply repressive, combined with primitive methods of contraception. In other ways, too, Pritchett was a young man in a hurry: professionally ambitious and socially on the make. That oil painting on the wall, a synecdoche for class which he put straight into *Clare Drummer*, had a lot to do with it. To him, Evelyn represented everything that wasn't Bromley. In some notebooks he kept in the 1930s, he was frank about the snobbish dimension of his attraction towards her and about his own eventual difficulties with its consequences: 'A man of humble origins but of ability, self-trained spends a lot of energy not merely in the instinctive expression of his talent but in conforming to the manners, mores etc. of his new class. . . . To be like other people releases a certain energy; but merely social or sociable energy . . . the cost in *strain* is immense.'[30]

This was not just a problem of superficial mimicry, at which Pritchett excelled. The Anglo-Irish were, he found, both elusive and demanding. In some of his reviews he was to describe these traits, but he sounds as if he's talking about his first wife's family as much as about the book he has been reading. He comments, for example, on T. E. Lawrence's 'instinct for mischief and intrigue, vanity and a core of diffidence, weakness, insecurity' as general characteristics of his world:

> History suggests that their insecurity as the lonely conquerors of a savage and treacherous country is a profound element in the general character of the Anglo-Irish. . . . There are the continuous histrionic touch and the remorse that follows – an unavailing remorse because it, also, is theatrical. There is the merciless mental energy which pours out endlessly in words or action, and turns upon the character with humiliating self-criticism. . . .[31]

And on the Anglo-Irish novelist duo Somerville and Ross:

> though *The Real Charlotte* is a novel about jealousy and the never-ceasing intrigue and treachery of Irish life, its main stuff is . . . snobbery. Not a plain, excluding snobbery that tells us where we may go and where we may not, but a snobbery that is in the blood . . . bedevilling the character with the pretensions of second cousins and the mildewed memories of better times. It is a snobbery that has become the meaning of life. It permeates everything: good sense, idealism, hatred, tenderness, religion – even pity.[32]

For now, though, Pritchett's energy was more in evidence than any social strains he felt. He was in love and, to Evelyn, his persuasiveness was enhanced not only by his enthusiasm but also by the fact that he was so out of favour with her father. Victor enjoyed this renegade status, but not unambiguously. He loved the stylish eccentricity of the upper classes in Ireland, at least on first acquaintance – the playfulness which led one landowner to carry a set of planks on his car, so that he could drive over the trenches dug in his drive by Republicans – and under the influence of such encounters, the young man became as 'sensitive, snobbish and fey' as someone out of the novels of Stendhal or Meredith.[33] Dandyism was part of the style, and Victor had more than a touch of it, inherited from his father. Tailors figure in his writings about Ireland – there's a particularly vivid piece about one measuring him for a dinner suit: 'All you heard was his small, accurate breathing near you as he walked round tugging you this way and that.'[34] *Nothing Like Leather* includes a scene in which the young Mathew Burkle becomes 'exalted' by the act of buying a suit in a 'brilliant mustard-coloured tweed'.[35] In *Midnight Oil*, Pritchett teases his young self about some of his more improbable outfits, such as the breeches which, after a country-house weekend at which he was persuaded to ride, he continued to wear in Dublin until someone told him he looked like a stable-boy.[36] In his journals he dwells on his social uncertainty and in *Clare Drummer* he fictionalises it.

His footing in the Vigorses' households was particularly rocky. While Evelyn and her sister had been frequent visitors at Burgage, the family's eighteenth-century house in County Carlow, Pritchett makes no appearance in the visitors' book and, after their marriage, Evelyn seems never to have returned to the place.[37] Most of her family broke off relations with them.[38] Although *Burke's Irish Family Records* assiduously pursues every other ramification of the Vigors family, Evelyn's first marriage is simply omitted.

Vigors resistance apart, Pritchett made friends easily, and was quickly at home in literary and artistic circles in Dublin. After an uncomfortable preliminary stay at a temperance hotel, he had moved first into lodgings in Waterloo Road and then to a service flat in Upper Pembroke Street, a Georgian terrace a short walk from St Stephen's Green. He read Irish writers – Douglas Hyde, Liam O'Flaherty, Katherine Tynan, as well as Joyce,[39] AE, J. M. Synge, James Stephens and W. B. Yeats, the last two of whom he interviewed for the *Monitor*.[40] He went often to the Abbey Theatre, sitting on the gallery benches with the dramatist and director-manager Lennox Robinson at performances of Yeats's *The Countess Cathleen* and Shaw's *The Showing-Up of Blanco Posnet*, and falling for the actresses: 'Shelah Richards, the quintessential young Dublin girl, decorous yet gay; the severe romantic, passionate Ria Mooney'.[41] Writers and painters became his friends, among them Sean O'Casey, Forrest Reid[42] and the artist Stephen Bone, son of Muirhead. He wrote about them all, at the time as well as later.[43] Meanwhile, although it seemed to him that Evelyn was hard to win round, she raised eyebrows by accompanying him on some of his Irish travels. Less than a year after they first met they were married.

On Evelyn's side, what bumped her into deciding was Victor's summons away from Ireland. The *Monitor* needed him in Spain, where its correspondent had died. In September 1923, a coup had brought a military dictatorship to power under General Miguel Primo de Rivera and it was clearly important for the paper to be covering events there. The prospect was as seductive to the restless Evelyn as to Victor, and their marriage took place quickly. Too quickly for Victor's parents to be present, though he later wrote that in any case his father had taken offence against his acting so independently, so precipitously. Perhaps Victor just didn't want him there. Whether as a joke or in an attempt at improving his position in his in-laws' eyes, he recorded Walter's occupation as 'Gentleman'.[44] The Church of Ireland ceremony was conducted by special licence at the house of friends in Elgin Road on 3 January 1924. Immediately afterwards the couple set off via London for Spain. 'There was a frost on the inside of the crowded third class compartment in which we travelled,' Pritchett was to write as if they were in a Russian story, '. . . and the fur collar of my wife's coat got stuck by ice to the window. She was silent and troubled. I was excited. . . . I did not take [her] to see my parents. I was on my high horse.'[45]

In Madrid, the Pritchetts settled into rooms off the broad slope of the Paseo de la Castellana, north of the city centre, started to take Spanish lessons, and embarked on a programme of reading and travel. As in Ireland, Victor was more serious about his journalism than he later recalled. In *Midnight Oil* he's eloquent about the intellectual awakening – described as a clearing of the romantic mists[46] – which he experienced in Spain; much less so about his work as a reporter. Typically, he got started straight away, filing his first article from Madrid on 15 January.[47] In the course of that year he was to write almost two hundred pieces, each carefully recorded in his notebook, on a wide range of topics: military developments in Morocco (where Spain was fighting a colonial war), the landscape of the Sierra Guadarrama in spring, the state of education, the atmosphere of a first night at a theatre in Madrid, attitudes to opposition parties under the dictatorship, the position of women.[48]

On politics, he continued to be detached, quietly ironic and clear-sighted. As with any reportage, the interest for later readers lies as much in how things seemed at the time as in the accuracy or otherwise of his predictions. Despite censorship, for example, Pritchett conveyed the strength of Spanish public feeling against the war in Morocco and relayed what he was able to learn about the colonialists' military retreats there – which many people, Lloyd George among them, hoped would lead to total withdrawal.[49] Pritchett also sceptically reported de Rivera's own versions of the situation: one piece appeared under the headline, 'Dictator Denies What He Calls "Fantastic Rumors"'.[50] Stories of Spanish setbacks may not have been fantastic, but they were no more dependable as prophecy than the happy notion that appeared on the same page as one of them: 'Adolf Hitler Asks Leisure for Writing – Organiser of Reich Nationalists Resigns to Take Up Literature'.[51]

In general, though, Pritchett correctly anticipated that extreme right-wing rule in Spain would continue.[52] The dictatorship gave him a metaphor for his travels: a map, he wrote, was a 'junta of unrelenting kilometers', humanised by the actualities of the landscape, harsh though they were.[53] In May he went south to Seville; in June to Segovia and Toledo; in August and September across the mountains of the north-west to Santander; in October back to Andalucía; the following March to Extremadura; and in April to Tetuán, capital of the Spanish-governed part of Morocco, where he met an Arab merchant who had diplomatic things to say about the benefits of Spanish rule ('we progress. Our women tend to drop the veil, and it is time they did'), while insisting that above all Moroccans wanted peace, and that in 'moral things, things of sensibility, bearing and character' they were superior to their temporary masters.[54] Pritchett returned by way of Catalonia. To foreigners, most of Spain seemed if anything more inhospitable than its southern neighbour, Morocco: remote from the rest of Europe, little visited by tourists. Sophisticated Barcelona was as hard as anywhere to comprehend: to Pritchett, Gaudí's new cathedral of the Sagrada Familia was 'a group of factory chimneys standing on a menagerie sculpted in dough'.[55]

It isn't always certain when and where Evelyn accompanied him. Pritchett still saw himself as more solitary than he actually was. Most, though far from all, of his travel pieces were written in the first person singular. In *Midnight Oil*, he wrote that Evelyn was not happy in Spain, felt isolated in its male-dominated literary society and returned often to Ireland.[56] But Evelyn herself, by contrast, later spoke about her love of Spain and of the intellectual company she and Victor enjoyed there together, as well as of their travels. (She defended bullfighting to one of her daughters, saying that it became comprehensible once you knew 'the heartbeat of the people'.)[57] She admitted that it had been difficult for her to become settled because they were so often on the move – but this in itself implies that they travelled together. Quite often, they had to. Victor never learned to drive and even in those days there were places which were least inaccessible by car. The *Monitor*, which carried a lot of advertising from motor manufacturers as well as from travel agencies, shipping lines and hotels, was keen to provide material for readers who might want to take motoring holidays.[58] In November 1924, 'Doña Evelyn Prichett' was granted a driving licence by the civil authorities in Madrid. With a touch of irony, she gave her profession as *conductora* – driver.[59]

Pritchett's Spanish travels were so important a part of his development, and his writing about Spain is intrinsically so interesting, that it needs a separate chapter – not least because the process continued over decades of changing circumstances, political as well as personal. As far as he and Evelyn were concerned as a couple, though, Spain was just one – albeit the first, most prolonged and most vivid – of several such experiences. By the middle of 1925 they were in North America.

The *Monitor* sent the Pritchetts to its own heartland in Boston and on through Rhode Island into Canada. They were given a dusty welcome, at first, by Quebec lumbermen unused to any kind of visitor, least of all a writer accompanied by his wife. One man, when Pritchett asked him for advice about somewhere to stay, told him drily, 'We don't have no hotels and spas.'[60] There's something surprisingly genteel and over-demanding, even lost, about the first American pieces of this hitherto robustly well-travelled writer: an inclination to complain about the smell of onions. This was partly, Pritchett said later, a matter of personal unhappiness in his marriage. It wouldn't have been surprising if Evelyn felt the strain of being in his tow and took it out on him. There were other sources of tension, too, as we shall see. But from the point of view of his work this wasn't all. Coming to the USA by way of the ancient, primitive economies of Ireland and Spain, Pritchett initially found himself at a loss. He hadn't expected immigrant working people in the Canadian forests to be so tough, so self-reliant, perhaps above all so unimpressed by yet another newcomer.

He found it even harder, at first, to know what to make of New York. He seems to have gone into a kind of three-day fugue on Riverside Drive, watching the movements of three women and, as if speeding up a film, writing about them as a dance rising out of the neighbourhood's miscellaneous other activities, like the Three Graces, a transformation in which his own reading and writing are acknowledged as elements:

> three ladies are dancing. Even here I can think of nothing else. . . . I see them. I seem to hear the petal-small feet pacing the earth and rising to a lilt; but that is all. There is no epilogue.
>
> This narrative is true to the most fragile detail. When that word epilogue, robust and shapely with wet ink, had dried on the page, a book fell suddenly from the shelf above my table. . . .[61]

The book was Walt Whitman's *Leaves of Grass*. At moments like this, Pritchett's writing in the mid 1920s is stuck in the prose poetry of the fin-de-siècle. But at the same time he increasingly, if confusedly, responded to the stimulus of the new; for example, to the science-fiction miracle of the mechanical lift (three years before Virginia Woolf wrote about it in *Orlando*): 'One feels like some explorer of the moon, being shot out of a Jules Verne cannon. . . . I expect to find myself beyond air or ether. The elevator bounces, selects its level, and I am left alone, vaguely mirrored in a glazed floor . . . thrown high and dry.'[62]

That article was immediately followed by other pieces in which Pritchett tests his feelings about modernity: about the lights of Broadway, about Greenwich Village – where he encountered members of the artistic avant-garde in a way that he hadn't in Paris – and about crossing the Hudson river near the newly constructed Bear Mountain bridge.[63] In each, he juxtaposes mass and individual, city and country, new technology and old crafts. He describes Broadway at night as a kind of verbal firework display: 'Giant words flow over the skyscrapers and off them, extinguishing into black air. The night swallows scores of golden words. . . .' He devotes a paragraph to the petrol being poured into his car. For all that, when he and Evelyn cross the Hudson, it is by the old ferry, not the new suspension bridge, and the countryside and its inhabitants provide the focus. The last words of the piece revert to an older idiom: 'The girl in the porch gets up, and, stepping into a pool of sun, picks three asters.' The piece about Broadway, similarly, ends by putting the modern world in its place. He falls into conversation with a man whom he has noticed reading poetry, and who turns out to have travelled all over the world. In this context, the 'sharp, electric brevity of the staged night', Pritchett wrote, 'appeared facile. . . .'

It is as if he was deciding where he stood before his coming journey to the poor whites of the Appalachian Mountains. Pritchett's eight articles about his travels there, published in the *Monitor* in October–November 1925, between them constitute an evocative, sustained essay. In its sympathetic focus on a harsh, simple, relatively unchanging way of life, it provides a strong answer to the questions he had been asking himself in New York. Even the focus on light seems to include a conscious response to the electrical extravagance of Broadway: in the southern mountains at night, by contrast, 'oil lamps burned sparingly' and people found their way by storm lanterns, partly by the light from a church porch, partly by the moon, 'yellow as candle light'. The men and women he met were, Pritchett approvingly believed, 'America's only peasantry' and, 'shut up in their loved mountains since the coming of the first settlers', had 'conserved their rough, antique modes of living', close in all respects to their natural surroundings, yet hospitable, genial and characterised by what, quoting the Spanish novelist Pío Baroja, Pritchett called a '"dynamic" sense of freedom'. It was in the Appalachians that Pritchett really learned how to write about Spain. Years later, summing up the Spanish philosopher Miguel de Unamuno, who had just died, he quoted a 'rough Baptist preacher' he had met a dozen years earlier in Tennessee, who told him, 'I belong to no one; I belong to myself.'

Perhaps it was at Evelyn's insistence that, by the end of the year, after a brief stay in Washington and a baffled visit to an American football match, they returned to Ireland.[64] Once again, subsequent accounts of their reasons are divided – as, indeed, the reasons themselves must have been. Victor later implied that Evelyn had been homesick. In her own occasional allusions to her first marriage in conversations with her children, she plausibly hinted that Victor had been restlessly driven from place to place by a hope that his writing would go better there, or there. (Later, when her son wanted to try to make his living as writer, she was keen to dissuade him.)[65] But of course these peregrinations were often required by his work. In 1926 the *Monitor* sent him back to Spain, and then to Tunisia, Algeria and southern Italy.[66] Evelyn accompanied him on the second trip. They responded to the deserts and mountains of North Africa but disliked the colonial postures into which their tourism forced them, especially when their French-speaking drivers raced through scenes which the Pritchetts would have preferred to have encountered differently:

> Grit spat up from our wheels. Our engines drummed in high monody.
>
> Homegoing Arabs riding their donkeys up the avenue of pale-bodied eucalyptus, overturned, jumped off, scattered before us . . . leathery, pole-boned limbs poking out of their robes like the sticks of a scarecrow.
>
> No word of protest came from the Arabs. They stood and turned, looking in chill silence like birds. . . .[67]

The couple were happier without minders and on foot, in southern Italy. They loved Capri, 'hurl[ing] its ashen and coppery-green precipices an odd thousand feet or two down into the sea'. They tiptoed through the town 'as if it were porcelain' before climbing the crumbling Phoenician steps to the next village, from which the island looked like 'a monstrous emerald fixed in sapphire'. In Sicily, near Palermo, Victor went in quest of someone with whom he had corresponded on business from the leather works in Bermondsey, seven years and an imaginative lifetime earlier:

> I ran into the courtyard and mounted a flight of stairs. My little fellow was waiting at the top at a door. He had pulled the bell. The door was opening. He had one foot on the step as I ran up. He was compact, well filled. His eyebrows were short, high and deprecatory. His yellow booted feet were discreet and small.
>
> As he turned to me inquiringly I suddenly realised I had thought of nothing to say to him. I had been too excited to think of even an opening phrase. . . . His discretion and composure rebuked me. Hotly I blundered out, fishing for words:

46

'I was told – I thought – Are you by any chance – You are not Signor Filippo?'

He shook his head sympathetically and said, 'I regret, I am not,' and the door closed behind him as he stepped into the house.[68]

It was Victor himself, of course, who had closed the door on the leather works, though his later work would often draw on his experiences there. Meanwhile, his second Irish stay lasted more than a year and in the course of it his fiction developed fast. He spent a good deal of time in a coastal cabin belonging to the D'Arcys at Mount Freer, Clifden, where he could write without distraction. In 1926 he submitted half a dozen short stories to magazines, among them 'Tragedy in a Greek Theatre'.[69] Several were rejected, but by the spring of 1927 he had done enough to be able to offer a potential collection to an agent who had taken him on, the up and coming A. D. Peters.[70] He was also, now, contributing more book reviews than reportage to the *Monitor* and – if unsuccessfully – trying to find a publisher for a travel book, under the putative title 'Irish Miles and Spanish Leagues'.[71]

Evelyn, meanwhile, revived her hopes of a theatrical career by getting a part at the Abbey which enabled her to use her Spanish observations, in Lennox Robinson's production of *The Two Shepherds*, by the Spanish dramatist Gregorio Martínez Sierra. Suddenly alone in the evenings in his study 'up among the chimneys' in Waterloo Road, Victor racked his brains for subjects for his weekly *Monitor* essay, and felt restless and put upon. He grumbled to Gordon that 'Evelyn flourishes like the green bay tree. And I wither away like the fig.'[72] He was also irritated by the effects of what seemed to other people to be his settled domesticity:

Now we have a flat everyone thinks we are respectable & nice to know, apparently. . . . It is curious how people like you to conform to *their* standards, and always distrust you when you stick to your own. Anything worse than that horrid, suety settled-down feeling is hard to imagine. I expect we shall be shifting around again soon. I hope so.

It is almost exactly a year since I was out of Ireland (when we went up to North Africa, in fact) and I'm just about feeling like another expedition if I can raise some money. I'm seriously thinking of shipping myself steerage to Spain again for a while.[73]

One outcome of his restlessness was the long walk through Extremadura and Old Castile described in his first book, *Marching Spain*.

This time, having persuaded Evelyn to move to London in search of more theatre work, he definitely travelled alone, leaving her behind at a new set of digs at 117 Charlotte Street. The tall Bloomsbury house was otherwise full of art students from the nearby Slade School and they all shared a single lavatory on a landing. Things were going badly between Victor and Evelyn. They were not helped by their surroundings: 'Two beds, one table, no other furniture,' he wrote in a later notebook. 'I worked at a tiny side table. Caught fleas.'[74] Though they were both later to have happy and fulfilled relationships with other people, they were unable to get on well together sexually. Naturally enough, neither of them went into detail about this, but both of them spoke about what Victor described to Gordon as 'years . . . of domestic infelicity'.[75] Much later, explaining to one of her daughters by her second husband why her marriage to Victor had not worked out, Evelyn talked of their incompatibility in a way that made clear that she meant something physical.[76] And Victor, both in his diaries and in letters to Gerald Brenan, said much the same, though more fiercely. In a journal entry on his fortieth birthday, writing about the happiness he had found with his second wife, he said that previously 'I had known only sexual misery and frustration. . . . What a monstrous egotism to accept with a sort of tortured complacency . . . that sexual misery of my first marriage.'[77]

There was a painful synergy between this frustration and Pritchett's often obsessive approach to his writing. As he admitted in a passage eventually cut from a draft of *Midnight Oil*:

I had become a fanatic; perhaps I [have] always been one. I was fanatical about art and writing. . . . My torment is clear to me now, in the passages of poetic exaggeration that suddenly break without warning or reason into my writing; they represent unsatisfied energies . . . I was something of a comic, an inverted poet or romantic, and, like all comics, I had a melancholy face and a scabrous or reckless tongue.[78]

It can't have been much fun for Evelyn, either, and it was understandable that in these circumstances she, in turn, withdrew from Victor. Each of them was miserable, lost and lonely. On the physical side, Victor was inclined to blame not so much his lack of sexual education in childhood as his 'anti-sexual education'.[79] He wrote well in *Nothing Like Leather* about how Mathew Burkle's inexperience is compounded by a clash between physical urgency and religiose hypocrisy. The only thing that made his own acquiescence in such difficulties possible, Pritchett told Brenan, had been 'foreign travel, a violent, immolating passion for foreign things, specially language and art, in which I could lose myself.'

Again, though, this seems to have been a retrospective simplification. One of the main themes of the fictions in which Pritchett most obviously drew on his life with Evelyn is not sexual incompatibility of itself, but the broader difficulties of relationships between independent women and relatively unreconstructed men. This is particularly true of Pritchett's second novel, *Shirley Sanz*[80] (published in the USA as *Elopement into Exile*).

The novel counterposes two young women: Shirley herself, who more or less forces the older Lewis Sanz into eloping with her to his home in southern Spain, and Cynthia Harte, who by way of various affairs ends up in the same neighbourhood and finds herself working as Shirley's nanny. Cynthia is ostensibly the freer of the two: unmarried, sexually casual, adroit at – and convincingly excited by – dumping partners once they've done whatever she needed them for: a knack she learned in part from how a man she once loved treated her. Shirley, by contrast, after her burst of rebellion-by-marriage against her possessive mother, seems at first to sink under the weight of her husband's large Anglo-Hispanic family with its intricately contending powers. Meanwhile, Lewis's own apparently bumbling conservatism, both as a patriarch and as a partner in his family's long-established business, is shown to be deceptive: he is shrewd, kind, surprisingly flexible and, in a situation where not only politics but political violence increasingly affects everyone's lives, his sympathies are on the right side. These qualities are apparent to Shirley, but she is also drawn to Lewis's less scrupulous cousin and business partner, James, a widower – an attraction sharpened by jealousy when she learns that something has been starting between James and Cynthia. In the end, while Shirley has her fling with James, it's Cynthia who is forced to move away.

As a whole, *Shirley Sanz* doesn't succeed: too many of its albeit sharply observed elements fail to coalesce, too much is begun and then forgotten. But in the interactions of the two main women, Pritchett absorbingly explores two kinds of female trajectory, for the most part within the same domestic sphere. In both cases the novel sees men's attempts to 'manage' the women with a mixture of sympathy and sharp satire: Cynthia's hapless onetime lover Geoffrey, spreading his clothes over every chair in the bedroom in a desperate bid for possession; the lecherous hotelier; the forlornly adoring émigré photographer, Augustus; the part-baffled, part-grateful, part-wretched Lewis himself. For the most part, though, the centre of consciousness is one or other of the women. Neither Shirley nor Cynthia 'is' Evelyn. But it doesn't seem far-fetched to suppose that in exploring the actions of both characters in relation to these and other men, and to their having burned their boats by choosing a way of life so far removed from their origins, Pritchett had learned from his marriage.

One guesses, too, that the substantial elements of happiness between Shirley and Lewis must also in part reflect aspects of Victor's life with Evelyn. While the marriage was often very difficult, and in due course ended badly, it lasted a long time – as far as actually living together was concerned, at least nine years, and officially twelve[81] – and it included many happy dimensions and episodes. Indeed, when it was time for Victor to set off on his solitary journey to Extremadura, he almost changed his mind.

The first entry in the notebook on which *Marching Spain* was closely based – an intensely immediate document, with its daily record of numbers of kilometres walked, and the maps and railway timetables folded into its pages – reads in part, 'Dismal London. . . . Breakfast. Sadness. Feeling not wanting to go. Do anything to get out of it; but some purposeful force within carries one through.'[82] The eventual book dramatises this mood. Evelyn (unnamed) has to push him out of bed and Victor keeps up a protesting refrain: ' "I can't go," I said miserably . . . "I shan't go," I said again' – all this as they travel on the underground from Warren Street to the main line station at Waterloo, where Evelyn sits with him in his train up to the minute of departure (' "Five to nine," I said. "Another five minutes," she said.') and then stands waving a handkerchief until he is out of sight.[83] It isn't the behaviour of people who know nothing but misery.

Still, that 'purposeful force' drove him hard. Within three months he had not only done his journey but written it up in a series of articles (they appeared immediately: in the *Christian Science Monitor*, the *Manchester Guardian* and *Outlook*),[84] and had delivered them in a fuller form to A. D. Peters.[85] The finished book, his first, was published at the beginning of February 1928.

Marching Spain is part of the story of Pritchett's dealings with a country, but it's also part of the story of his first marriage. The book is punctuated with tales of difficult relationships and other people's homilies about how relationships should be: a man running away from his marriage; a blacksmith and his wife who, like the Pritchetts, are childless ('How lonely life is without children. . . . And you wander alone? Like the shepherds who never see their families. What a life for them');[86] a railwayman who lives much of his time apart from his wife and who not only 'artlessly' tells Pritchett that having children is the most important thing – the only thing which will make an otherwise disaffected woman stay with her husband – but announces Pritchett's childlessness to all the other railwaymen, as they arrive;[87] a group of women who gossip about him and his childlessness, thinking he is asleep; a pathetic waiter who enlists Pritchett's help over his embattled engagement; above all, a lonely Basque woman who remembers having met him before when he passed that way with Evelyn and who, learning that the couple's families came from different countries, is prompted to pour out a lament about her own rows with her Castilian husband: 'So they opposed,' Pritchett wrote sympathetically, 'like two goats head to head, mind to mind, locked silently month after month in the silence below the pass.'[88]

All this external unhappiness prepares the ground for his own bitter disappointment, when he arrives exhausted at his poste restante at Salamanca, to find letters from home which spell nothing but bitterness, nothing but *nada*: 'my letters were abomination and misery, nothing . . . the pains of misfortune like a broken spring dug into me. The café stamped itself upon the mind as hard as the stare of clear misery. . . .'[89]

The period after Pritchett's return to London from Extremadura was among the hardest of his life. He was extremely worried about money, and he and Evelyn were forced to move often from one set of cheap lodgings to another: after Charlotte Street, to a nearby place with a 'stinking sink' at 8 Fitzroy Square, let to them by a painter who endlessly dunned them for rent.[90] Some of the intensity of his experience of poverty was conveyed a couple of years later in *Clare Drummer*:

The terrible complacency of people when their pockets were jingling with money. The prison-like banks. In a restaurant he saw one till full of half-crowns, and another stuffed with green notes, and the sight disgusted him. From his window the windows of the houses gaped like unfed mouths; and the houses themselves were grey, shrunken paupers, tinkers, huddled beggars, smoking away at the chimneys as though they had in despair picked up a few cigarette ends to compensate for the shrinking emptiness inside them. Keegan's grocery van slid alongside the curb on the opposite side of the canal, and that was a preposterous sight: hams, oatmeals, pickles, butter, flour all going into one house! . . . The black, shiny well-fed procession of cars into the city! He would like to attack a car, puncture its tyres, break its windows. . . .[91]

At times, Victor was forced to do commercial translations for which he was paid a farthing a word.[92] Evelyn found more theatre work, first in a short season for the London Repertory Company (she played a maid, a waitress and other walk-on roles), then in an Arts Theatre Guild Christmas entertainment called *Tod the Tailor*, a loose update of *The Knight of the Burning Pestle* starring the young Richard Goolden, in which 'Mr Evelyn Vigors' was mentioned by the *Era* among half a dozen actors who had 'cleverly differentiated' their respective parts as supporting tailors: more cleverly than the reporter knew.[93]

Around now, Victor spent some time in the country. Cyril was living in the thatched gamekeeper's cottage of a big house at Marlow, in Buckinghamshire, and Victor rented the converted stables beside it, where he struggled with his first novel. Evelyn came and went. A neighbour had a gramophone which distracted Victor and also worried him: 'If we can hear so much through the wall, how much can they hear of what E & I say?' He had temporarily lost interest in working as a reporter but seemed surprised when, in November 1927, the *Monitor* stopped his retainer. He trailed around publishers begging for work as a reader: 'Cassell No Hutchinson No. . . . Hodder Stoughton No.'[94] By the end of the month his savings were down to £3. 'Still no news of a job. . . . It is impossible to think about the novel with all this financial worry hanging over one. . . .' He was saved by unexpected bits and pieces. Some of his stories were anthologised in E. J. O'Brien's *Best Short Stories of the Year*.[95] The *Monitor* resumed sending him books for review and soon he was again appearing there on average at least once a week. Early December brought a cheque for £14, by which he was so relieved that he bought a new hat and took Evelyn, Cyril and a friend dancing in Covent Garden. Then Evelyn got her part in *Tod the Tailor*. Victor swung between mild elation, frequent illnesses and a general sense of drudgery and inadequacy. Getting up the Spanish novelist Benito Pérez Galdós for the *New Statesman*, he felt 'mediocre, impotent, & fit merely to fill up ledgers. . . .'[96] Within days, he was broke again, but then another cheque arrived, some of it to be spent on Christmas presents for Evelyn as she left for Liverpool: grease paints, a hot-water bottle.[97] The couple were apart at Christmas, Evelyn in her show, Victor back with his parents in Bromley. His diary entry on Christmas Day says how sorry he was that she wasn't there.

Soon, though, he was back on his emotional switchback. In January 1928 he is desperate for a job; in February the *Monitor* makes him a sub-editor of the literary section at a salary of £250 a year. Early in June, in a wild diary entry, almost illegible even by his own taxing standards, he talks of being 'weighted with a desire that embitters', and of Evelyn's apparent lack of feeling, even comprehension, concerning it.[98] 'I may & will get rid of her,' he recklessly scrawled, 'but am I afraid to? What would I do? Would I be any better off? Why in God's name would I find the perfect love? Shall I never no [sic] one moment of sexual ecstasy?' That autumn, in the country, he worked on *Clare Drummer* eleven hours a day and Evelyn took a room of her own in Bloomsbury.[99] At last, at the end of December 1928, the book was finished, but he was 'Terribly depressed by it. It is jejune, tedious, faulty, all the characters are alike . . . the novel is a hopeless form.' He added, 'Something different must be started, a sort of autobiographical record of the lying type' – like, he suggested, George Borrow's mid-nineteenth-century novel-cum-memoir, *Lavengro*, about a life of vagabondage and literary journeywork.

Despite his earlier longings for separation, Victor now lamented that Evelyn was

> away again. She is always away. Sometimes I think I'd give anything for a home – a proper home – with children. All this healthy modern wife working business is terribly trying. I sometimes dream of a woman who is physically & intellectually satisfying – a mistress. But I only dream. Silly fool.
>
> But the plain fact is I suppose we cant afford children & decent comfort on £250 a year and it is agreed that she has gone away because at least she is earning a little money & is happy – which is more than she [is] doing nothing with me.[100]

A less positive view of Evelyn's theatrical life emerges from

Pritchett's novella 'The Spanish Virgin', which he wrote at this time. The main character, a girl called Crystal, escapes from her mother into a career on the stage. The earlier stages of the book are set in Spain, and are vivid and full of surprise. But the two-thirds which involve a travelling repertory company, despite fresh glimpses of the physical surroundings of backstage life, are mainly hackneyed and, in every sense, stagy. Whereas the main Spanish character is made enjoyable fun of through an essentially sympathetic grasp of his hidden and not-so-hidden yearnings and confusions, Pritchett is too impatient with the actor-manager Fontenoy Dufaux and his ex-leading lady, Miss O'Malley, to give them anything more than a caricatural life, and the Fontenoy–Crystal affair is both over-contrived and under-imagined.

Did Victor, as the novel may suggest, suspect Evelyn of having had an affair? He himself slept with other women around now, though all that he confided to some notes made much later was that one of them lived in Chelsea, one in Maida Vale. While the written records of most periods of Pritchett's adult life are exceptionally full, they become very patchy at this time. Between 1929 and 1936 he either stopped writing his journals or, if he wrote them, they were subsequently thrown away. It seems impossible that he and Evelyn never sent letters to each other, yet only one has survived from any time in their relationship and that is a carbon copy of a letter from Victor to her about their divorce settlement.[101] A few letters remain which were written *to* them, as a couple, by close friends: the artists Stephen and Mary Bone, the novelist Richard Church and his wife Rina.[102] And there are several entries about them in the diaries of Olga Martin – wife of the *New Statesman* editor Kingsley Martin – who remained a close friend of Evelyn's after both of their marriages had broken up.[103]

Documents like these can be hard to interpret, especially when, as is often the case, they speak warmly of the Pritchetts' marriage. Were their friends ignorant of how badly things were going, or were they trying to jolly them along? Ten years later Pritchett himself gave 1930 as the date when the marriage ended. But in August of that year Church wrote to the couple he nicknamed 'Evening and Vesper', congratulating them on getting a new flat and wishing them 'a deluge of life in it; work, and desire for more work; and indescribable little indolences together, and sudden gusts of misery bursting into secret love together. . . .'[104] In March and May of 1931 he wrote again, with similar confidence that there was a 'them' to write to ('probably you are gazing into the sun on the beach, Evelyn a sight such as was seen only in pagan Rome, or at the Aphrodisiac rites on the hills above Corinth').[105] A letter of July 1932 may have been aimed at bolstering the marriage: 'You are the happiest people in the world, & both true artists of life. Perhaps you don't believe it; but you have the love of many people as a proof!'[106] (To Gordon Pritchett, too, the description 'artists of life' seemed apt: he attributed the fact that the couple's living arrangements included little furniture beyond cushions on the floor to the influence of their Moroccan travels.) Unless the Churches were totally out of touch, the Pritchetts were still together that October, when Richard sends 'little Eva' his love; and again in February and May 1933, when Rina joins him in sending love to them 'both'.[107] That summer, or even later, they took Evelyn's schoolboy nephew, David Willison, on the first of two holidays on the Norfolk Broads (Evelyn was a proficient sailor). To the teenager, it was obvious that the couple were getting on badly. Looking back, he thought their kindness to him at least partly an attempt 'to keep the show on the road'. If so, the effort was a lot more persistent and long lasting than Victor later recalled.[108]

Whatever was happening in Pritchett's private life, his work was gathering momentum. *Clare Drummer* appeared in 1929; *The Spanish Virgin and other stories* (with a cover design by Mary Bone) in 1930; a second novel, *Shirley Sanz*, in 1932. All three books were dedicated 'To Evelyn'. He was reviewing a great deal: for the *New Statesman*, the *Spectator* and the *Fortnightly Review*, now, as well as the *Monitor*. Short stories were appearing at some rate: at least ten new ones between 1930 and 1933.

One of the striking things about these early writings is how firmly they were disavowed by Pritchett later. Like other prolific authors, he wrote stories which he didn't publish, and published stories in magazines which he didn't put into collections, and published stories in collections which he didn't put into *collected* collections. The *Collected Stories* of 1956 contains thirty-seven items; that of 1982 just twenty-nine. The earliest of the stories in either book first appeared in 1932.[109] In the preface to the second volume, Pritchett, meditating briefly on the processes of fiction, writes, 'only once – and that was when I was twenty-three and beginning – did I take down the scene, the character and the conversation straight from life, as I listened to a man in Dublin trying to persuade a barman to give him a dozen oysters without paying for them.'[110] Yet not only does this story, 'Fishy', not appear in either book, but nor do any of the others which he put together in *The Spanish*

Virgin. The much ampler *Complete Short Stories* of 1990 contains everything from all of Pritchett's collections after *The Spanish Virgin*, plus
nine previously uncollected items, making a total of eighty-two stories.
But again it includes neither 'Fishy' nor anything else from that book,
let alone several other early stories which never made it into book
form.[111] Pritchett's mature view of this work was that it was no more
than a learning process in which 'I was . . . seduced by many influences,
and had not yet found a distinctive voice'. But it was better than that
and there was another reason for his having distanced himself from
some of it. The copy of the 1982 volume which he gave to his second
wife is inscribed: 'I wrote all these stories from the time we came
together in 1934.' This was not strictly true, but it suggests a motive for
some of the exclusions.

If Pritchett drew promiscuously on his experiences in his fictional
writing, his relationship with Evelyn was no exception. Aspects of her
went into *Clare Drummer*, into 'The Spanish Virgin' and also into
Shirley Sanz. But while there's plenty of biographical interest in these
early long fictions – in the writer's developing skills and preoccupations,
and how he reveals, conceals and otherwise shapes his personal life
story – few readers would feel that they are neglected masterpieces, or
even that they deserve to be reprinted. Some of the early short stories,
on the other hand, have much stronger claims but have similarly been
forgotten: an oblivion which Pritchett at the very least connived in.
Among the rejected stories are some which touch on his marital
unhappiness. 'Agranti, for Lisbon', for example, published in 1930 in
the *Fortnightly Review* and never reprinted, fictionalises the sea voyage
he describes in the second chapter of *Marching Spain*, but with a
different vein of personal metaphor. At the moment when the boat is
about to leave the dockside it is seen as a bride, and the journey as the
alarming first stage of a marriage: 'It is a moment of fear; the bottom of
the world has fallen out. A man who boards her at this moment takes a
risk: she is not there. He is climbing into a mirage of iron. . . . There is
no escape now. She is a harsh and unaccustomed bride. . . .'[112] The hint
becomes the main subject of another story published soon afterwards,
'A Serious Question', a sharp, Lawrentianly symbolic episode about a
sexual mismatch, childlessness and emotional immaturity.[113] Though,
again, never reprinted in Pritchett's lifetime, it is among the most
complex and fully realised of his early fictions, as well as a painful
encryption of aspects of his marriage.

James Harkaway and his wife sleep in separate rooms. At night, they talk to each other through an open door, 'never saying what they meant, keeping it all on the surface and only letting glints of real intent and buried brooding appear'. (This describes, too, how the story itself operates.) Harkaway is a rent collector, a cautious man but one with 'a fanciful desire to be suspected of passion'. There may be an echo of that recent self-description by Victor as 'impotent, & fit merely to fill up ledgers'.[114] Harkaway's wife resists his wish for a child: she does not 'regard herself as the vehicle of nature, the tool of a fate'. From the safe seclusion of her bedroom she is talkative and in her domestic anxiety reveals more than she may mean to: 'Did you put the guard round the fire?' she asks him. 'Did you shut the gate?' Reassured, she becomes flirtatious, a little reckless. There's a suggestion that she comes into his room, or perhaps it's just that they think this may happen: at any rate, he reacts coldly and their conversation shifts to gossip, in part about a neighbour's dogs. 'Lovely boys,' Mrs Harkaway calls them. She says she wishes they had a dog. Other ventures are hinted at, other risks that they won't take. They talk on, she feeling that 'every mocking sentence was like a dip of the paddle which shot her boat wildly forward, more sharply every time into the mists and uncertainties of a quarrel which could, after all, be stopped in a moment'. She turns to the fact that they have no children, then realises she has gone too far. 'She had said something real to him by accident, when the only way she could be happy with him was by inventing a fairyland of pretence. Their talk became painful, bitter, and spasmodic.'[115] Banal, also. Bathos is an important part of Pritchett's art and, now, Harkaway becomes pre-occupied with other pains: 'Lord, but bicycling didn't half play up the calves of your legs!' He sleeps but she stays awake, wondering about spiders and mice, and missing his voice: 'Now he was asleep, she could passionately love her husband. Tears were in her eyes.'

At last she, too, goes to sleep. She dreams of an invasion, a strange man in her room, then several strangers. She wakes and hears real noises: 'Men walking in the garden. She screamed out: "Darling there are men in the garden." ' In fact, they are horses.

'In the garden,' exclaimed his wife. There was a scuffle of clothes, and a thump like one of those apples as she jumped out of bed . . .

'The naughty boys!' she cried, as he pulled the door open. 'Look at them.' . . .

The creatures stopped like gawky louts who had been caught robbing an orchard. Sardonic in their nakedness, swishing their tails,

and the smell of hide, manure and bruised grass steaming on them.
. . . Harkaway squared his shoulders and delivered them a final notice
in his professional way.

'Go on. Get out of this. Gee up,' he shouted. . . .

'Go along, you naughty boys . . .' cried Mrs Harkaway.

For a moment, husband and wife are stirred: she pulls a spider's web
from his hair, he suddenly, passionately, picks her up and takes her to
her bed. But the moment passes:

As she lay there quickly curled up like a feather, looking at him with
a kind of fear, he suddenly became timid, tender, pitiful, apologetic
. . . he sneezed. . . . Misery stamped out his fire and almost with tears
of desolation he kissed her and went to his own room and the
tepidity of his bed. She called to him through the wall:

'You did leave the gate open. That is how they got in, the cheeky
boys.'

That serious question of the open gate came rushing into his mind
to add to his perplexities . . . but, his children, they had vanished.

*

The Pritchetts' separation was at first indecisive: much less clear-cut (as
well as less early) than Victor later remembered it as having been. But
it seems certain that by the beginning of 1934 they had embarked on
the split which events later that year would make final. Evelyn's acting
career had come to nothing, and she was working in the office of a
literary and dramatic agent, John Quill, in Adelphi, south of the Strand
– an agency like the one bleakly depicted in 'The Spanish Virgin'.[116]
Not only her marriage but her whole life seemed to have failed and she
sank into a deep depression.

For all his imaginative and professional strength, Victor himself
didn't go unscathed. He published only one story in 1933, none in
1934. Early in 1934, Victor Gollancz turned down *Nothing Like Leather*
despite a reader's report which, though negative, concluded that 'if you
decline this book you will be doing something which I know you will,
for personal reasons, deplore . . . and may make a check in the career of
a man who has brilliant possibilities and is still young and feeling his
way'.[117] Pritchett later often mentioned his misery during these years
and there is a revealing deleted passage in one of the drafts of *Shirley
Sanz*, where he speaks of Lewis Sanz's surprise at how things have gone

wrong with Shirley: 'He was astonished that he had deluded himself with his love. It had occurred to him that in marriage there must be disillusion, but he had never thought it possible that if one lived passionately any other consideration . . . could jeopardise it.'[118]

Pritchett was not Lewis Sanz and living passionately was only one of his rules of life, though an important one. He also believed in living for his work and had come to understand what he had always intuitively known, that this required imaginative solitude. The condition is figured in another tale he never reissued, 'The Sack of Lights', written as early as 1928,[119] about a deluded London vagrant with her song, 'Valencia, land of oranges', her mysterious mission to 'git me lights', and her mad story of rockets and a general:

> No one else could hear what her mind heard. No one else could see what her eyes saw. Alight with it, she walked from her room at the back of Euston to Piccadilly Circus with a sack on her back – the sack which she always carried in case there was anything worth having in the gutters – and 'Valencia, land of oranges' twiddling like a ballroom of dancers in her head.
>
> . . . The façades of the buildings were tall mirrors framed in gold, speeding lights. 'Chucking it about,' she cried out. The crowds did not even hear her in the roar.[120]

'The Sack of Lights' has a quality which Pritchett liked to find in other writers: Flannery O'Connor, for example, with her fidelity to what he called 'the inner riot that may possess the lonely man or woman at some unwary moment in the hours of their day'.[121] Whatever his unhappiness in the late 1920s and early 1930s, he himself had this 'inner riot' to keep him going.

3

A so beautiful country spoiled
by politique!

Unlike so many of his contemporaries, V. S. Pritchett didn't become a
'Spanish Civil War writer'. Yet no one publishing in the English
language at the time knew Spain more intimately.[1] During his first stay,
in 1924–5, he filed for the *Christian Science Monitor* almost every day of
the week. He wrote on Miguel Primo de Rivera's dictatorship; on the
opposition, whose politicians Pritchett interviewed and some of whose
intellectual leaders became his friends; on the war in Morocco and the
emergence of General Franco during it. He did pieces on developments
in Catalonia; on social issues such as education, the women's movement, the economic position of the middle classes. As in Ireland, he saw
what the country was like on the ground, travelling on foot as well as by
train, bus and car, meeting considerable hardship, and overcoming
human barriers by his enthusiasm, classless ease and curiosity. Few of
the people he met can have encountered another stranger who was so
truly interested in them and in what they thought. But Pritchett's
concerns were not only those of a wandering amateur anthropologist
with a liking for a simple way of life. He approached Spain, more than
Ireland or America, in an intellectual spirit as well as a romantic one.

Among the most lasting, if indirect, influences on him was the
cultural renaissance of late nineteenth- and early twentieth-century
Spain, partly under the influence of the radical philosopher Francisco
Giner de los Ríos. Giner, himself influenced by German Romanticism,
had been involved in setting up a new college in Madrid, the Institución
Libre de Enseñanza, dedicated to secular, socially beneficial, rational
(rather than religiously based) ideas, including freedom of enquiry and
the equality of women. One of its offshoots was a kind of liberal
interdisciplinary think-tank called the Residencia de Estudiantes, set

among chestnuts and acacias on a rise of land above the Paseo de la Castellana, where Victor and Evelyn lived when they first arrived in the city. Among those whom the Residencia nurtured were the philosophers Miguel de Unamuno and José Ortega y Gasset, the novelist Pío Baroja (like Unamuno, a Basque), and the poets Antonio Machado and Federico García Lorca. It naturally became a stopping-off place for intellectuals from all over Europe.[2]

One of the first articles which Pritchett filed from Spain was about the liberalising impact of educational change there,[3] and the Residencia had a direct effect on him personally. It became his university. Having made a quick start on learning the language, he soon began to read work by some of the people he met, as well as books that they recommended. He took part in Pío Baroja's *tertulia* (a distinctively Spanish kind of informal salon), heard Lorca read, often visited the liberal politician Melquiades Alvarez – who, like Lorca, would meet a violent death in the Civil War. Most important, he read Unamuno's *Del Sentimiento Trágico de la Vida*, responding with almost physical excitement to its 'opening peal':

Ni lo humano, ni la humanidad, ni el adjetivo simple, ni el adjetivo sustantivado, sino el sustantivo concreto; el hombre. El hombre de carne y hueso, el que nace, sufre y muere – sobre todo muere – el que come y bebe y juega y duerme y piensa y quiere, el hombre que se ve y quien se oye, el hermano, el verdadero hermano.

[Neither 'the human' nor 'humanity', neither the simple adjective nor the substantivised adjective, but the concrete substantive – man. The man of flesh and bone; the man who is born, suffers and dies – above all, who dies; the man who eats and drinks and plays and sleeps and thinks and wills; the man who is seen and heard; the brother, the real brother.][4]

Here was an answer to his father's sentimental mysticism and a partial antidote to his own more fin-de-siècle posturings. It was also a focus, a justification, for the human curiosity which had underpinned all of his best early writing. 'Unamuno showed me my own world turned upside down,' he later recalled:

I began to see European history for the first time. No one had taught me *European* history. I saw England from the outside. And in Spain one begins with the elementary things of life: hunger to begin with. Hunger for bread, and all the human hungers. From the stark basis of Spanish realism, carnal and unaffected, I painfully began to build my own picture of the world.[5]

The first of Pritchett's two non-fictional books about Spain takes Unamuno as its starting point. Like everything Pritchett wrote, *Marching Spain* looks at and listens to its human subjects on level terms. But it is unusual in having an agenda: the idea that such attention to other people is better than religion. This becomes explicit at the end of the book, when he makes a dutiful attempt to visit the famous cathedral of León. It is closing time – 'se van a cerrar', he is told (they're about to shut). So – and the symbolism can't be missed – he finds himself back on the street: the street, with its vivid, sacrilegious human energy:

Children were kicking a football against the Cathedral door. Under the Holy Family and the saints and the prophets, the leather thudded. . . . Outside his shop an idle, floury baker sat hotly reading his paper. Down the street wobbled a man learning to ride a bicycle. . . . There were old women carrying water-jars and men trailing in the dust of donkeys. . . .[6]

In the early chapters of *Marching Spain*, from the moment of the boat's first mooring at La Coruña in the midst of the Good Friday processions, Pritchett's encounters have been dominated – to his frustration but also his unavoidable fascination – by religion. Or rather by religions, heterodox, individualistic: the evangelical button seller, Don Benito, with his illicit copy of the Book of Genesis; the Scottish Protestant missionary and his assistant Don Francisco, the latter ferociously gratified by the fates that have overtaken his detractors – this man shot in a quarrel, that one dead of syphilis.[7] Unexpectedness of these kinds gratifies the narrator's anarchic humanism: no one behaves as they are expected to; nothing goes quite to plan, or by the book. In Spain, even the most rigid-seeming of doctrines breaks down.

Pritchett, too, as a travel writer, had his own form of antinomianism: 'I carried no Baedeker.'[8] Until his abortive attempt to see the cathedral in León, he made no effort to touch the customary bases, or even to find out what they were. He has nothing to say about the architecture of Extremadura and Old Castile, about the Roman and Moorish inheritance and the elaborations of churrigueresque, about the region's great monasteries or the paintings inside them. *Marching Spain* is explicit in its prioritisation of flesh and blood over buildings, its preference for 'human architecture'.[9]

There's something overemphatic about this approach. Pritchett seems to be briefly in danger of a doctrinalism very much of his time. But he is never hypocritical. What we remember of *Marching Spain* is precisely its 'human architecture': the young man from Málaga, loud and long in his patriotic denunciations of Seville when Pritchett has thoughtlessly mentioned both towns in the same breath; or the old man he meets in the foothills of the Sierra de Béjar, with his exultant claim that he thinks *nada* of life: 'Nothing! Nothing, nothing, nothing. When it is good, good. When it is bad, good too, for who can change it?'[10]

In his relish of human oddity, Pritchett can sometimes come close to caricature. The notebooks he kept in Spain are full of half-comic

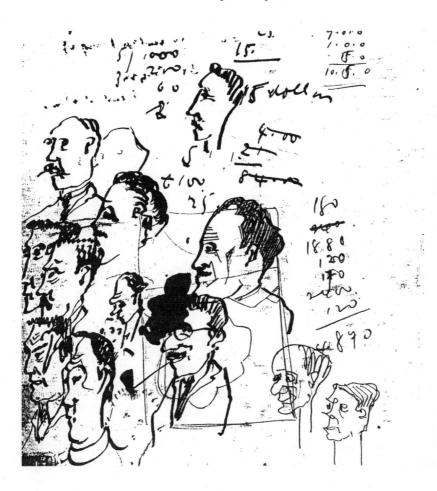

sketches of people he has seen. But this doesn't mean that he fails to treat others as equals. By giving them an identity which, as in Dickens's novels or in the paintings of Goya, exaggerates characteristic traits, Pritchett forces us to look at them. And he deals with himself the same way. The book's opening – Victor's wretchedness at leaving Evelyn behind and his nervousness about the rigours which he plans to inflict on himself – is full of self-mockery. When Don Benito tells him that he's mad to undertake his walk, Pritchett counters, 'Don Quixote was mad', to which Don Benito replies that Cervantes's book is overrated and that anyway very few people have finished it. Don Benito doesn't know, as the reader does, that Pritchett himself had not yet read all of it either.[11] The author sets up another fall for himself when, in answer to Don Benito's question why he has chosen his particular route, he extemporises that it was the one taken by Wellington in the Peninsular War. This is the first and last time the historical precedent is mentioned. Not only is Pritchett no conquering hero, he doesn't give Wellington another thought. By the end of his journey, undecided between going west to Galicia or north to León, he is guided by nothing loftier than an arbitrary decision to take the opposite route from a blind woman on a donkey who has asked him the way. Pritchett is a haphazard traveller, a man who takes *Tristram Shandy* with him rather than a guidebook, and who also follows Sterne in saying not only a lot about little, but also, sometimes, very little about something. Chapter 4 is called 'Nothing About Portugal'. It consists of five and a half lines.

If Pritchett's self-awareness is caricatural, it's also, like his caricatures of other people, essentially serious. He compares his project to selling matches: 'I was going to sell Spain.' This not only mocks both his poverty and his opportunism, but also asks a question of himself, one which his seemingly offhand description of the contents of his Fitzrovia flat, as he leaves it, helps to answer. 'I looked at the sink, the gas ring, the newspaper bought with lively excitement the day before and now fallen loosely on the floor, the brief flood of adventure ebbed out of the print. . . .'[12] The discarded newspaper reminds him that, for the first time, what he is setting out to sell as a travel writer is intended to last.

Marching Spain has lasted partly as a consequence of its sheer vividness. This is, to some extent, a matter of its fictionality. The story is set up as a voyage of exploration, as if the narrator has never been to these parts before – but, of course, he already knew them well. The strengths are mainly descriptive. Pritchett can make even a train journey as strange as a riddle: 'some lines we gathered together under our wheels and others we threw aside in armfuls with a crash into the main stream. . . . We slid up and down against another train.'[13] Or there is the fantastical sense, as much Gulliver as Tristram Shandy, that in Cáceres he is walking over a giant's body:[14]

> already I had begun to feel the tilt of Spain's central tableland beneath my feet, mounting like the heat-breathing body of some gigantic animal to the Gredos, the backbone which cuts the peninsula in two. The Gredos were a hundred miles away, four days' march, but all roads like the bones of a vast body lead to the great spine.

More than half a century later, it was the physicality of *Marching Spain* which astonished Eudora Welty: 'What a stunning announcement of a new writer. . . . Everything in Spain, every element, has its voice . . . and its physical touch.'[15] And if one is often physically aware of the narrator's presence, Pritchett also stands back and lets his people tell their own stories. Sing their own songs, too: the book is full of song. 'The man who is seen and heard', indeed: one can go back to Unamuno's list and tick off all the elements. Eating, drinking, playing, and also dying – a funeral is described with the same brio as a wedding.

With its repeated attacks on organised religion, *Marching Spain* was, in the late 1920s, a political book. The influence of the Residencia is audible again in what Pritchett has to say about the decay of Salamanca, once among 'the great University cities of the world', but now 'squeezed dry by the theologians'.[16] But his politics are far from the revolutionary socialism which was soon to be associated with the Republic, especially by English writers. Like Unamuno, Pritchett was his own man, and the value he put on taking other people at their own self-estimate and letting them get on with their lives was liberal in an essentially conservative sense. 'Every new idea is a war,' he wrote, 'every old one peace.'[17]

The Spanish peninsula provided settings and characters for much of Pritchett's early fiction, as well as for his travel writing and journalism: for 'The Spanish Virgin', for *Shirley Sanz* and for a handful of short stories including 'The Evils of Spain', first published in the *New Statesman and Nation* in 1935 – a story of comic individualism and anarchy.[18] In the spring of 1935 he was there again, reporting for the *Fortnightly Review*, as well as acting as a temporary stringer for the

BBC.[19] The Second Republic, ever since it came to power in 1931, had been in a state of economic and factional crisis which made most programmes of reform unworkable. In 1933, what had been, in effect, a series of unstable coalition governments shifted sharply to the right. Socialists, anticipating a takeover by their similarly faction-ridden and diverse opponents, attempted an armed revolution in October 1934. Pritchett was uniquely well placed, not only imaginatively but through his experience and contacts, to interpret the situation as it unfolded. Yet, having researched his piece with his usual thoroughness, he chose to go straight home to England. In the following months and years, when people from all over the world rushed to take sides, and take active part, in a conflict most of them knew little or nothing about, he stayed put. He didn't return to Continental Europe until the end of the Second World War.

Victor Pritchett was in love. It wasn't the only reason for his abstention, but it was a big one and its consequences were everywhere. Dorothy Roberts was nineteen, strongly built, passionate, intelligent and ambitious. She came from the hilly borders between Welsh Montgomeryshire and English Shropshire: the kind of country, and the kind of family, in which prosperous master butchers doubled as masters of foxhounds. She had a queue of local admirers but she wanted a larger world, was well-read and, having trained as a secretary in London, she had taken a job in the agent's office where Evelyn happened to be working. It was through Evelyn, who liked her, that Dorothy and Victor first met. Unknown at first to Evelyn was the fact that, in the autumn of 1934, they became lovers.

The story of how the relationship began needs its own chapter, but it has a bearing on Pritchett's dealings with the Spanish Civil War. When 'VSP' – as Dorothy, like everyone else by now, always called him – was sent back to Spain by the *Fortnightly Review* in 1935, she begged to go with him. But he was still married and she was legally a minor. However liberated Dorothy was, she was also a daughter of Welsh churchgoers and it would in every sense have been going too far. So a simple, but inadequate, explanation for Pritchett's not having taken part in the war is that he wanted to return to his girlfriend and to push through his divorce from Evelyn. Victor and Dorothy married in October 1936, shortly after Spain's 'Tragic Summer'. Their first child was born at the end of the following year. It was no time to be getting shot at.

This wasn't, though, the whole story. There were other reasons behind Pritchett's decision to stay in England. One was that he knew too much about Spain not to find most other foreign writers' opinions and actions in relation to it simplistic. There's no doubt about his essential sympathies. He expressed them in the *Left Review*'s famous 1937 symposium, *Authors Take Sides on the Spanish War*: 'I am heart and soul for the People of Spain in their brave and stoical resistance to Franco and Fascism. The lesson of Spain for the rest of western Europe, even before this struggle, lay in the innate simplicity and nobility of the uncorrupted common people. They have now burned this lesson upon the imagination of us all.' At this level of generalisation, he was content to join a long and illustrious list of Republican supporters, among them W. H. Auden, Samuel Beckett, C. Day Lewis, Victor Gollancz, Aldous Huxley, C. L. R. James, Storm Jameson, Arthur Koestler, John and Rosamond Lehmann, Louis MacNeice, Naomi Mitchison, Raymond Mortimer, John Middleton Murry, Sean O'Casey, Herbert Read, Edward Sackville-West, Naomi Royde-Smith, Stephen Spender, Sylvia Townsend Warner, Rebecca West and Leonard Woolf. But, as even Pritchett's brief statement betrays, his feelings were complicated. The 'innate simplicity and nobility of the uncorrupted common people' is a concept with which hardly anyone in any of the rival factions could have quarrelled. Much of what appealed to him in his Spanish travels was a consequence of centuries of feudalism. He was to confess many years later,

> The attraction of Spain to the northerner is its rejection of modern life, its refusal of the Reformation, the French Revolution, of all that we call Progress; this rejection is not entirely negative by any means. By indolence and recalcitrance, the Spaniards have preserved their individuality, a creature unashamedly himself, whose only notion of social obligation is what old custom dictates.[20]

The Spain with which he had fallen in love in the mid-1920s was ruled over by a military dictator and was fighting an imperialist war. His dispatches had been subject to censorship. Yet he deplored what he called the 'naïve, Soviet poster-fed lyricism' of politically engaged Spanish writers of the 1930s.[21] And, though an enthusiastic advocate of most of Orwell's other works, when *Homage to Catalonia* appeared in 1938, he was to write, 'There are many strong arguments for keeping creative writers out of politics, and Mr George Orwell is one of them.'[22]

Pritchett praised Orwell's account of his day-to-day experiences in the Civil War, but unsparingly diagnosed what he saw as the book's 'perverse' take on their political context. In particular, Pritchett's first-hand knowledge of Franco's career in Morocco made him sceptical of the idea that a Moroccan uprising in support of the Republic would have been feasible.

> it was surely clear from the very moment of foreign intervention – which was at the beginning of the war – that the Spaniards had tragically but undoubtedly missed the revolutionary tide. Mr. Orwell disagrees. Yet what grounds are there for believing that the democratic moderate line was unrealistic and even strategically unsound? . . . Is it credible that without the 'tainted' Russian arms, there would have been any Government Spain left to which revolutionaries behind Franco's lines could rally? And once Franco had collared the Moors first for a Holy War, what hope was there of a Moroccan rising, all question of French feeling apart? Given the situation, I see no reason to believe in any of these possibilities.

There's a subtext to this review. Orwell and the *New Statesman*, or at any rate Orwell and the magazine's editor, Kingsley Martin, had been at odds since the previous year, when Martin turned down a piece by Orwell which exposed the suppression by Spanish Communists of a rival left-wing faction. Martin sent Orwell Borkenau's *The Spanish Cockpit* for review instead, but in the event that piece was also spiked, and another copy of the book was turned over to Pritchett. Orwell claimed that Martin was in effect censoring anything critical of the Left in case it should lend support to Franco,* but it seems no less likely that, as Martin himself said, he didn't want a review to be used as a political platform at the expense of the book itself, and that in this as in other ways he found Pritchett a better critic than Orwell.

*Orwell's views on the spat appear in Sonia Orwell and Ian Angus (eds.), *The Collected Essays, Journalism and Letters of George Orwell*, vol. 1, *An Age Like This, 1920–1940*, 1968, pp. 276–8, 297–302. (See also C. H. Rolph, *Kingsley: The Life, Letters and Diaries of Kingsley Martin*, 1973, Penguin edn 1978, pp. 241–7.) The Borkenau piece could have been disqualified on the ground that Orwell had already reviewed the book for *Time and Tide*, but Martin's main objection seems to have been that it aired Orwell's views more than giving an account of the book. Orwell claimed that Martin's letter to him made clear that it was on political grounds that the 1937 piece was rejected and his editors confirm this, saying that they have the letter itself. Oddly, though, they do not quote from it. (Martin's own editorial papers from the period were among those lost when the magazine's office was bombed in the Blitz.) Although Orwell continued to grumble about the *New Statesman*'s line on the Civil War, he soon resumed reviewing for the paper.

Partly because of this history, Pritchett's review of *Homage to Catalonia* has been reprinted[23] – uniquely among the very many pieces about Spain which he published in the 1930s. The others also deserve to be read. After *Marching Spain* appeared, he was in demand to write on Spanish topics for the *Fortnightly Review*, the *London Mercury*, the *Manchester Guardian*, the *News Chronicle*, the *Spectator* and several other papers in addition to the *New Statesman* and the *Christian Science Monitor*. Any book with a Spanish element was sent his way. He reviewed Hemingway's *Death in the Afternoon*, Somerset Maugham's *Don Fernando*, the memoirs of the bullfighter, Juan Belmonte (whom he knew), a book on fifteenth-century Spain's expulsion of the Jews.[24] In the last instance, the comparison with Nazi Germany looks obvious, now, but in 1936 not everybody would have made it, as Pritchett eloquently did. More and more, as British attention was drawn to how events in Spain were related to what was going on in Germany and Italy, the books he was sent and the way he treated them had a political bearing. He reviewed a history of the Spanish monarchy in terms much more critical of the subject than the author, whom he took to task for not mentioning that Alfonso XIII, who had abandoned the throne when the Republic came to power (and whom Pritchett was summoned to interview on the King's arrival in Britain)[25] had been 'factious in the worst nineteenth-century tradition', playing politicians against the army in a way which had contributed to Spain's current troubles.[26] In April 1934, in an admiring review of J. B. Trend's *The Origins of Modern Spain*, Pritchett pointed out that while 'the educated Spaniard was inevitably a revolutionary', ideas about revolution there were deeply bound up with, and complicated by, nationalism, religion and tradition.[27] The British Left were at best misled, Pritchett asserted, in regarding Spanish intellectuals 'as an Iberian branch of the Fabian Society'. He was to attack British ignorance more witheringly in August 1935, in a review of Leah Manning's *What I Saw In Spain*, published by Gollancz.[28] Manning, he wrote,

> has the easily-raised emotions of the ill-informed . . . she did not speak Spanish, she saw mainly Socialists; she accepted her facts from them. . . . Visiting Spain for the first time and having the usual blindness to character endemic in the politically minded, she seems to have been carried away by the facial fervour of her friends, their flashing eyes and fervent gestures. She might have seen the same exalted manner in Fascists, priests and peanut vendors.

If the piece was tough on credulity, it was the opposite of complacent. By 1936, Pritchett was writing that the next European war would have its origins in Spain.[29]

He continued to insist on the complexities and contradictions of Spanish life: especially its ambiguous relationship with Europe and modernity, the intensity of its regional differences ('there is no such country as Spain'),[30] and the way they were replicated in party political terms and affected any military action. Some of these ideas, lumped together under the general heading of 'Spanish exceptionalism', have since become tainted by association with Fascism.[31] But it wasn't from Fascists that Pritchett learned them. Among the people who influenced him, for example, was Fernando de los Ríos, a moderate socialist who was among the founders of the Republic and who became Spanish ambassador to the USA.[32] In a wider and longer historical perspective, exceptionalism is helpful to an understanding of Spain and the country's recent success as an integral part of Europe doesn't contradict the idea as clearly as it might seem to. Modern Spain is in part a result of its history – a history which includes the fact that, in the Second World War, this right-wing dictatorship remained neutral, to the advantage, as Pritchett saw, not only of itself but of the Allied democracies.

None of this could have been clearly foreseen at the time and, in his own thinking, Pritchett inevitably sometimes contradicted himself. The revolutionary autumn of 1934 found him in northern Spain. Despite his later claim, in the Orwell piece, that democracy and moderation might have prevailed, Pritchett wrote then that 'It is useless to counsel or expect moderation in Spanish political life. It is irrelevant to remind Spaniards that they are forgetting the decencies of true democracy. . . . They have never had these delights.'[33] Everywhere he travelled in 1934 and 1935, he encountered an extreme, reckless kind of disillusion with the Republic. He speculated that the Left, despite its optimism, also embodied the nihilistic element in Spanish life. 'I think the Left were very conscious when they took up arms that they would perhaps smash themselves and the Republic irretrievably. I think they felt that their honour as well as their intransigence demanded martyrdom.'

This article, published in the *Fortnightly Review* in December 1934, is one of many in which Pritchett's pessimism comes close to conservatism – a conservatism reflected, as in his writing about Ireland, in the frequent pull away from political reportage towards description of what always appealed to him more: the permanencies of the landscape and of its inhabitants, with their ancient occupations, their near-indistinguishability from their surroundings, people 'burned by the sun to the colour of soil, men of adobe rather than men of flesh, pieces of earth walking'. They could be figures in a painting by Ignacio Zuloaga, the most internationally celebrated Spanish artist of his day. Zuloaga had much in common with the younger Pritchett, whom he knew, and who visited the artist in the course of his 1934 trip. 'Poor Spain!' Zuloaga wrote to him afterwards. 'What a pity! all these stupid, and cruel revolutions! A so beautiful country spoiled by politique!'[34]

The Burgos peasants Pritchett depicts feelingly in his 1934 *Fortnightly Review* article, like the Appalachian farmers he had met a decade earlier, are often hungry, but they are self-sufficient, own their own land, are patriotic towards their region and bitterly opposed 'to anything which means change'. Such sentiments attracted the man who, as a child, despite his parents' rural origins, had never lived long in the same place. Pritchett aspired to self-reliance, and would not accept reflex contemporary identifications between poverty and 'oppression'. The real loser in the Civil War, he came to believe, was not the working class but liberalism. Not all Spanish peasants, of course, corresponded to his ideal. Many were the vassals of absentee landlords, and Pritchett wrote about their needs sympathetically and out of long observation. He believed that the Republicans were doing no better by this underclass than their predecessors had. In the spring of 1935 he encountered a director of a lunatic asylum who claimed that in recent years he had taken in 500 people whose only affliction was that they were starving.[35] On this tour, Pritchett kept his eye firmly and unromantically on politics under the Republicans: on the balance of payments crisis and high unemployment, on the huge number of people imprisoned for political reasons and on the influence of, and shifts in policy by, different elements of the Catholic right wing. Meanwhile, in a series of articles and reviews, Pritchett continued to question the orthodoxies about Spain which prevailed among the British Left, whose version of events when war came was as much an importation, he argued, as the weapons and troops of the Italian and German Right. Spain itself was a place to which these foreign polarities did not apply, a country 'always in a situation where the main facts are much less important than the imponderables, where conditions and individuals

are more important than ideas. It is one of those countries which, with
Ireland and Russia, break the heart and ruin the minds and lives of the
logical foreigner.'[36]

There was a personal sense, of course, in which Ireland had broken
Pritchett's heart. But he was recovering, and in other ways he loved
what he saw both there and in Spain – above all because it produced
something even more important to him than usual at this time: the kind
of writing he loved. The development of Pritchett's aesthetic, in his
fiction and also in his accounts of others' work, is in more than one
sense the story of his life. Pritchett saw himself above all as a working
writer but within that, at this time, as a novelist first, a short-story
writer second and the rest third. He had every artist's fear that his gifts
were under threat. But he also saw that current developments in his
private life could change his writing for the better. The sense of
liberation and honesty which he instantly found with Dorothy, and his
scorn at the conformist attitudinising of many writers about the Spanish
Civil War, converged in some particularly intense reflections about his
own work.

These went beyond, though they involved, his conviction that when
an artist hands himself over to a cause, the results no longer belong to
art. He deplored, for example, the effects of Republican activism on the
work of Ramón Pérez de Ayala, whom he regarded as the most brilliant
of contemporary Spanish novelists.[37] And in a 1937 essay he praised
Turgenev's shoulder-shrugging reaction to the collapse of the
revolutions of 1848, and explored the lessons offered by Turgenev's
Rudin to current circumstances: 'How seductive is the foreign
barricade, how exotic the international, as distinct from the national,
situation! How curious the society which uproots its intellectuals and
sends them abroad to discover their wills!'[38] In Pritchett's own case,
though, there was more than politics to contend with. On the one hand
he saw that it wasn't always easy for an artist to distinguish between
propaganda and a more impartial creative engagement with events in
the world. He longed for the latter and sometimes reproached himself
with failing in it. Too much of his effort, he confided to a journal begun
in June 1936, had gone into chasing originality: 'An impatience with
the usual and normal, therefore always going off at a tangent from it.'[39]
Part of the reason, he feared, was egotism, a self-preoccupation that
kept him from pursuing 'other experience'. He was appalled 'by the lack
of interest of my experience. The things I don't know. Always preserving the self. Thus I don't go to Spain, to the Spanish war, because I

am preserving my peace . . . my private world. The Spanish world would break into it and distract.'

He wasn't the first or last writer to castigate himself on grounds like these, and in any case he was being too hard on himself: it wasn't as if he had never let Spain into his work. (In a more self-confident frame of mind, he grumbled in a 1937 review that 'you were called an escapist if you went to Spain before August, 1936, but not an escapist if you joined the International Brigade or became some kind of British delegate afterwards'.)[40] But other things, too, had previously invaded his writing. 'My fight in the past few years,' he wrote in his journal, 'really since the break up with Evelyn has been against . . . conformity, an attempt to recover this earlier natural [*word illegible*] which the social (and in the long run political) requirements of upper middle class society had diverted, distracted and weakened.'[41] There's a clear link between this resistance to conformity and his unwillingness – however guilty he felt about it – to campaign in Spain.

The resulting shift in Pritchett's writing took some time. He was distracted, as we shall see, by his new marriage, by having young children, by official work in the Second World War, by reviewing. Besides, although in future he was always to talk down what he had written while he was with Evelyn, there was a lot in it that was of lasting value. In some essential respects, too, especially the obliqueness which momentarily worried him in 1936 but which is an important, even defining, element of much of his best work, his voice happily stayed the same. Still, he felt he had to embark on something still truer to himself and to his origins, including the country he came from, than his work had always been. As he put it, with his keen ear for the truths that lie in clichés, in a story published the following year; 'You Make Your Own Life'. One of the headings in the 1936 notebook is 'An *autobiography*'. Among the main patterns in his career is the way that, encouraged by the new confidence he acquired in the mid 1930s, he engaged more and more directly with the experiences of his early years and also with Englishness.

Pritchett's withdrawal from Spain was incomplete, and temporary. During the Civil War he closely followed what was going on, not least through Spanish and Hispanophile friends who came to London, most of whom were liberal-leftists, some of whom surprised him by thinking 'the Caudillo' (Franco) the least bad of the available options and one of whom brought news of support for him even within parts of the radical Frente Popular.[42] Unamuno was among those liberals who ultimately took Franco's side, but Pritchett's friends included unswerving

Republicans, too, among them the novelist and former Swindon railway worker Ralph Bates, who had first gone to Spain in 1930 and joined the International Brigades.[43] Pritchett continued to review books relating to the Civil War and his judgements have stood up well: his praise, for example, of Franz Borkenau's *The Spanish Cockpit* and of Elliot Paul's *The Life and Death of a Spanish Town*, about the effects of the war on the then primitive and little-known island of Ibiza.[44] Above all, he wrote several long, judicious, simplification-resistant essays on the subject between 1936 and 1938.[45]

A similar independence characterised Gerald Brenan, whom Pritchett first got to know at this time. Brenan came from an upper-middle-class colonial military background of a kind familiar to Victor through the Vigorses. He had served with distinction in the First World War, but was determined to shake off his upbringing. In pursuit of a career as a poet and novelist, he had moved in 1919 to a remote mountain village in southern Spain, where he lived intermittently for several years during his equally intermittent affair with Dora Carrington. Like Pritchett, he had travelled widely in the peninsula, was fascinated by its people and its history, and compensated for not having been to university by an almost fanatically industrious and systematic approach to study.

The two men met at a party at the Spanish embassy in London shortly before Christmas 1936. They liked each other instantly and dined together soon afterwards at the Mallorca, in Soho.[46] Immediately before being driven out by the Civil War, Brenan had been living at a house which he and his American wife, Gamel, had bought at Churriana, near Málaga. (They were among the last expatriates to leave.) He was now at work on a personal account of his Civil War experiences. After much reading – not least of articles by his new friend Pritchett – and many changes of narrative approach, this became his authoritative study, *The Spanish Labyrinth: An Account of the Social and Political Background of the Spanish Civil War*, published in 1943. Brenan's Spain was different from Pritchett's. Though he had travelled, he had mainly lived in one region, and – at least by local standards – in seigneurial style. Most of Brenan's friends in Andalucía, as Jonathan Gathorne-Hardy shows in his vivid biography,[47] were other expatriates. But he had had direct contact with the war. Churriana was often bombed, on the false information that it contained a munitions dump, and Spanish people whom Gerald and Gamel knew were killed. For a while, in 1936, Brenan reported on events around Málaga for the *Manchester Guardian*. He remained intensely involved in everything that was going on in Spain, but, like Pritchett, he knew the country too well to accept the prevailing attitude to it of the British intellectual Left. Gathorne-Hardy writes that 'his feelings were for the Republicans', but

> these feelings did not have the same left-wing ideology – romantic, proletarian-worshipping and often fuelled by class guilt – as those of so many of his contemporaries. . . . Also, for some time, he backed non-intervention. His reading rapidly showed him that the Civil War was a Peninsular problem, not an extension of European conflicts; and the violence he so minded . . . would be exacerbated if other nations poured in arms and munitions.[48]

*

In 1950 Brenan published a second book on the peninsula, *The Face of Spain*, and around this time both he and Pritchett went back: Brenan, with Gamel, to Churriana, which from now on was his main home; Pritchett to research *The Spanish Temper*.

Pritchett's second book on Spain, like Brenan's, is the fruit of thirty years' travel, reading and contemplation. As if anxious about being thought to have repeated *Marching Spain*, Pritchett goes out of his way in his preface to dismiss the earlier volume as 'a juvenile book . . . now happily out of print'.[49] But although there are points of overlap, the new work is immediately more spacious, more comprehensive, less idiosyncratic. The author has grown up: not only can he see the point of architecture, now – even of Gaudí[50] – but he has developed a suspicion of travel writing as a form of romantic voyeurism. He expressed similar doubts in his 1945 introduction to a selection of writings by his earlier hero, Robert Louis Stevenson. Pritchett now thought that most of Stevenson's travel writing had 'worn very badly' and attributed this to what he saw – unfairly (he showed no sign of having read Stevenson's engaged works of political anthropology, *In the South Seas* and *A Footnote to History*) – as an essential dandyism in Stevenson's approach.[51]

The world had moved on. This time, Pritchett arrived in Spain by air and in ways other than the merely visual there's a new expansiveness to his view:

> Spain is the great producer of exiles, a country unable to tolerate its own people. The Moors, the Jews, the Protestants, the reformers –

out with them; and out, at different periods, with the liberals, the atheists, the priests, the kings, the presidents, the generals, the socialists, the anarchists, fascists, and communists; out with the Right, out with the Left, out with every government.[52]

The Second World War had prompted some caution even in Pritchett about such lumpings together. 'It is absurd of course,' he acknowledges, 'to generalise about a nation from the sight of two people on a railway platform.' But he was an intuitive writer, less reliant than Brenan on bookish sources, and more willing to take risks: 'we are travellers,' he reminds the reader, '– let us correct one generalisation by adding a great many more.'[53] The book's frame remains that of a journey, described in the present tense. In its course, in a talkative, casual-seeming yet underlyingly systematic way it contrives to introduce key elements of the topography, language, culture, history and politics of Spain and its different regions. The scope is wide: Pritchett is particularly alert, for example, to Basque issues. And, partly under Brenan's influence, there is a much stronger historical underpinning than in *Marching Spain*. He writes about imperial Spain and its decline, about great figures of the Spanish Church such as St Ignatius Loyola. Meanwhile, he observes the changes that have come with Franco and with modernity: the kinds of urban development that were springing up all over the world, as well as forms of intellectual and artistic suppression that were peculiar to dictatorships, whether of the Right or the Left.

He has a lot to say about Franco, most of it bad. The previous dictator, Primo de Rivera, by contrast, who died in 1930, now seems to him 'a benevolent and practical despot'.[54] Pritchett acknowledges, though, the shrewd pragmatism of Franco's policy in the Second World War ('to get valuable pickings from both sides and to keep out of Europe'), as well as the fact that the Allies had a lot to be grateful for in Spanish neutrality. And, with his usual fair-mindedness, he continues to insist that much of what is wrong with post-war Spain has to be laid at the door of the Republicans:

The history of the Republic from 1931 to 1939 has disillusioned Spaniards about themselves. The early achievements of the Republic were important, but savage intolerance soon swept them away. It was mad to open an all-out attack on the Catholic Church, it was mad to potter with the land question; but each section of the Right and Left wanted its own absolute, without compromise and without even some small show of practical sense. Each party fell into the hands of its own extremists.

Now Spain is exhausted and cynical and silenced by guilt about the Civil War. . . .[55]

Such thoughts are prompted in part by the setting of this part of the book: Madrid. Throughout, topography is artfully linked to wider issues, among them the extent to which writing about Spain has always been a form of cultural fiction. Romantic 'Andalusia', Pritchett points out, is an invention of the French: of Gauthier, Mérimée and other authors. And the two great mythical figures given to the world by the peninsula are themselves fictional: Don Quixote and Don Juan. He delves brilliantly into both stories (no guilty mutterings, now, about not having finished Cervantes), and into differences in attitudes to them inside and outside Spain.

Don Juan leads him naturally into a section on the country's sexual mores: naturally, but not always convincingly. While it was true that the Spanish imagination 'runs easily to the thought of orgy',[56] Pritchett's observations about prostitutes and brothels owed more to his conversations with Brenan, an aficionado, than to any direct researches of his own. (Brenan talked a lot about brothels, which, to Pritchett's amusement, he pronounced 'bruthels'. Comparing Pritchett with Chekhov in a letter to Dorothy, Brenan said, 'They both write admirable short stories, they are both good raconteurs, they both twitch in bed. The only difference I see is that Chekov also had piles and went the round of brothels in every town he visited. I doubt if V.S.P. has done that at Murcia or Almeria, and I fear his book will be the worse for it.')[57] Pritchett is more self-assured on bullfighting, about which he writes appreciatively as well as with a sane grasp of the arguments pro and con.[58] And he is similarly commonsensical about the rise of tourism. Aware that even the most sophisticated travel writer is in part both a tourist and a professional guide, he's enough of a relativist to see, also, that what can appear irritatingly or even despicably new is often no more than a version of the past: 'The tourist is part of the landscape of our civilisation,' he writes of the Alhambra, 'as the pilgrim was in the Middle Ages.'[59]

The Spanish Temper is still one of the best introductions to Spain and it has often been reprinted. It is not a long book, but no important region, movement, theme or issue is left out. And with all its range and subtlety there are many personal elements: an encounter with an urchin who acts as 'secretary' to the bullfighter Belmonte, or with a highflown unemployed Francoist lawyer; and characteristically intense descriptions of the landscape:

> the colouring of iron, blue steel, violet and ochreous ores, metallic purples, and all the burned, vegetable pigments. These landscapes frighten by their scale and by the suggestion of furrowed age, geological madness, malevolence, and grandeur. . . . Nature has died and . . . only its spectre, geology, remains. It is simply chaos. Ravines are gashed out, sudden pinnacles of rock shoot up five hundred feet into the air; their tops seem to have been twisted by whirlwind, the Ice Age has eaten into their sides, the Great Flood has broken their splitting foundations into gullies. This amphitheatre is the abandoned home of fire and water. . . .[60]

Even fiction isn't absent: the blind woman on her way to Vigo, first described in *Marching Spain*, becomes three blind women here.[61] Sometimes – as was pointed out in *Time and Tide* by the young Alan Ross, himself a good travel writer as well as a poet – Pritchett seems to have had difficulty in re-energising his old theme. Others were more enthusiastic. Frances Partridge was so absorbed in the book on a train journey to London 'that it gave me quite a shock when I happened to look up passing that very English-looking elbow of the Thames near Reading, & see a single oarsman, & some louts kicking about a football in the softest of green fields'.[62] Later, Robert Lowell used *The Spanish Temper* as a companion guide and found it like 'a perfect short novel . . . it is so well composed, so unexpected and so understated'.[63] There were Spanish admirers, too, not least the liberal socialist Luis Araquistáin who, once he had got over finding himself described in it as a Communist, called it 'a forceful and true portrait'.[64] Still, there's some truth in what Alan Ross said. *The Spanish Temper* was the end of a cycle in Pritchett's work as a travel writer.[65] It also emerged from a particularly complicated phase of his second marriage. If his earliest encounters with Spain owed more to Evelyn than he later acknowledged, he was always happy to admit how much the maturing of his work, not only on that country but in general, owed to Dorothy.

4

The Marvellous Girl

When Victor Pritchett and Dorothy Roberts met in 1934, he was thirty-three, she nineteen. Almost forty years later, Victor wrote about their falling in love in a story called 'The Marvellous Girl'.[1] The narrator, Francis, has been separated from his wife for a couple of years but bumps into her, together with the Dorothy character, in a restaurant. The younger woman (the story doesn't give her a name) is 'tall, calm . . . with dark blue eyes', and she works for Francis's wife, who describes her as 'the marvellous girl . . . [the] only one I have ever been able to get on with'. Francis has already met her more than once. But it's when she says 'Goodbye' in the restaurant that he really notices her for the first time. The word becomes a challenge and he pursues her to a public meeting where, through a crowd, they catch sight of each other again:

> there was a gap between the ranks of heads and shoulders and he saw her brown hair and her broad pale face with its white rose look, its good-humoured chin and the laugh beginning on it. She turned round and she saw him as he saw her. There are glances that are collisions, scattering the air between like glass. . . .

The lights in the hall fail and, as everyone leaves in the confusion, they catch hold of each other. She says, 'I have been looking for you,' and either he says the same, or she repeats it – there's an ambiguity. The conversation goes on in this delicately loaded, Noël Cowardish way: 'Are you with your wife?' she says. 'No,' he says.

In real life, what happened next was that Dorothy and Victor went back to the studio he was now renting in Rudall Crescent, Hampstead, where he played 'St James Infirmary' on the gramophone while cooking them both an unseductive-sounding dinner of fish in milk.[2] The date was 5 November 1934: Guy Fawkes Night. Subsequently, it was a joke between them that the fireworks had gone off not only metaphorically in the flat but also literally, on nearby Hampstead Heath. All the rest of their lives together, until Victor lost his memory in his nineties, they commemorated – the word is too solemn: they relived – that first time. One anniversary during the Second World War, he wrote her a five-page letter beginning:

> Dearest Dorf,
> The night of nights. I'm thinking of all of it. What do I remember? Your soft, anxious voice on the telephone, your overcoat buttoned across because of the cold, your lips the first time I kissed you. . . . Then the very young way you said, Marvellous. Your rich breasts. Your lovely long legs. Then going into you and being overcome by the sight of your eyes, which seemed to have melted into a blurred blue radiance.[3]

(That 'Marvellous' is remembered in the story's title.) Even in letters to other people written on the same day, these memories could come to the surface, echoing, and echoed by, the ritual annual explosions that were going off all over England. On 5 November 1944, Pritchett wrote to Gerald Brenan, 'I have been so violently in love during the last ten years, and so prolongedly and deeply so, that the subject deafens me.'[4]

The affair was both passionate and, at first, very guilty. Sexually, they were instantly compatible. For Victor, this was an exhilarating liberation after the years of muddle and unfulfilment with Evelyn. He and Dorothy also liked, amused and respected each other. They shared various enthusiasms (especially, when they first met, for D. H. Lawrence), as well as predicaments: it was soon clear to both of them that Dorothy was almost as keen to escape her upbringing as he had been. On her side, Dorothy was strongly attracted by Victor's being a writer, and also by what he wrote – not always the same thing. Their instant, deep intimacy was overhung, though, by the fact that as long as Dorothy was still working with Evelyn (she was looking for another job) it had to remain a secret. 'God Almighty – How Evelyn will loathe & despise me when she's told about "*us*",' Dorothy wrote from the office.

> She's just been telling me a long story without names – which I was able to supply myself with – about everything. Oh Christ. Darling its worse than ever. I do wish I'd had the guts to tell her then but it

perhaps would not have been a good idea, especially as I shall be going very soon. We must wait till then & tell her quickly. *Please....*[5]

Another source of tension was the reaction in Welshpool. Victor, after all, may have been a writer highly regarded in London, but he was also that nightmare of the parents of teenaged girls, an older married man, and one with no money. Dorothy had had plenty of boyfriends, so, although her parents were particularly dismayed by the idea of this one, they had some hope that he wouldn't last. The longer things went on, though, the more vocal Dorothy's religiously devout mother, Elsie, became about her objections, especially when she was told that the couple planned to marry. Her 'line', Dorothy told Victor with a surprising note of surprise the following spring, was that 'you were married and I had *no right* to be in love with you! . . . She said I wont really be married to you, its wicked, & I'm a hypocrite 'cos I've been to church this morning when I knew I wanted to marry you.' Elsie told Dorothy, 'You wouldn't even be married to him if you went to fifty registry offices. If he's left one wife he'll soon leave someone who isn't his wife.'[6] Undaunted, Victor took Dorothy out to Rules restaurant, where he gave her a ring he had bought in Tottenham Court Road.

Meanwhile, Dorothy's father became very ill. One morning, as he sat talking to Dorothy, he 'suddenly made a most terrifying noise & fell off his chair on to the floor', cutting his eye and his ear. 'I suppose its all the result of drink,' Dorothy added in her letter to Victor.[7] Her father had had a stroke. He was fifty-six.[8]

The handsome Richard Samuel Roberts was a prominent man in Welshpool. He had inherited a farm, mainly sheep and cattle, from his father, and ran it with the help of a manager who lived on the land. But his main source of income was a wholesale butchery business, supplying retailers along a line westwards to the coast below Harlech. He sang in the church choir – all the family went to church at least once every Sunday – and, like his wife and their forebears, he rode to hounds. The family lived in a three-storey Georgian house at 28 Severn Street. Mary, born in 1911, was three years older than Dorothy. After them came John, the only son; the sensitive Jean; and sceptical Edith. In intelligence, most of the girls, with their mild, part Welsh, part educated-middle-class voices, took after their mother. One of Elsie's best friends, later, was Frances Pitt, a successful author of books about country life. The two women rode a lot together: point-to-points and steeplechases, as well as hunts. They also bred horses.[9] The main childhood recreation of Dorothy and her siblings had always been horses, Edith recalled. They were 'mad on horses. Dorothy was a very good horsewoman in her younger days. My father thought the world of Dorothy. She was his favourite, I'm sure.'[10]

If Richard did have a favourite, it's easy to see why Dorothy might have been the one. She was full of life and good at most things. Her younger sisters adored her. Even in old age, Jean liked to remember seeing Dorothy in a shaft of sunlight the day she became a house captain at their school in Welshpool, 'and being overwhelmed by how beautiful she was'. She was bright and outgoing, 'always in any plays that were going on', and extremely successful with boys – which was a source of worry to her parents ('Mother had her work cut out trying to keep her in,' Jean recalled) and of envy and apprehension on the part of Mary, who, as the eldest, was expected to marry first. Even Victor confessed that he was jealous of Dorothy's previous lovers. She was energetic as well as good-looking, and among the things that made her popular was that she had inherited her father's liking for drink: one of the teenager's nicknames was 'Sherry'. In those days, as she explained to Victor, she drank mainly on impulse. When people she didn't like came round, she 'had a lot to drink because they aren't so tiresome when one has had a lot to drink . . .'[11] Or, on a Sunday, when the pubs were closed but she happened to be on a train home to Welshpool, she went to the restaurant car for 'tea &, for some unknown reason, two whiskies & sodas. Probably because I felt cock-a-hoop about drinking when I couldn't have had a drink in a pub. And I felt reckless.'[12] On an earlier journey home at Christmas 1934, as she told Victor in a letter written late that night, she had several neat gins '– so far without result!'[13] When the train arrived at Shrewsbury, she and some relations and friends were met at the station 'by sundry odd people & cars & had a terrific race home & arrived at 12.30.' A day or two later, exuberant with her new romance, she shook off a cold to play mixed hockey, scored four of her team's six goals and went to a dance the same evening.

Evelyn, meanwhile, finally learned how things stood. She had been living alone, in a deep depression about the failure of her marriage, but with the help of Jungian analysis her spirits improved and she, too, fell in love with someone much younger. Donald Maxwell was in his late teens when they met at a party. As with Victor and Dorothy, it was a case not only of first sight but of ever after. Evelyn told her children that when she first met Donald and stood beside him, she felt 'completely at peace'.[14] In strange symmetry with Victor and Dorothy, the pair went back to Donald's flat in Hampstead and from then on were inseparable. They were to die within weeks of each other, forty-odd years later.

It isn't known exactly when Evelyn and Donald first met.[15] But from people's letters to Victor complaining about missed appointments and unanswered correspondence it's evident that, as might be supposed, his life became hard to manage in the autumn of 1935.[16] And that once Evelyn learned about Dorothy, there were many scenes. Although she and Victor had been living apart, there were still strong ties between them (Evelyn's family still has the copy of *Nothing Like Leather* which he inscribed to her at the beginning of 1935). At home, trying to write, Victor was vulnerable to that relatively new instrument of emotional torture, the telephone. He told Dorothy that if he didn't pick up the phone, it would ring '40 times'; if he did, Evelyn called over and over again. Her situation was intolerable, she told him. Once, in the middle of the night, she rang to say she must come up to the studio immediately 'because she was in great trouble'. Only later did the worried Victor realise, or guess, that she was in the middle of a row with the 'new man' and that it was he who was her main audience.[17]

As quickly as Dorothy could, she moved to another job, as editorial assistant on the *Air Annual of the British Empire*, which had its office in Holborn.[18] She did well there and when a possibility came up of the firm's becoming involved in an air taxi business, two of the directors took her to lunch at the Savoy to sound her out about a bigger role.[19] But all her thoughts were on Victor and marriage. While his divorce was crawling through the courts, they needed a discreet place where they could get away together. Friends of Victor's came to their aid. A wealthy fan in St John's Wood who knew his situation pressed £20 on him to take Dorothy on holiday.[20] And another philanthropist came up with a longer-term solution.

Harry Roberts was a well-known author and contributor to the *Spectator* and *New Statesman* (which is how he and Pritchett became friends), who combined social activism with working as a doctor. A charismatic man in his mid sixties, he practised several days a week at his clinic in the slums of Stepney, while writing books and articles on social policy.[21] As a young physician in Cornwall, Roberts had become part of the artistic and intellectual set in St Ives. Now, with his partner Winifred Stamp, he ran a utopian commune-cum-salon of his own at a stone-flagged house they had built in thirty acres of wooded countryside at Lower Oakshott, near Hawkley, Hampshire, where he spent long weekends. The main room was furnished with a long table, a big dresser, a couple of divans, plain linen curtains and a lot of bookshelves. There were two bedrooms above and half a dozen wooden huts outside, each with a bed, table, washstand and chairs.

Pritchett later wrote of Roberts, 'Human love, I mean particularly love affairs and distresses, moved him to such an extent that the mere listening to some story of it, sad or happy, appeared to put him in a state of love himself.'[22] He was intense, spontaneous, impulsive, immoderate in everything – especially drink, smoking and argument – while maintaining a rigid respect 'for the delicate, the shy, the elusive, the private, in human life'. When Victor introduced them, he and Dorothy took to each other immediately. The couple went to Lower Oakshott together a lot (Victor's later memories often turned to a winter night when they made love in a garden folly there, moonlight shining in off the snow outside).[23] When Victor was away in Spain for the *Fortnightly Review*, Dorothy stayed there, 'picking cowslips, bottling cyder & drinking & talking to Harry'.[24] Later that year, Pritchett moved in completely for six months to work on *Dead Man Leading*.

The book was to be published by Chatto and Windus, which had picked up *Nothing Like Leather* after the novel was rejected by Gollancz. It was the beginning of a lifelong association, but no one knew that at the time and Pritchett's editor at Chatto, Ian Parsons, became concerned that his recently acquired author almost immediately fell behind schedule. Pritchett had begun *Dead Man Leading* in the summer of 1935, but truthfully explained in November that 'domestic upheavals paralysed it for a while'. He was, he told Parsons, 'one of those novelists who write about three hundred thousand words in order to produce a hundred thousand'.[25]

Among the domestic upheavals was Dorothy's father's stroke, which proved fatal. All the family gathered. Undertakers hovered like Welsh birds of prey. Dorothy wrote in misery to Victor about her emotional confusion – fear, bewilderment at not being able to tell whether her father felt anything or knew what was happening, revulsion at the collective intensity, guilt that she was not feeling the 'right' things and finally overwhelming grief: 'My daddy's gone VSP. He died. Dead, dead. Oh VSP he's dead and I can't believe it.'[26]

The family's bereavement put Dorothy's own situation into the background as far as the rest of them were concerned. It also opened up a solution over the wedding. While her mother minded very much that

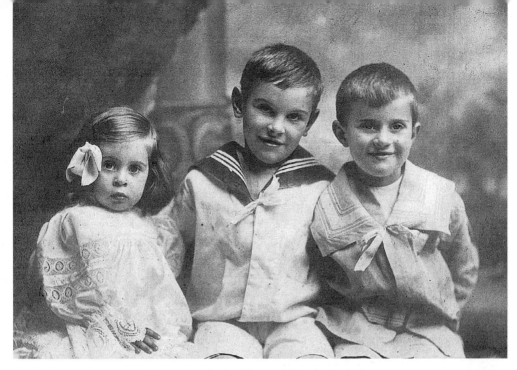

1. Victor, flanked by Kathleen and Cyril

2. Walter Sawdon Pritchett, VSP's father,
in his prime

3. Walter and Beatrice in old age

4. William Pritchett, Congregationalist Minister of Sedbergh, VSP's grandfather

5. At Alleyn's School, Dulwich

6. Victor in the Paris photographer's studio where he worked as a clerk, together with the messenger boys whom he later described as 'a nimble little guttersnipe from Montmartre called Pierre, and a gangling, hot-faced Breton'

7. In Paris, 1921

8. The dandy in Ireland, mid 1920s

(*Above left*) 9. Evelyn's Spanish driving licence. Pritchett never learned to drive and his wife gave her profession as 'conductora', driver (*Above right*) 10. In the 1930s

11. Cover by Mary Adshead (wife of Stephen Bone) for Pritchett's third book *The Spanish Virgin and other stories*, 1930

12. Victor and Dorothy on their wedding day, 1936

(*Above left*) 13. With Josephine in the garden of Maidencourt, *c*.1939
(*Above right*) 14. With Oliver at Maidencourt

15. Wartime austerity design: the cover of
In My Good Books, 1942

V·S·PRITCHETT·

In my
good
books

Recommended by the Book Society

16. In the office of the *New Statesman* in Holborn, *c.* 1946

Dorothy could not be married in church (and her elder sister Mary that she was going to be married at all), the fact that they would all be in mourning made the notion of a quiet register office ceremony, away from home, less unacceptable. Victor's divorce decree 'nisi' was expected in February 1936.[27] It was time for him to be invited to Welshpool.

Dorothy went on ahead, leaving him alone at Lower Oakshott. He wrote her a series of comically piteous love letters about their separation and his helplessness. 'You are with me at 4.15; you are not at 4.30 – what has happened to these you's and me's? . . . I've become a dabster at frying sausages and a terror with the teapot; the only trouble is that I am sordid in my habits and melodramatic in the stage effects that I obtain. I told you, I think, that I set fire to a tomatoe [*sic*].'[28]

Meanwhile, he tried to reassure her, and perhaps also himself, about how determined he was to make a good impression on her family: 'I'll behave,' he promised. 'I'll wear four suits. I'll buy a new hat.' He tried to imagine Welshpool, wondering whether it resembled Kirkbymoorside. The letters are full of cartoons and cartoon sequences: Victor sitting naked and morose on the edge of the bath; Victor as he imagined his prospective in-laws might see him, as a down-and-out or a villainous seducer; Victor as he saw himself, scratching his head purposelessly; Victor undergoing forced baptism in Wales; 'St. Victor' *triumphans*, leaving Welshpool at the head of a military band. Meanwhile, he pressed ahead with *Dead Man Leading* as well as with various essays, especially on Spain,[29] and ideas for stories, among them one about a family of undertakers which was to become a favourite with his readers, 'Sense of Humour'.[30] He took stock of his feelings. 'It is good for me being here among these kind and delightful people and in this cosy place,' he wrote to her from Oakshott near the end of January 1936,

> because I can get *clear* about you & me. I need to go away to let the electric excitement of my nerves to [*sic*] subside, and to allow my feelings & instincts freedom to pursue their logic. I see how urgently I need you.
>
> Does this solemnity frighten you? I am a terribly *serious* person, you know. I don't mean intellectual. I should be serious if I were a tightrope walker, or a barman, or a tram conductor, or an aeroplane man. I am also gay with love of you.[31]

The letters between Victor and Dorothy, none of which have as yet been published, are among the great surviving records of a love affair and a lasting marriage. (One remembers Henry and Mary in *Mr Beluncle*: 'The letters he wrote to her! "You'll have to get a new drawer, Mary," Sis said.' It's no surprise that Pritchett wrote well about Thomas and Jane Carlyle, with what he called 'their craving for each other's voice'.)[32] The correspondence began in 1934 and continued into Victor's old age, and each of them kept most of the other's letters. Because of his travels – to write books about different countries and also, later, to lecture and attend conferences – the couple were often apart. But even when they were in the same house, Victor wrote often to Dorothy: after a quarrel, on a birthday or an anniversary, or occasionally for no reason other than that she was asleep and he wanted to talk to her. When they were apart, each of them described the day's events in full detail: what they and people they were with had done, said, eaten; the progress of their moods and thoughts.[33] Sometimes there was serious emotional business. Though the marriage ended as it began, in exceptional happiness, it went through some long difficulties in between. And there were the usual domestic practicalities. But above all, the sense one gets is of a conversation between lovers who were also friends: gossipy, funny, affectionate and often frankly sexy. 'Your Sunday letter *roused* me,' Dorothy once wrote from Welshpool in the early days, 'yes really!' – and she went on to describe the sensation.[34] Writing the letter as well as getting her reply must have aroused him, too. It was around this time that Victor wrote to her, 'I can feel your lovely dark crisp secret hair pressed against me, the lovely ardent little mound above your cunt, and then the hot, licking gripping little mouth of your cunt, like lips, around my sliding cock. . . .'[35]

Very many of their letters, then and later, refer not only to their sex lives together, but to the sustaining erotic effect of the correspondence on each of them.[36] If it seemed a poor substitute for the real thing, the letters have lasted: devotedly preserved traces of what both partners, as long as they could write, continued to describe as a love affair. One important component was evidently the exactitude with which both of them described their experiences. Yet another, of course, was the sheer pleasure Victor took in entertaining. His letters are often very funny, not least, early on, in parodying the contrast between their sexual freedom and traditional notions of courtship:

Dear Miss Roberts,

Or may I call you Dorothy? May I dare? May I permit myself? Or rather the question is can I stop myself. And again, Can you stop me? Alas you cannot now be ignorant of my sentiments. Am I only to see you on the most formal occasions – taking off your nightgown, putting on your nightgown, or modestly shrinking in the bath? . . .[37]

This epistolary exuberance was to become a problem later, when she was stuck unhappily at home and he was away for long periods and kept telling her about the good times he was having. But for the most part each found the other endlessly interesting and amusing. 'There is nothing in the world so lovely as kissing you,' Victor wrote in the elation of finishing *Dead Man Leading*,

And now I'm a free man, a no novel man, I shall do a lot of it. I have also bought you today one Bentley, one Berlei corset, a persian rug, a marvellous machine for undressing you very quickly – the clothes just fall off one by one in proportion to your excitement, on the sprinkler valve principle – and two gallons of perfume. Also a false moustache for myself to enhance my powers! . . .[38]

The drawings are similarly effervescent. A one-legged woman whom Pritchett meets is fantastically turned into a Cyclops, too. Victor himself is shown, peering into a mirror while trying to improve a posture thrown off-balance by his pendulous balls, or as a hypocritical saint watching smugly as a strong-legged Dorothy dances for him naked.

While letters like these poured through the letter box at 28 Severn Street, Dorothy was preparing the ground with her family, talking up Victor's work and telling them that it was through his friend Harry Roberts that she had got her new job. (This seems to have been a fiction to explain her Lower Oakshott address. She promised to brief Victor if there were any other white lies he needed to know about.) In the event, his visit went both as badly and as well as they had anticipated. There was a gruelling series of dinner parties at which he met aunts from Rhyl, uncles from Builth Wells, cousins, family friends. One of the latter, a farmer called Cyril, asked him, 'What be you, then?' Victor said, 'I'm an author.' As Victor later told the story, Cyril pondered. 'Well, damn it all, there's a bit of etiquette about me but I never heard of an *author*.'[39] Mrs Roberts's etiquette was less narrow, but she remained tight-lipped about her daughter's having chosen so poorly, when she could have had the pick of Montgomeryshire. Dorothy's younger sisters, on the other hand, were enchanted and amused by Victor. 'The only men we knew were schoolmasters, bank managers, farming people,' Jean remembered later. 'I adored him on sight. He entertained.'

In September, the divorce decree 'absolute' came through.[40] There were still some tangles to sort out. Although Evelyn had inherited a considerable sum from her father, she tried to secure a third of Victor's earnings as a settlement.[41] But on 2 October 1936 Victor and Dorothy – the 'two dears', as Harry Roberts called them – were married at Hampstead Town Hall in the company of a crowd of friends. By March, Dorothy was pregnant. The artist Mark Gertler (who was already a parent) sent a comic letter of anxious congratulation: 'I am glad to hear that Dorothy is going to have a baby – I hope she is having a good doctor to look at her every now & then – *most important* – otherwise there can be trouble – I don't know what to say about being a father – a child is still another cause for worry and anxiety in life – more complications – But I *suppose it has its "compensations"*.'[42] Gertler must

How d'you do?

But when she was 21 she danced in the nude to tantalise the little saint because he had.

she

saint

have known that, to them, there seemed nothing to be compensated for. Victor had made clear to Dorothy early on that he wanted children as much as she did. '[S]upposing we took a house near Dartington' (the famous liberal school), he fantasised, 'and sent Humphrey, Hector, Hermione and Hippocrates there and kept Hippolytus at home – in view of his well-known incest trouble.'[43] The birth of their daughter – Josephine, not Hermione – on 28 December 1937 prompted another flurry of delighted cartoons: Victor dancing naked with a wineglass balanced on his nose, phoning all his friends, struggling with the laundry, having lunch with an eighteen-year-old Josephine in Paris. There's a sequence about nappies: Victor imposing military order on a pile of them ('Nappies! Shun! Form Fours!'); puns on the word: 'Taking a Nap', 'Schnapps', 'Nap-o-leon' (a lion in a diaper). One drawing, captioned 'what it feels like to be a father', shows Victor as a suited and haloed god ruling over both London and the sun and moon.

From the point of view of his fiction writing, these first years of real family life were also among the most productive of Pritchett's career. Dorothy was keen to be helpful and her encouragement was sharpened by jealousy. She was still very wary of Evelyn and also of Victor's intellectual women friends: people like his fellow *New Statesman* critic Janet Adam Smith, despite her imminent marriage to the poet Michael Roberts; or the much sought-after Margaret Gardiner, who ran a pressure group with which Harry Roberts was connected called For Intellectual Liberty, where Dorothy had sometimes helped out as a secretary. Above all, she was possessive about Victor's writing. The fact that work was still coming out which he had written when he was with Evelyn made her doubly eager that he should now write 'something that's "ours"'.[44]

He showed no reluctance, publishing about twenty new short stories between 1935 and 1939, fourteen of them included in his second collection, *You Make Your Own Life* (1938). The novel which he was working on at Lower Oakshott, *Dead Man Leading*, appeared in 1937. (*Nothing Like Leather*, published in January 1935, was finished shortly before they met.) Dorothy's family tended to give her much of the credit for Victor's success: 'she made him', her sisters often said, later. In fact, of course, through his own gifts and intensely hard work (and with help from a number of other people – Evelyn among them) he had already reached the point in the career of many successful artists when struggle almost imperceptibly mutates into fame. But it's also true that from now on he owed a huge amount to Dorothy. 'In the thirties, my

life changed completely,' he was to write in *Midnight Oil*. He had fallen 'happily and deeply in love. There is, I am sure, a direct connection between passionate love and the firing of the creative power of the mind.' Something of what he meant is conveyed in a transparently autobiographical story written early in the Second World War, called 'A New World':[45]

> If they came out on the sunny side of the house and looked up into the sun's face, the light striped and drenched them from head to foot, making their toes spread in their shoes. . . .
>
> What was this new world? It was their love for each other. . . . He watched her. She watched him. He was a small man who looked as though he was going to spring after something new every minute; and she was a big girl who looked as though she was about to run after something which made her laugh. Even when they were still, even when they were in different rooms, they were planning to run towards each other. To run after their love, of course. . . . [He] would get up and open his door an inch and look at her; and immensely satisfied, return to his room again. When this palled they jeered at each other, and once or twice they had terrible quarrels. . . . But there was a core of their peculiar ecstasy in it.

This ecstasy seemed not only to re-create the present but to wipe out the past. There are only three exceptions to his erasure of the work he had done pre-Dorothy: the stories 'X-Ray' and 'The Upright Man'; and *Marching Spain*. The first is an almost purely documentary account of its subject, combined with a meditation on illness and its institutionalisation. (Pritchett, as he mentions in *Midnight Oil*, had suffered various psychosomatic complaints during his break-up with Evelyn.) In his story, the fate of anyone in hospital, especially in those days – loss of individual self-determination; denial even of the right to know about one's own condition; separation from the domestic world which gives one security and meaning – is neatly summed up in a patient's response to someone's asking whether 'they let you see yourself' in the X-ray: 'Nao,' he replies scornfully. 'What do you think you are inside? A family group?'[46]

'The Upright Man' is an equally touching but more pessimistic fable about a repressed clerk in an office such as the one where Pritchett worked from 1916, and about his departure for, and death in, the First World War. It asks an indignant question: 'what can a man do in the world who cannot bend his head?' Both pieces first appeared in the *New Statesman* in 1932[47] and their dark mood may have owed something to the deteriorating situation with Evelyn. From Dorothy's point of view, though, as well as Victor's, they were free of anything else that might have been associated with the earlier relationship. *Marching Spain*, written when he was married to Evelyn, was reissued subsequently; but then his marital unhappiness pervades this narrative – and it is the only one of his books published during the marriage which he didn't dedicate to Evelyn.

Two new emphases are evident in the work he wrote in his early years with Dorothy: the relatively high proportion of it that was non-autobiographical (though his life continued to provide him with plenty of material)[48] and, relatedly, an increased, almost exhilarated sense of the fictiveness of all aspects of life.

Dead Man Leading is the most obvious case in point, a new departure both in subject and handling. The story concerns three men on an expedition in Brazil, where Pritchett had not yet been. The characters and their situations – for some of which there was a real basis in the search for a lost explorer in Brazil described in Peter Fleming's 1933 book *Brazilian Adventure*[49] – are sharply imagined. Harry Johnson is on a quest for his father, a former missionary in the region, or at least for an explanation of his disappearance and presumed death when Harry was a child. Gilbert Phillips, a journalist (Pritchett drew satirically on his own experiences here),[50] is his rival for a girl in England, Lucy, step-daughter of the expedition's leader. Pritchett was freed by writing the novel. In letters to Dorothy, he talked about his sheer practical fascination with how to handle his imaginary material: 'you have to avoid writing a travel book and yet remember that whatever the private problems of people in the midst of Brazil, Brazil will be the major thing, because it's the present moment.' He resolved these technical problems not only with the help of his wide reading of books about South America, but by making a model of the terrain in the garden. Some howlers remained: there are no orang-utans in the Amazon and, even in their own habitat, they don't make a noise like the one described in chapter 14. But the editor of a Brazilian newspaper whom he met in Rio much later pleased him by telling him he had got the atmosphere absolutely right. And John Updike was to write,

It is almost my favourite kind of book, the poetic/exotic, especially good when the author hasn't been to the place described. Nabokov's descriptions in *The Gift* of central Asia have something of the power and bone-deep authenticity of your descriptions of the Amazon jungle. I was enchanted by sentence after sentence, e.g., 'Only half of the day had gone, and now once more the rain had stopped, and the hot blue body of sky thrust limbs and shoulders through the cloud.'[51]

Updike could have found many other examples. Pritchett brilliantly ransacked his imagination, his reading and any half-relevant experiences of his own to supply touches which, from the first page, convey an illusion of belonging to Brazil: the foam behind the launch, for example, which makes the boat resemble 'a mongrel worrying a dirty mat'.[52] Much of what he wrote derived from his other travels, not only in hot countries but in the forests of Quebec. A lot, too, came from the travel books which were a staple of his reviewing at this time.[53] (And there is more than a touch of *Heart of Darkness*.) More fascinating still are the intimate sources of his imagery: the way, for example, that Sawdon Pritchett's business seems to have been worked into the Amazonian rainforest: 'one seemed to be passing show cases of fantastic drapery and millinery, in an overheated shop, green unfolding upon green . . .'[54] or the sudden introduction of some of the surroundings of Victor's early years in Congregationalist Sedbergh as a metaphor for Harry Johnson's sexual paranoia: 'Is the heart a little Bethel [chapel] – some sectarian organ which has lost its religion, the texts on the wall and the Israelitish fantasies, but not the fear and the guilt which were the root of the religion?'[55] The basis of the story, after all, is a man's search for his father – a search in which he himself becomes lost; and a preoccupation that runs through it is the difficulty of shedding one's origins, however far one travels. Calcott, for example, urged by his employee Silva to communicate with Shakespeare's Hamlet when Silva conjures him up at a seance in the heart of Brazil, finds that Hamlet has been eating steak and onions. As the narrative points out, this says less about the Prince of Denmark than about 'Calcott's subconscious mind, with its nostalgic memories of the Old Kent Road'.[56] Such elisions work in both directions. In the book's last paragraph, Phillips finds the England to which he has returned alone very like the Amazon: 'Nothing could have been more like the river and the jungle and the sudden squawk of birds to his unaccustomed sight and ear, than the street light-daubed in the rain, the impenetrable forest of lives of people in the houses and the weird hoot and flash of the cars.'[57]

The plot – and *Dead Man Leading* has more suspense and more 'action', in the conventional sense, than any other of Pritchett's fictions – is moved forward with a narrative suppleness enhanced by its own musings on, and exemplification of, the undependability of stories, especially in flashes forward to later accounts of 'the Wright expedition', which in turn act to heighten the suspense of the main action.[58] There are various uncertainties along the way, several of them compounded by Silva, with his 'artist's irresponsibility, his weakness for getting the facts slightly wrong'.[59] Does anyone have a true sense of the missing missionary and is he dead or alive? Does the expedition have a mercenary aspect – for example, as Silva suspects, a search for gold? Is Lucy pregnant and, if so, by whom? Psychological tensions and personal realignments compound all this: each of the characters is in a state of flux. But Pritchett's long interest in people's fantasies and the stories they tell themselves and others is developed here as something beyond a quirk of individual personality.

The new emphasis is particularly noticeable in a short story written around this time, 'You Make Your Own Life'.[60] Its setting is a barber's shop in a small town through which the narrator happens to be passing and the title, with its metafictional nuances, refers both to the barber himself and to his present customer, both of whom the narrator observes and listens to as he waits his turn. From the outset, the mood is curious, sceptical: 'Take a seat, just finishing,' the barber tells the narrator, who silently comments, 'It was a lie. He wasn't anywhere near finishing.' He picks up a newspaper, full of stories of personal tragedies that have happened elsewhere. Then he turns back to observing barber and client. Impatience – he has a train to catch – heightens his interest: the haircut is unusually elaborate and when the client, Albert, leaves, he doesn't pay. Now, the narrator takes his seat and the barber starts to gossip:

> 'That man!' he said. He mused to himself with growing satisfaction. He worked away in long silence . . . The result of his meditation was to make him change his scissors for a finer pair.
> 'He ought to be dead,' he said.

The barber's story takes over. Albert has had tuberculosis and tried to commit suicide with a cut-throat razor. He and the barber have linked histories: they went to school together and the barber is married to a former girlfriend of Albert's. This last bit of information is introduced by one of those conversational clichés (such as the title itself) to whose deceptive resonances Pritchett is so alert: 'Matter of fact . . .'

With the narrator, we listen and we watch – and feel we are watched: 'I saw the barber's forehead and his dull blue eyes looking up for a moment over my head in the mirror. . . . He glanced sardonically at the door as if expecting to see the man standing there.' The barber tells more about his amatory contest, and the risks his rival took with his health. The narrator says idly that the barber must have wished he could have killed Albert. The reply is indignant: ' "Kill him?" he said. "Me kill him?" He smiled scornfully at me: I was an outsider in this. "He tried to kill *me*," he said.' Albert ('matter of fact') poisoned his whisky. But the barber outwitted him and went off with the girl. This was when Albert tried to cut his throat. He failed, life goes on, the barber and his wife have children, Albert takes the occasional girl to the cinema: 'It's a dead place, this,' the barber concludes,

> '. . . all right in the summer on the river. You make your own life. The only thing is he don't like shaving himself now, I have to go over every morning and do it for him.'
>
> He stood with his small grin, his steady eyes amused and resolute. 'I never charge him,' he said. He brushed my coat, he brought my hat.

This is where the tale ends, one loose end neatly tied (so that's why Albert didn't pay), but half a dozen previously invisible knots exposed, unravelled. Has the barber ('You make your own life') made the whole thing up, to pass the time in this 'dead place'? Or is it the narrator who has invented it for himself, and for us?

'You Make Your Own Life' gave its enigmatic title to the collection in which it reappeared in 1938. If at one level it obviously refers to fiction as an essential aspect of human existence, it also voices a different but related, and no less fundamental, belief and experience of Pritchett's. For many years and in various senses, including that of being a 'self-made man', he had been making his own life. Now for the first time the process was turning out well. He was a success in his work; he was happy; he believed that he was becoming more 'himself'; and, of course, all of this was being remade in his writing. While much of his work in these years was inventive, imaginative, metafictional, he continued to write straightforwardly about his own immediate experiences, including – for the first time at any length since he described his Paris landlady – his experiences at home. Two long items of this kind appeared in the *New Statesman* in 1936 and 1937, neither of which has been reprinted: 'The Chimney' and 'The Storm'.[61] The first applies the documentary observation he had developed abroad to two English workmen. One of the men has built a new chimney for the house in the country where Victor and Dorothy are living, the other cuts their firewood. Pritchett simply describes their work, their habits, the contrasts between them, not least in nuances of status, and their inter-actions. Nothing 'happens', except that the chimney is built and the fire burns. But by the end we know the men as well as if it were us they had been working for.

The second piece also concerns status, among other things. It vividly describes a storm which flooded a mill in Langstone Harbour, on the Hampshire coast, where Victor and Dorothy stayed during the summer of 1937.[62] The house stands on brick stilts in reedy tidal water full of birds:

> the gulls, the dunlin, the curlew; and . . . the swans, which come down in slender and silent flotillas when there is enough water to bring them, or rise on a new impulse, thrash the sea and pass like a flight of mad, white violins to the other shore. Further away, like a scattering of little black commas, are the duck and the teal, and soon, when the weather is colder, the wild geese will arrive.

As compelling as the birds is the water itself, which is a main subject of conversation and speculation in the pub. 'No mind is empty that considers the sea,' Pritchett observes. One of the keenest of the local marine soothsayers is a retired naval man 'with little hair, a dyspeptic eye, inclined to colourless assurance, unemphatic despair and general fussiness'. His prophecies also turn out to be the least reliable: he's still shouting 'It's all right' as the pub and the houses on the waterfront are inundated. The events themselves are powerfully and comically described:

> The trouble with this kind of tide when it has a gale behind it, is that you may keep it out of your doors and windows and live an aquarium life in the strange white water-light and stillness of your room; but after the water has swept by it will come in through a mouse-hole in the wall or through the cracks of the wainscot and floor-boards. That is what happened to us. Very soon one of our floors became convex,

and the furniture began to rock on it. The wainscot parted from the boards as if someone underneath were prising us open with a hammer. . . . Then down the steps into the mill room poured a mild stream that did not stop for two or three hours.

 We had gone to an upper room by now . . . The bathroom rose and fell – it is no gimcrack structure – and the verandah, which is on this side of the house, rose and fell with it. Presently a bigger wave . . . like a hippopotamus or an enormous gladstone bag, threw boulders against the brick pillars, there was a scream of wrenched wood, and the verandah left us. There are twenty feet of it. Complete with floor and rails it sidled out like a pleasure steamer from a quay, and, ducking pleasantly, went out to sea . . . turned skilfully some hundred yards from the shore and then steamed back, circling in a leisurely way until it found the lee of the mill. There its character changed. From a frolicking cruiser it became a battering-ram in these narrower waters. Down went its bows like a bull's horns, and it charged the house. . . . Was it going to batter down the door and let in the full stream of the sea? We could merely barricade the door and bet on its chances. I had read my Victor Hugo on the man and the gun too recently to wade waist-deep into the swirl and tackle a verandah at the crowning moment of its life.

Part of the fun in all this are the deft metamorphoses by which, amid the colloquial ease, the narrator and his wife are briefly transformed into fish in an aquarium, then into part of the structure of the house ('as if someone . . . were prising us open with a hammer'), and other such changes affect the water ('like a hippopotamus or a . . . gladstone bag') and the veranda itself, turning the latter into a pleasure boat and then an assault craft, and finally an exultant human being. This 'crowning moment' is also the narrator's, in the hierarchy of village experience and village storytelling. Until then, 'I had never been able to say in places where the experienced gather: "This is the worst gale on this coast since '07." But now . . . I have graduated in calamity. I have become a wiseacre at last.'

So 'The Storm', for all its superficial simplicity, is another story about storytelling. But, like 'The Chimney' and 'You Make Your Own Life', it's about watching, too: full of different ways of, and motives for, seeing. There are the 'we' who watch the birds and who join other local people in watching the sea. There's the pensioner who feels it's his duty to 'keep an eye' on the mill. There's the publican who (watched, of course, by the narrator), at the height of the storm 'came out in grey bloomers – her skirt flew over her head at once – and went down what had been a path, waist-deep in water and clinging to the wall. She said she did this because she "wanted to see what it was like outside".' And there are voyeur outsiders: artists who come to paint; visitors after the storm, who look at the veranda washed up on the shore and wonder where it came from; above all, the friend who writes film scripts and who tells the narrator, 'What copy!' The story pretends to repudiate this notion: 'Copy, of course, is what you have not seen.' But copy, of course, is exactly what the narrator *has* seen, and has given us.

The dexterous movements in Pritchett's best writing of these years – between recording and imagining; between standing aside from and commenting on the processes of narrative, and with seeming unself-consciousness immersing himself in them; between looking outside himself and drawing on what is most important to his private life – all these come together in one of his most memorable stories, 'Sense of Humour', published in the same year, 1937, but written at least twelve months earlier.[63] It's about an undertaker's son, the girl he falls in love with and his rivalry with her former boyfriend, who stalks them (though the term's implications of stealth and silence are scarcely right for Colin's ostentatiously noisy pursuits on his motorbike). The personal aspect may seem the least obvious. But Dorothy had been upset by her dealings with the undertakers at the time of her father's death; and the couple had felt harassed by Evelyn. 'Sense of Humour' was not Victor's original title, but it perfectly fits the tone of the piece, which was, among other things, a salve for some of what they had been going through.

Like all Pritchett's best writing, the story is instantly accessible and yet exceptionally dense in texture. Its complexity is partly psycho-logical, partly tonal. Colin is killed in pursuit of Muriel and Arthur, an event dealt with intricately, not least in Muriel's response: Arthur notices that she is sexually stirred by it. It is Arthur Humphrey who narrates the story, with his cockney wisecracks and his clichés, but much of it is revealed through the dialogue of people who don't mean to be funny, but are – for example, when he takes Muriel MacFarlane home to his parents' for a Bank Holiday weekend (a passage closely based on Victor's introduction of Dorothy to his own parents):

'The Glen Hotel at Swansea, I don't suppose you know that?' my father said.

'I wondered if you did being in the catering line,' he said.

'It doesn't follow she knows every hotel,' my mother said.

'Forty years ago,' the old man said, 'I was staying at the Glen in Swansea and the head waiter . . .'

'Oh no, not that one, I'm sure Miss MacFarlane doesn't want to hear that one,' my mother said.

'How's business with you, Mr Humphrey?' said Muriel. 'We passed a large cemetery near the station.'

'Dad's Ledger,' I said.

Talking and hearing are not always the same thing here, but both are as important to the story as looking is to 'The Storm'. 'Listen to that rain,' Muriel says to Arthur, early in their acquaintance, and much of their relationship moves forward through sounds: through Arthur's attentiveness to others' accents, as well as the reader's to Arthur's self-revealing patter ('it pays in these small towns to turn up at church'), and through innocuous-seeming phrases which are preparing big effects. Muriel tells Arthur that her father was 'on the railway'. Arthur responds with a music-hall couplet: 'The engine gave a squeal. . . . The driver took out his pocket-knife and scraped him off the wheel.' We half remember that squeal when Colin and his red motorbike go under the Birmingham bus – that, and other noises which have been more overtly connected with him, not least on his outings with Muriel in the firm's little Morris (he's a commercial traveller): 'we'd hear him popping and backfiring close behind us,' Arthur irritably recalls. 'We could hear him banging away behind us'; 'We would hear that scarlet thing roar by like a horse-stinger'.

There is a class dimension. Even a little Morris, in this world, is not only quieter than a motorbike but, as Arthur isn't averse to hinting, a step up for Muriel. She makes a bigger one after Colin has died when, in her confused emotions, she makes love with Arthur. ('Ever noticed how hot a woman's breath gets when she's crying?' he observes coolly.) For various reasons – practicality, economy, a kind of guilty respect (' "It would look nice," my father said'), Arthur agrees to drive the corpse home in his father's hearse; and, out of similarly mixed motives, Muriel insists on occupying the passenger seat. While the quiet, well-sprung limousine makes its way through the streets, people raise their hats, as they used to for hearses; and Muriel, who has been tearful, begins to cheer up. 'It's like being the King and Queen,' she says – and is quick to notice whenever suitable obeisances aren't forthcoming. 'Look at that man there,' she says as the story ends. 'Why doesn't he raise his hat? People ought to show respect for the dead.'

In the case of the couple themselves such respect has been mixed. There are ambiguities. Muriel says she was never exactly Colin's girlfriend – 'he'd no sense of humour' – but the strength of her feelings when he dies seems to confirm Colin's own claim that there was more to it. Arthur, meanwhile, is convincing in his frank mixture of opportunism, callousness and a limited kind of sympathy:

> She put her arms around my neck and cried, 'Colin. Colin,' as if I were Colin and clung to me. I was feeling sick myself. I held her tight and I kissed her and I thought 'Holiday ruined.'
> 'Damn fool man,' I thought. 'Poor devil,' I thought.
> 'I knew he'd do something like this.'
> 'There, there,' I said to her. 'Don't think about Colin.'

In the end, the story does justice to all three main characters, though it is Arthur who dominates, with his knowing proverbs and his all-pervading commercialism. ('I told her I could do her better stockings than the ones she'd got on. She got a good reduction on everything. Twenty-five or thirty-three and a third. She had her expenses cut right back.')

'Commercial Traveller' was what the story was called when Pritchett first offered it to John Lehmann for his magazine *New Writing*. This was almost a year after Dorothy's father's death, but the tale had already been doing the rounds of better-paying magazines. 'It's about 7000 words long and this and either its manner or its subject or both, give it little chance as far as I can see with the monthly reviews,' Pritchett told Lehmann.[64] Lehmann was happy to take it, but had already committed himself to a piece called 'The Commercial Agent' for the same issue and asked Pritchett to come up with a different title which 'would please you equally well'.[65] Once it had been chosen, 'Sense of Humour' was obviously right. The phrase runs like a refrain, cropping up first in an early exchange between Muriel and Arthur: ' "Don't mind me", she said. "I'm Irish." "Oh, I see," I said. ". . . Got a sense of humour." ' Like father like son: when Arthur first mentions Muriel's Irishness to his father, Mr Humphrey's response is identical: ' "Oh," said the old man. "Irish! Got a sense of humour, eh?" ' Meanwhile, Muriel shrugs off

Arthur's solicitousness that Colin may be annoying her with, 'He's not annoying me . . . I've got a sense of humour.' But a sense of humour is what Colin himself fatally lacks.

None of this, of course, is as obvious on a first reading as it becomes in a summary. But the title lightly jogs the phrase whenever it occurs, so that – as with a refrain – we have a sense that its meanings move around whenever the context shifts. When one looks back, it becomes clear that, despite their protestations, the characters in the story are in fact almost entirely humourless (though Muriel finds it very funny that Arthur's father is an undertaker). Arthur thinks himself quick and makes a few 'jokes', but they are as laboriously calculated as his decision to go to church. And while all the characters are to some extent measured by the stereotypical ways they use the phrase, and – at least in Muriel's case – perhaps catch it from each other, the story is also playing with the reader's reactions to it.

Still, 'Commercial Traveller' would have been a good title, too. Pritchett's satire on Arthur's money-based values and on how they distort his relationships was rooted not only in his own upbringing, but in worries about his current development. He told Brenan, 'if I do not succeed [as a writer], then I am nothing but a thwarted shopkeeper who would be much better [sic] person keeping shop than worrying about art & literature. . . . I stand, perforce, with one foot in the Montaigne-Freud territory and the other in a sort of spiritual Selfridges . . .'[66]

Now that he had a family, making a steady income was even more of a preoccupation than it had always been. Pritchett repeatedly grumbled to John Lehmann about the fees paid by *New Writing*: 'Can you suggest any way I can earn my living? I cant do it by writing!'[67] And again, 'Sorry to write this greedy sort of letter because I know N.W. isn't rich; but neither am I and while I don't expect you to give what the Americans will give me, I do want to buy a staircarpet and pay the doctor and drink for my troubles.'[68]

In March 1939, Dorothy became pregnant again. Cyril Connolly was not the only contemporary writer of the time preoccupied by 'the pram in the hall'. Some time around now, Victor did a new caricature of himself.[69] A board fastened across his shoulders carries books on one side, balanced by a pile of nappies and a chamber pot on the other. Strapped to his chest are a clock and a cigarette machine, while his right knee operates a kind of lid to 'cover up Josephine'. With one hand he's writing a novel, with the other, reviews, while his feet are scribbling letters and a biography. The head of the bespectacled figure is haloed but he's also endowed with a clearly visible though not immodestly sized pair of testicles. The picture is captioned, 'Guilty, or The Perfect Husband'.

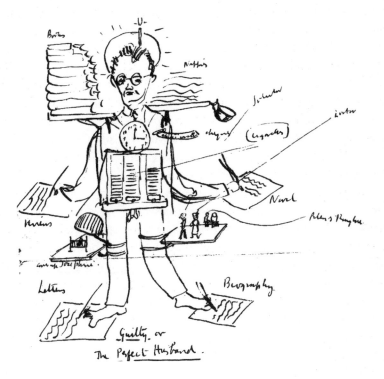

5

What else is there to do but write?

Pritchett's emergence during the Second World War as not only Britain's leading 'man of letters', but the greatest writer-critic since Virginia Woolf, was based on long years of preparation. His newspaper and magazine cuttings, patiently preserved throughout his travels and household moves, now cram six fat boxes in the New York Public Library. The most vivid evidence of his early labours, though, is a ledger which he kept for thirteen years from 4 August 1922.[1] He had not been a clerk for nothing. Here, in hand-ruled columns, is his systematic record of everything he submitted for publication: date, subject, publication, whether the fee had been paid and, sometimes, how much it was. The last entry reads '24.9.35 R. Gino Watkins Time & Tide £1-3-0.' 'R.' stood for 'Review', and *Gino Watkins* was the title of a biography of the then-famous Arctic explorer. The reason the ledger ends in September 1935 is that from now on, Dorothy kept the books. Up to that point, Pritchett managed his own business affairs, and his 'List of Articles', as he modestly called it (it actually included books and short stories, too), is a vivid record of the routines of an ambitious young professional writer of his day.

Time and Tide was one of half a dozen publications for which, by 1935, he was writing in full spate. He contributed five reviews to the magazine that year; ten to the *New Statesman*, including one of his first major critical essays, on Tolstoy; and eight pieces to the *Fortnightly Review*, among them one of his important articles about Spain, where he had returned that spring. He was also still writing occasionally for the *Christian Science Monitor* and, in March 1935, made his first appearance in the *London Mercury*, with a story, 'Miss Baker'. As it happened, he didn't appear in the *Spectator* in 1935, though he did in every other year between 1929 and 1939. While Pritchett wrote occasionally for the socialist *New Statesman* from as early as 1927, and by the Second World War it had become his main journalistic home, its Conservative opposite number, the *Spectator*, was the first English paper to give him a regular niche.

The most obvious effect of the gradual expansion of his outlets from the *Monitor* to all of the leading London weeklies and fortnightlies was a new freedom to be sharp and ironic – and, with that, the development of Pritchett's fictionalising, sometimes fantastical, response to his reading: 'What a week-end!' he wrote in the *Spectator* in March 1930,

> I have startling memories of ranging through the Finnish night cheek by jowl with a werewolf; of contemplating with fascinated disgust the garbage heaps and slime of the Thames estuary; within a few hours I was off across the Channel to be titillated by the amorousness of lower-class Germany; thence to Florence in the company of a masquerading footman; and finally northward again to 'go native' among the Eskimos of the Arctic Circle.[2]

This, of course, was a review of new fiction. Books about travel and exploration, meanwhile, were a staple of British publishing and Pritchett was an obvious person to write about them. In 1935 alone, he reviewed new books about journeys in countries ranging from Abyssinia to Venezuela, as well as about French slang, France in the heyday of Modernism, mountaineering, Spain, and Spanish America in the age of Columbus.[3] Autobiography was another of his specialities, especially working-class memoirs such as Jack Hilton's *Caliban Shrieks*.[4] His sympathy for the social underdog extended to Jews – a feeling not universal in the literary London of his day and one which found its way into his fiction as well as his reviews[5] – and is seen, too, in his pioneering pieces on writers from British colonies and, later, ex-colonies, from Mulk Raj Anand in the 1930s, through Wole Soyinka and Shiva Naipaul to, in the 1980s, Salman Rushdie.*

*When Pritchett reviewed Mulk Raj Anand's *The Coolie* (1936) in the *London Mercury*, the Indian novelist wrote that the piece 'gave me enough happiness to requite me for all the pain and torment that had been wrung out of me by the passion of that book' (Mulk Raj Anand to VSP, nd, OP). Later, Pritchett wrote of Wole Soyinka, 'Confusing though he is, he bursts with promise; he gets into the imagination of his people; he is really inside' (VSP to unidentified correspondent, 19.11. ny, NS Archive). In 1971 he wrote to Anthony Thwaite about his enthusiasm for Shiva Naipaul: 'I suppose the Indian émigrés have most of the go at the moment. They have something of the Jewish intelligence, I mean something that corresponds to it in their situation. . . .' (VSP to Anthony Thwaite, 1.12.71, Berg). Pritchett's early sympathies on this score were at home in Kingsley Martin's *New Statesman*, which was markedly supportive of colonial independence movements.

Though his range was wide, it was a long time before he was able to get off the treadmill of reviewing new fiction. The first fiction review he wrote had been as early as 1925, for the *Monitor*, of a translation of Karel Čapek's *Krakatit*, about the inventor of a nuclear explosive. Čapek's was the only title reviewed in that piece but within a few years other papers were putting Pritchett through the standard apprenticeship-cum-initiation rite of English literary journalism: 'batch' pieces, for which the reviewer is sent the week's entire output of novels and short-story collections to choose between – apart, that is, from any volumes picked out by the literary editor for solo treatment by a more established critic. Later, Pritchett was among the writers most in demand for these individual pieces and his long review-essays on current fiction became an important part of his critical work. Meanwhile, though, in his first six months as a *Spectator* critic, he hectically covered forty-seven fiction titles, mostly four or five at a time. In the following year, 1930, his twenty-five pieces for the magazine involved about a hundred new novels and collections of short stories, as well as other books. Meanwhile, he also wrote for the *Fortnightly Review*, where, too, fiction was part of his brief. Soon, he was doing batches for the *New Statesman* as well and at an even more demanding pitch: six new novels in one review, seven in the next, six in the one after that. Over all, for different publications in 1932 – a year in which he published a novel (*Shirley Sanz*) and two short stories – he wrote at least sixty-six reviews, dispatching fifty-four titles among just eight of them.

Plainly, he couldn't have done justice to everything he was supposed to have read and he was honest enough to admit it. 'Presumably one reason for the fact that the public reads long novels is that the reviewers praise them,' he hazarded wryly in an early *New Statesman* piece, 'and reviewers praise them because there is no time to read them through.'[6] So subversive an admission wouldn't have been allowed in the pages of the *Christian Science Monitor*, but if he thought that being printed in the *New Statesman* meant that it would be heeded by his editors there, he was wrong. He had a new ally at the paper in the brilliant and redoubtable Kingsley Martin, who became editor in 1930 after being a leader writer at the *Manchester Guardian*, where Pritchett had been an occasional contributor since 1924.[7] (Later, although the credit wasn't Martin's at all, he would boast, 'I have always been proud to regard [VSP] as my greatest literary discovery.')[8] Martin's support was welcome, because Pritchett's first dealings with the *Statesman* had been far from easy. David Garnett, literary editor until 1931, once wrote him a four-page letter saying bluntly, 'I didn't like your novel review & finally decided to scrap it. My criticisms of it are as follows. . . .' His comprehensive list of objections included Pritchett's ignorance of a book which Garnett thought he should have read, 'sloppy & careless' writing, unsubstantiated generalisations and 'slapdash judgement'.[9] Chastened but undaunted, Pritchett kept going and learned from his mistakes, while Garnett was soon succeeded by Raymond Mortimer, who became a friend as well as a mentor and ally. Later, Pritchett often acknowledged how important Mortimer's combination of imaginative commissioning and editorial rigour had been in his development as a critic.[10]

It was Mortimer who, at a time when the *Statesman*'s sales and reputation were rising fast,[11] first used Pritchett on a regular basis in the magazine, though without at first remitting his ordeal by fiction. In some weeks of 1933, it seems as if there was a conspiracy between editor and reviewer to parody the whole process, Pritchett covering seven titles at a go, then eight, then nine.[12] But by 1935 even the *New Statesman* had to concede that his apprenticeship was nearing its end. For some years, other magazines had been publishing substantial pieces by him on major works and authors. For the *Fortnightly Review*, in particular, his topics had included *The Tale of Genji*, Montaigne, Hazlitt, Shaw and D. H. Lawrence.[13] In 1932 the *Fortnightly* published a particularly strong piece by him attacking the censored version of *Lady Chatterley's Lover*, which had just appeared. 'We used not to be so squeamish nor so genteel,' Pritchett wrote. Lawrence, he argued powerfully, had tried

> to rescue those colloquialisms from the dirt into which hatred of life had thrown them. . . . Because of its irrelevant issues censorship has not only made it difficult to see Lawrence whole and to put all these silly charges of pornography in their place, but it has artfully succeeded in making this question seem the most important one. . . .
> This expurgated edition is the final crime against him.[14]

Pritchett also spread his critical wings with a substantial essay as early as 1930 on Latin-American verse for the *Spectator*.[15] And in 1933 the *Spectator* published a full-page polemical piece by him, responding to one by the older, well-established novelist Rose Macaulay, which had appeared the previous week. Macaulay had deplored what she archly called 'horridness' in literature. Pritchett pointed out that another name for the phenomenon was realism. Good novelists, he said, do not set out to please readers, 'but to note a set of experiences'.[16] It was not only an aesthetic argument but a territorial claim.

The following year the *Fortnightly* published a 3500-word essay by him on the Spanish novel.[17] The *New Statesman* – by now well on the way to becoming established as the leading political-cultural weekly in the world – at last responded by handing over most of the fiction round-ups to Peter Quennell, Cyril Connolly and others. Pritchett was too good a fiction reviewer to be let off this chore entirely – as late as 1938 he reviewed six batches of new fiction in the *Statesman*, averaging five titles per piece – but from 1935 he was given much wider scope in the magazine and wrote correspondingly less for its main rivals, especially the other weeklies.[18] On 28 December 1935 he published the first of what were to be many volumes'-worth of long *New Statesman* essays on major writers of the past: on Tolstoy's late political and religious work.

Ever since, as a teenager, he discovered Ruskin, Hazlitt and Stevenson, Pritchett had been drawn to the essay as a form. Collections of essays were the subjects of some of his earliest reviews for the *Christian Science Monitor*, where he argued that the genre was under pressure from the accelerating pace of life and the compression of all kinds of journalism. Despite that – or so he wrote when he was still only twenty-four – the essay 'hints at the leisure we desire, and this hint deludes us almost into the belief that we are actually enjoying a deep inward leisure'.[19] There was some wishful, not to say whimsical, thinking in this, and pieces he wrote on the same subject in his later twenties and early thirties are less optimistic. He took the opportunity provided by Leonard Woolf's *Essays on Literature, History and Politics* in 1927, for example, to express his frustration at how constricted most literary journalism was.[20] A sympathetic sub-editor gave this piece the heading, 'Wanted – Elbow Room', but as soon as Pritchett began to be given the room he thought he needed, he found that yet more problems were involved, to do with the limitations of his knowledge and lack of time to prepare, as much as of length. '[H]umbug is the essence of the essayist's temperament,' he told readers of the *New Statesman* frankly, in 1933.[21]

Whatever corner-cutting he had to do in the early years, though, Pritchett's criticism gained from the sheer cumulative experience of writing it. Over his long lifetime he wrote on many subjects several times, while continually adding new ones. Two further major pieces on

Tolstoy would appear in his various collections of essays; and – to focus on classic Russian writers alone – no fewer than five on Dostoevsky, four on Turgenev (about whom he also wrote an entire book), two on both Goncharov and Pushkin, one each on Aksakov, Chekhov (eventually also the subject of a book), Gogol, Gorky and Shchedrin. This is to say nothing of reviews, lectures and radio talks which he never republished in book form, or of the hundreds of authors of other nationalities about whom he wrote. From the beginning, he had seen reviewing as a way not only to earn a living, but to catch up with all the reading he imagined others, 'better educated', had already done. And because he had a good memory, in the process he built up an unequalled range of reference. When, in 1969, he lectured at Cambridge on the novelist George Meredith, it was on the basis of more than forty years' contemplation. The first of his several journalistic articles on Meredith had been written for the *Monitor* in 1928.[22]

Besides, his reviewing was not only an intellectual activity but an imaginative one. He often said that because he had not been to university, he had no preconceptions about a literary pecking order; and that because he was a practising fiction writer, he approached other writers in the spirit of wanting to find out exactly what they were doing, and why. There is no more sympathetic or more catholic literary critic in the English language. As his younger friend A. Alvarez was to say, 'Pritchett wasn't talking about literature, he was talking about family.'[23] In that first big Tolstoy piece – which, in common with almost all his other criticism published before 1939, has never been reprinted – he set his mark high. The occasion was the twenty-fifth anniversary of Tolstoy's death, a fact which in itself reminds one of a practical reason for Pritchett's range: his longevity. In one of his last pieces for the *New Statesman* he reminisced:

> How touching and hapless one's elders looked when one spotted them on their own: lonely Shaw looking into the window of the gun shop in the Strand, Wells with a fly button undone in a club, Yeats with a detective novel fallen on his chest, Chesterton at the window of a pub restaurant off Leicester Square, also asleep, with his head on the table-top marble – the clown in all the passive dignity of private life.[24]

By then, Martin Amis, Julian Barnes, Christopher Hitchens and James Fenton were on the magazine's staff, and the authors about whom

Pritchett was writing included Bruce Chatwin and Ian McEwan. Yet when Pritchett was a boy, Tolstoy was still alive.

There's no missing the intimacy and fluidity with which his early piece on the Russian writer begins: 'Twenty-five years have passed since Tolstoy fled from his wife and home at Yasnaya Polyana to seek isolation and to die.' If Pritchett was a child at the time he was writing about, it's as if by association that the next sentence flashes back to something that happened to Tolstoy in his own childhood, before attention shifts to how Maxim Gorky thought of him, and then to the Communist ban on his Christian writings and the more recent ban by the Nazis. In a couple of dozen lines, a passage of literary history has been sketched, in vivid and immediate human terms, and Tolstoy has been set before Pritchett's readers both as a man and as a sage whose writings speak to, and offend, the contemporary world. How, Pritchett asks, does Tolstoy's pacifism – so big an influence on conscientious objectors during the First World War – look from the perspective of 1935? Pacifism was a pressing question about which Pritchett had been writing separately, for example, in a review of Bertrand Russell's *In Praise of Idleness*.[25] Now, he related it to the specific situation of the artist (his own non-participation in the Spanish Civil War was certainly in his mind),[26] as well as to the octogenarian Tolstoy's complex psychology, and its no less complex effects on readers of his fiction:

> Our instincts rebel against his idealism because we see in it the expression of the desire for death in a man who, vigorous and joyous in sensual life and excelling in describing physical action and the sensuous surface of life, has turned to rend the physical. He was obsessed with the physical. Why should he force upon us the doctrine of escape that sprang from his revulsions?

The essay puts biographical and textual flesh on these abstractions, and ends by answering its own question: the late Tolstoy was 'a master of didactic persuasion and one of the few readable preachers'.

Ved Mehta, a *New Yorker* writer in the later decades when Pritchett himself contributed often to the magazine, would praise the way that his critical pieces generally 'had a striking image or told a story'.[27] Eventually, Pritchett's impressionism was to be used as a stick to beat him with, but already, by the 1930s, his use of the technique was often self-aware, even para-fictional: 'In Paris the afternoon of the 26th of July 1848 had that kind of sultriness which novelists are very fond of noting when violence is in the air, the tightened nerve snaps, and a cause is lost.' So he starts the first essay he wrote on Turgenev, in 1936.[28] Again and again, his criticism sets out like a piece of fiction:

> The world would be poor without the antics of clergymen. The Dean [Jonathan Swift], for example, wished he was a horse. A very Irish wish which a solid Englishwoman very properly came down on; Lady Mary Wortley Montagu was one of the few hostile critics of *Gulliver* . . .[29]

or:

> The English humorists! Through a fog compounded of tobacco smoke, the stink of spirits and the breath of bailiffs, we see their melancholy faces. Look at Thomas Hood, his eyes swollen with the cardiac's solemnity, his mouth pouting after tears . . .[30]

or this lead-in to a piece on Russian fiction, particularly Shchedrin's *The Golovylov Family*, with its understanding of human loneliness and inertia:

> We walk down a street in the dead hours of the afternoon, looking at the windows of the villas as we pass by. They are glass cases: they are the domestic aquarium, and what our idle eye is seeking is a sight of the human fish within. And presently we are taken by surprise. We see a face in one of those rooms. Agape, bemused, suspended like some torpid trout, a man or woman is standing alone there, doing nothing, and sunk in the formidable pathos of human inertia, isolation and *ennui*. . . .[31]

The interplay between his fiction and his critical writing went back to Pritchett's earliest days. He was usually, after all, doing both on the same desk. Once again, his ledger shows how this worked in practice. To take 1935 again: his novel *Nothing Like Leather* was published by Chatto and Windus at the end of January. In that month Pritchett wrote four reviews and set one of the *New Statesman*'s regular parody competitions. (Characteristically of him, this one invited entrants to find ways of reviving seven specific clichés.)[32] In February, as well as three reviews, he finished the manuscript of his autobiographical article 'Beginning to Write' for Nelson's and was also sending around various stories, including 'Miss Baker', which was taken by the *London Mercury*.[33] The tally for March was three reviews, two literary articles, another competition, and one rejected story. In April, negotiations were going on over no fewer than seven stories: some new, such as 'The Aristocrat', others, like 'X-Ray' and 'The Upright Man', being offered for reissue or for first American publication. Meanwhile, he wrote three more reviews. In May he was in Spain for the *Fortnightly*, but managed also to write a review and another competition entry. In June he submitted his Spanish article and two reviews, while finishing 'The Evils of Spain', which was rejected at first by the *New Statesman* and then also by *Encounter*, but which Mortimer eventually ran the following December.[34]

July was no less busy: six reviews, two essays, various short items based on his travels and two competitions. One of the latter invited advertising slogans for writers, on the analogy of 'Guinness is Good for You'. (Among those he picked were 'Freud: Don'ts for Dreamers', 'Henry James: Caviare to the Particular' and, for Mrs Beaton, 'Good Reading for Good Feeding.')[35] As the year went on, he began work on some new stories, as well as on *Dead Man Leading*. But however much Dorothy wanted Victor to write 'something that's "ours"',[36] he had a living to make and, while doing his best to reassure her, he also tried (unsuccessfully) to persuade Ian Parsons at Chatto to reissue *The Spanish Virgin*, which Ernest Benn had remaindered.

From the start of their relationship the literary agent in Dorothy had begun to organise Victor, as well as to take an active critical role in his writing. She not only answered the telephone and took over his typing, filing and record-keeping, but began to make suggestions about his stories. 'My very dear Friend,' she wrote to him some time in 1935, about the story eventually called 'The Evils of Spain',

> I took you at your word & did Conversation Piece very roughly & very quickly – just a draft for you to correct. I thought perhaps you might do it this afternoon so I'll give it to you at lunch time.
>
> I did enjoy it & roared with laughter. It does most definitely 'come off' – most successfully. I only thought one thing & that was Is it possible somehow to explain why Angel was wearing the Ambassador's pyjamas? I say this not because its really necessary but I thought it might make it even funnier. . . .[37]

She also recommended new outlets for his work ('is Good House-keeping a market for you. I see that A. J. Cronin, R. C. Sherriff, Richard Aldington & Osbert Sitwell have things appearing in it. You might try it. . . .').[38] And she arranged his timetable. He should take a little time off on Sundays, she urged, and confine his reviewing to the evenings so as to leave the days free for imaginative work.

The last seemed a particularly good idea but in practice was not so straightforward. Pritchett's view of writing was traditionally hier-archical. He saw novels as the highest form, followed by short stories and then travel writing. Everything else was essentially journeywork – left-handed writing. He eventually came to accept that he wasn't primarily a novelist. But although he wrote persuasively about the distinctive merits of the short story, his novels' relative lack of success didn't lead him to adjust his criteria. Above all, he chafed at the amount of time he spent on reviews (and also, in his later years, on lucrative but undemanding tourism features, especially for *Holiday* magazine). He had a living to earn and journalism was a necessary way of subsidising, as well as indirectly publicising, his fiction. But he couldn't bring himself to see that in relation to his whole oeuvre, he was being too hard on himself; that his journalism was some of his most important work. As with his account of his childhood, there was an element of myth making, here, which helped keep him going. But it was a myth that sometimes got him into difficulties, particularly when others believed it and tried to help. It was reinforced during the Second World War, when most British writers and other artists were enlisted, one way or another, for tasks other than those which they regarded as their main work.

To many people at the time, Pritchett's wartime *New Statesman* essays were a literary education. The aspiring young novelist Peter Vansittart, for example, saw him as 'a great god', and the 'Books in General' series (begun by Desmond MacCarthy, but by now almost synonymous with Pritchett) as 'a one-man university'. It was a common view, especially among the many readers who came (unlike Vansittart) from working-class, 'elementary-school' backgrounds, for whom the *New Statesman* was part of the educational ambition and, ultimately, transformation of mid-century Britain. Another engine of this social change was the BBC which, acting on a recommendation from Stephen Spender, first approached Pritchett as a possible broadcaster in 1935[39] and for which he did more than eighty talks during the Second World War.

*

In the autumn of 1939, as a precaution against air raids, but also in the hope of making a life more like the one they had known with Harry Roberts at Lower Oakshott, Victor, the pregnant Dorothy and two-year-old Josephine moved out of the flat the couple had been renting in Maida Vale to a rented farmhouse near Great Shefford, Berkshire, about fifty miles south-west of London and ten from where the Brenans lived in Aldbourne.

Victor was not among those husbands who take easily to their wives' childbearing. As he wrote to Gerald, 'pregnancy & the subsequent feeding is a terrible time and I shall be glad when Dorothy & I can begin again to have some life together. I get bored without the active company of women; I get depressed and become just a factory turning out anxieties. . . .'[40] Waiting for her to go into labour, he joked, was 'like waiting for an air raid'.[41] But Maidencourt provided consolations of its own. It was, and still is, a beautiful place, a substantial four-square early nineteenth-century manor house of red brick, its gently sloping gardens bisected by a clear stretch of the River Lambourn, running shallowly over gravel and chalk from East Garston, just up the valley. The orchard was enclosed by a crumbling eight-foot wall. Downstream are meadows which often flooded in those days and, on raised ground, visible from the bedrooms, the distinctive cylindrical flint tower of the parish church, surmounted by its octagonal parapet. The South Downs rise gently at front and rear, concealing, behind the farm, a railway cutting whose single-track line carried trains from Lambourn to Great Shefford's little station and – a main advantage of the location for Pritchett – on via Newbury to London. The Brenans often cycled over. The Pritchetts, too, acquired bicycles and Victor joked about the development of their calves.

When they arrived at Maidencourt, the surrounding farm was in poor shape, heavily mortgaged by an absentee landlord who had recently died. In 1941, a new owner brought in an enterprising young tenant farmer, David Rabbitts, who for the time being lived in a smaller house immediately behind the Pritchetts. The war brought some protection to struggling British farmers and soon the place was flourishing: fields of corn, sheep, a few cows. To Josephine, as she grew conscious of her surroundings and of the distant presence of the war, it was a place of utter safety, freedom and happiness. To Dorothy, though, it was very hard work. There was no electricity. While the large rooms with their high windows were full of light in the summer, in winter just keeping warm and dry was a substantial task. Writing to John Lehmann, Victor half grumbled, half boasted about living in 'a mansion . . . with a walled garden, full of rats, a few fleas, bird's nests, long corridors like the way back to the womb, squares of damp on the wall and a kitchen the size of a Wesleyan chapel'.[42] When Oliver was born at Maidencourt, the pipes froze and they had to fetch their water from the stream. Soon, Josephine developed bronchitis and Oliver suffered severe digestive complications. It was lucky that Victor was a hardened walker. Three times in a single day he struggled the four miles to Lambourn through snow and ice, in search of medical help.[43] When the bluff local GP warned Dorothy not to get too fond of her baby she collapsed.

Oliver survived and the doctor's advice later became a family joke. (Dorothy would ask her grandchildren whether they thought she could risk getting fond of their father now.) Domestic dramas apart, a combination of rural isolation and early wartime fears made Victor feel superstitious, and Maidencourt was at first haunted for him by various nervous anticipations and associations. He worried that the place was beyond his means, not only financially (the rent of one pound a week was far from cheap, by rural standards)[44] but socially. Was he tempting fate by living out of tune with the times? Maidencourt had no right to exist, he wrote in his journal, 'Its day is done. But I must be the first man who has lived in it who has thought this. . . . Already there is a decline. Such a house cant be "kept up": it is only partly furnished and by poor stuff. We have no maid. . . . No carriage and no car.'[45]

The house was on the route taken to Oxford by Hardy's Jude the Obscure: in his intellectual ambition a talismanic figure for Pritchett, but in his tragic end a very frightening one. (Pritchett seems not to have known about another literary association. Five centuries earlier the Maidencourt estate had briefly belonged to the Tudor poet, Sir Thomas Wyatt.)[46] Pritchett was suddenly less confident of his gifts and especially about how well they would withstand the pressures of war. For a time he abandoned *Mr Beluncle*, and this made him worry even more about possible analogies between himself and his father who, as he later wrote, 'had seen his energies dispersed in the 1914 war and at precisely my age, in 1939. At first our family history seemed to be repeating itself.'[47] But if he was worried about the effects of the war on his work, he also felt guilty about missing the main action: 'Here at Maidencourt,' he wrote in a notebook, 'the sun, the green . . . buttercups on the stream like a petal strewn lane between the willows . . . – over there, appalling violence & pain. Over the wireless that voice like teeth coming slowly towards me, threatening, eating a bite off peace, happiness & freedom to which you feel you have no right and which yet seem the only reasons worth fighting for.'[48]

Such mixed feelings were common enough and Pritchett was not alone among artists of the time in having difficulty deciding where his main duty lay. It seemed obvious that the least useful thing he could do would be to enlist, though both of his brothers did and Victor himself was rated Grade 1 as fit for possible service.[49] Still, he joined the Home Guard in Newbury and, while worrying about what would happen if he were conscripted into the real army, wrote wryly to Brenan (another volunteer) about the frustrating limitations of his duties:[50]

we are proud of having 1) had our post bombed the night before last 2) of having bombs within 300 yards of it 3) of having bombs about a mile from it. I give these details in the order as they were given to me by chaps reluctantly and yet very English-ly toiling towards accuracy and truth. . . . Our report book – I quote from a secret document at my own risk – reads something like this:

Monday	Nothing to report
Tuesday	Smith failed to report for duty
Wednesday	Nothing to report
Thursday	Nothing to report
Friday	Nothing
Saturday	No sugar, no tea, no wick in lamp
Sunday	Loud explosion

No less improbably, he became a member of the Hungerford Rural District Council. Meanwhile, he travelled often to London, partly on *New Statesman* business, partly to keep an eye on his parents, though it turned out that they didn't need him. 'Mother I expected to be ill . . . from fear of air raids,' he wrote in his journal. 'She was almost exhilarated.'[51] He found his father busy with his own form of preventative action: 'while the bombs fall he prays and they are "guided" away from his house and fall – well, I'm sorry to say, sometimes on other people's houses.'[52]

Inevitably, Victor's not unamused sense of futility, compounded by the distractions of day-to-day life, affected his writing. Unable to plan in the long term, he was also easily drawn away from the shortest imaginative effort. As he listened to aeroplanes groaning overhead, he castigated himself for wondering 'what will be the last sentence I shall write if by any chance a bomb blows me up. . . .'[53] It wasn't an idle preoccupation. In London, he took his turns as a fire watcher at the *New Statesman*, whose office was hit in the autumn of 1940. Of course, the situation gave him copy. 'One likes to see damage,' he noted with his characteristic honesty,[54] and he was to see plenty of it – some near his home (where, aiming for the main railway line between London and Bristol, the Luftwaffe dropped a surprising number of bombs),[55] but mainly in London. On one occasion he found himself on the seventh floor of Broadcasting House in an air raid; on another, spending the night with a hundred others on mattresses in the BBC's concert hall in Langham Place.[56] The London streets, Pritchett wrote in December 1940, 'look like jaws which have been mutilated by the dentist, fantastic examples of decay at the roots, neglected cavities'.[57] When one unexpected raid began he found himself hesitating about which shelter to go into: 'it is like choosing where one is going to die. . . . For – it never occurs to me I shall be *safe* in a shelter. I only feel *safe* outside.'[58] He was to use some of these experiences in stories, among them 'The Voice', about a disgraced preacher being rescued from a bombed church.

Meanwhile, like other writers, he began to get used to the wartime version of literary life, taking on official tasks for the Ministry of Information and other government bodies, and reviewing and broad-casting on increasingly topical themes. He was, he told John Lehmann, 'Harassed by every kind of interruption, distracted by every kind of journalistic red-herring, pursued by the BBC, the M.O.I. [Ministry of Information], the M. of Transport, the Home Office, Foreign Office, District Council, Fire Watchers, Home Guard & the Board of Education'.[59] Despite wartime privations, the environs of Broadcasting House in Fitzrovia – home ground to Pritchett ever since he and Evelyn lived there in the late 1920s – had a new cosmopolitanism, thanks to a large influx of intellectual refugees from Continental Europe and also from India and other parts of the still vast British Empire.[60] The BBC's labyrinthine corridors were full of writers and artists, and its canteen became a kind of international cultural club. Pritchett's regular dashes on foot between Broadcasting House in Langham Place and the *New Statesman* in Lincoln's Inn Fields – journeys hard to make without being bumped into by Dylan Thomas, Julian Maclaren-Ross or another of the local literary pub crawlers – often involved a detour to the Ministry of Information in Malet Street, where yet another, overlapping team of writers was based, including Pritchett's agent A. D. Peters and also, in the early part of the war, Graham Greene. The MOI, Pritchett told Brenan, was 'like a lunatic asylum, a life of taxis, telephones and everyone's office like a street corner with people coming in and out and shouting'.[61] Some other writers, meanwhile, were in the London fire service: Henry Green, William Sansom, Stephen Spender. In this crowded scene, literary impresarios like John Lehmann and Cyril Connolly – both of whom were editing magazines – found it even easier than usual to attract talented people to their parties and Pritchett was among their favourite guests.

Often, though, he was hurrying to catch a train – whether home to Maidencourt or, more often than he would have liked, to one of the documentary assignments in various parts of Great Britain which his grasp of the details of ordinary work ensured he was picked for. He described marshalling yards in East Anglia and interviewed station masters and quarrymen. He collaborated with film makers, recording 'days in the life of a bus driver and a small suburban couple', and found it 'amazing what the process could discover'.[62] There was a bureaucratic, jargon-laden aspect to the world of propaganda, of course. Writing a pamphlet on 'Transport in War Time', he told Brenan, involved sitting at Waterloo Station 'while "chiefs" give me the "dope", I "approach angles" and so on'.[63] But he was too serious a writer simply to put down what he was told to. To him, such projects meant the kind of research Zola had done in preparation for *Germinal*.[64] In a single year, as he recorded in a journal entry written at Christmas 1942, he went 'to Liverpool twice, Yorkshire, Wales (4 times) Southampton, Edinburgh, York, Birmingham, Chippenham, Bath, Bristol. . . .'[65] The journey to Bristol was made on a goods lorry. He spent weeks in the shipyards of Clydeside and the north-east of England. He already knew some of what he described – for example, that all kinds of work are like writing in that they involve 'a sinking and absence of the self, a merging in the rhythm of the job'.[66] But, as with his earlier travels, the investigations he undertook were careful and sustained, and, despite some sentimental-propagandist touches, his accounts of what he saw, especially in the anonymous sixty-four-page illustrated booklet *Build the Ships: The Official Story of the Shipyards in Wartime*, are still absorbing.

As in Manhattan twenty years earlier, he responded with equivocal vividness to modern technology: 'A submarine flatters human intelligence in a superlative degree. It is a brilliant, sinister brainwave, a shaft of sheer intellectual satisfaction. It is like living inside a brain.'[67] But his main attention is on the workers. With a pang of sympathy, he notices among blacksmiths at work a boy who 'two months ago . . . was thirteen and at school'. Still: better a boy than a girl, in Pritchett's terms. Always a traditionalist in matters of gender, he remarked on 'one of the most extraordinary sights of the shipyard, the first sign of civilisation – a woman in overalls, sweeping up!'[68] The first chapter of *Build the Ships* is titled 'A Man's Job'. The book does its dutiful best to acknowledge women's role in the wartime shipyards and Pritchett allows that women he met who had previously been domestic servants or shop assistants seemed to prefer their industrial jobs. But he confided to Dorothy that he thought it was 'wrong' for women to do this kind of work. Men's reaction against it, he guessed, was

> not jealousy of their taking men's jobs, cashing in freely on generations of men's experiences & habits, but simply jealousy of the employer who has power over them. . . . I believe the men (who do not like the women working there and ridicule them in private) really feel a confusion of emotion. . . . I'm not saying they're right, but all sorts of queer things are mixed up in it.[69]

The husband and father added conscientiously, 'I should like to see you and all the overworked mothers who get no time off go off to Mr Bevin' (the minister of labour in Churchill's coalition government) 'and demand people to be directed into *your* industry!!'[70]

In *Build the Ships* – a straightforward, powerfully immediate account of the industrial process from design to launch, complete with the nuances of the difference between welding and riveting, geared turbines and older engines – Pritchett particularly relished the evidence of human resilience and adaptability that was provided by the repairing side of the shipyards' work: the conversion of merchantmen to aircraft carriers, the salvage of damaged ships, especially the welding together of one that had been blown in half. Above all, both in his official writings and in letters home, he simply described. In the repair works, 'Everyone looked green . . . because of the coloured lights & the blaze of oxy-acetylene welding. . . . The noise was frantic, a hum broken by metallic shrieks and bell-like beatings and spittings.' Outside in the town, 'The Army . . . race about with popping eyes, as if chasing their short moustaches. The sailors stand about loose-jointedly.'

He was as self-deprecating about his wartime projects as about everything else. People listening to the BBC's World Service in China and Africa, he said, 'hearing a noise like the quacking of ducks, realise that we are talking about literature'.[71] 'We' included George Orwell, who was at Broadcasting House a lot, producing his regular series *The Voice* for the Eastern Service and working on his wartime commentaries. He and Pritchett recorded a discussion on 'What's Wrong with the Modern Short Story' in 1941 – the first of several successful radio collaborations between them. Pritchett's first impression of Orwell was of 'a thin ill looking man with a mackintosh and a sunken grin at the corner of his mouth . . . camped in a one roomed service flat with a teacup and a typewriter'.[72] He liked him instantly and, despite the longstanding hostilities between Orwell and Kingsley Martin, and the fact that, as Pritchett quickly saw, Orwell kept his acquaintances compartmentalised, they became friends. They had much in common, not least having lived rough in Paris and Spain. Both were serving in the Home Guard and Orwell, who had only recently moved back into London from the country, was keen to advise Pritchett about how to handle his relatively new bucolic existence. Pritchett relished his prickliness and puritanism, whether about rural life or about social divisions and politics more generally:

> He was an expert in living on the bare necessities and a keen hand at making them barer . . . I remember once being advised by him to go in for goat-keeping, partly I think because it was a sure road to trouble and semi-starvation; but as he set out the alluring disadvantages, it seemed to dawn on him that he was arguing for some rural Arcadia . . .; goats began to look like escapism and, turning aside as we walked to buy some shag [tobacco] at a struggling Wellsian small trader's shop, he switched the subject sharply to the dangerous Fascistic tendencies of the St John's Wood Home Guard who were marching to imaginary battle under the Old School Tie.[73]

One of the things he appreciated in Orwell was that, for all his quirky patriotism, he was a cosmopolitan: 'closer to Camus, Silone, and Koestler than . . . to any English contemporaries'. More important still, 'he was "in life"'.[74]

The BBC was quick to realise that, like Orwell, Pritchett had more than merely 'literary' skills to offer and, given the newly egalitarian demands of the time, fewer disqualifications than many other available writers. Pritchett 'was trained as a journalist . . . and has a quick pen', one producer wrote to another in recommendation. 'He also has a sincere and sensible voice and manner – not too cultivated.'[75] This represented a big change of tack since Pritchett's first encounters with the organisation in 1935. At that time, having been gravely warned that it would be necessary for him 'to be auditioned at the microphone before your name could be put before the English Committee of this Council as a possible broadcaster', he was given a trial which was adjudicated by 'Miss Somerville and Miss H. V. Stuart, of Sherborne School for Girls and Chairman of the English Committee of this Council'. The verdict was negative: 'Although your voice reproduced quite well, it was felt that it did not possess quite the power and enthusiasm needed for a series of talks to elementary school children.'[76] For 'power and enthusiasm', one should probably understand something to do with elocution. In wartime England, by contrast, the BBC's former fruitiness was less in demand. Pritchett took part in some of the first discussion programmes which used working-class participants, helping to find appropriate speakers in his country neighbourhood and explaining the costs involved – 'hire of car, hire of room, supper, drinks, etc.'[77] – to producers who seem to have thought that working men, unlike intellectuals, would be happy to take part not only without fees, but paying their own expenses.

The social changes represented by such events were also directly addressed by Pritchett in talks about language, slang, national identity and, especially, about the need for 'a new common culture, a common language, which does not separate the educated from the less educated'.[78] He was delighted, though not unamused, by some of the results, telling Frances Partridge that a docker had told him, 'I've been reading nothing but Kant these last three years.'[79] Meanwhile, he threw himself into live broadcast discussions with people who had had the kind of education he himself had longed for, like the philosopher G. M. Young and the critics Clive Bell and Kenneth Clark, against whom he relished pitting his wits. 'How we think is by talking and arguing,' Pritchett said in one of these programmes, and talking is 'the basis of most human relations'.[80] He had always been not only an enthusiastic conversationalist but an observer of conversation – of its social and intellectual rules, as well as (from a fiction writer's point of view) what it revealed about people. One of his most original essays discusses conversation as a discipline and an art.[81] These broadcasts enabled him to practise it constructively and, at the same time, to speak publicly on behalf of, as well as about, those less well equipped to speak for themselves. Pritchett stayed close to the world of most listeners, telling the sculptor Henry Moore, for example, that he thought the 'average' viewer would find some of his work 'fairly remote from human experience' (a point whose implications the grammar-school-educated Moore dealt with well), or reminding other participants that the very capacity to think is bound up with the socio-economic system.[82] At the same time, in the course of these conversations he increasingly articulated and defined aspects of his cultural conservatism. When the radical Scottish poet Edwin Muir produced the facile claim that all good writers are 'rebelling violently' against the values of their time, Pritchett responded sharply, 'Are Thackeray and Trollope bad writers?'[83]

Pritchett's BBC work brought not only new subjects, but wider reputation and influence. 'Chap down here welcomed me like Aston Villa,' he boasted to a producer friend, after returning home from one of his assignments.[84] To Brenan, he later confessed an addiction to the 'secret, guilty exhibitionism of the microphone'.[85] Even the most straightforwardly literary assignments reached relatively big audiences. Broadcasting on writers from Mark Twain to W. E. Henley, E. M. Forster to Ernest Hemingway, he was often able to develop ideas originally conceived with a relatively small readership in mind, for example, by turning one of his 'Books in General' pieces, 'Gibbon Joins the Home Guard', into a radio programme.[86]

The Gibbon essay first appeared in August 1941. The title refers to the fact that, early in the Seven Years War, the future historian of the decline and fall of the Roman Empire ingloriously – and, though Pritchett doesn't say this, not unlike Pritchett himself – joined the Hampshire Militia. As in all of his criticism, behind a mixture of topical reference, gossip and light aphorism, Pritchett gets across a lot of historical and literary information, while unintimidatingly leaving the impression that all he has done is remind us of what we already at some level knew. He makes us want to read Gibbon's autobiography and journal, as well as his most famous work. He tells us something about his subject's life, and about how his character and experiences were reflected in his writing. ('The qualities we expect of Gibbon are sense, balance and judiciousness. No man is more likely to . . . extract the value from his disappointments, to gather in, perhaps complacently, all the compensations.') One phrase links Gibbon to Bacon, Swift, Johnson; another deftly sums up an aspect of his attitude to Rousseau. But Pritchett isn't showing off. His eye is always on Gibbon himself, and on how to convey both what makes him distinctive and what will make us want to know him better. He quotes one of the funniest of Gibbon's own aphorisms: 'Few perhaps are the children who, after the expiration of some months or years, would sincerely rejoice in the resurrection of their parents.' He sums up pithily: 'Gibbon has a taste for the truth that is melancholy, for seeing life as a series of epitaphs. And yet in [Joshua] Reynolds' portrait the fat little scholar with the second roll of chin, and the lips which seem set for the discharge of some destructive epigram, is not as sober as he looks. He is, in fact, cutting a dash.'

That last touch takes Pritchett back to the Home Guard: in Gibbon's day, members of the Militia dashingly wore scarlet. The shape of the piece is satisfying in itself. Pritchett often said that a short story should be the prose version of a sonnet, with all its compression and sense of completeness, and there's a similar formal artistry in his non-fiction. Behind the connections he makes, too, between Gibbon as a man and as a writer, lies Pritchett himself, keeping his own dutiful watch on the Berkshire Downs while his young children slept. What difference might it have made if Gibbon had been married? the father in Pritchett idly wonders – 'we might be reading of the Birth and Rise, rather than of the Decline and Fall of the Roman Empire.'

More important, how does a sense of duty affect a writer? Gibbon 'was . . . thorough, industrious and responsible, and some part of his suffering was due to his conscientiousness'. Conscientiousness took the form of unremitting work: 'Sooner or later, the great men turn out to be all alike. They never stop working. They never lose a minute. It is very depressing.' Depressing – but also reassuring. The Gibbon piece is the first in Pritchett's *Collected Essays*. The last, 1300 pages and forty-odd years later, has something similar to say, this time about Virginia Woolf: 'she worked harder than ever when she became famous, as gifted writers do – what else is there to do but write?'[87]

Pritchett knew that the virtues of industry could be illusory, especially for someone from his kind of background. 'I realise what escapists we who rely on our own efforts are,' he told Brenan, 'any effort, to us, is valid just because it is an effort.'[88] Still, 'work' is a key word for him and so, too, is 'great'. In private, to Dorothy, he made no secret of his ambition. 'How necessary it is now that I should do something great in my life and in my work,' he wrote to her on a train journey in October 1942, 'not falter any more, but harden off and decide and impose what I want.'[89] He still made fun of his own solemnity, especially in his drawings. In one of his early letters to her the words 'I am always saying to myself I will be a great man' are illustrated by drawings of him

posturing in his underpants in front of a looking glass, then with top hat and cigar, riding on an elephant, accompanied by Dorothy on a camel with a military band, and finally scribbling at his desk, casually spilling his wineglass over the scrawny, supine figure of an 'Editor crawling'. But seeing the funny side of his dreams didn't mean that he wasn't serious about them. There's a sense in the essay on Gibbon that Pritchett is telling himself that his own capacity for hard work just might be a capacity for the greatness he, too, aspired to.

So, even more than before, he worked and worked, and Dorothy worked, too, running the house, keeping the accounts, answering the phone, and typing and retyping his frequently corrected drafts: stories, sections of the once-again-resumed novel, essays, talks. Fortunately for her, most of Victor's correspondence at this stage was still done in longhand. Even so, among household chores and attending to the children, it wasn't unknown for her to be at the typewriter from nine in the morning until six in the evening. The Pritchetts' next-door neighbour, the farmer David Rabbitts, had to come into the house sometimes to use the phone and still gasps at how much she smoked: 'She had a packet of Gold Flake in the kitchen, another packet in the sitting room: cigarettes everywhere!'[90] In the midst of everything she made time to write a story of her own. Victor encouraged her and sent the result to John Lehmann, saying 'it struck me as very promising but I'm prejudiced and we'd be glad to get an official opinion'.[91] Lehmann didn't take it and it seems that the manuscript hasn't survived. The sheer fact of Dorothy's having written it, and in such circumstances, provides a painful glimpse of hopes whose suppression was already contributing to her frequent unhappiness – an unhappiness which would gradually spread to her family.

Pritchett's own career continued to flourish on almost every front. In April 1941 he wrote to his current editor at Chatto, Harold Raymond, suggesting that a selection of his *New Statesman* pieces might make a book. Raymond agreed and various possible titles were aired. Pritchett said that at one point early in the war, when he had been worried about running out of subjects, Kingsley Martin had told him, 'Don't worry. Just wade your way through the Classics.' Perhaps 'Wading through the Best Authors' might make a good name for the book. Eventually, as so often, he found his title in a popular cliché: *In My Good Books*. It's only a small selection of the essays he had written by the time the book went to press, but it gives an idea of his range. The two opening pieces are specifically war-related: the one on Gibbon and an account of *Histoires d'un Conscrit de 1813*, Emile Erckmann and Alexandre Chatrian's fictional memoir of an ordinary Frenchman serving under Napoleon in the first conscript army in modern Europe. From there Pritchett turns to the Romantic-period Swiss novelist and autobiographer, Benjamin Constant, and to the early French detective, Eugène-François Vidocq (another piece which begins like a novel: 'The time of the year and the year itself are unknown, but one day, well before the French Revolution, a tall, good-looking, fair-haired youth was hanging about dejectedly on the quay at Ostend seeking for a boat which would take him to America'). The remaining topics in this loose group – it isn't treated as a separate section – are also French: Zola's *Germinal* and Alain-René Le Sage's *Gil Blas*. Then the book turns to Russia, to Lermontov, Gogol, Turgenev and Dostoevsky, and on to Italy (Svevo), before coming back to England with a handful of essays on Victorian authors, others on the eighteenth century and on Irish writers, and a final group on puritans of one sort and another, including Americans.

The book's cosmopolitanism is striking, given the inevitable insularity of wartime Britain. There has been a myth that Cyril Connolly's *Horizon* was a lone beacon of cultural internationalism in its time, but the myth makers have evidently not read the *New Statesman*.[92] From the point of view of Pritchett's own development, though, an interesting element – encouraged by the wartime climate and one which the BBC, as well as the *New Statesman*, was eager to give him opportunities to explore – is the extent of his concern, too, with English subjects and with the nature and history of Englishness.[93] It is represented in this collection not only by predictable writers such as Henry Fielding, Elizabeth Gaskell and Thomas Hardy, but also by Francis Kilvert (whose diaries were first published in the late 1930s) and by the Leicestershire puritan George Fox. About Fox, Pritchett movingly concludes: 'He was English. One sees him, the big man from a dull flat country, a peasant shrewd and, yet, in a massive way, naif; sober yet obstinate; gentle yet immovably blunt; a man who has made his mind up, who has the inordinate pride and yet the inordinate humility of the saints.' As so often in Pritchett's criticism, there was a personal element in this. Fox, like Pritchett's grandfather, had preached (in Fox's own words, 'declared the Day of the Lord') in Sedbergh.[94]

Englishness was scarcely a new subject for Pritchett, of course. From the beginning, the people in his fiction more often than not came from the English lower middle class: clerks and shopkeepers, publicans and pub-goers, selfish people slightly above themselves in their own minds, quick to censure opportunism in others. Because he had spent the formative years of his writing career outside England, he saw his country partly with an outsider's eye. The emphasis continued in his wartime stories: for example, in 'The Invader', a vignette (not included in his *Complete Short Stories*) about a group of soldiers on their home turf, repelling a tramp whom, though they pay lip service to his having fought in the First World War, they are determined not to let into their hut.[95] In many of Pritchett's critical essays of the same period – on Priestley, on H. G. Wells, on A. L. Rowse's *The English Spirit*, on Harold Nicolson's *England: An Anthology*, on Pierre Maillaud's *The English Way* – he is frankly curious about the origins of what he sees as national quirks. His sense that religion, and particularly puritanism, is a formative aspect of secular English life is developed in several wartime pieces published after those selected for *In My Good Books*. In these explorations, he often confesses ignorance and incapacity. It's yet another of the qualities which draw readers in. 'When lately I was reading *The Mystery of Edwin Drood* I felt extremely the want of some sort of guidance on the Victorian fascination with violent crime,' he wrote in 1944. 'What explains the exorbitant preoccupation with murder, above all?'[96] And again, 'My eye has been often baffled by lack of the words which would define the poor streets of the East End, as they used to be before the war.'[97]

These admissions were genuine. As his knowledge grew, so did his sense of his own ignorance. He read avidly, was endlessly inquisitive and observant, and relished new situations in which he could eavesdrop. The commissions which war brought to him, however irksome he professed to find them, were rewarding in these ways. But there was a new reason why he sometimes felt at a loss when faced with the things he had known best. His past – so important a theme to him – was increasingly at odds with his present kind of life: that of a well-known professional writer, married with two children, living in a farmhouse in the Home Counties, on equal terms both with the local establishment and with high-cultural society in London. It's startling to turn from 'The Invader' and his essays on George Fox and on Arthur Morrison's *Tales of Mean Streets*, to his journal for 1943 and to see – whatever his reservations and ironies about his new surroundings – just how far V. S. Pritchett has come:

Went to Lady Colefax's 'Salon'. Present: Rosamond Lehmann &

John, Stephen Spender in AFS uniform. . . . Lord Esher; a Pompadourish lady with electric blue eyes & a black spot under one, an eye in italics. Lady C with the springing cat look of the voracious hostess . . . A General with a monocle and tapering trousers. Talk: workers' discussions. Bolted through the blackout afterwards and just caught the 7.40 from Paddington as it was going out, my heart going like hell. I like this dimmed light, soft, chattering evening and hoped I'd be asked again and wished D had come. But she wouldn't: 'nothing to put on, darling.'. . .

. . . Ruth let us have one month of her ration of wine. What a delight. 2 bottles whisky, 1 bottle rum, 1 champagne, 1 bottle sherry, 1 Claret. Bless her. One ought not to despise Ruth. . . .[98]

There are sophisticated lunches – at the Athenaeum, at the Café Royal, at the Etoile; with Orwell, Kenneth Clark, John Piper, John Pope-Hennessy (who said 'how frightfully funny' about everything) and Malcolm Sargent. There are famous visitors to the offices of the *New Statesman*, Father D'Arcy among them, the 'Jesuit with silver hair and, as it seems, painted face, handsome, a dandy, a sort of actor, oozes social charm'. It's not surprising to find Pritchett confiding to his journal that, living in the country, 'I get intensely over excited by company in London.'[99]

Of course, another selection from the journal tells a more domestic side of the story. The day before Victor's thirty-ninth birthday, on 15 December 1939 (a cold, damp day, 'as though the earth were giving off steam from a hundred damp bonfires'), Oliver had been born at Maidencourt while, downstairs, Victor washed the dishes and paced up and down.[100] January was exceptionally cold and they were soon snowed in. 'We remain perfectly healthy,' he told his publisher, 'but the Ivory Tower is not in it. I suppose the perfect example of the aesthete is the goldfish frozen into the middle of an iceberg.'[101] Fourteen months later, Victor recorded, 'Oliver suddenly stood up in the middle of the sitting room a long way from land, so to speak, and walked three steps and then stood still, knees bent & rather astonished.'[102] There had been another surprise, recently, when Victor took Josephine snowballing: 'She was astonished to see how peeing on the snow melts it – & so am I! A proud moment. . . .'[103] Around the time when, in London, Victor was first being lionised at Sybil Colefax's salon, Josephine got pneumonia and he spent hours repairing her doll; Dorothy was 'working herself to the bone' and was often unwell, but consoled herself with Ruth's drink ration; Victor himself got 'the worst cough & cold I have had for years'; a German raider hit the school next to Newbury station, killing two children ('On the station in the dark one felt the grit of the . . . glass underfoot in the damp'); Victor went to Glasgow to do some of his research on shipbuilding. The summer came and London was depressing and muggy. At Maidencourt, 'Dorothy & I wilted in the garden & were happy. . . . A duck is sitting . . . by the pond on 10 eggs. Great hopes. Will a fox get her?' The children fretted, '"Make me an animal. I want the Trike. . . . etc." They're in bed now thank heaven & looking rosy & angelic.'[104]

It isn't misleading to divide the journal like this. Although the entries are chronologically interwoven, Pritchett had begun to lead two lives, at home and away. He loved Dorothy's company. Their wartime letters to each other were still as intimate and sexually charged as those of their courtship. 'It is so vital and dynamic, our marriage,' Victor wrote on yet another train, in June 1942: 'I never adored your body as much as I do now. . . . I very much like seeing you at doors, especially when you are naked at the bathroom door. I could never tell you what your soft, white, wild smelling, wild tasting body means to me but my cock goes hard as I write this to you.'[105] This was soon after Dorothy had sent him a cartoon of how she thought he too often saw himself – a brain on a pair of legs. She contrasted this with a picture captioned 'As I see him': a much smaller brain, sketchily flanked by the words 'mind' and 'heart', above a distinctly locker-room depiction of an erect penis, beside which she wrote the words 'exquisite sensibility – I think this fits in here'. 'Darling – I love you,' she added. 'I *loved* last night & I wish I could make you delighted with yourself.'[106]

If sex continued to be one staple of their letters, Josephine and Oliver are increasingly another. Victor compared his feelings with those of his friend Richard Church, who had said that being a father made writing seem unnecessary, even impossible. Certainly, Pritchett wrote, 'One falls in love with one's children. To touch them, play with them, talk to them gives me that helpless, mindless, alive physical feeling of love. They are like the spring in the house. . . .'[107] On his research trip to Tyneside, watching some local children swinging on railings outside a bombed-out pub, his thoughts about them merged with his feelings for his own children. He told Dorothy that through his love both for her and for Josephine and Oliver, he had reached a new level of responsiveness. Previously (or so he thought, as he wrote), other people had just been 'designs & patterns' to him.[108]

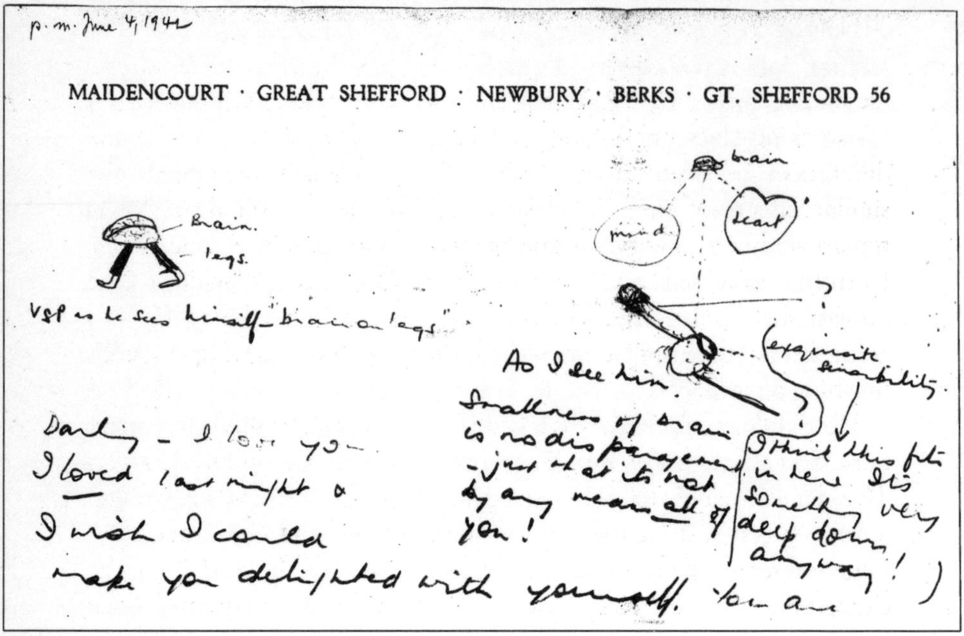

p. m. June 4, 1942

MAIDENCOURT · GREAT SHEFFORD : NEWBURY, · BERKS · GT. SHEFFORD 56

[handwritten diagram and note: brain, legs — "VSP as he sees himself 'brain on legs'"; mind, heart, brain diagram; and handwritten message]

Darling — I love you — I loved last night & I wish I could make you delighted with yourself. You are...

In their tender eroticism and domesticity, these wartime letters were clearly meant to help overcome physical separation, but in some ways, of course, they added to it. Victor's, in particular, are full of cheerful, almost boastfully Walter-like news about what he has been doing, whom he has been meeting, this lunch, that hotel. Dorothy sometimes came to London with him,[109] but that earlier reference to her not having gone with him to Sybil Colefax's is telling. It's as if the couple were doomed to repeat some of the aspects of Victor's parents' relationship which he most deplored and feared.

The journal Pritchett began in 1940 ends on 9 February 1942. Its last words are, 'This has been the happiest time of all in my very happy marriage with Dorothy.' Happy it may often have been, but it was becoming much less simple and straightforward. Again, he made light of the difficulties in his letters:

marriage obviously is a sacrament because it is such a violent state. To call it an agreement between two people to live together – à la Bertrand Russell – would be a masterpiece of understatement. It's a civil war, with victory celebrations, banquets, enormous advances, inexplicable retreats, persistent guerrilla work, comfortable lengths of blitzkrieg, marvellous intelligence work & plenty of stretcher bearing. . . .[110]

He had been reading the All Souls historian A. L. Rowse's account of his working-class upbringing, *A Cornish Childhood* and, for all the differences between the two men, Pritchett easily recognised the similar effects of their early struggles on their personalities: 'The remarkable fact of survival and getting anywhere makes one smug.' Dorothy, he added, had gone to London for a break, which, 'God knows, she urgently needed. She really is a prisoner here.' He was going to take the opportunity to heat up some stew and sit up all night finishing a piece.

He didn't mention that he had found an opportunity of another kind. Some time in the spring or summer of 1942 he started an affair. The details – including the woman's identity – are not known: no journal survives from the period between then and late November. (This seems unlikely to have just been a coincidence, though the expectation of a German invasion in those months may have been another factor, including in the affair itself.)[111] Dorothy, however, was a more powerful and independent wife than her mother-in-law. It was one of the reasons Victor was attracted to her. He well knew that she was attractive to, and attracted by, other men and – in theory, at least – there was an understanding between them about this. Early in the war he had written to her about his sense that, on her side, 'something new was going to happen':

> – that in mind, intention and talk with people you did not see why you should keep yourself to me. This has often made me cold with wretchedness and fear and loss . . . and very afraid of the adjustment that would have to be made; but I have thought that if this is inevitable, that a sort of mature feeling, a ripening would come to us because we love each other . . .[112]

Now it was the twenty-seven-year-old Dorothy's turn to be so mature. Victor had decided – rather offhandedly, at least as he presented the position to her[113] – to end his affair on her account. Dorothy answered with humility but also with a dignified sense of their mutual independence. She had, she told him, been sitting up late, thinking about the fact that writers are extraordinary & special people – no, *don't laugh* – & that they're so many, many different people & shades of people & therefore have special licence, because it is important for them to develop every aspect of themselves & they cant do this on one poor ordinary female. And I dont – & never did – want to stunt your life at all by interfering with any other relationships you need. I'm sad that I didn't tell you all this before you wrote your letter. I was going to tell you but I hadn't got it tidy. Now I dont know what to do to make things right for you. . . . I really think, you see, that your decision to break wasn't made freely & that it isn't what you want. And doing something you don't want to do makes me less of a person to be respected & considered & you therefore do it in a way that is disloyal to me & shows me in a bad light. Now I think we must strengthen what *we* have when we can be truthful about it, & then we will both be more free. . . .

This is the most I've ever loved you & cared for you & your happiness so I do hope that you will accept it & do & be what you want & what is in your heart. Its difficult for me because I don't want to exaggerate or minimise your affair or make it into something it isn't. But if you still want it, whatever it is, have it, darling. I'm truly sad I didn't say all this before but I'm sure you could make it right in spite of your letter, if you want to.[114]

It was a brave position for anyone to take, let alone a woman with no independent means, stuck in the country with two small children in the middle of a war. And of course it made Victor feel even more tied to her. But for all her rationalisations and strength of purpose, the situation made Dorothy extremely miserable. No less inevitably, the pain lasted much longer than the affair. A few months after the crisis, Victor sat downstairs at Maidencourt one night, writing to her. They had quarrelled and she had gone to bed. He didn't know if she was asleep.

I thought about writing a story about you. I often do this, and I draw back afraid. For it often seems to me, though not always, that works of art are written because something is lost or finished. They are like memorials. . . .

Whenever I think of writing a story about you I think at once of the snow falling at Oakshott & us going to the Folly & undressing in that cold hut and clinging to each other, mouth to mouth, on that little hard bed. The snow light was on your skin. . . . Really it is a poem not a story.

> . . . Come out of this trance of unhappiness, my darling. . . .[115]

She did emerge but, more often than before, she was prone to deep depressions. Her sister Jean later recalled babysitting at Maidencourt for a couple of days while Dorothy made a rare trip to London – perhaps the trip Victor referred to in his letter to Brenan. On her return, Dorothy burst into tears while bathing one of the children, 'because you go away and have a nice time but you always have to return to the children's baths'. She smoked even more heavily, these days: 'you smoke & smoke,' Victor wrote to her anxiously, '& cough & cough just because there is something reckless about you that likes to be independent of me.'[116] There was also something reckless about how she drank – especially on Monday and Tuesday nights which, to Dorothy's despair, Victor now often spent at the *New Statesman*.[117]

For the Pritchetts, of course, as for others in similar circumstances at the time, marital damage was to some extent put into proportion by the war which had helped cause it, and if Dorothy was often depressed, she was also practical, generous and outgoing. In the winter of 1944, when a friend who already had two young children went into labour with twins, Dorothy had the older children to stay at Maidencourt along with Josephine and Oliver. ('Have you crawled on the floor,' Victor asked Gerald rhetorically, 'dressing four young children who cant stand still, whose noses are running, and may at any moment pee in your ear? If only children were taller.')[118] Victor, meanwhile, continued to travel widely on various commissions. Early in 1945, he was put into uniform and sent in the wake of the Allied armies in France and Germany. To Brenan, he was jaunty about the prospect:

> A British civilian with status of Captain, tetanus injection, willing to be buried in a Protestant cemetery and owning about 2 tons of military equipment, is addressing you. . . . I still touch wood about the expedition; a last minute cancellation or postponement would not surprise me. The official world is a drunken man's world; everything is just out of focus. But not my identity photograph. With glaring accuracy it has picked out the dirtyness of my beard, my puddled eyes, my sensual snout, my degraded lower lip and my obscene second chin . . . There never was a clearer picture of a man who cant be trusted a yard. . . .[119]

He assumed that, once again, he would be having a much better time than Dorothy (his metaphors of drink and excess may have been prompted by some half-conscious sense that his absences and her drinking were linked): 'The war is a kind of debauch of experience for writers. . . . But no one says anything about the wretched lot of the married woman with children trudging all day from the stove to the sink, and getting no uniform even.' In the event, to relieve Dorothy, the Brenans had Josephine and Oliver to stay for a couple of days. And Victor, meanwhile, saw plenty of wretchedness at first hand, plenty of places to which, as he recorded in his notebook, the troops' acronym 'FUBAR' applied: 'fucked up beyond all recognition'. He described his increasingly grim journey in a *New Statesman* article headed 'In Desert Germany'. It doesn't appear in any of his books.[120]

. . . Between Winchester and Wantage one had seen this kind of country, but here it was on a larger scale . . . There were beech woods with their red floors and the long, bearded parades of the victorious pine. And then we saw the first wounds: a branch stripped off an apple tree, the grass roughed up by mortar fire, the fantastic scroll of tank tracks like the ritual images made by primitive man. The litter of fighting began; torn paper in the turf and the ration tins thrown down. The war looked like Box Hill after a Bank Holiday, a picnic or paper chase that ended in a village with its roofs blown off and its rafters sticking up like fish bones.

. . . The white tapes of the engineers were fixed along the roadside. . . . Little Keep-off-the-grass notices were posted. 'Mines Cleared to Ditch,' they said. What happened where the tapes ended? A countryside which hitherto seemed to be the victim, now became hostile and without innocence. 'Stay in the truck,' it said. 'Do not get out on the road. It will burn you. Do not touch anything.' . . .

. . . I remember the sweet stench of the destroyed villages, pale German children jeering, cattle loose among the ruins, the peasants with pick and shovel digging a wide deep grave. . . .

. . . But now we came to the town which was our destination.

It was a place about the size of Reading. Three days before, though it was nearly surrounded, the Germans had occupied the town. They had been told to surrender or the town would be destroyed. They did not give in until it was too late. The white flags sagged vainly from the attic windows of the few surviving houses. We have become connoisseurs of ruin in this war. We have learned to distinguish between the bombed, the shelled, the burned, the blasted. But in England we have never seen a town that has been killed, completely written off and abandoned, a place as empty as Pompeii, that has the sour stench of a rubbish heap from one end to the other, and where the only sound is the drip of water from the broken roofs. Large areas of the town were waves of chocolate rubble and in the streets that remained the walls had bulged and the roofs capsized. There can have been few habitable houses left; no doors or windows remained; inside the houses one climbed – one did not step – from room to room. Outside, where it had been cleared for traffic, the rubble was shovelled into embankments. From what was left of one street one looked into the ruin of the next, and to streets beyond framed in the fretwork of destruction. . . .

*

He was home in time for the victory celebrations, which he described with a mixture of exuberance and mild satire ('the English folk singers sturdily dug the grave of English song').[121] Pieces on national events were to become an important part of his journalistic repertoire: the mood in the London streets on the day of the coronation of Queen Elizabeth II in June 1953, or of Winston Churchill's funeral twelve years later.[122]

The war had established Pritchett as the most eagerly read English literary critic and essayist of his time. He maintained and extended this position, not least in the USA. In 1952, he did his first review for *The New Yorker* (which had already begun publishing his short stories). The subject was Henry Green's novel, *Doting*, and it elicited not only a letter from the editor, William Shawn, thanking him for his 'extraordinarily good article' and expressing the hope that he would 'do more book pieces for us', but also a telegram in the magazine's extravagantly untelegraphic prose: 'WE WERE DELIGHTED WITH YOUR HENRY GREEN ARTICLE AND WOULD LIKE TO RUN IT IN THE ISSUE GOING TO PRESS THIS WEEK IF IT IS ALL RIGHT WITH YOU COMMA . . .' Shawn also sent the ration-bound Pritchetts what Victor described as 'a momentous ham'.[123] Pritchett's connection with *The New Yorker* was to become as important to him as with the *New Statesman*; financially much more so. He also became a frequent reviewer for the books section of the *New York Times* and, when the *New York Review of Books* was launched in 1963, was among its earliest and most popular writers, contributing well over a hundred long items over the last quarter-century of his working life.[124] Meanwhile, he continued to broadcast frequently and was in increasing demand as a lecturer, especially in the United States.

For now, though, in the mid 1940s, it was on the top floor of the *New Statesman*'s ramshackle offices that Pritchett was most at home. Immediately after the end of the war he was persuaded to take on the job of literary editor. The experiment wasn't a success and didn't last. He relished the built-in social life of the job, but the modest organisational skills it required – selecting books for review, making sure that not too many or too few pieces were commissioned, setting deadlines – were beyond him. He found it particularly hard to choose reviewers, saying he thought everyone was either too good or not good enough. Looking at his pages today, though, despite his encouragement of one or two relative newcomers – particularly Naomi Lewis, for whom he had more than a literary fondness[125] – most of his contributors seem to have more or less chosen themselves from the well-established ranks of *New Statesman* staffers and regular critics: Richard Crossman, Harold Laski, Kingsley Martin, Ralph Partridge, Peter Quennell, Philip Toynbee, Hugh Trevor-Roper, Leonard Woolf . . .

Pritchett was also unprepared for the attempts at outside interference which any editor has to deal with, from a friend's casual-seeming word of influence, through the more overt pressures of authors and publishers, to the angry complaints of the famous when they feel an injustice has been done. No one in the last category was more vociferous than Edith Sitwell, who turned her ire on Pritchett when he dared to publish a scathing review by Giles Romilly of the *Collected Poems* of Lilian Bowes-Lyon. Rarely can the work of an English poet have been defended in a way to which the word 'clinical' seems so literally apt yet also so open to physiological scepticism. 'Both this unhappy lady's legs have had to be amputated,' Sitwell wrote,

after a year or more of intense agony. She is now in agony with both arms.

Her terrible fate is the result of a kick received from a hysterical woman in an air-raid, while Miss Bowes-Lyon was living in the slums in order to work among the people.

I am glad to hear that Mr Romilly was unaware of this . . . But under the circumstances, the terms 'blanched mash', 'bloodless' etc. have, and I think naturally, outraged those who know the circumstances.[126]

At least such episodes made for enjoyable gossip, as also did the amatory entanglements of Pritchett's contributors, about which he wrote with relish to Brenan:

> Reviewer No 1 who wants only what other people have got, takes Reviewer No 2's girl from him. Reviewer No 2 goes for consolation to see Reviewer No 3. He, upset by the sadness of his friend, invites him into bed with his wife. Reviewer No 3's wife now leaves [for] Reviewer No 2. Reviewer No 1 deeply shocked, gets married quickly. The rest are left to argue it all out, day & night, on sacred Existentialist principles. [127]

Meanwhile, though, the lack of editorial supervision over his own pieces made him lose confidence in them. 'With you encouraging and informing me and Raymond [Mortimer] discouraging me, I was quite a passable writer,' he told Brenan, 'on my own I begin to show that incompetence which affected God . . . after he had got rid of Satan.'[128] Worst of all, the work got in the way of the still unfinished *Mr Beluncle*.

6

The pleasures of privilege

Everyone wanted him to finish the novel, Gerald Brenan in particular. The relationship between the two men was deeply important to both of them as writers. They met as often as they could. They wrote to each other regularly: so regularly that they considered publishing some of their correspondence, perhaps focusing on the war. ('It would be better than Stephen Spender's journal which suffers from solitariness,' Pritchett claimed, 'everyone has become isolated by the war.')[1] They read and commented on each other's work, and talked it up to literary friends, Pritchett helping Brenan to get published and reviewed, and giving him advice about other professional literary matters, such as taxation.[2] Not all of their conversation was about themselves. They had wide mutual interests and, because both were extremely gregarious and found similar things funny, the friendship included a lot of gossip and jokes, as well as serious interchanges on history, politics and especially on what they were reading. To each, the other was someone to whom frustrations and self-doubts could be freely confided, and who could be depended on to provide encouragement and praise, as well as criticism.

In Pritchett's case the correspondence, like his conversation, had a fantastical aspect, which enabled him to try out ideas for stories. 'One should write stories about feasts,' he said in March 1941, by way of a protest against food rationing (he had just been on a shopping expedition):

> . . . of how a man sacrificed a beautiful girl for a chop, or seduced another by promises of unlimited tinned salmon. What love affairs the directors of the Home and Colonial [Stores] must be having; imagine the insinuation which accompanies the sausages slipped into the carrier bag, the terrible wink that goes with cheese.[3]

He took his own advice, while giving it a different twist, in 'The Satisfactory', a slightly over-determined tale about a gluttonous antique dealer seduced by his secretary's rations.[4] But while the correspondence was, in some respects, an extension of Pritchett's notebooks, it also allowed him to unburden himself of some of his deepest worries and neuroses. Much of what he confided to Brenan was about his sense that he was almost deliberately wasting his true vocation. As he had put it in May 1938, 'I get a curious masochistic and nonconformist pleasure out of excessive work and especially out of work of the wrong kind. I get a cussed kick out of earning my living; and the artist in me is in perpetual harangue with the tradesman.'[5] This was only a few months after the men first met, and Pritchett quickly apologised, reminding himself that other writers – like his friend James Hanley – had known much worse situations. Still, eleven years and a long war later, the story was still the same:

> It is my great difficulty as a novelist – if I have any serious right to call myself that – that my mind burns too quickly, consumes too many ideas & scenes & people and could rush through them all in one fierce fizzing gorse blaze, leaving me with the ashes of people. This defect combines fatally with the impersonal and summary, hit or miss training of journalism. I try to damp it down and learn patience and slowness. . . .[6]

Now, though, there was a more pressing reason for him to explain himself to Brenan, and to change his habits. Brenan had taken at face value Pritchett's worries about having to work as a 'tradesman', and in particular his complaints about the burdens of being literary editor of the *New Statesman*. Brenan remembered what it had been like to be poor and how much the generosity of other people – in his case an aunt, as well as his reluctant father – had meant to him in his at first unsuccessful efforts as a young poet and novelist. Thanks to these handouts and to occasional inheritances, he had never had to take a job, and he imagined that most people were in a similar situation. 'Nearly everyone I know has *some* unearned income,' he told Pritchett soon after they first met.[7] Finding that Pritchett was an exception to this dubious rule, he solved his friend's problem, or tried to, with a gift of £1000. Pritchett drew back, partly because he had received a big lump sum from his agent only a few years earlier, which had also been intended to enable him to 'drop sundry journalism and write a novel'.[8]

But eventually he accepted Gerald's offer, while insisting both that he should ask if ever he needed the money back, and that he, Victor, would in any case repay it when he could.

This was in 1948.[9] It changed the whole family's life, though not entirely in the intended ways or for the better. When the war ended, the owner of Maidencourt had decided that his tenant farmer, the Pritchetts' neighbour David Rabbitts, who was making a success of the business, should have the main house. (Subsequently, he bought the whole farm.)[10] So the Pritchetts returned to London, to a tall Victorian house in Parkhill Road, on the Camden–Hampstead border, in walking distance of the BBC on the other side of Regent's Park and within relatively easy reach of the *New Statesman*. Pritchett was always more at home in the city. He joked to Brenan, 'Oh the wind on the heath (Hampstead Heath). . . . Or even better, Oh the wind on the Hampstead tube or the air-conditioning hurricane that blows up your trousers at Gloucester Rd. Why look at flowers in the garden when you can buy them?'[11] And he found material for many of his best stories in his day-to-day life there. His story of post-war London, 'When My Girl Comes Home', for example, was prompted by something told him by their cleaning woman.[12] But he and Dorothy had come to love the Berkshire Downs, too. By now, they had many friends in the area and it also seemed a better place for the children to grow up. If only Victor could be freed from his regular office ties they would move out again.

A glamorous, vivacious friend of Raymond Mortimer's, Mary Dunn, had a few years earlier divorced her rich husband and married a war hero and dilettante artist called Robin Campbell. They and Mary's young daughters lived in Savernake Forest at Stokke Manor: a ramshackle, leaky, many-roomed mansion of every period and none, its maze of long corridors all eventually leading back to a galleried central drawing room. Mary vaguely ran the market garden, Robin vaguely painted, and meanwhile they entertained a large London-bohemian-cum-rural-aristocratic circle.[13] Donald Maclean, soon to be exposed as a Soviet spy, was among the more riotous of their visitors, though he had strong competition, not least from Philip Toynbee. The Campbells' friends also included several people whom the Pritchetts already knew well: especially Cyril Connolly, Kitty West, the critic Robert Kee, the stage designer Jocelyn Herbert and their respective partners of the time. Guests were put up – sometimes for lengthy periods – in one or other of the farm cottages close to the main house, especially a high-gabled Victorian place with a small garden which adjoined the wide back lawn of the main house, surrounded by dense woodland. In 1947, shortly after the Pritchetts returned to London from a holiday in Ireland,[14] Mary offered this cottage to them as 'a taking off place for finding one for yourself'. She added reassuringly, 'everything is electrified. (Farm produce.)'.[15] Brenan's gift freed them to take the house and they were to be there for four years.

It was small for a family and Pritchett, spoiled by his time in radio studios, increasingly required absolute silence where he wrote. So an attic study was found for him in the manor house: a long room with two windows facing over the farm buildings, its sloping ceilings wood-panelled against cold, damp and noise. Here a mountain of review copies grew up, to the awe of the domestic staff and to the occasional despair of Victor himself. 'A terrible hatred of books is descending on me,' he told John Lehmann, 'they choke me. Better to write than to read.'[16] The remains of Pritchett's 1950s library are still in the house today. Dorothy stayed behind in the cottage, typing his manuscripts and making sure his copy was put on the right train. (On one occasion during the war, the script of a talk Pritchett was to deliver live had gone astray in Broadcasting House. The producer telephoned to ask him to bring his own copy up from the country, but he was already in London. Dorothy travelled up by train with it.)[17] She also acted as a first reader for his choices as one of the Book Society's selectors and did various research projects for him, including digging out possible items for a *New Statesman* anthology which he edited.[18] And she cooked, made jam and cheese, missed her children in term-time, found them exhausting in the holidays, smoked and drank whisky.

Beneath the surface the marriage was becoming rocky. Sometimes on the surface, too. Several people who knew Stokke well at the time have memories of a trial separation between the Pritchetts, an adventure from which he, for once, seems to have returned more miserable than she.[19] On the whole, though, Dorothy was far the more troubled. Victor was immensely adaptable and, by now, very sure of himself. If there were worlds he didn't fit into, he rarely noticed the fact. Yet even he seemed to Frances Partridge not always at ease in the bohemocratic environment of Stokke at its wildest, and Dorothy often either felt left out, or pre-emptively excluded herself.

Perhaps the most telling example of her increasing inner isolation is that she cut herself off from the aspect of Stokke with which she would otherwise have been most at home: horses. Everyone at Stokke rode. Steeplechases were one of the main entertainments. Yet Dorothy never gave any sign of having any such interest and those who knew her then were amazed to learn, later, that she had come from a hunting family and was an excellent horsewoman.[20] Perhaps in marrying out of Montgomeryshire, she had renounced its secular religion, just as Victor had renounced Christian Science. She may, too, have feared that if she started riding, she wouldn't be able to stop Josephine catching the habit and that it would prove too expensive for them. But something deeper was surely also involved.

Her own excuse was that she was just too busy and this was true enough. Victor was very conscious of the demands he made on her. The copy of his first collection of essays, which he had given her in 1942, is inscribed, 'To darling Dorothy – thanking you for making this book possible, for keeping the peace while I wrote it and working so hard yourself.'[21] Consciousness of how hard he made her work, though, wasn't the same as avoidance. Eventually *Mr Beluncle* was finished. Pritchett delivered the typescript to the relieved A. D. Peters in the summer of 1950. Meanwhile, whatever his intentions when he had accepted Brenan's £1000, the effect of giving up his editorial job at the *Statesman* was that he wrote for the paper even more: twenty-eight pieces in 1949, thirty-five in 1950 – a return to his wartime level of activity. Gerald didn't complain about this but, privately, after what Jonathan Gathorne-Hardy describes as 'a stunned pause' in reaction to his own generosity, he came to regret the gift, spending the next twenty years 'intermittently tortured by . . . longings for the vanished sum', until Victor – who had been unaware of these feelings – repaid it. In the short term, meanwhile, Victor and Dorothy were themselves tormented by a sense that they needed to explain themselves to Gerald every time they spent any money – buying a much-needed car, for example, or going on holiday.

Just as Victor was unwilling to acknowledge not only that he enjoyed journalism but that it was one of the most valuable dimensions of his work, so he tended to minimise what became a distinctly above-average level of prosperity, and the pleasure he, as well as Dorothy, took in it. Gerald Brenan wrote a vivid encomium of them at their happiest and although it dates from their later marital heyday, it was based on, and unqualified by, almost forty years of earlier close acquaintance:

> V.S.P. is short but sturdily built, tough and wiry. He is both a very sensual man and a demon for work. He likes good food and plenty of it – meat, cheese and pudding with plenty of cream on it – and to

watch him eating is like watching an engine being fuelled with coal, for what he takes in is at once converted into intellectual energy. Every morning he works from breakfast till lunch and then, after a short siesta, is at his desk again and writing hard till supper and often after that till midnight. . . .

Essentially he is a family man, wrapped up in his wife and children. . . . [Dorothy] is a tall, handsome buxom woman with a vivacity and clearness of colouring that make her seem many years younger than her age, and the best wife any hard-working writer ever had. She types all her husband's business letters and manuscripts – no easy task since his handwriting is almost illegible – criticizes his work and reads books for him. She is also a splendid cook and housekeeper and a lively and amusing talker. But it is her warmth, generosity and exuberant hospitality that I would like to single out. . . .[22]

The couple banked at Coutts', ate in good restaurants when they were in town and went to Harley Street when they needed medical treatment. Dorothy dressed well. Victor had his club, the Savile. Both children were soon sent to boarding schools. By the standards of some of the Pritchetts' friends, these days, all this was modest enough – and, by comparison with a salaried job, it was never secure. But solid sums of money were coming in. In 1944 Victor's Suffolk Aunt Ada had left him £1341 13s. 4d.[23] (Financial comparisons across time are never simple, but to translate this into the values of sixty years later one needs to multiply by at least twenty-five.) His second book of literary essays, *The Living Novel*, published in 1946 and hailed by Edmund Wilson as more interesting than the criticism of Virginia Woolf or E. M. Forster,[24] earned £650, an extraordinary success for a work of its kind.[25] Most of his short stories sold several times: to magazines on both sides of the Atlantic, sometimes to anthologies and then to his book publishers as collections, which in turn were generally bought by book clubs like the Readers Union. Radio broadcasts paid well, including for repeats, and their texts often appeared in the *Listener* – that is, when they hadn't already started out as magazine pieces. Travel articles were another good source of income. In addition, Pritchett was paid a retainer by the *New Statesman*: together with fees for individual items, his income from that source alone came to £1500 a year in the mid 1940s.[26] He was in demand to judge literary prizes and helped set up the Somerset Maugham award, making a persuasive case for establishing a separate fund for the judges' fees, rather than taking them out of the money available for the prize itself, which he also got increased.[27] In 1953 he was invited to give the Gauss Seminars at Princeton: the first of several well-paid visiting appointments and guest lectures at prestigious American universities – Smith, Brandeis, Columbia, Vanderbilt. From the mid 1950s he also had a regular retainer from *The New Yorker*, guaranteeing the magazine first refusal on all his short stories, in addition to its high payments for the work they published.

Despite all this, he always worried about money and continued to work unremittingly. His children thought of every house they lived in as a 'word factory'. The contrast between his efforts and the relative ease and indolence of better-selling writers such as Graham Greene is painful to see. Greene often said that but for an encouraging review of *It's A Battlefield* by Pritchett, he would have given up writing altogether in 1934.[28] But, having agreed to take part in a written debate with Pritchett and Elizabeth Bowen in the late 1940s under the title *Why Do I Write?*, Greene was barely able to rouse himself to make his irony-laden and self-contradictory contributions, while Pritchett, in the course of pushing the public correspondence along, had to point out that even now, after twenty years as a professional writer and with ten books to his name, he still couldn't make a living without journalism.* Two years later, when Pritchett and Greene were supposed to be working together on a radio discussion about Robert Louis Stevenson for the latter's centenary in 1950, Greene kept disappearing to the Aegean. The producer, P. H. Newby, wrote apologetically to Pritchett – who had finished his own share of the work well on time – explaining that Greene still hadn't done the required revisions to his part of the script. 'He said he hadn't looked at it, felt lazy, but promised he'd pull himself together. . . . I envy him, don't you?'[29]

Pritchett did envy him. Even spending a single day in bed with flu filled him with guilt:

> have a terrible conscience feeling that someone will find out and imprison me for not finishing all my books, reviews, etc. etc. and that

---

* *Why Do I Write?*, 1948, pp. 39–44. Among the issues Pritchett raised here was the way that the free public library system in Britain – intrinsically admirable though it was – had not (in these years before the long-campaigned-for advent of Public Lending Right) found a way of compensating authors of books which were multiply borrowed. And he returned to his familiar guilty theme: 'Instead of solving one's own problems, how much easier it is to edit, review and do any reputable second-hand work on the problems of other writers!'

the Bank will write me a snooty letter and all the tradesmen will arrive in a charabanc and gather in deputation to say, 'We don't like you not paying your bills, but we can put up with it; what we cant put up with is your just slacking at the same time. Get out of bed.'

And driving the charabanc is an official of the Inland Revenue. . . [30]

He knew all too well that if he were to ease up on his writing, his income would drop. But he didn't ease up, and many of his later literary acquaintances were surprised by the style and comfort in which the couple increasingly lived.

Holidays apart, Victor was sometimes able to take Dorothy on his writing trips. In 1951, when he was researching *The Spanish Temper*, they flew to Spain together. 'Is it the clear pure air, the wine, the food, the sensation of living in a heavenly nightclub without Philip Toynbee . . .?' he asked Gerald, re-infatuated. 'Dorothy wants to live here forever & eat prawns and crayfish and drink sherry for the rest of her life and I had to hold her down in her zest at the bullfight, she was so exalted & wanted to sing Land of My Fathers.'[31] At Stokke, too, there were many happy times. Victor wrote seductively to his friend, 'It's been a day after your heart. A dozen beautiful half naked girls have been chattering all day in Mary's black currants, picking them and sunbathing under my window . . . there is nothing like adjacent sex for putting champagne into the mind.'[32] Dorothy, it was true, had been 'unwell' and Victor apologised for their both having struck Gerald as glum. Still, he himself had been much cheered by going to one of the summer garden parties at Buckingham Palace: 'The thing itself was boring of course except as a wonderful useless spectacle, but what was wonderful, I own, was the terrific snobbish pleasure of privilege. Oh to be a toff, a real nob. Oh to live in a sort of Royal Enclosure. . . .' Stokke was not quite that, but was the next best thing, and Pritchett filled his diaries with the quirks of upper-class life. He found his human surroundings endlessly amusing: the volatile writer Philip Toynbee, for example, who, Victor told Gerald, was no doubt 'at this moment . . . shooting a) a servant b) his host c) himself in a torrent of explanation', or the equestrian Robin and Julia Mount, whom he described as 'neighing across the room', and whose 'connubial conversation sounds like a rough game of lacrosse', full of 'throw-away lines, like "I hear Joybells is behaving badly among the ground nuts", or "I hope you will come to our point à point."'[33] Then there was the chatelaine Mary

Campbell's 'hysteria' when her maid became ill and the housework wasn't done ('Tells the doctor "I want her up by Monday" '); or the time when she was fined for speeding, gossip columnists turned up at the house, and she got rid of them by pretending that she was a farm worker and that Mrs Campbell was away. Victor was a little in love with Mary and he put something of her into his imperious femme fatale, Mrs Brackett, in *The Key to My Heart*.

The Pritchetts' children also loved it at Stokke, surrounded as they were by the freedom of Savernake Forest, as well as the companionship not only of the various children who came and went, but also of Mary's daughters, the slightly older Nell and Serena Dunn. The Dunn girls in turn adored Dorothy and Victor. For Nell, who later became a successful writer, 'Dorothy had something particularly special about her. She had huge warmth. And she was always smiling and always wanting you to be around her . . . in the kitchen garden picking peas, or having a drink on the lawn or something.'[34] Victor, as both Nell and Serena fondly recalled, organised treasure hunts for them all with rhyming clues, and an indoor hiding and chasing game called 'Cocky Olly', specially devised for Stokke with its two sets of staircases.

Looking back on her parents' lives, Nell Dunn nostalgically described 'this idea of people having interesting conversations with each other in a very relaxed way on a lawn and making an omelette and salad for supper and sitting at the kitchen table. It was a wonderful country bohemianism.' A bit too bohemian for Victor, sometimes. He tended to exaggerate his own puritanism, but there was a physical aspect to his moderation in drink. Although he had developed a taste for good wine when he lived in France and, later in life, would regularly drink a serious martini or two before meals, he always felt sick well before any other sign of becoming drunk, so he held back. This contributed to his sense of being an outsider, as well as to the sharpness of some his observations. He sent Brenan a long account of a dance at Stokke: 'drunken peers out for fucking', an Austrian princess glittering 'like a ballet dancer', Robin 'Randy' Mount boasting about a woman who, ever since he accidentally shot her, wrote to him every week, Philip Toynbee sobbing and threatening suicide, Benedict Nicholson with his head in his hands, Julia Strachey moaning 'Oh dear'.[35] At least it was a distraction from winter days at the cottage, which reminded him of Chekhov:

By the samovar, Dorothea Petrovna broods on the tempest in her soul, remembers the wolf hunts of her childhood, the schoolmaster who read her his essays and blew his brains out . . . Victor Petrov-ovich-aski spits into the fire, beats his breast, exclaims that he must kill a few serfs and makes remarks like 'There was a sanitary inspector in our town . . .' or 'Who knows, in a hundred years' time there will be no such thing as February. . . .'[36]

They began to feel that they needed, and could now afford, somewhere both larger and more private, where Victor would have his own study and also, implicitly, where there might be fewer alcoholic temptations in Dorothy's way. Everyone knew about her 'secret' drinking, though Victor and the children didn't realise that they knew.[37] In a notebook begun in 1945, he had jotted down what seem to be some ideas for a story provisionally titled 'Infidelity', in which the starting point would be a wife's drinking:

> she always has a reaction after wine, becomes gloomy, irritable touchy & quickly finds an excuse for a quarrel
> The quarrel any wild thing that comes into her head
> Sexual reconciliation.
> All the result of boredom, isolation in the country, ten years of marriage, hard work, work & work, no friends.
> It always begins with 'Entertain me. Say something to me.' Then he knows there is going to be a quarrel.[38]

In the autumn of 1952, buoyed up by the success of *Mr Beluncle*, they took a handsome red-brick house in a valley above the village of St Mary Bourne, fourteen miles south of Newbury. Wadwick House reminded them of Maidencourt, but was grander. It had been built in the early nineteenth century for a local man who, like Dorothy's father, had prospered as a master butcher. Reached by a steep curving drive to the confident front door, it stands on rising ground above an old drove road, facing a slope of farmland. It had a walled kitchen garden, barns and other farm buildings, and, above and behind, five acres of rough paddock and woods. It was a distinct step up from Stokke Farm Cottage, but even more remote. Three or four houses are scattered on the long lane that leads to it from St Mary Bourne, but they aren't visible from Wadwick House and the road ends there, so no one other than the occasional walker came past. And the Brenans had gone back to Spain.

These disadvantages weren't at first apparent. Although Victor professed to find it 'odd and unreal that a writer is allowed to live in a house', and was appalled by the expense and distraction of the move, both he and Dorothy enjoyed the place's pretensions. Raymond Mortimer made them suitably lavish presents of a chest of drawers painted by the Bloomsbury artist Roger Fry, and a case of tropical butterflies.[39] The gardens were known as 'the Park', Victor boasted, and the lawn was mowed by someone who had been waiter at the Savoy: 'we shall be able to invite Eddie [Sackville-]West.'[40]

He didn't waste long on such fantasies. Soon, he was back at work. 'I have written 3 Books in General, one short story, two broadcasts, three reviews in the last few weeks and I'm about to write on Eliot's poetry for The New York Times, a terrifying job for me.'[41]

A railwayman faced with an earnest set of questions from Pritchett for a wartime documentary had told him abruptly, 'put down I have shocking dreams.' Pritchett often repeated his words later – for example, in the preface to Why Do I Write?, the public exchange with Elizabeth Bowen and Graham Greene, which he began during a family holiday at Welshpool (this was his idea of taking time off). The book was published in 1948: a period, in Britain, of radical socialist government and of severe rationing – not least of paper. Should they all 'be putting their shoulders to some wheel or other?' Pritchett asked his fellow authors. Or is the writer 'simply the incurable instance that cuts across the general pattern; the man with shocking dreams'?[42]

He had continued to put his own shoulder to the cultural wheel, since the war. He was involved in the new United Nations Educational, Scientific and Cultural Organisation, UNESCO ('Question:' he irreverently asked Brenan. 'Unesco is a) a suppository b) a Rumanian courtesan c) a Californian fruit d) one of the American states e) a desert animal').[43] He chaired a committee planning an exhibition of modern British books and writers for the National Book League. He campaigned for Public Lending Right. Despite all this, he was sceptical about efforts 'to "do" anything with the writer', and ever more critical of the kinds of formal declaration and manifesto that had polarised and stereotyped cultural discussion in the 1930s. As he once summarised his position, 'I do not want to say anything. I write because I see.'[44] In private, as time went by, this view hardened, along with his increasing impatience with socialism, at least as it was turning out in practice. He had always had his doubts about the Left, not only in Spain but in the Britain of the 1920s and 1930s. As early as 1926 he wrote to his brother

Gordon, 'I used to be a Socialist, then became a violent Conservative, and finally I am joining my own party and calling it "the party of the enlightened Pritchetts".'[45] Some time in 1939 he told John Lehmann, 'I get waves of rage about the Party Line now & then, so perhaps I was wishing you are not of that persuasion; but, like myself, a crypto-Tory, anarchist free trade liberal with strong Socialist bias. . . .'[46] Ten years later still, he expostulated to Brenan, 'by successful socialism, we have made plain automatic liveableness into the scum of all good. . . .'[47] Now, in 1951, he wrote about his exasperation at having been invited

> to a meeting to discuss how writers could help to preserve peace in the world! Good lord – writers no longer have influence on govern-ments. They are, if anything, the mere tools of them, if they once commit themselves to a political utterance. How childish people are to believe in that wonderful, non-existent inspired, shamelessly influential Bohemian of [the] last century: the Artist, the Writer. Imagine trying to influence a successful Chinese revolutionary . . . or a McCarthy. . . .[48]

There was a difference, he insisted, between believing and imagining, and changes of tack by some of the more conspicuous literary ideologues of the 1930s had strengthened his opinion. Always suspicious of the initially fellow-travelling but later politically mobile group associated with W. H. Auden and Stephen Spender, he said in 1951 that Spender now looked '*professionally* naïve, professionally ashamed'.[49] After the long years of wartime political realism, Pritchett needed to return to his fantasies – particularly the recurring dream of childhood.

Mr Beluncle appeared in October 1951. The following year, Pritchett wrote his first critical piece for *The New Yorker*, an enthusiastic review of *Doting*, by Henry Green. *Doting* turned out to be Green's last novel, just as *Mr Beluncle* turned out to be Pritchett's. While he would always regret what he saw as the failure of his ambition to be a novelist, in his case (unlike Green's) the process can be seen as one of shedding a heavy launching rocket, which had enabled his career to accelerate in other forms. But this was not how it seemed at the time. Pritchett was widely admired as a novelist. Five of his eleven books, to date, were novels and, from his publishers' point of view, collections of short stories were, as his editors at Chatto and Windus, Ian Parsons and Harold Raymond, kept stressing, mainly a way of helping keep public interest alive between novels.[50]

His earlier novels had been well received. *Clare Drummer*, it's true, had not been much of a success, though the *Spectator* described it as a 'good study' of a possessive mother and a daughter desperate to escape her clutches, and the Irish poet and dramatist Austin Clarke, writing anonymously in the *TLS*, called it a 'clever comedy of the emotions' and applauded its satirical insight into Anglo-Irish life.[51] The novella 'The Spanish Virgin', on the other hand, was highly praised, including by L. P. Hartley,[52] and Pritchett's other long fiction set in Spain, *Shirley Sanz*, was generally seen as a serious advance in his work.[53] By the mid 1930s he was treated as not only a rising novelist, but an impressively diverse one. *Nothing Like Leather* was compared with work by Arnold Bennett,[54] and was reprinted in 1938. With *Dead Man Leading*, Pritchett was favourably contrasted with Aldous Huxley as having a talent which was 'specifically that of a novelist; that is to say, his perceptions, interpreted by an acute intelligence, clothe themselves in characters, in human situations, in stories'.[55] According to this reviewer, *Dead Man Leading* was 'charged with terrific vitality . . . a rich, a deeply-assimilated, original and satisfying book', an opinion which was again supported by his publishers: Chatto reissued the novel in 1949.[56]

From the perspective of how Pritchett was regarded by the critical establishment in his early fifties, then, part of the interest of *Mr Beluncle* was that it was his first novel for eleven years.[57] Commercially, it was also one of the most successful books he had yet written, the attractive little volume with its cover by Edward Ardizzone selling over 7000 copies within a couple of months and paying off the entire debt that Pritchett had built up to Chatto in advances on his other recent books.[58] Although critics were divided about it, Elizabeth Bowen described it in a 'Books in General' piece for the *New Statesman* as restoring strength and energy to English fiction, which – like many others at the time – she saw as having become etiolated, self-conscious and lacking in 'the necessary obsession'.[59] Pritchett professed embarrassment at the book's being given so much space not only in his own paper but in what was now generally seen as his own column. It was 'like getting double one's meat ration by mistake', he said.[60] But he can't have minded Bowen's praise. In the character of Mr Beluncle, she memorably wrote, 'We have a figure heaving forward at us out of the print, a dense, florid, abundant, intolerable physical personality, collecting detail, fusing extraordinary attributes into itself as the book proceeds.'

Raymond Mortimer, meanwhile, told Pritchett in his clubmanly way that he had 'somehow metamorphosed cabbage-water into Montrachet'.[61] And Kingsley Martin characteristically took his own share of the credit: 'Looking back over a good many years, I recall that I always believed you would some day be England's leading author.'[62] Some others, though, were less sure. The *TLS*'s anonymous reviewer, given the middle page for an assessment of Pritchett's whole fictional output to date, argued that, having created Mr Beluncle, the novel doesn't know what to do with him, and that 'a suitable form for [Pritchett's] talents has somehow consistently evaded Mr. Pritchett the novelist' – while the short-story writer, by contrast, had produced some of the best work of the previous twenty years.[63] Pritchett affected to shrug off this piece, but it rankled. The author, he said, was evidently 'one of those schoolmaster critics who think that books should be written to their measurements'.[64] In fact, he was Julian Symons, who had been a friend of Orwell's until the latter's death the previous year and was one of the sharpest young writers in Britain: a detective novelist and editor, and a determined freelance.[65] In time, Symons's view that Pritchett was essentially a short-story writer was to become so prevalent that it was accepted even by Pritchett himself. But it is an oversimplification. In their uneven ways, *Shirley Sanz* and *Dead Man Leading* still have strong claims on readers, as does *Nothing Like Leather* (which Symons regarded as the best of his novels, while acknowledging that in some aspects it's a first draft for *Mr Beluncle*). *Mr Beluncle* itself is among the outstanding novels of its time: one which not only creates the strongest and strangest individual character in English fiction of the mid century, but also maps a crucial phase of lower-middle-class English patriarchy. As Erik de Mauny wrote three years later, in another *TLS* appraisal of Pritchett's work, it was difficult to think of any English novelist of the time who 'picked off the exactions of . . . domestic tyranny with more wincing accuracy'.[66]

In manipulation of tone as well as delineation of social class, this is the territory of the film director Mike Leigh, a quarter of a century before Leigh first explored it. *Mr Beluncle* attends to the ordinariness of human misery with a mix of brutality, tenderness and high comedy: in Beluncle's mad old mother, for example, with her desperate longings for the dead husband with whom she never really got on and her attempts to send parcels of stale cake to her long-lost daughter by throwing them out of the window; or in the Beluncles' ordeal by family Sunday lunch and the hilarious panic that takes over when, in the course of it, someone knocks at the door ('I don't want people to see how we live,' says Beluncle).[67] It's a novel in which houses become extensions of individual neuroses, not only – though most intensely – in the expansive property-owning ambitions of Beluncle himself (based on Walter Pritchett, of course, with some additional colouring from Cyril Connolly),[68] but also in many points of exposure between characters on different sides of a door, a wall or a window. The cliché of an old woman watching the outside world from behind her curtain is understood not as voyeurism, but as a limited attempt at self-analysis, or self-therapy: it provides her 'with soothing, harmless comparisons with her own life: she was looking for events in the lives of others which would match and explain events in her own life'.[69]

Despite the power and centrality of Mr Beluncle himself, the novel is densely and sympathetically populated. His sons – so closely based on Victor and his own brothers that their sister was a little indignant at having been left out[70] – are often the main focus, but several of the most memorable characters are found outside the family: Mr O'Malley, the frenzied schoolmaster, in denial of his Irish origins; Mr Phibbs, the railway stationmaster, torn between socialism and an individuality which mainly consists of automatic opposition to anyone else on any issue; Granger and Vogg, evangelist rivals of the Church of the Last Purification, Toronto, the sect to which Mr Beluncle belongs; that group's local leader, Lady Roads; Mrs Truslove's crippled sister, whose belief in the possibility of cure the book, against its own grain, will allow to be confirmed; and Mrs Truslove herself, Beluncle's business partner, with her mix of deep affection and sadness about how she has wasted her life in being involved with him.

Then there's Beluncle's wife, Ethel, simultaneously cowed and rebellious, and the way that for her and other characters (though not for her husband, who lives entirely in fantasies of the future), grievances and regrets about the past dominate the present. Pritchett's long brooding over his book contributed to its understanding of process – what, in one of his essays on Turgenev, he calls the novelist's 'tenderness, this capacity to observe the growth of characters and the changes of the heart'.[71] In Mr Beluncle these processes include self-invention, conscious and half so. Mrs Truslove has 'only lately taken to wearing glasses and was forming the habit of taking them off when she talked of private matters';[72] Mary is 'training herself to show Henry that she could read what was in his mind'.[73] Beluncle, though, remains the central character: preposterous, yet seen with vivid sympathy for his vanities and obsessions, the wobbling barometer of his feelings (and lack of them) about others; above all his financial greed and improvidence, and how they are mingled with the optimism of his religious 'beliefs'. 'The story of our money and of our religion has yet to be written,' Pritchett had argued a few years earlier, in an essay contrasting Russian and English fiction.[74] In *Mr Beluncle*, he wrote part of it.

Julian Symons objected that, though Pritchett's is the world of H. G. Wells, 'the amiable self-deception of Wells's little man . . . has become an ugly growth of deceit and egotism'. He was right, except in objecting to it. Deceit and egotism do characterise Beluncle, and the damage they inflict is far-reaching. Nothing could be more tenderly realised than the muddle of longing, fear and disappointment in Henry's courtship of Mary, with the dark shadow cast over it by his father. The novel is a study of abusive relationships (the narrator himself calls them that).[75] Part of its truth lies in the submissive love which Beluncle elicits.[76] His selfish capriciousness is a form of violence, as the no less vulnerable Henry recognises: 'happiness, serenity, trust and truth were less after violence. . . . Another rock crumbled off the island on which one tried to live.'[77] The father wields his power through a hypnotic mix of affection and false sympathy – he even seems to pity the joint of meat he is carving. And part of the novel's force lies in showing the complicity of his victims, alternately charmed and bullied into taking a scared pride in their predicament. In a time of nostalgia for family values, it's salutary to be reminded what the nuclear family could be like and what were some of the reasons for its erosion.[78]

Mr Beluncle might have been a different novel. In one of its threads, Henry's escape not only from his father and his religion but from his class, it anticipates several better-known English fictions of the 1950s. (This aspect is more emphasised in some of the many drafts.)[79] Again, though not a novel of action, it contains plenty of suspense. Will either Henry or Mrs Truslove get out from under? Will Mr Beluncle's profligacy finally catch up with him, or will he succeed in charming yet another backer into ruin? Part of the novel's strength is that not all of these questions are answered, though we're left with our own hunches. There are things in it that don't work: Miss Dykes's self-cure, the dangling side plot involving Beluncle's dissolute sister.[80] Nonetheless, it is one of the most vivid, funny and painful British novels of the mid-twentieth century and among the most neglected.[81]

7

Empty Bed Blues

The appearance of *Mr Beluncle* ironically coincided with a new flurry of anxieties about Walter's finances and Beatrice's health. Not the least of the problems was that it was never entirely clear what they amounted to. Cyril Pritchett wrote in frustration to Victor, 'I have always felt that if only one member of the family had the facts and absolute truth in regard to [Walter's] affairs – well we might between us all arrange some workable scheme of salvage.'[1] No one knew whether the couple's capital was exhausted, as Walter claimed it was. His work as a Christian Science 'practitioner', or faith healer, brought in a little. Gordon created some fictitious clerical tasks for him as a face-saving way of giving him money, but this led to anxious phone calls about tax, which suggested that Walter, despite his denials, still had a taxable level of income.[2] Cyril admired what he tried to persuade Victor was 'the great struggle the old man has made since 1936 – especially when you consider that for all practical purposes his age alone has closed every door of hope or opportunity'. Eventually, all three brothers decided to give him a small regular allowance, but they couldn't think of any way of making him realistic about what it amounted to ('£25 each quarter would look like £50 to him,' Gordon lamented, 'and would promptly be spent on something foolish'). They settled on £5 per month apiece. For now, Walter's worries abated, Beatrice's health improved, and Victor and his siblings relaxed.

Victor was a conscientious son and brother, but, given the choice, he preferred dealing with these relationships on the page to having to confront them in actuality, and in any case his literary material was changing. For a time, he planned other novels.[3] One was to have been a sequel to *Dead Man Leading*, though Dorothy squashed the idea, joking that it sounded as if he meant to 'do a Henry Green' (Green was famous for his participial titles) with 'a Leading, Following Groping, etc.

etc.'.[4] There had already been many signs, though, not least in the difficulty he experienced in completing *Mr Beluncle*, that his novel writing was at an end. In his criticism Pritchett is particularly alert to the practical and psychological obstacles novelists have to face. He said of Sheridan Le Fanu, for example, that the journalist 'could not be trusted to *accumulate* a novel . . . the process bored him'.[5] And there's a clear element of autobiography in a dialogue he wrote under the title 'Novelist', in which the speakers are a writer and his typist. 'People say a bank clerk's life is monotonous,' the writer complains,

> but it is nothing to compare with a novelist's. He goes to his desk every morning. He writes for 3 or 4 hours, he has his lunch; after lunch, the afternoon depression and exhaustion set in. He goes for a walk and doesn't see or hear anything because his novel is in his mind. Back he comes to read & correct what he has done in the morning or to read and to do some journalism. And in the next few months he knows he will have weeks of blank mindedness, followed by impulses to suicide, to find a respectable job. . . .[6]

Pritchett often referred to how easily bored he was, how fearful of boredom and how, despite his attempts to 'learn patience and slowness', his temperament was best suited to the economy and the quick, distracting results of journalism and short fiction.[7] 'I do not make enough of myself', he lamented to Brenan in 1950.

> So much is shut up in well-appointed little rooms. It's as if I could not get drunk.
> What is it that releases one psychologically, imaginatively at 49? Too late isn't it? . . . Or is one self-deluded? . . . It is no doubt one of the major sadness[es] of writers: to be haunted by the harrowing suggestion that they have powers unfulfilled, when in fact their powers were fulfilled long ago. . . .[8]

Pritchett complained a lot about feeling middle aged, these days, and about his increasingly frequent attacks of gout. There was a bigger, secret worry, half revealed in his reference to not being able to get drunk. Dorothy's drinking dominated the family's day-to-day life. The clinking of bottles had become one of the background noises of the house, like squeaking door latches and creaking stairs. When Victor spent a day in London, Dorothy was as often as not drunk by the time

he returned. She was sometimes violent, or just embarrassingly confused, and confusing. Josephine and Oliver didn't feel they could bring
friends from boarding school home to stay, so had to refuse otherwise
welcome invitations because they wouldn't be able to return them. On
one occasion, when Victor suggested to Oliver that he might ask
somebody back, the boy burst into tears, sobbing that he preferred to be
alone.[9] As with the strange, psychologically violent enclosed order in
which the Beluncle family live, with its mixture of dread and love and
secrecy, they felt themselves locked up in concealment – a
concealment which, in fact, fooled nobody. There's a revealing hint of
the depth and reach of the repressions involved on Pritchett's part in
the fact that, two decades later, describing the writing of *Mr Beluncle*,
he said that it had been much influenced by *The Golovlyov Family*.[10]
Shchedrin's novel is about life on a matriarchal aristocratic rural
Russian estate at the time of the abolition of serfdom. There's so little
like *Mr Beluncle* in it that, at first, one suspects a slip of the pen: did
Pritchett have another source in mind? But he tended not to make
mistakes of this kind and, when he did, it was for a reason. What *The
Golovlyov Family* is mainly about is the destructive effects of alcoholism
in a family: not a prominent theme in *Mr Beluncle* (though it's touched
on in the character of Beluncle's sister Connie), but decidedly one in
Pritchett's private life during the novel's long gestation.

By 1951, when Josephine was fourteen, her existence outside school
had come to seem totally unpredictable. She was eventually to become
a social worker, specialising in family situations so desperate that
responsibility for the children has been taken over by the courts. So
there is more than autobiography in her frank account, given after both
her parents had died, of a predicament in which 'You don't know from
one day to the next whether somebody will be sober or not.'[11]

> It's something you're collectively ashamed of – the family secret.
> And of course these things are not secret: everybody knows. I don't
> know whether [our father] was trying to protect us or himself or
> what, really, but often when it was perfectly obvious to me that she
> was drunk he would say things like 'Mummy's a bit tired'.
>
> Obviously it affects you in all kinds of ways. If your parent is an
> alcoholic you know they are not available to you, emotionally or
> sometimes physically, so you can't trust them.

'The family secret' is the phrase used by Oliver, too. He compares the situation wryly to 'not owning up that you'd stopped believing in Father Christmas' and speaks, like his sister, about a regime of euphemism:

> My father wouldn't say that my mother had a drinking problem or was a bit peculiar last night. I knew but I wouldn't say. Occasionally he'd say, 'She's not very well,' and I would say, 'Yes, so I see.' So there was a certain period of non-frankness on all sides, everybody trying to spare everybody's feelings.

Both children longed for conventionality. At their boarding schools, almost everyone was automatically prepared for Anglican con-firmation. To be confirmed, you had first to have been baptised and Josephine easily persuaded Oliver that this, at least, was something they could take under their own control. Their father was surprised by but tolerant of their decision and a christening party was organised. 'The great event of our lives has been the determination of Jo & Oliver to be christened,' he wrote immediately afterwards to Gerald, in Spain.

> We cant get at why, but they announced it and so off they went to the local church for adult baptism and did it with great composure. We had a gay party afterwards. The Stones [the engraver Reynolds Stone and his wife Janet] uttering Betjemanly remarks about gravestones and chancels and with Janet (bishop's daughter) snubbing the vicar as only a bishop's daughter can.
> It was Trollopian. Mary Campbell turned up with a delicious pi look on her face and was amusing. Robin behaved with the dignity of the sort of elder brother I ought to have had. . . . It was delightful, from the champagne to the conjuring tricks afterwards.[12]

Would this turn out for Oliver to be 'the beginning of a traditional Pritchett religious career', he wondered light-heartedly? Surely for both him and Josephine it was more likely to lead to scepticism, as Dorothy's religious upbringing had. 'The only religious remark I ever heard Dorothy make', he recalled with, again, unconscious-seeming insight, 'was in Rome when she was allured by the Roman Catholic faith "because it gives women something to do".'

To the adolescent Josephine the whole event seemed to have been hijacked into 'a bit of a piss-up for the grown-ups, really'. She sat upstairs in her bedroom, 'feeling sulky and pious'. Back at school, both she and Oliver soon became disillusioned with God, who seemed no more able than they were to improve the situation at home. Victor, meanwhile, so dependent on Dorothy's secretarial side, had a more practical reason for anxiety, though it seems that she never actually let his work down. Like many alcoholics, she maintained a dimension of rigid discipline. It would eventually save her and also, by a hair's breadth, the marriage.

For Victor, meanwhile, there was above all loneliness: the loneliness of not being able to rely on the person he most loved, and of having a secret. He still didn't admit it even to Gerald – who knew perfectly well but never mentioned it. What Victor did speak about, and with a vehemence all the stronger for its obliquity, was his hatred of heavy drinking in other people, especially Celts (of whom Dorothy was one). 'I'm odd about drink, I suppose,' he told Gerald in 1948:

> I think Dylan Thomas would be a better poet without it; indeed I cant think of any writer, poet or prose writer, who is improved by the bottle and who does not indeed deteriorate as a result of it. . . . To the Welsh & the Irish drink is fatal, it throws them back into the wilderness. . . . Also, while drink improves some men for a while, it disimproves women, because it creates the ham actress. . . . But then – I'm simply damning a sin I've no mind to. I'm a puritan, I resent the expense, I see no value in the results, and the experience is painful.[13]

In another letter, written at Stokke after a series of parties full of what he called 'alcoholic violence', he said, 'I can stand the abuse of alcohol less than anything. I hate the coarseness, the vulgarity, the madness in it. I hate to see people transformed into puppets, and ugly ones at that . . . Only one or two people I know are the better for a lot to drink. The rest fill me with what I can only call dread. . . .'[14]

Still, there had been many good times since the end of the war, not least for the children. They had originally gone to school at an experimental boarding establishment, Beltane, in nearby Melksham, where the Brenans sent their daughter Miranda and the Mark Gertlers their son Luke. A hobby of the amiably eccentric headmaster was to collect large relics from past wars – pontoons, for example, and glider fuselages, the noses of which the children turned into wigwams. Oliver jokes that the school had given up on providing meals, 'leaving food in accessible places for children to steal and cook themselves'. Victor was too conscious of what he saw as the deficiencies of his own education to let the situation continue and, having found a tutor in the village to bring the children's formal skills up to scratch, he and Dorothy moved them to better organised though still liberal institutions, Josephine to Cranborne Chase, Oliver to Port Regis and then Bryanston: unstuffy schools, but ones whose more dependable regimes appealed to both children.

At home, for all the unpredictability of their mother's behaviour, Josephine and Oliver had friends near Wadwick (the four children of Jocelyn Herbert and Anthony Lousada in particular) and – as through-out most of their childhoods – beautiful surroundings which gave them a lot of freedom. Their father's study was on the ground floor, beside the front door and adjoining the dining room, so, when he was working, they had to be quiet around the house. His study also doubled as a guest bedroom. After Norah Smallwood had stayed there at Christmas 1952, Victor pretended to be worried that she would suppose he never did any work:

> My study – you will be pardonably relieved to hear – has been returned to me once more, complete with windows and Pritchett's Universal Desk-Bed, Easily Convertible into Guests' Wardrobe, Bathroom and Ornamental Walk. My two Fountain Pens have been taken off the Christmas Tree. . . . I reckon I can now get in my full eight hours of daily sleep and write without interference on the walls. I congratulate myself that this System of mine has enabled me to keep up a High Level of Production and when I hear that you are publishing a book of mine [*Books in General*] this month I can only say what a remarkable Contraption the Pritchett Mobile Author adaptor is.[15]

In school holidays, there were riotous games of table tennis and billiards, and outings to the cinema in Newbury or Andover. Visits to the Partridges at Ham Spray meant croquet and swimming. And there were family seaside holidays in Cornwall, in Brittany – where they were almost as amused by the self-conscious picturesqueness of the much-painted fishermen in Bénodet as they were horrified by the war damage[16] – or at Dalkey, near Dublin. Like most refugees from English rationing, the Pritchetts appreciated the amplitude of Irish cooking, though in other ways Victor noticed 'an obvious deterioration . . . since the collapse of the Anglo-Irish. The country is now ruled by fat commercial travellers and priests . . . The old sullen, stupid Ireland is on top.'[17] On holiday, as always, he was an affectionate, enthusiastic, inventive father, but he was also still an eavesdropping writer. During one journey back from Ireland via Fishguard, the family stopped for a meal at a hotel in Monmouth. Victor came back from the bar, delighted: 'I've just overheard a man in the bar saying that he's going to climb halfway up Mount Snowdon.' The moment went into his story 'The Snag'.[18]

Victor and Dorothy also often went on trips together without the children, sometimes on impulse, more often connected with pieces he was writing. Once, Dorothy found she had £30 in unspent travellers' cheques so, 'We did a mad thing . . . at a moment's notice we dashed off to Paris & blewed it.'[19] The British Council sent him on a lecture tour in Italy, where they visited Graham Greene ('extraordinary, a fanatical worker . . . and a hard drinker') and went to a party at which the British vice-consul sat on Pritchett's knee.[20] Increasingly, invitations came for him to teach further afield: a year at Bennington, six months in Melbourne, a British Council tour in Canada. Partly out of concern for Dorothy, he turned most of these suggestions down, but in June 1953 they decided that he should take a visiting appointment as Gauss lecturer at Princeton, to be held over the coming autumn and winter, and that Dorothy should use his absence to attempt a cure. That autumn, once the children were safely back at school, she went into a private ward at University College Hospital in Bloomsbury, for what was described as 'rest, observation and treatment'. Pritchett, apprehensive and suffering from a new attack of gout, set sail on the SS *Ile de France*.

Perhaps it was only his imperviousness to literary fashion that prevented him from subsequently writing a campus novel. He had the material. His stay at Princeton is among the most fully documented periods of his life. He wrote almost daily to Dorothy, and often to Gerald and to other friends. Though he didn't keep a journal, he took a lot of notes, especially of visits to some of the more illustrious people he met, among them Hannah Arendt, Albert Einstein and Adlai Stevenson. And the friendship he made there with the young English writer A. Alvarez is also recorded in Alvarez's vivid memoir, *Where Did It All Go Right?*[21]

Pritchett dreaded going away to Princeton, he told Brenan. He was very worried about Dorothy, telling his friend vaguely that her health 'hasn't been good . . . nothing urgently, seriously wrong, but things which ought long ago to have been put right'.[22] And he was apprehensive about his new audience. He still had some of the anxieties of an autodidact. His friendships in the Madrid Residencia, his years on the *New Statesman*, his BBC discussions with some of the leading British intellectuals of the day, his work as a literary editor, much of it with contributors who were well-known scholars, the success of his critical books (he had been invited to write a history of English literature since 1880),[23] British Council lecture tours, dinners at Oxford colleges with friends like David Cecil – from all this he knew that he was most people's match. But until now he had never taught formally, or in a purely academic setting. His assignment was well within his powers (the topic he chose for his lectures was contemporary British fiction), but the annual Christian Gauss series was extremely prestigious and he was nervous about it. In mid-Atlantic, his gout took a turn for the worse, his toe developing 'a sullen flushed sexy look. . . . [Y]ou shall be in love, it says, with *me*.'[24] Limping into his rooms with their Oxbridge austerity, confronted with a 'miserable 2′6″ bed' and realising that he would have to occupy it for three months, he felt suicidal.

At first, things didn't improve. The Graduate College at Princeton was in those days still an all-male institution, a 'rather raucous monastery occupied by young bullocks getting their Ph.Ds'.[25] Victor's situation there struck him as like having to live at school with Oliver. His first encounters with American food were discouraging: clams seemed to him like 'snot on shells'. Nor were his first impressions of his new colleagues much more appealing. After taking tea with the Dean, he wrote, 'The Princeton voice I can only describe as the low, polite gurgle of an in-growing toe-nail if it could talk.'[26] Then there were the onslaughts of 'a drunken professor called Blackmur' – the eminent poet and 'New Critic', R. P. Blackmur. Later, having spent some enjoyable evenings with him over dinner at Lahière's in Witherspoon Street, Pritchett acknowledged that the 'pungent & fervent & knowledgeable' Blackmur had his good points. But for the most part he seemed 'a terrible embarrassment' . . . 'bitter, petulant, defensive and difficult', not least when he stood up during one of Pritchett's lectures and, for no apparent reason, bellowed, 'VSP is like me: he's a Tory Anarchist.'[27]

Some of these stories, of course, were for the amusement of Dorothy, who seemed at first to be making a good recovery. 'Just got your letter,' Victor wrote to her on 14 October: 'Oh lovely, lovely . . . I hate being separated from you . . . Your letter delighted me & made me laugh like you and I laughed together. I love you so much. Perhaps we have gone mad about money, you and I, do you think. I mean to sell oneself into a monastery for £1800.' He missed her deeply and, although Pritchett tantalised the libidinous Brenan with accounts of how attractive he found black women and speculations about whether he would take an American mistress, it's clear that separation from home made him even more than usually conscious of how much his successes owed to Dorothy, and how much they had cost her. 'What a dangerous thing marriage is,' he wrote to Gerald. 'It envelopes one, protects one, it's the wonderful hothouse in which one grows year after year; but taken out of it, how exposed . . . one is, what a horrible self or ego appears. What, one says, is this the creature my poor wife has to endure every day – this panicky, aggressive, self-pitying preying mantis. Ugh.'[28]

He was too cheerful and gregarious, though, to succumb to such broodings for long. He quickly made friends with Al Alvarez, who had just moved from Oxford to a fellowship at Princeton. Almost thirty years Pritchett's junior, the short, funny, highly intelligent, 'excitable and incoherent' young poet became a proxy extra son. The two men had a lot in common. Alvarez's family were in the rag trade and his father was chronically reckless with money: 'insolvency', Alvarez later wrote, 'was the element he swam in.'[29] Alvarez loved literature but was unsure what to do about it. Although he was well on course for a successful academic career, the prospect didn't excite him. Like Victor, he was a romantic and, although there were many differences between the things they felt romantic about (in Alvarez's case, extreme physical and psychological challenges: mountaineering, poker, contact sports – he helped coach the college rugby team), they were united in their love of good writing and their sense that universities were not necessarily the best setting for it. Pritchett was the first professional writer, as distinct from literary teacher, Alvarez had known and he communicated to the younger man not only some of his specific literary enthusiasms, but the idea that they could provide a way of life – one to which Alvarez, too, could aspire.

Wherever Pritchett went, Alvarez later wrote,

> he created his own microclimate, fizzing with energy and appetite. He was addicted to writing like some people are to the bottle. He wrote every day and seemed able to write anywhere – in the waiting room of Grand Central Station, on the train and, probably, in his head as he walked the last few hundred yards to wherever he was going. . . .

One important aspect of this microclimate, for Alvarez, was that it was clear of the usual English fog of class and rank: 'He was always on the lookout for signs of life – the college janitors interested him as much as the professors, or possibly more – and he refused to take the high ground with anyone. He was a famous writer . . . but he treated me as an equal from the moment we met.'

Pritchett's first impressions of Alvarez were more cautious. To Dorothy, he described 'a very captious but giggling and kindly boy . . . always washing his pants to save laundry. . . . He has a sacred packet of Lux.'[30] Before long, though, he had seen enough of his talent to recommend him to Janet Adam Smith, now literary editor of the *New Statesman*. For Victor, stuck in a strange small town thousands of miles from his wife, children and friends, Al's conversation, and especially his anecdotes about his much-thwarted sexual exploits, were a lifebelt.

Soon enough, the New Jersey Transit was taking Pritchett into, and also bringing out to his lectures, a world which he found a lot more fun. Although even literary Manhattan struck him at first as 'small and drab', he quickly changed his mind – except about the fact that some of its inmates suffered from too much closeness to university life. He described Lionel Trilling as 'a quiet Herbert Readish fellow, with a whining, martyred wife with all psycho-analysis popping out of her harrowed eyes'.[31] But others in the *Partisan Review* circle appealed to him straight away. Philip Rahv was 'a breath of fresh air', because he was 'a man, not a professor'.[32] This was even more true of Norman Mailer ('intelligent, charming, drunk').[33] Among those who came to his first lecture, along with John Berryman and the publisher Robert Giroux, was Mary McCarthy: 'Ah, what a woman she is. Forty, I suppose, beautiful, a little bony across the chest for my taste, but full of charm, original intelligence and with a terrifying tongue. One could feel the knife going into one's back as one turned away, though I was flattered to hear she liked me. . . .' And there was also, as he later told Brenan, 'a nice man-eating woman with huge blue eyes, like a car's headlights'.[34]

Typically, Pritchett seems to have had no idea what a celebrity he already was among the New York intelligentsia. As W. H. Auden and many others had found long before, the United States welcomed clever people off the boat with an enthusiasm to which they were unaccustomed at home, and which their own countries rarely offered to anyone travelling in the opposite direction. Pritchett's books not only came out in America at the same time as in England, but were already sometimes suggested by his US publishers: it was Blanche Knopf, for example, who first proposed *The Spanish Temper*, which he had just finished writing.[35] Several of his short stories had by now appeared in *The New Yorker*, where he also had a fast-growing reputation as a critic.

Not that American outlets were all that mattered. At the time, the *New Statesman* and the *Listener* were read on the East Coast as avidly as the (then unborn) *New York Review of Books* is today in Europe. Susan Sontag, for example, subscribed to both when she was a graduate student at Harvard only a couple of years later, and found in Pritchett's reviews 'my first introduction to a more relaxed kind of criticism (I hadn't then read Virginia Woolf's essays) – not academic, and without the high moralism of Trilling'.[36] To Sontag, as to many others before and since, Pritchett was 'a revelation. I didn't know you could write about literature in such a way, that you could be lyrical and precise and not carry a huge burden of judgement.' So no one other than himself was surprised that he was given lunch by *The New Yorker* and by *Holiday* magazine, and a cocktail party by the Knopfs, and a dinner chez Lillian Hellman, where he met Arthur Miller, 'a thin, straying creature who became rather amusing'.[37] (Hellman, who was to become a close friend, he described at the time as 'a half naked genial harridan of 60 with dyed yellow hair, a tremendous nose, tigerish eyes, a man's voice, and the most . . . well-educated, mild person'.)

In that autumn of 1953, V. S. Pritchett was a transatlantic hit. 'Everybody is falling in love with him,' Blanche Knopf reported to Ian Parsons.[38] Back in London, meanwhile, Dorothy was deep in a depression and was kept in hospital longer than had been planned. Despite Victor's best intentions and his most passionate declarations, and whatever pleasure Dorothy took in his anecdotes in other circumstances, his letters regaling her with his successes can't have helped. Not, of course, that he was anything but sympathetic. 'I'm so afraid that when you get out you will run into depression or flu,' he wrote solicitously when she was allowed to go home,

> especially down at cold Wadwick. For God's sake, coddle yourself, please darling, because I love every inch of you and you are terribly precious. . . . It's nearing Nov 5 and 6th, the most important & beautiful days in my life, when that miraculous burst of love came to us which has got into my blood & bones for ever.[39]

Almost immediately, though, the same letter returned to his New York news. And within three days he was writing brightly about a party where 'I was a draw', and where he once again met the lady with the headlamp eyes, 'a coquettish divorcée (Mrs Kerr) who was tremendously arch – still, I rather liked her'.[40]

While Victor was making the most of his freedom he often, and increasingly with reason, felt guilty about it. 'I feel just inadequate & small as a pea,' he told Dorothy, later in the letter about this particular party, 'and I think of nothing but my bad character. It becomes clear to me that I must be terribly depressing & frustrating to live with and I feel it is very largely my fault that you have gradually got ill & unhappy.' This didn't remove Dorothy's apprehensions, though her friends were doing all they could to look after her – Jocelyn Herbert and Norah Smallwood in particular. Victor responded enthusiastically to news of a party of George Weidenfeld's she had been to. He was assiduous in shopping for presents for her and the children, and in attending, from a distance, to their finances. He hoped, he told Dorothy, to bring home £400 or £500 from Princeton and £275 from Knopf, 'So we wont be at all badly off. Don't worry. . . . It is marvellous, don't you think, to pay £750 in income tax & school fees & *not notice* it.'[41]

Yet at the same time, almost every letter told Dorothy, one way or another, that Victor was not only doing things she might also have liked to be doing (he met Greta Garbo at a party, 'looking white & wizened in a corner', and John Steinbeck, who announced that all the Father Christmases in the Manhattan stores were women),[42] but also managing to do things for which, hitherto, she had seemed indispensable – even to the extent of typing his own lectures.[43] And if all this made her jealous, worse still was the evidence which, in his ebullience, he rarely managed to disguise, that he was doing some things which, had she been there, she would decidedly have put a stop to. He could be persuasive and amusing about the monastic nature of his existence at Princeton ('Alvarez & I are thinking of calling ourselves Brother Al & Brother Pritchett, of the Order of the Off-Whitefriars, or Off-White Sepulchre. . . . I've burned my pants on the radiator and made the colourful error of washing my socks with them.').[44] But there was not much to convince her in the studied off-handedness with which he mentioned a 'prim restful dinner' at 'Mrs Kerr's', or in the attempted reassurance with which he described the lady as 'very slow, very nice', adding that 'these people are so encased in good manners and elaborate phrases that one doesn't know how to take them'. If Mrs Kerr was so prim, and her world so artificial, why was he so soon having dinner in her company again – this time, 'a warm, homely, friendly evening'?[45]

Over Christmas and New Year, while Dorothy had the children home from school at Wadwick, Victor, somewhat to her relief, was laid up at Princeton with a bad attack of gout, 'exhausted with pain' and irritated by what he called 'cash payment doctoring' (though not too ill to joke about having had to pay for a urine test. 'You do a specimen with a jar & the girl says "2 dollars": I thought *they* ought to pay *me*.').[46] The college's kitchens were closed for the holiday, so Al brought in salami and bread and marmalade and even, on one occasion, 'a couple of hot steaks in a brown paper parcel'. He also entertained the invalid with song titles suited to his condition: 'You've been a good old wagon, Daddy, but you done broke down', and 'Empty Bed Blues – the Princeton national anthem'.[47] The younger man was about to travel to Poughkeepsie and Victor thought that without him he might have to go into hospital. At the last minute, though, 'with that superb American hospitality', a trip to Virginia materialised. He had previously spoken of Mrs Kerr's Virginian connections, so Dorothy may have guessed, though Victor didn't say, where the idea had originated. Soon, he was disingenuously full of how his health had improved: 'masses of energy and one gets infected with the general American feeling of excitement about nothing in particular'.[48] So infected, in fact, that when he launched the latest of his critiques of his parents' marriage, he seems not to have noticed that, to the resentful Dorothy, he might have seemed to be talking about himself: 'one person has knocked the life out of another in the interest of his own egotism,' he told her. 'It makes me so angry.'

The slender, blue-eyed Barbara Kerr was a Wendell. Ancestors of both her parents had come to America in the early seventeenth century and the family was long established in Boston – though one of her grandmothers had scandalised society there by leaving her husband and four children for a man fourteen years younger, with whom she went to live in Paris. (Edith Wharton is said to have had her in mind in the character of Mrs Lidcote in her story 'Autres Temps . . .')[49] Barbara herself was brought up in Chicago, where her banker father had moved on business, and she had made a career in journalism, most recently as an editorial writer for the *Boston Traveller*. Later, she was to become founding editor of *People* magazine and editor of *Mademoiselle*. At the time when she met Victor she was in her early forties, twice divorced, with a dry, frank wit: 'I'm not gifted matrimonially,' she would say. She was on the rebound from an affair with a prominent journalist whom she had met on an assignment for *Time* magazine. Though she was often sad about the turn her life had taken, the first impression she made on Victor was one of gaiety: 'You wrinkled your nose,' he told her later, 'you were amused. Your gloom was a charming sort of coquetry.'[50]

Victor, Barbara later recalled,

> was totally different from anybody whom I had ever met before. He fitted in; it's a pity he couldn't have lived in America, he fitted in so well. He had a remarkable ability to draw out people and to empathise with them, to discover what was inside them in a way that most American men, at that date especially, were not able to do. He was the most sympathetic person to talk to that I've ever been involved with. . . . We just happened to strike it off and when we were together we were happy. I was fascinated by him because he was totally different and he had a marvellous gift of expression, marvellous mind, a marvellous observation of the world. I adored the way he would look at people and react to people. . . . He absorbed every detail of street life. . . . [51]

They went to parties together and she introduced him to some of her friends, among them – in the course of a trip to Chicago, where Pritchett was lecturing – Adlai Stevenson, who had just been beaten to the presidency by Eisenhower. (Pritchett found him 'an energetic man with startled eyes . . . very intelligent & witty, perhaps a little naïve, but very concerned, thoughtful and melancholy . . . not interested in political power'.)[52] Political gossip was among the pleasures Victor and Barbara shared. Meanwhile, with the atavistic pursuit of innocence that can make the guilty seem so infantile to outsiders, they went to Central Park Zoo and took the double-decker bus down Fifth Avenue. On Victor's increasingly frequent trips into the city from New Jersey, he had begun to stay over at Barbara's house on the upper east side. In Virginia, he was a hit with her cousins, though they were astounded that he couldn't drive. Barbara gave him a fountain pen which he used regularly for years afterwards.[53]

January ended and, with it, Victor's appointment at Princeton. He had enjoyed his break from the more attritional aspects of his home life and he didn't want to leave Barbara. She had given him 'so much mad life', he wrote to her later, 'and that, in the end, is surely what makes our lives worth living & memorable'.[54] At the same time he had missed Dorothy very much and was looking forward to being back with her.

'Get us a table at the Etoile, darling,' he wrote (adding, with a dash of Henry Green, 'It will be heaven to have my delicious, cunty wife in my arms').[55] When Barbara said she would see him on to the boat, he enlisted Al to come along and to take her home afterwards. It was evident to Al that, until the last minute, Barbara hoped Victor might stay. For her, it was too early a replay of what had happened with her previous lover. Unlike him, though, Victor promised to see her as soon as she could get to London. In the meantime, he asked her to keep in touch partly through Al, partly through letters sent care of the Savile Club.

Back in England, at the beginning of 1954, Dorothy's abstinence was more or less sticking, though Jocelyn Herbert noticed that she still kept 'a little cache' of drink at home.[56] Generally, she was in much better health. When Victor arrived in London from Southampton docks, the children were away at school, so the couple had themselves to themselves. At home at Wadwick, both were soon caught up with arrangements for him to repeat his Princeton lecture series at London University and, in abbreviated form, on the radio, as well as with the publication of *The Spanish Temper* and with new plans for a trip to Portugal for *Holiday*. They did their best to settle back into country life. That July the Brenans came to stay at Ham Spray and Ralph Partridge drove them over to Wadwick.[57] Though it rained throughout most of the summer, Victor seemed in high spirits. When Frances Partridge told him of an Oxford doctor's comment that the weather was causing depression among several of his patients, he told her cheerfully, 'Oh yes, I have my revolver always at my elbow.'[58]

Already, Barbara Kerr had made more than one trip to London. In the spring, recapitulating their New York outings, Victor took her to Kew Gardens and the Zoo and the Tower. They went to the House of Commons and heard Hugh Gaitskell speak.[59] Victor brought the city alive in a way that was completely new to her, though she had been there often and had relatives as well as friends in England. It may have been around this time that, under the heading 'The Love Affair', Victor wrote in a notebook, 'It came into my head this morning that the successful, happy adultery is not now often described.'[60] Lacking an immediate excuse to go back to the States, he got in touch with R. P. Blackmur about teaching possibilities there the following year.[61] He told Blackmur to send his reply to the Savile, but this was not as safe as he had assumed. Soon, one of Barbara's letters was forwarded by the club to Wadwick, where Dorothy, in her secretarial role, opened it. It's not difficult to imagine her reaction. According to Barbara, Victor said that his wife 'was walking around with a pistol and would shoot [her] on sight'. (As Barbara later put it, 'I found that rather awkward.') Firearms were not Dorothy's style, in fact, but trying to contact members of Barbara's family was. For a time, the lovers stopped communicating. Victor pretended – perhaps he believed – that the affair was over.

Soon, though, they were seeing each other again in London. They had already begun to talk seriously about whether they might marry. To Barbara, it seemed clear that the main obstacle on Victor's side was his devotion to his children. She knew, though, that she would face problems of her own. She was no housewife and had seen enough of Victor to understand that someone from his background might have domestic expectations which she wouldn't be able to meet. She also wondered whether he would find things difficult with her family and vice versa. Her parents, she was sure, 'would not have been happy about it and would not have gotten on with Victor'. On this score, Victor wasn't troubled. He had come up in the world since his struggles with Evelyn's father and there were few circles in which he felt socially unconfident. Besides, as he told Al Alvarez that summer, he found it 'superb to be in love and to have friends who are [on] one's side'. Barbara was 'the most glorious woman I have ever known'.[62] At home, with no one to confide in, he felt like 'a bursting volcano'.[63]

After discovering the affair, Dorothy went back to drinking hard. Victor often despairingly felt that he was solely responsible for her condition: that simply by being who he was, he made her miserable. But he also knew – partly because he was by profession an observer rather than a man of action, partly just from years of bitter experience – that there was nothing he could do about it. Nothing except, perhaps, to leave her.

Barbara was right that the children were his strongest reason for not giving up his marriage, but he began to think that even they might be better off if he brought matters to a head. They were now sixteen and fourteen years old. What was their opinion? He took them on an outing to Andover and asked them gently whether he and Dorothy should separate. He didn't mention that he was involved with anyone else, though Josephine had heard her mother fly into 'quite jealous rages', accusing him of having affairs. In scenes like this, Dorothy would sometimes pick up the phone and talk, or pretend to talk, to a man in London whom she seemed to be threatening to go to. Josephine felt deeply protective of her father at such times, particularly when, as happened increasingly often, Dorothy attacked him physically. Once, when he hurt his back in a fall on some steps, Dorothy punched his bruises, 'shouting and screaming and yelling'. But Josephine was angry with Victor, too, 'Because: why is he pretending that she's tired? She's not tired, she's drunk, and he ought to be telling her she's drunk and to stop it.'

In answer to their father's question about splitting up with their mother, Josephine was hesitantly in favour, but Oliver said no. To Victor, Oliver's response was in effect a veto. Other things, though, kept the marriage still hanging by a thread, especially Dorothy's continuing, if sporadic, efforts to pull herself round. On one occasion when she was driving Oliver to school, she was so shocked by how drunk she was that immediately afterwards she got herself readmitted into hospital. When she re-emerged, the couple tried various practical solutions, such as an evening routine of going out together to the local pub to play bar billiards, which encouraged the competitive Dorothy to keep a clear head and also contained her behaviour by making it more publicly visible. Every day, though, was a struggle. Their trip to Portugal together turned out to be hurried, fractious and exhausting. After it, Dorothy – whose fortieth birthday was looming – was again in what Victor described as 'a poor way'.[64] Spurred by Gamel Brenan's translation of Pérez Galdós's *La De Bringas*, which had recently appeared,[65] she once again tried to do some writing of her own, but wouldn't show Victor the results. 'Its hard,' he acknowledged, 'if you want to write, to be married to a writer, specially when you type [h]is awful stuff, as Dorothy does for me.'[66]

Certainly, being married to that particular writer, with his huge output and zest, must have been part of the problem, but it wasn't easy, either, being surrounded as Dorothy was by women who enjoyed much more independence – whether through artistic work, like Gamel and the stage designer Jocelyn Herbert, or through having money of their own, like Mary Campbell and Frances Partridge, or both. Any self-comparisons on such scores were compounded by her sense that her friendships were at least as much Victor's as her own: wasn't it him that these women really came to see, invited to supper, enjoyed having around? In any case, Dorothy's drinking went back a long way: to her father, to her own adolescence and to those wartime years, a decade earlier, stuck in the country with her young children while Victor went wherever he went. However guilty Victor felt about his part in her predicament, and however hard he tried to help, ultimately any remedy had to be her own.

In January 1955, just before Dorothy's birthday, Victor moved out of home and into the Savile. Dorothy pursued him by phone. Robert Kee was startled by his friend's undisguised horror when a club servant interrupted a conversation between them to say that there was a call from Mrs Pritchett: 'No, no, no,' Pritchett said, in a panic-stricken voice: 'Tell her I'm not here.'[67] From the Savile he resumed his efforts to find some teaching in the States, but had left his enquiries too late.[68] That spring he was back at Wadwick, trying once more to make the best of things and sometimes persuading Dorothy to join in his social life in London. Despite, or because of, his personal turmoil, Pritchett was professionally even busier than usual. There were the usual literary events, described to Gerald with a mix of critical perception and graphic social satire: a 'very sticky' party for the once pioneering Vorticist writer and artist Wyndham Lewis, for example, now in his seventies, 'who sat like a flaccid, deaf and expiring tortoise on a sofa'.

I said how much I admired *Tarr*[69] – which I do; it still makes me laugh – he told me I had insulted him! There he sat, torpid, almost asleep, in his manias. I noticed his small, white hands. I suppose to many writers there comes a moment when they give up. [T. S.] Eliot said he (W.L.) had matured & become humane – as if that were a good thing. So it might be for some of us, but mellowing has meant the softening of W.L.'s talent I think. His talent lay in the incapacity to mature, in dissociation, in lack of heart and an astonishing short-circuiting of feeling, so that he was wired only to head and eye. If he is a bore because he lacks a sense of proportion, it was also the basis of his originality as a satirical writer. His mistake was to try to be Swift without Gulliver, or describe a wonderland without Alice....[70]

Some nervous to-ings and fro-ings were prompted by a threat of litigation from the Spanish socialist Luis Araquistáin, whom Pritchett had mistakenly described in *The Spanish Temper* as a Communist. Emollient letters from both Pritchett and his publishers calmed Araquistáin down. Pritchett began putting together his first volume of *Collected Stories*, for which Chatto advanced him £350 against generous royalties.[71] His publishers also tried to persuade him to write a book about Greece, which he declined, suggesting Mexico instead, for which they offered an advance of £500.[72] This idea gradually turned into a project on Central and South America for *Holiday* magazine, which would arrange and pay for the travel. The results would in turn be used for some radio talks as well as in the book.

While his travel plans took shape, Pritchett belatedly finished a radio talk on Portugal[73] and embarked on a series of broadcast conversations suggested by the philosopher A. J. Ayer, who took part, together with the biologist Peter Medawar, the poet Rex Warner and others. Their subjects included 'Puritanism and what it involves' and 'Games'. (Pritchett confessed that he knew nothing about the latter and had never wanted to distinguish himself at any game except once when he was ten and would have liked to have been injured at football, 'in front of a very pretty girl'.)[74] In the summer of 1955 he did a radio talk on Arthur Morrison, the author of *Tales of Mean Streets*, in a series on neglected novelists.[75] He was also thinking about a possible sequel to *Mr Beluncle*[76] and about some short stories.

If all this weren't enough, in the course of the same privately desperate year Pritchett wrote no fewer than thirty-five items for the *New Statesman*, reviewing books on Simenon, Shelley, Bunyan, Maupassant and Hogarth among others, and contributing essays on whatever caught his eye: tourists, the Law Courts, an ice show, a visit to Stratford on Shakespeare's birthday, an encounter in the Andes. It would be interesting to know what Dorothy felt as she typed the opening words of one of these pieces, on Mary Wollstonecraft and women's rights. 'The great battles for the emancipation of women are over,' her husband asserted. 'There are now only skirmishings and frontier incidents between different but equal powers. . . .' But the same article may carry a clue to the survival of their marriage, when Pritchett says that Wollstonecraft underestimated 'the reviving power of sexual love'.[77]

Sexual passion was something Victor and Dorothy had almost always shared, and they did what they could to distract themselves back into it, together. In June 1955 they went to Paris, partly to arrange for Josephine, who was leaving Cranborne Chase, to spend six months in France, partly on a working holiday for a *New Statesman* article. They went to an exhibition at Versailles, a new gangster movie (*Du Rififi chez les Hommes*), several plays, a performance by the Peking opera which they found thrilling.[78] The school holidays gave them another lift. Dorothy again stopped drinking.[79] Josephine took off for France. Oliver, who was doing well at school, had developed a gift for clowning which, Victor said, made them spend a lot of the summer in laughter.[80]

Victor, though, was secretly still very much caught up with Barbara and saw her whenever she managed to get to London: at the flat of one of her friends, at various hotels. His friends were beginning to find out about the situation – among them Richard Crossman, the Labour politician and *New Statesman* staffer, with whom Victor sometimes stayed when he was in town and who, like many people, had imagined him to be a model of marital fidelity.[81] A probing letter from Gerald, soon after the Pritchetts got back from Paris, stirred Victor into a sudden confession which mixed a competitive kind of sexual frankness with hard-won self-knowledge:

> Sexual puritanism is unknown to me; the only check upon my sexual adventures is my sense of responsibility which I think has always been a nuisance to me. . . . I am peaceable, a non-quarreller, amiable – really a hedonist you know. But I notice people prefer jealousy to love, unhappiness to happiness, power over others to pleasure for themselves, unkindness to kindness. . . . Of course I'm romantic. I like to be in love – the arts of love then become more ingenious and exciting. . . . You must not mention it in any letter you write to Wadwick but an American woman with whom I had a most deeply moving affair in America, is arriving in London this coming week and, God knows what will happen. It is difficult & painful & torturing because I adore her. I'll tell you about it one day. It has caused I suppose naturally, boundless distress at Wadwick. So if you do write about it, send it to this club, not there. . . .[82]

Just over three weeks later, groaning with gout like a cartoon clubman, he wrote from the Savile to tell Gerald that he had broken the relationship off. He didn't know whether he would ever get over it, he said. It wasn't a passing affair, 'but a devastating deep love which was returned'.[83] Prompted by Ralph Partridge who, encouraged by Frances, had eventually broached the subject with him, Victor now told Gerald what he already knew about Dorothy's nine-year alcoholism. He said that despite everything, he could not face another divorce. The letter was the first of a desperate series in which lamentations about having stuck to his marriage for so long alternated with fears that, at fifty-four, he would never regain his old optimism and strength.[84] 'Dreams, hopes are cruelties,' he wrote, cliché-bound in his misery. 'Curse everything.'[85]

As in the closing phase of his marriage to Evelyn, unhappiness made

Victor painfully indecisive. If he even momentarily thought he had finished the affair in the summer of 1955, Barbara wasn't aware of it. 'There was no big scene of break-up,' she later said. It gradually became clear to her that he was not going to get divorced – that 'he would be miserable and he would regret me and regret the children. And God knows what Dorothy would have done. It was, I guess, star-crossed.' According to Barbara's recollection, she and Victor just gradually saw less of each other. Whatever transpired between them that summer, the autumn brought Pritchett's next journey for *Holiday*, to South America via New York. This time he flew. Again, Dorothy stayed behind.

Was the trip another attempt by Victor to bring things to a head? If so, it was only at an unconscious level. Gerald had urged accommodation rather than confrontation, and Victor's letters home resumed his oblivious-seeming antiphon of boisterous, entertaining news from abroad with solicitousness about Dorothy's condition. 'I wonder all the time how you are,' he wrote, 'above all whether you are well and have thrown off your attacks and are enjoying yourself. I expand, as you do, by being free for a while but that doesn't mean I don't love you. I do.'[86] This was on the writing paper of the Hotel St Regis, 55th Street and Fifth Avenue, Manhattan, an address which she must have realised was within easy reach of Barbara. He enthusiastically recounted some of what he was doing: a meeting at Knopf about a planned selection of his stories; dinner at Sardi's (with whom?); a visit to Birdland (alone, he said); an amusing lunch with Wystan Auden 'in his filthy dirty flat – I cant tell you of the dust & disorder – in a sort of Camden Town part of New York, a Polish semi-slum of pretty houses falling to pieces'.

Pritchett's travels in South America were sponsored by Pan-Am, which treated him well but was slow in making the final arrangements, so that his time in New York was extended by a week. At last, in mid October, he headed south, wiring home from Cartagena, 'GOOD FLIGHTS BOILED ALIVE WELL LOVE VESPER.' From Lima he let Dorothy know that he was staying at 'a real Ritz, famous throughout S. America for its food and rightly so'. A few days later he sent a description of a meeting with the Chilean poet Pablo Neruda and his 'wonderful third wife with huge mouth, enormous breasts and vermillion [*sic*] hair'. He included a sketch of the Nerudas' house. Victor found the Communist poet 'a great charmer . . . solemn yet amusing'.[87] In Chile he was again staying at 'a super hotel . . . with a lovely modern room right over the sea'. Though he went to a nightclub with the local British Council representative, he guessed that Gerald's reports of the brothels had been exaggerated: 'I haven't visited one, nobody seems to go to them.'[88] But there were plenty of other excitements: meetings with yet more new people – the Argentinian author and editor, Victoria Ocampo; 'a writer called Borges' – samba at a bar in Rio, where he stayed up until dawn; the theft of his pipe by a monkey.

A little earlier Victor had suffered a virus, running a high temperature. To Dorothy, its effects may have been more reassuring than his more calculated attempts to cheer her up. She had written to him about the enforced break between Princess Margaret and the divorced Peter Townsend, and he had replied with a passionate six-page letter, interpreting this peculiarly English drama in the exotic context of the culture surrounding him ('Primitive magic sacrifices the son [King Edward VIII] in one generation; now, to expiate the sins of the nation, the virgin is given to the dragon'), while also seeing it as an attack on their own situation – one against which he mounted a feverish defence:

> The absurd archbishop [of Canterbury] is telling you and me that we are not married, whereas we both know that his opinion is nasty and lacking in dignity and true belief in life. He's a death-wisher. Ordinary people display a lovelier and warmer regard for human nature and a more fitting belief in it.[89]

In a calmer frame of mind he regularly asked for Dorothy's news which, unsurprisingly, was very different from his own. She was very low and, although she was not drinking, the medication she had been prescribed was preventing her from sleeping.[90] Perhaps, she wrote, she should have travelled with him, rather than attempting another cure alone. Victor stepped up his pleas:

> I am sorry you get so depressed and tired. It sounds to me that you have started your 'turns' again. My darling, if you have, please, please I beg you to go to a doctor. They will destroy you; they will destroy Jo, Olly & me too. You *must* get them put right. Darling, don't you understand we all *love* you? And that I want you. Its mad to go on being so unhappy, so ill, so tired. Please, don't be self-destructive. You are yourself happiness, gaiety, fulfillment. Don't throw the days of life away in pointless regrets. . . . [91]

Poor Dorothy's wretchedness was intensified by yet another episode involving her children. A son of some Spanish friends of the Pritchetts was at school with Oliver. The boy let slip that his mother had told him that Mrs Pritchett had been 'in an institution'. Oliver asked Dorothy whether it was true. In the context of what she imagined to have been total secrecy, the exposure was hurtful in itself, but knowing that she was being talked about by their friends – even by her children and *their* friends – made her suicidal. Her paranoia was compounded by new suspicions about Victor's extramarital life. Was it from Victor that the boy's mother had heard? Were she and Victor having an affair? For the time being, helped by tranquillisers, Dorothy suppressed such feelings, and, when Victor at last returned home, their rapprochement, though strained, was at first not unhopeful. He found her 'peaceable, normal, kindly and almost completely well'. Both of them wanted to stay together and longed to recover their early happiness. Both, too, though, were growing resigned to something very different. 'I sit industriously, defeated, in my trap,' Victor wrote sadly to Gerald, soon after what he said had been a successful family Christmas.[92] 'She has no notion of what she has done to me or to Josephine (especially); but I am sure also that I must have done harm to her. Such is marriage.'

8

London Retrieved

Although people drink, in Pritchett's fictions, and there are even a few
alcoholics in them (such as Calcott in *Dead Man Leading*, the 'colonel's
daughter' in 'The Sailor', and Mr Beluncle's sister), the last time he
used alcoholism as a main subject was in 'Pocock Passes', published in
1939. Once Dorothy's problem had come to dominate his life, it was the
last thing he wanted to write about. Even an essay about the
temperance movement dating from as late as 1971 is strangely
detached.[1] He did, though, explore other aspects of his recent personal
experiences in a small number of fictions concerning failed marriages,
jealousy and infidelity. 'The Snag', for example, which appeared in
Encounter in 1956,[2] is about the middle-aged narrator's affair with a
scandalous divorcée with 'ice-blue eyes' named Sophia, and is full of
sharp, half-satirical perceptions about her, such as how, in the luxury of
her flat, she had 'wrung out of interior decoration the things that she
had failed to get from marriage'. She eventually goes off with an old
acquaintance of his. This man – like the stranger Pritchett encountered
on the way back from holiday in Ireland – will climb halfway up
Snowdon, but the person who really only gets halfway is the narrator,
with Sophia. The story ends, 'she was the scandal I could never have
made the most of and I was the hole-in-corner despair from whom he
had saved her. But for him she might now be having rows with me in
cinema queues on Saturday nights.'[3]

The narrator of 'The Snag' is unmarried, but 'The Ladder', reissued
in the 1956 *Collected Stories*,[4] explores a teenaged daughter's reaction
to her father's second marriage, and the eventual complicity of father
with daughter in driving out the new woman. It is in 'The Sniff',
though, first published as early as 1948, that Pritchett got closest to
diagnosing at least one main aspect of the long turbulence in his
relationship with Dorothy.[5]

'The Sniff' is about a shop assistant who, to the delight of his children but the confusion and growing jealousy of his wife, develops a secret life as a painter. The psychology is vivid and complicated, particularly in the relationship's accrued processes and assumptions. The wife has previously been irritated by her husband's lack of ambition at work, but this is also part of what she has come to live by: 'One of the satisfying things about him was that he was always reproachable.' His new hobby feels to her like an infidelity, not only to herself but to her previous understanding of him. In an attempt to regain control, she offers to sit to him, but finds that in this situation the control startlingly becomes his:

> It was terrible. The way his astonished eyes looked at her, how composed his astonishment was. The way he measured her, as though she was in some way wrong. . . . He grunted as he drew.
> 'You have a hard life,' he said . . . 'Shut up with three children, always at the stove or at the sink. You don't have a chance. I often think,' he said, 'you never have a life, not to call it life.'
> Her lips straightened.
> 'Go on telling me,' she said.
> 'You need a rest, a change,' he said, measuring the shoulders with the pencil.
> 'You don't say,' she said. 'And who's going to give it me?'
> And then she slowly came to see what it was that she hated about this painting of his. *He* had a life, a life she couldn't share, a secret life she could not enter. Wonderfully kind, he sounded – wonderfully kind, just like a man who is being unfaithful to you. Telling her. Telling her to go and have a life of her own.

This seems over-explained: the interpretative critic in Pritchett can sometimes be overheard in his fiction. But, seen biographically, the story clearly represents a sympathetic effort not only to understand but to give voice to a point of view not far from Dorothy's. In doing this, it also articulates the husband's priorities, which are very like Pritchett's own. There's an interesting ambiguity in how the forceful wife's resentments modulate into a final subservience on her part. The story leaves us sympathising with her, but it is the husband's art which has clearly triumphed:

> she can't understand why she does this, why she should enslave

herself to this new mistress of his – she tiptoes to his room at dinner-time with a tray; if he is working she puts the tray down without a word, so as not to disturb him, and goes out. She asks no questions. She makes no difficulties. She keeps the children away. . . .

The skill lies not only in the way this transition is managed, but in how the reader has been led to it from the opening words, so tantalisingly unspecific when they are read for the first time: 'It is hard to say what the present situation is, whether it is improving or whether it is becoming one of those everlasting situations that mark the characters and memories of children.' The ending can only be seen properly under the light of this beginning.

Reviewing the 1956 *Collected Stories* (published in the USA as *The Sailor, Sense of Humor, and Other Stories*) for the *Observer*, John Raymond called Pritchett 'incomparably the finest short story writer of our time'.[6] He may have been the finest, but in the early 1950s he was far from the most productive. In these difficult years, although he was doing a lot of literary journalism and travel writing, Pritchett's short fiction – at least by his own standards – had come near to a standstill. He published no new stories in 1951, only one in 1952, one in 1953,[7] none in 1954. While the appearance of the *Collected Stories* (which sold a modestly encouraging 2400 copies in Britain within two months) drew attention away from the effects of his private life on his work – effects which were beginning to frustrate his publishers, as well as himself – it also gave him a much-needed boost. Pritchett's fiction writing picked up a little in 1955 and 1956.[8] But at home, things continued to be very difficult and, because it was there that he worked, his imaginative writing suffered correspondingly. The 1956 collection was dedicated, as usual, to Dorothy and in the copy he gave her he wrote, 'To darling Dorothy with love from VSP.'[9] But the remission of hostilities when he got back from South America was no more long-lived than after his return from Princeton.

Dorothy was bitterly angry, bereft and jealous: the last, it seems, without current cause. While Victor had not broken with Barbara when he intended to the previous August, his letters to Al Alvarez and Gerald Brenan early the following year, 1956, make no reference to her. Nor does he mention anything else that might have been a threat to his marriage – other, that is, than sheer lonely unhappiness and remorse. Whether or not he had simply become more discreet (he later ruefully described Alvarez as 'leaky'),[10] he assured Dorothy, with less tact towards her than pain, exasperation and guilt on his own account, that her fears were 'a morbid fantasy'. He had, he claimed, 'utterly finished' with Barbara, 'ages ago'.[11] In mid February 1956 he yet again delivered an ultimatum over Dorothy's drinking by moving back into his club, saying that this situation would last until she took steps to get herself 'really cured'. He refused to see her except in the presence of a doctor. Dorothy's wretchedness was compounded, now, by regrets about at least one love affair of her own which she had given up on his account. The details are not known, except that Victor readily sympathised. '[You] have, everyone has, a great need for love,' he wrote and promised her that she could depend on his love for her. 'I hate to see your beauty being wasted in this ugliness,' he added, 'and my talents too. I have a responsibility to my gifts and you to your grace and attraction as a woman.'[12]

With his friends, Victor was more pessimistic. He felt 'blasted', he told Gerald, by what he described as Dorothy's 'lies & fantasies'. And to Al he wrote from the Savile Club on 23 April 1956,

> Things have been very black with me and, though I get patches of respite, the outlook continues to be grim and to get grimmer. I brought Dorothy to her senses by leaving her, got doctors to explode all the lies and effect a second 'cure'. I *think* it's working, but am uncertain for the old instability and violence remain. I now spend more time in London which gives me some relief, but many calamities – all rooted in that disastrous visit to the U.S. – stun me and cage me. My health has been dreadful. . . .[13]

Middle age was a bad time, he warned Al. 'Avoid it. Hibernate between 45 and 65 if you can.'

In all this, Pritchett didn't entirely lose either his sense of humour or his capacity to think constructively about the future. He found some wry amusement in the fact that Dorothy, with the benefit of her latest cure, was radiant with good health, while he had been suffering from a new attack of gout (the result, he supposed, of 'repressed acidity, bitterness and general irascibility'), as well as from prolonged depression and anxiety for which he was getting psychiatric help.[14] He was beginning to wonder whether their life at Wadwick, 'the Russian isolation of the country', was contributing to their difficulties. They were both increasingly cut off by their personal predicament, but Victor – his language showing the effects of psychotherapy – thought he might be more able to 'reintegrate' in London.[15] Perhaps Dorothy might be able to 'reconstruct herself' if they moved back to town.

Meanwhile, he had been working day and night, not least on his 25,000-word article on South America for *Holiday*. And, in his bachelor state at the Savile, he managed to see more of his friends – gleefully reporting to Alvarez, for example, a conversation between Cyril Connolly, 'a New York hostessy lady called Mrs Ryan' and himself:

MRS R: Mr Connolly, *did* you ever meet Mrs Virginia Woolf? What did you think of her?
C.C.:   I disliked her. She asked embarrassing questions.
MRS R: What questions?
C.C.:   She asked me 'What do lesbians do?' Since she had all that with Vita Sackville West she might have known. If she didn't, she was being naïve and embarrassing.
VSP: You could have replied 'They do good.'
C.C. (*lighting up*): Ah, you mean that they have a green finger?[16]

By June 1956, Victor was back behind what he now saw as the 'prison bars' of Wadwick. 'I wish I had a sundial mind that recalled only the sunny hours,' he wrote sentimentally to Al. 'Of course I rattle the bars of the cage violently from time to time, but now I know they wont break.'[17] His thoughts had been full of nostalgia about America. Typically, though, his mood quickly lightened. In the same letter he confesses that he has become obsessed with money, and elaborates a comic fantasy about simultaneously having a sex change and dying, thereby becoming his own widow and inheriting his own life insurance.

If Pritchett wasn't writing much fiction, he could at least apply his imagination to everyday life. Together, he and Dorothy began to look for a house in London, soon finding what they wanted in a run-down but potentially still elegant terrace between Regent's Park and Camden Town. To enable him to buy it, the *New Statesman* lent him £2500 at three per cent annual interest.[18]

Several years were to pass, and several setbacks would have to be got through, before Dorothy finally and permanently stopped drinking. But in moving to London the couple took what proved to be a decisive step towards a new life. As a result, everything good they had known together would eventually come back to them, and more. Some time before he met Barbara, in a letter commenting on what he saw as the limitations of the moral world in which Graham Greene allowed his characters to function ('how careful he is to keep his people below par'), Victor had passionately spoken up for 'the amount of moral energy, even heroism that ordinary people put into making their love & marriages survive the attacks of contemporary life'.[19] Far from everything between him and Dorothy managed to live up to that standard. But, separately and together, they went on aiming for it.

Meanwhile, the struggle was often bitterly hard. Dorothy's mother's death in 1956 was a new setback. In the summer of 1957, soon after Oliver finished his A-levels, Victor again left home, pleading with Dorothy in letters to get more help, and – in a desperate echo of his father's idiom – to 'decide now for happiness'.[20] Around this time, a young doctor called Emmett Dalton was recommended to Dorothy. Dalton was aware of the positive results that were being achieved by Alcoholics Anonymous. Though the organisation was still relatively little known outside the USA, it was beginning to make headway in England, its reputation helped by a recent Oscar-winning movie, *I'll Cry Tomorrow*, based on the best-selling confessions of one of the programme's more famous successes, the actress and singer Lillian Roth.[21] On Dr Dalton's advice, Dorothy agreed to try AA. She was sceptical and – for the first time – she didn't consult Victor in advance. He soon came to know that she was going to meetings, but when she talked about them to him, it was obliquely. Instead of describing her own confessional statements to the group, for example, she attributed them to other people. The ruse was transparent, but any fiction writer would have realised the importance of going along with it. Gradually, Dorothy grew reassured about the extent of Victor's commitment to her, as well as to her recovery. She began to rediscover her own strength of will, finding that AA bolstered it and provided her with new scope, outside her family. If she needed help, so, too, did other people she began to meet, at the Baker Street meetings and elsewhere. She persevered with the programme, gave a successful talk at Holloway women's prison and her confidence began to grow.[22] At a stroke, she gave up her sixty-a-day cigarette habit.

One of the factors which contributed to Dorothy's eventual recovery may have been the fact that the Pritchetts were no longer mere tenants of the house they were living in. Buying 12 Regent's Park Terrace was a concrete investment in each other and in their future, as well as a return to an environment which, at bottom, suited both of them better than the country. Until they moved in, Victor had been unaware how much difference it would make to him to be permanently back in London. Now, he was overwhelmed by it: 'The richness of London life, the interiors one discovers, the people, the names! There is no city like it.'[23] Regent's Park Terrace was, he wrote, 'an ideal frontier', perfectly situated between his aspirations and his origins.

The Terrace modestly echoes the spacious acres and sweeping architectural façades of Regent's Park itself. A long rectangular common garden partly screens the road's elegantly uniform flat front-age, a hint of *piano nobile* emphasised by a necklace of metal balconies. Pritchett soon afterwards affectionately described streets like it, in *London Perceived*: 'three- or four-storey houses, with their arched or porticoed doorways, their fan-lights, their long windows . . . their base-ments, and their railings. Rows of doorways, rows of windows, each house like a mild and spectacled face.'

At the back, small individual gardens overlook the larger, Italianate houses on the west side of Gloucester Crescent. Within earshot is London Zoo. In spring, at night, the Pritchetts could hear 'the hippos mating and roaring . . . and the parrots, monkeys, seals . . . screaming with love'. It sounded 'like a huge laughing party'.[24] But if the enclave is close to Regent's Park, it is separated from it by the wide railway line running north from Euston ('to me . . . not the romantic terminal,' Pritchett wrote, relishing his new opportunities for such connoisseur-ship. 'I'm a Paddington man or, even more, a Liverpool Streeter').[25] So it is more strongly claimed by Camden Town, on the same side of the tracks: by the busy shops and then-handsome cinema of Camden Parkway, by the market of Inverness Street and by run-down Arlington Road, with its huge Victorian doss-house for homeless men.

Today the Terrace, like nearby Primrose Hill, has gone up in the world, though it still has some of the marginal feel of the Dublin streets where Pritchett had lived in the 1920s, which it visually resembles. In the mid 1950s, though, it was only just beginning its ascent and there was much to remind Pritchett that, if the grandeur of Regent's Park was a short walk to the south-west, the shop where his parents had both worked in Kentish Town was no further away in the opposite direction. Many houses in the neighbourhood were essentially 'rooming' places, given over to multiple short-term occupancy. Two of them were brothels, or so Pritchett liked to believe.[26] He took a literary pleasure in disreputable associations. (Some years later, the journalist Nicholas Tomalin – by then, with his wife Claire, a near neighbour of the Pritchetts – found a dead cat and carried it in a sack to the nearby canal. He met Pritchett on the way. 'Got a body in there, Nick?' Pritchett asked and was only a little surprised when Tomalin answered, 'Yes.')[27]

For Pritchett, the area's associations with Gissing's *New Grub Street* were still strong. At various times during the couple's forty years there, their neighbours included Angus Wilson and P. N. Furbank, both of whom were to rent flats in number 2, and A. J. Ayer and his wife, Dee Wells, at number 10. Round the corner in Gloucester Crescent were the Tomalins, Alan Bennett, Jonathan Miller and his wife, and the publisher Colin Haycraft and his wife, the novelist Alice Thomas Ellis. Arthur Crook (a former printer's son who, like Pritchett, had left school at sixteen, but who in 1959 became editor of the *TLS*) moved into a nearby flat in Regent's Park Road and the novelist Elizabeth Jane Howard also lived nearby for a time. Derwent May, the poet and literary editor of the *Listener*, bought a house in Albany Street, the other side of Parkway.

It had been many years since there had been so near-perfect a convergence between Pritchett's marriage, his work and his social life. That he and Dorothy were not only finding it again, but that it would last, wasn't, of course, clear from the beginning. Besides, there were difficulties to deal with other than Dorothy's not drinking. Victor's beloved mother died soon after their arrival at Regent's Park Terrace. He grieved for her, and worried about what would become of his still lively, expansive and spendthrift father. It wasn't Walter, though, but Victor himself who was now plunged into unexpected financial embarrassment. In 1957 the *New Statesman* became a public company. Its accountants advised that the directors – of whom he was one – should repay any loans the magazine had made them. Pritchett had already paid back £1000 of the original £2500, but he had to tell Kingsley Martin that he couldn't quickly find the rest. He saw no option but to offer to resign his directorship, though it was worth £200 a year to him. Martin was anxious that the magazine shouldn't lose Pritchett and suggested to his fellow board member Leonard Woolf that they make him a private loan to cover his debt to the magazine.[28] Woolf was a philanthropic man, but often only reluctantly so. Though he agreed to Martin's suggestion, he soon regretted it and began to pursue his share of Pritchett's debt, scarcely relenting even when Martin told him about Pritchett's domestic difficulties.

In December 1957 Pritchett managed to sell a story to *The New Yorker*,[29] which enabled him to give Woolf back £375 of what he owed him. Woolf now asked for six per cent interest on the rest: double what Pritchett had been paying on the original loan. Thanks to a run of successes with *The New Yorker* as well as to his work for *Holiday* magazine and other American commissions, Pritchett eventually managed, to his relief, to reduce what he owed both Woolf and Martin, making his final repayment to Woolf in June 1961. But the experience was a harsh reminder of the realities of freelance life: one which put extra strain on both Victor and Dorothy at a time when they could have done without it.

The children were still very much on their hands. Josephine came back to live at home while she did a secretarial course and then reluctantly took a job at Spinks, the antiquarian art dealer in St James's. Josephine was not the biddable middle-class girl that these choices – however desirable to her parents – might have suggested she was, but independent and with a strong social conscience. Cranborne Chase had got her through a wretched period in her parents' life, while giving her its own questioning liberal ethos. She had republican views, started to learn Russian and decided to make a trip to the Soviet Union. There was some friction over this. Victor and Dorothy thought a stay in Italy would be more the thing – a conventional preference but also in part a political one. Victor pointed out to Jo that the Russians 'last year committed one of the major crimes of history in suppressing Hungarian freedom', though he conceded that there might have been some Russians who disapproved of this.[30]

Oliver, meanwhile, on the brink of leaving Bryanston, was the subject of different anxieties, partly about whether he would have to go into the army (in the event, National Service ended just before he would have been called up), but also because he thought he wanted a career as an actor. Victor took pains to help him with the few theatrical contacts he had – mainly with theatre critics – but he was privately aghast. (Ironically, and unknown to Victor, his ex-wife Evelyn was at the same time discouraging her own son from becoming a professional writer.)[31]

In his work, Pritchett was once again stuck. His thoughts about another novel went nowhere. The reputation of his criticism still didn't prevent him from feeling he was wasting his energy on it. This discouragement increased when *The New Yorker* (more, it seems, for reasons to do with its relationship with another author than out of any intrinsic dissatisfaction with the piece in question) asked for major cuts and alterations in his essay on a new translation of *Madame Bovary*.

'Really I have nothing to say about Flaubert,' he wrote exasperatedly to Gerald Brenan. 'I cannot get interested in these great writers any longer. I regard them as monstrous robbers of one's time if one is a writer, however modest, oneself.'[32] *Holiday* magazine, meanwhile, wanted to send him to Eastern Europe. But he and Dorothy were getting on better, she was keeping off drink, and he was keen not to leave her alone for any length of time. Besides, he was becoming frustrated by the superficiality of this way of writing: sketches of individual countries, a few pages to each, of the sort he had recently done about Latin America – vivid, fluent, stylish, but with little depth or originality. His thoughts were focused on England and, in a notebook which he began early in 1957, he planned a book about it: one which would explore his home country through social class.[33]

As far as short stories were concerned, Pritchett unblocked himself by adopting a fictional mainstay: a plot involving a stolen necklace. The result succeeded well enough to be taken by *The New Yorker*.[34] Now, to his relief, ideas started to flow again.

Soon after finishing 'The Necklace', Pritchett wrote a new episode in the saga of his father. He called it – it called itself – 'Just a Little More'. For some years after Beatrice's death, Walter had lived with Gordon and his wife. 'Father spent most of his time in the kitchen,' Gordon later recalled, 'reading cookery books and saying, "This would be nice, wouldn't it?" '[35] In Victor's muted, subtle handling, a combination of bereavement and liberation in the recent widower, and his feelings about how to manage his new life, are revealed through his attitude to food: guilty, greedy, reminiscential. The narrative point of view is mainly that of the widower's daughter-in-law, with the effect that while the old man holds the stage, our eyes are frequently drawn to his polite but slightly impatient grandchildren and, more, to their anxious, also grieving father. There's some muted comedy in this, especially when the old man drops a hint that his sons may find enough money to send him on a world cruise, or to buy him a large house he has taken a liking to. There is pathos, too. The widower's greed, vanity and posturing don't deprive him of sympathy when he says, ambiguously, 'you look in the larder and you can't be bothered. There's a chop, a bit of bread and cheese, perhaps. And you think, well, if this is all there is in life, you may as well finish it.'[36] Portions, after all – the piece of fat the old man likes with his beef; the extra spoonfuls of sugar – are an ancient metaphor for life's span and in wanting 'just a little more', the widower also reminds himself and his family that he is no more immortal than his wife was. In ways like this, the story's characteristically downplayed, nuanced, familial tenderness offers an alternative to what Pritchett had described in *Mr Beluncle*. 'Just a Little More' is a story about three generations and their interactions, variously selfish, courteous, sceptical, worried, amused, within the walls of a true home.

The *New Yorker* fiction editor with whom Pritchett had mainly worked until the mid 1950s was Gus Lobrano. In 1956 Lobrano died and his place was temporarily taken by Katherine White. In these nervous times for Pritchett, he wasn't reassured when White almost immediately turned down 'The Snag'.[37] Soon, though, to his delight, White's son Roger Angell, who had been his enthusiastic editor at *Holiday* magazine, moved to *The New Yorker*. It was Angell who took 'The Necklace' and, although he declined Pritchett's next story, 'The Insult', 'Just a Little More' prompted a telegram of acceptance from him in 1958.[38] Encouraged, Pritchett was soon at work on a new story, one which would eventually become part of a loose sequence about English country life (prompted, perhaps, by the huge success of H. E. Bates's *Darling Buds of May*, which appeared to instant acclaim in 1958. Pritchett had known Bates since the early 1930s).[39] In these comedies – subsequently collected under the title of the first of them, 'The Key to My Heart' – he drew directly on the life he and Dorothy had recently left behind at Stokke and Wadwick while, among other things, exploring the effects of class-consciousness on English behaviour.[40] Angell accepted this story, too, which Edmund Wilson was to call 'a comic masterpiece as well as an acute *tableau de moeurs*'.[41]

Still uncertain about the directions his fiction was taking, Pritchett now returned, as so often, to something he had been working on several years earlier. 'Citizen' is a story of the mid-life psychological breakdown of an artist – the narrator's daughter, Effie – whose history of falling in love with unavailable men culminates, in a modern version of the myth of Praxiteles, in a delusion that she's being pursued by a Roman statue, the *Cittadino Essemplare* alluded to in the title. Other than the statue, Effie's latest impossible man is a schoolmaster and the nature of his impossibility is that he is homosexual. William Shawn's *New Yorker* was famously prudish and Roger Angell was charged with communicating to Pritchett that, although Shawn wanted to publish the story,

we are all a little concerned about the line on page 13, where Wilkins says, 'There has really only been one man in [my life].' When one couples this with the narrator's observation that this is 'the kind of subject that one did not discuss in my generation', it seems to indicate that this is a confession of homosexuality on the part of Wilkins. If this is what you do mean, we earnestly hope that you will consider dropping that theme.[42]

According to Angell, the problem was not 'the touchiness of the subject' but that it was irrelevant. But it was far from irrelevant and a better approach might have been to have got Pritchett to make Wilkins a more likeable character. What really doesn't work about him is the crude way in which the story guys his schoolmasterliness. From his earliest fiction, Pritchett had been drawn to exploring different kinds of sexual incompatibility and, in 'Citizen', he almost succeeds in imagining it in a new way, in relation not only to homosexuality but to the unconscious influence of a strong father on his daughter's sexuality. For the sake of the story's appearance in *The New Yorker*, he gave in to Angell's suggestions without any fuss, while – not much more satisfactorily – restoring the penultimate version when 'Citizen' appeared in book form.[43]

Pritchett's relationship with Angell was very productive and became a close friendship as well as a collaboration.[44] Angell, naturally enough, appreciated Pritchett's amenability to editorial suggestions:

In time, I came to understand that the amiable attention he gave to even the smallest cut or rephrasing in his text was not a sign of politesse or modesty, but came from the intense, almost sensual pleasure he took in every part of the writing business. . . . Writing is hard work, and Pritchett was a practitioner who didn't resent its ditchdigging days.[45]

But in situations like the one which arose over 'Citizen', such professionalism – partly imposed by the Pritchetts' financial predicament – could come close to capitulation. There were related pressures, arising from the near-insatiable appetite of the weekly *New Yorker* for good material. The acceptance of 'Citizen' soon after 'The Key to My Heart' meant that Pritchett was close to qualifying for the magazine's 'bonus for quantity', payable if three stories were taken within a twelve-month period. This bonus (there was an even bigger one for six stories in the same period) amounted to a twenty-five-per-cent increase in the fee paid, not only for the qualifying story but for the previous two.

Encouraged by Angell, and slightly bullied by his creditor Leonard Woolf, Pritchett now began to behave like a gambler.

In July his US agent, Peter Matson, sent Angell a new story, 'The Wheelbarrow'.[46] It was one of Pritchett's best – a pregnant encounter between a contained Englishwoman and a voluble Welshman, Evans, whom she hires to help clear out the house of her recently dead aunt. Through Angell, Shawn again raised questions of sexual propriety. There is a moment in the original version when Evans admires Miss Freshwater's niece's legs. It's scarcely sensational. Miss Freshwater's niece is trying on some old shoes she has found and Evans says, 'look at those legs, boy!' In its innocent relish, this rhymes convincingly with when we first saw him, in the garden, pushing a wheelbarrow, 'sometimes tipping it a little to one side to see how the rubber-tyred wheel was running and to admire it'. But Mr Shawn was unhappy about the legs and wanted them removed. Again, while the stick of potential rejection was not brandished, the carrot of yet further bonuses was: Pritchett was reminded that he still had four full months in which he could earn the higher bonus for six stories. He was about to leave for Bulgaria and Romania on a commission from *Holiday* and hurriedly conceded, joking to Angell, 'I seem to remember in one of Mary McCarthy's novels that we British are felt to be disturbingly freespoken about the body.'[47] In the book version of 'The Wheelbarrow' the legs are restored.[48]

Pritchett now quickly offered the magazine a number of stories which weren't really ready, such as 'On the Scent' – later published in *Encounter* – and what was eventually to prove one of his most successful fictions about the Second World War, 'When My Girl Comes Home'. Both were turned down, but in December 1960 *The New Yorker* renewed its 'first-reading' agreement with Pritchett, now worth $500 a year.

All this was during the Pritchetts' first five years back in London. Not since the mid 1930s had his short fiction been so fertile or so varied. Between 1956 and 1961 he published eleven stories. 'When My Girl Comes Home' gave its title to a new collection which appeared in 1961, his first since *It May Never Happen*, sixteen years earlier. Writing in the *Listener*, the young poet John Fuller described Pritchett as a 'master of the subtlest fears and aspirations of all social classes, casting them into significant detail with a patient skill that one pines for in the dull stretches of reporting that too often pass for social realism'.[49] His stories, Fuller said, 'have more poetic originality in them than satire, without losing their edge or relevance'. Meanwhile, Pritchett's new line in bucolic comedy, featuring the volatile relationship between the caddish Noisy Brackett and his impetuous wife, made up a further, overlapping volume, *The Key to My Heart*, published in 1963. Between now and his eighties, he was to bring out new collections of short stories roughly every five years, as well as a further 'Collected' and a selection.[50] He also, of course, still wrote extensively on the art of the short story both in reviews and essays.

Martin Amis was to write that Pritchett's 'method' involves an attempt 'to interpret the world through the romantic, nervous and mystical thoughts of his own characters, who are seldom remarkable except in their peculiar ordinariness. If one thing underlies his work it is the constantly dramatised proposition that ordinary people are really extraordinarily strange.'[51] If it was a method, it was one derived from empirical observation. More often than not, Pritchett had encountered in real life the strangenesses he turned into fiction. 'The Fall', first published in 1960, is a good example.[52] For years he had been mulling over something he had seen at a party for Compton Mackenzie's seventieth birthday in 1953. 'A grotesque incident took place . . .' he wrote to Brenan at the time:

> A haunted looking middle aged film producer, quite sober, threw himself on the floor and then got up. Again, he threw himself down. He was demonstrating a stage fall to anyone who happened to be interested. He did it about a dozen times which exhausted the interest of the guests; and afterwards I found him doing it alone, for his own pleasure, in another room.[53]

Pritchett's fictional version transposes the scene to the annual dinner of an association of accountants, one of whose members is a shy but vain man, first seen moving from mirror to mirror as he puts on his evening clothes. Charles Peacock's brother is a well-known actor and Charles in a way emulates him, putting on funny voices for his acquaintances, adding colour to stories about their family. 'One was entitled to a little rake off – an accountant's charges – from the fame that so often annoyed.'[54] At the party, as Charles drinks, fending off the other accountants' enquiries about his brother, he broods on their differences, especially the way that his brother, secure in his fame, tends to run down their mutual background: the father who kept a fish and chip shop, and who went bankrupt. (Was there a personal dimension, for Pritchett, to do with his siblings' feelings about his exposure of their upbringing in *Mr Beluncle*?) At any rate, Charles is caught up in his memories, so much more absorbing than the company at dinner – at least until conversation turns to the subject of the association's president, who has had a fall.

After the toasts, as people are getting ready to leave, Charles begins to face his loneliness: 'He, who feared occasions, feared even more their dissolution.'[55] One thing he has learned from his brother is how to do a stage fall. Now, with the thin pretext of the president's accident, he looks around dignifiedly, lets 'the expression die on his face' and measures his length on the floor. Before anyone can speak, he is up again, only to repeat the process once, twice, five times.

The episode is thickly textured. There's Charles's physical pleasure, on a hot evening after a lot of food and drink, in simply lying on the carpet. And there are his undulations of mood as he both responds to and despises his new audience – especially an inoffensive man who earlier befriended him, and who enrages him by trying to persuade him not to do the fall yet again and offering him a lift home. Charles escapes into a private room, where, alone, he repeats his little exploit in front of a picture of Queen Victoria: his own version of the Loyal Toast.

That private room in 'The Fall' seems like a metaphor for the writer's study: 'a small, high room, quite empty and yet (one would have said), packed with voices. . . .'[56] Like Charles, Pritchett himself still combined a performative sort of sociability with a keen need to be alone. In his case, solitude enabled him to absorb and reorder the imaginative stimuli which the slightest encounter generally gave him. He was always on the lookout for behavioural surprises, promising scraps of conversation, in the street, in a shop. He had plenty of time for strangers – people like the ones he described in *London Perceived*: a woman who dances on the pavement in Haymarket, or another who collects ecclesiastical rarities and old books and newspapers, and whom Pritchett often helped to carry her bundles from the bus stop.[57] It was in his study, though, that Pritchett made these people and situations most real to himself, dealing with the world by escaping from it. He told Brenan, 'I remember vividly thinking when I was reading something in my teens and was very unhappy, that I need never be *totally* unhappy in life, because I could read or write.'[58] Perhaps they were bad habits: 'literature is such a dream world. It closes the doors. One is shut in comfortably with self-love.' Still, he continued to insist on them.

The routine at 12 Regent's Park Terrace was absolutely regular.

Oliver Pritchett calls it 'the working method'. Some time between 7 and 7.30, Victor went downstairs and made the morning tea. *The Times* and the *Daily Mail* had already been pushed through the letter box, and he took them and the tea tray back to bed where, with Dorothy, he caught up with the news and made a first attempt at the *Times* crossword. Then he returned to the kitchen and, in a haphazard way, made his own breakfast. It was the only meal he cooked – usually bacon and egg with toast, the egg yolk often broken, the toast often burned. Next, he took another pot of tea to Dorothy, had a bath and, around 9, in his own phrase, 'clocked on'. From then on his surroundings had to be quiet. In the early years at Regent's Park Terrace his study was a little room at the rear, on the first floor. But this was too noisy when children played in the gardens behind, so he moved his main workplace to the top of the house, a steep climb to the third floor, with its view over 'the flaking plane trees, the seeding poplars, the weeping elms, the chestnuts'.[59]

Wherever V. S. Pritchett worked, his first ritual was to light a pipe. (He smoked Gold Block and surrounded himself, as the day went on, with dead matches.) Second, he arranged an old pastry board across the arms of his comfortable chair. There he wrote all morning while, in the ground-floor dining room, Dorothy followed her own long-familiar routines in the partnership, typing at the window, keeping an eye on the Terrace's comings and goings, dealing with correspondence and telephone calls, and cooking. At around 1, Dorothy, or – when they were at home – Josephine or Oliver, would call Victor down for an old-fashioned English meat-and-vegetables lunch, preceded on his part by a martini. The crossword was resumed. After this, the couple rested, Dorothy upstairs in bed for most of the afternoon, Victor – generally in the first-floor library – for about an hour. Then he made more tea, before going round the corner to the Cypriot grocers ('The Brothers Karamazov') in Parkway, or to the tobacconist ('Much Obliged'). Peter Vansittart, who lived nearby, often used to see him queuing with his shopping bags, 'chatting enormously to everyone around'.

The remaining two hours before supper at 7 were spent working – as also, very often, was the time between supper and bed. When Josephine and Oliver were around, there might be games in the sitting room: Scrabble, or cards – Racing Demon, and a game called Spite and Malice. When they were alone, Dorothy liked to watch television in the evenings, Victor less so, but he usually saw the news and enjoyed David Attenborough's natural history programmes and the occasional football match. He also had an appetite for comedy shows and was a particular fan of the lewdly insinuating entertainer Benny Hill. (When an admirer of Pritchett's, the jazz musician, librettist and critic Benny Green, asked him to inscribe one of his books, Green found to his mild mortification that Pritchett had written 'To Benny Hill . . .').[60]

About once a week Victor lunched or dined at the Savile. He also usually went to the monthly literary lunch club at Bertorelli's in Charlotte Street, along with Al Alvarez, Stephen Spender, Freddie Ayer and another philosopher, Richard Wollheim, the travel writer Patrick Leigh Fermor, the painter William Coldstream, the novelist Peter Vansittart and occasionally Graham Greene. Dorothy liked to get him out of the house: it was good for him and she had engagements of her own, not least to do with AA. There would be an errand for him on the way back – dry cleaning to pick up, coffee to buy. With the knack for these things that he had inherited from Walter, he stopped some-times to buy Dorothy a dress, or a piece of jewellery. (He was 'brilliant' at this, his granddaughter Georgia later recalled.) He often went on foot, retreading long-familiar paths: Charlotte Street itself was where, in another world, he had once lived with Evelyn. On his return, Dorothy seemed always avid for his 'news' and he would give an animated account of whom he had met and what they had said: 'quite a cabaret', according to Oliver.

The couple also regularly went out for dinner together, either to a restaurant – L'Escargot in Greek Street, L'Etoile in Charlotte Street, Chez Victor in Wardour Street, or to his club. There were occasional literary parties and receptions: book launches, prize givings. And they were favourite guests of their many friends, not least Margot Walmsley, with her Earls Court salon. There were, too, dinner parties and lunch parties of their own: for the Brenans, the Partridges, Victor's old *New Statesman* colleague Janet Adam Smith, the historian Veronica Wedgwood, Al Alvarez and his new wife, Arthur Crook of the *TLS* and his partner Juliet Wrightson, American visitors like the Angells and Pritchett's US publisher, Jason Epstein. They took pains on these occasions. The food, which Dorothy always cooked, was traditional and good, and the wine well chosen by Victor from the cellar of his club. Alvarez says that his first experience of 'great wine' was a claret Victor produced over dinner in Regent's Park Terrace. Peter Vansittart also recalled 'excellent wines, and a good deal of drink beforehand. Dorothy and V.S. unobtrusively kept everything sort of in control.'

One aspect of the quiet control noticed by Vansittart was, of course, that Dorothy now never drank alcohol – though she seemed to enjoy parties more than ever. Another was the fact that, for Victor, any social event was something that came both after and before work. He was always attentive to his guests. But, as Roger Angell put it, while he 'never showed the dazed, half-there look of the mid-book author – he was too considerate for that – . . . it was understood by everyone who cared about him that his main engagement always awaited him'.[61]

Defended by these routines, back in the seclusion of his smoke-filled study, Pritchett studied his notebooks and contemplated what he could use from them. Often, as with 'The Fall', such ruminations went on over years. His 1960 story, 'When My Girl Comes Home', is another example, having originated in a chance conversation as long ago as 1948. The Pritchetts had been living at the time in Parkhill Road, near Camden, and perhaps it was their return to the area which reminded him of it now. The woman who cleaned for them in those days had told Pritchett how her elderly, poor sister-in-law had been 'slaving to the bone' to welcome home her prodigal daughter, who had been away for twenty-five years in Japan. When she arrived, far from falling on her mother's mercy, the supposedly helpless woman astonished everyone by being confident, beautiful, apparently well educated, with excellent manners and 'speaking three languages'. She had had two children by different fathers, one Indian, one Japanese.[62]

It took Pritchett so long to develop this situation imaginatively that one of the objections to the finished story at The New Yorker was that it seemed dated.[63] It's true that its immediate circumstances and confusions derived from the Second World War. What if the daughter's family had imagined that, during the war, she had been imprisoned by the Japanese? There might have been a campaign to get her back, friends and neighbours writing to the Red Cross. The newspapers might have taken it up. How would these people have felt, what would they have done, if the emaciated victim of their imaginings turned out to be this healthy, vivid adventuress – turned out, in fact, to have been a collaborator, married to a rich Japanese? And how, in turn, would she respond as she not only learned about her family's wartime privations and losses, but discovered that their sense of her own situation had been so far from the truth?

These musings developed into one of the richest and longest of his stories. Some of its details arrived entirely by accident. The natural confusion in Hilda Johnson's family between her first husband, Singh, and her second, Shinji, for example, was suggested by the name of an art historian in Tokyo which Pritchett happened on in a book about Japanese sculpture, on the shelves of the *New Statesman*.[64] Through the story's attention to such minutiae, the reader comes to know a family, even a small neighbourhood: what its members have experienced, their resentments and imaginings and inconsequentialities, and what they reveal about the operations of anyone's mind. A passage Pritchett wrote not long afterwards about Hogarth's cartoons can be applied to his own technique:

> His people have the subdued hum of mundane living in their ears. . . . At first sight he is prosaic; then we notice the subtlety of texture, the minute sensuous brilliance of selected detail. He respects his subjects. Ordinary or uncouth, his women breathe. He draws the person. He has the Londoner's ruminative satisfaction in character and in the comedies of self-respect.

He could be describing his own sense, in 'When My Girl Comes Home', of the worked-up little drama and of people's wish to get in on the act – people like Hilda's uncle and aunt, the Fulminos:

> 'She was in the last coach of the train, wasn't she Mother?' Mr Fulmino said to Mrs Johnson. He called her 'mother' for the occasion, celebrating her joy.
> 'Yes,' said Mrs Johnson. 'Yes,' Her voice scraped and trembled.
> 'In the last coach, next the van. We went right up the platform, we thought we'd missed her, didn't we? She was,' he exclaimed with acquisitive pride, 'in the First Class.'
> 'Like you missed me coming from Penzance,' said Mrs Fulmino swelling powerfully. . . . [65]

One of the story's main themes is the human need, expressed in conversations like this, for a sense of emotional significance in which concepts of what's relevant, what truly 'matters', even what's truly true, don't apply. (Harold Pinter, whose plays first began to appear in the late 1950s, seems to have learned from Pritchett's use of this device.)[66] Mrs Johnson's faith that her girl would come home, a matter of admiring pity among her friends, hasn't been misplaced, though everything she and, in different ways, they attached to it was: its factual basis, its moral meaning. And, whatever each of them comes to understand individually from Hilda's mix of frankness and fantasy, they collectively choose to sustain their mutual dream – a decision reinforced by equally fictional newspaper headlines: 'A Mother's Faith. Four Years in Japanese Torture Camp. London Girl's Ordeal'.

It could easily have been no more than another ingenious story about self-delusion, individual and collective, but something else is going on. In Pritchett's fiction, as he put it much later to Al Alvarez, 'The cat is never quite on the mat, as far as I am concerned.'[67] The collision which seems to have been set up between Hilda and Bill Williams, who has been in a labour camp, turns into something more conspiratorial. Bill, it transpires, has a second career as a thief. Even this war hero can't be taken at face value – a subdued revelation which ties in with another thread, about war, enmity and guilt.

Most of those who learn the truth about Hilda have something on their own post-war conscience, even if it's only a ration-book fraud. And to the characters who saw most of the action – Bill Williams, Jack Draper – the issue between the two sides is at a human level much less clear-cut than the others want it to be. As the narrator says, 'where we thought of the war as something done to us and our side, Jack thought of it as something done to everybody.'[68] This powerfully sympathetic, non-moralising sense of who does what to whom is in turn linked to another dimension, often hinted at in Pritchett's work (and here perhaps a shade too explicit), about colonialism. Hilda's sexual adventures began with that already colonised man, Mr Singh; later, back in London, she takes up with a West Indian.

Meanwhile, in appropriating her story to their own wishes, her family and their friends have been doing a kind of colonising of their own, about which the narrator is explicit – for example, when he refers to 'Mr Fulmino's uncontrollable . . . gift for colonising' and says that his attitude to Hilda, his niece, is as if she were 'a secret fortification somewhere east of Suez'.[69] These are, the story suggests, connections and procedures characteristic of England, and especially of London. 'Knock on the doors of half the houses in London and you will find people with relations all over the world,' we are told,[70] and the tale is in part an exploration of the paradoxical link between this cosmopolitanism and the city's intense localness: the fact that any permutation of street, pub, bus route, can form a world.

The post-colonial dimension of 'When My Girl Comes Home' may have been influenced by a trip to India on which Pritchett was sent by the British Council in 1960, to attend a series of literary events in which the other participants included Vladimir Nabokov, as well as Pritchett's friend Stephen Spender and the young John Wain. Pritchett particularly enjoyed Nabokov's irreverent company. Whatever the sympathies of Pritchett's fiction, and also of his criticism – which had always been responsive to writers from former British colonies – he found the Indians he met in person antipathetic. 'So far I just hate . . . their smoky whispers and twitterings and their awful sofa-like softness,' he wrote to Dorothy. 'I can't get used to the men's nappies.' He was delighted that Nabokov felt similarly, bellowing in their hotel bar that 'there is a Russian phrase for their writhing whispering manner which, translated, is "working your finger up your arse without soap"'.[71]

'When My Girl Comes Home' is about many different things, and has an original take on the theme of post-war return and adjustment, but it's above all a story – a prose poem – about London. Increasingly, the city to which Pritchett had at last returned from his wanderings, and other cities which had mattered to him, were to become his main preoccupation. He was, he had often felt, essentially 'a documentary writer'. It puzzled him when critics said that his fictional characters were bizarre or extravagant, because, to him, '"normal" people of the lower middle class – which is my country – have the characteristics I describe'.[72] He had come to recognise, if only because others so often saw it this way, that his work was 'naturally intense, romantic & fantastic'. He once told Brenan that he saw Frances Partridge's husband Ralph

> not as [a] well-built grey-haired man with a booming voice, but as an elephant trumpeting, a bishop sly in canonicals who has been fiddling about with the Real Presence, or when he wears his check overcoat, as a dangerous thing in charge of a concentration camp. Untrue impressions, damaging, fantastic – though not damaging from my point of view. They make him seem more alive. The satire is meant to be festive, an amplification of life.[73]

And he enjoyed the Irish writer Frank O'Connor's joke that he, Pritchett, wrote about English people anthropologically, as if they were South American tribes being interpreted to educated Russians.

At heart, though, what Pritchett was interested in was what he saw as the truth. In London in his late fifties and early sixties he rediscovered a kind of truth which he had known since childhood: one in which the humdrum and the caricatural merged. In 1960 Walter died and, although Victor would write about him again, especially in his memoirs, the event freed him of the compulsion to do so, while heightening his imaginative absorption in the wider physical and human world father and son had shared.

In October 1960, an opportunity to write factually about London fell into his lap. Mary McCarthy had had a success with a book about Florence, the text accompanied by pictures taken by Evelyn Hofer, a gifted photographer just starting her career. Its publisher, William Jovanovich at Harcourt Brace, proposed to Ian Parsons at Chatto and Windus a Pritchett–Hofer collaboration on London.[74] Parsons saw various obstacles. Chatto were still waiting for the book on Latin America for which they had paid Pritchett an advance. Besides, Parsons anticipated that Pritchett's main publisher in the USA, Alfred Knopf, might not take kindly to this involvement with another house. Apart from the 1956 *Collected Stories* (for the most part made up of work published in other books), neither publisher had had anything new from Pritchett since *The Spanish Temper* in 1954. In the nick of time, Pritchett delivered a strong new collection, made up entirely of work done since the move to Regent's Park Terrace. It took its title from 'When My Girl Comes Home' and included eight other stories. Knopf was sufficiently appeased not to obstruct the Harcourt Brace proposal. The London end of the publishing deal, Heinemann, agreed to co-publish with Chatto and the Americans came up with a handsome $5000 advance. With relief, Pritchett paid back the last instalments of what he owed Leonard Woolf and Kingsley Martin.

Meanwhile, he met Evelyn Hofer and they instantly got on. Short, slightly jowly, reserved but expressive, with immensely lively eyes, she could have been Pritchett's younger sister, but for a German accent unaltered by decades abroad. Her anti-Nazi businessman father had taken the family away from Hesse in the 1930s, and they had subsequently lived in Republican Spain and then in Mexico. Evelyn had gone on alone to the United States to make a career as a photographer at *Harper's Bazaar*, and had married an Englishman. Her previous book, which Mary McCarthy, with a nod to Ruskin, called *The Stones of Florence*, had appeared in 1959.

First published in 1962 and several times reprinted,[75] *London Perceived* (as far as the author's own situation was concerned, 'London Retrieved' might have been a better title) is one of the main fruits of half a century's thinking about the city where Pritchett was brought up. The other is *A Cab at the Door*, published six years later. As Pritchett put it himself, he was old enough to have ridden in a horse tram and to have been run over by a hansom cab, while having lived to see the effects on the city of the triumph of the welfare state, as well as of the end of the British Empire.[76] Between these two London-based books, he published meditations on other cities, also with pictures by Evelyn Hofer: *New York Proclaimed* in 1965, *Dublin: A Portrait* in 1967. A collection of shorter pieces, published in Britain under the title *Foreign Faces* and in the USA as *The Offensive Traveller* (1964), included essays on Seville and Madrid. And in 1971, Pritchett's love affair with Paris would be commemorated in *Midnight Oil*. These books represent the larger part of his output over a decade – albeit a decade in which he also published new volumes of literary criticism and of short stories, as well as an unreduced tally of journalism.

He continued to travel widely, but the long, adventurous explorations of his early days were behind him. Inevitably, too, these city books have a literary aspect: over the years, fictional encounters with London – those of characters in Dickens, or in stories by the Wapping-born humorist W. W. Jacobs – had become almost as real to Pritchett as historical ones. But *London Perceived* isn't a view from an armchair. If the narrator is more a flâneur than a hiker, much of the book's drama, especially in the long middle section following the Thames upstream from its estuary, comes from movement. With its echoes of Dickens, Conrad and Eliot, this is the last important account in which the Thames could still be treated as a busy thoroughfare, and all the more elegiac for its unawareness that what's being described with such vivid life will, any year now, be gone for ever:

Twenty-three miles of industrial racket, twenty-three miles of cement works, paper-mills, power stations, dock basins, cranes and conveyors shattering to the ear. From now on, no silence. In the bar at the Clarendon Royal, at Gravesend, once a house built for a duke's mistress, it is all talk of up-anchoring, and everyone has one eye on the ships going down as the ebb begins, at the rate of two a minute. The tugs blaspheme. One lives in an orchestra of chuggings, whinings, the clanking and croaking of anchors, the spinning of winches, the fizz of steam, and all kinds of shovellings, rattlings, and whistlings, broken once in a while by a loud human voice shouting an unprintable word. Opposite are the liners like hotels, waiting to go to Africa, India, the Far East; down come all the traders of Europe and all the flags from Finland to Japan. . . .

Inevitably, as a book originally intended for American readers, *London Perceived* covers ground which some natives find overfamiliar: London as an aggregation of villages; the *rus in urbe* aspect – parks, squares, gardens; cockney rhyming slang. And after the extraordinarily flexible shifts of vantage point in the first eighty pages, the second half seems too tied to chronology: one could do with the playful freedom of Virginia Woolf's *Orlando*, with which the history often intersects. There's another problem, common to all the books Pritchett did with Hofer: although the text and the pictures are generally in sympathy, they aren't directly tied to each other. Pritchett suggested a few subjects and, in the case of the pictures of servants in the Garrick Club, may have helped to make the arrangements. He certainly fixed up the wonderful one of a man in a bowler hat – part gentleman, part gentleman's gentleman – sitting at the bar of the Red Lion in Duke of York Street, cufflinks and tie perfectly calculated, cigarette in mouth, hand round a pewter mug, umbrella hanging beside him, his gaze solid, yet melancholy, and firmly averted from a riot of cut-glass mirrors in the background. The subject was Victor's brother Cyril. For the most part, though, writer and photographer were both jealous of their independence and, while they became friends, they didn't work together and didn't discuss the projects. (Hofer, in fact, never read the books, though she enjoyed Pritchett's stories. And Pritchett said he regarded himself as 'my own inner photographer'.)[77]

The book avoids the merely dutiful – indeed, avoids altogether many of the more usual destinations of a tourist guide: art galleries and museums, for example – and is often very original. Pritchett's Betjemanesque enthusiasm for the London of the Victorian Gothic revival was ahead of its time and is conveyed, even by his own standards, with outstanding brio: Tower Bridge as 'a cross between a pair of Baptist chapels and Rhineland fortresses . . . a bridge suitable for King Arthur',[78] or the mix of dignity and frivolity in Barry and Pugin's Houses of Parliament:

> Its aspect changes with the hours of the day, so that it has a processional and transient lightness. From the river the long sand-brown façade has restraint and regularity, is serious, yet without heaviness. Then the eye is raised to the roof level, and the spires and turrets seem to break out into a pageant-like trooping of lances and banners, at some fantastic Field of the Cloth of Gold. They glitter. One can imagine the trumpets of heralds. . . .[79]

With his traveller's eye for what's so obvious at home that it goes unnoticed, Pritchett points out in this passage, near the book's end, that the Houses of Parliament have 'members', not representatives – which brings him back to where he began: with the paradox of London's clubbable privacy, its visible gardens open only to residents, the social nuances of the different bars in pubs, the monastic separateness of the ancient inns of court, the deceptiveness of gentlemen's clubs, their wide steps leading up to misleadingly open front doors.[80] It was a theme which Pritchett was well placed to write about. He was one of those people who, though they have come, as the English used to say, 'from nowhere', have found – as his father had longed but failed to find – that there is room for talent and industry in those closed gardens and up the club steps.[81]

Pritchett's work was going well, Dorothy was still not drinking and the children were on their way. But his new stability wasn't invulnerable. In December 1960, Barbara Kerr got in touch. She wondered whether Victor might be coming to New York and suggested that, if so, she might see him – perhaps with Dorothy. His reply was uncharacteristically blunt:

Dear Barbara,

I am glad to hear that things are going well for you. They are also, for me. What else can I say? A lot, of course, but I've no idea what you are like these days, nor have you any idea of what I am except that I'm 60 and very glad the Fifties are over. . . . I have no notion of coming to New York and, of course (if you will reflect upon it for a moment) you will understand that it is impossible that you should meet Dorothy & me there or anywhere ever. I have no news that you would understand. Love from

Victor.[82]

More than forty years later, and five years after Victor's death, whenever Barbara recalled this letter her eyes would fill with tears.

Some of the news that he so woundingly told Barbara she wouldn't have understood was communicated, instead, to Gerald. Oliver had gone to Oxford 'and already his mind expands'. Josephine, to her parents' surprise, married an army officer working in Military Intelligence. Victor described Brian Murphy as 'a gay, intelligent fellow, fat, short-sighted and a bit of a dandy, a very odd sort of soldier and very nice'.[83] Soon, the couple moved to Cyprus, where Brian was stationed.

When Jo had her first child – a boy named Justin – Dorothy went out to help. Victor stayed behind at Regent's Park Road, with Oliver to look after him. Olly was a very capable cook, Victor told Dorothy ('Stands in front of the grill with a pack of cards in his hand, overheats the plates in the best tradition and is very cheerful'), while adding that they had eaten out often, at Bertorelli's, L'Escargot, the French Club and the Swiss restaurant, as well as at the Savile.[84] Dorothy, meanwhile, was amused to bump into a member of her Alcoholics Anonymous group at Athens airport. For a time, the couple's roles were reversed – 'It is strange *you* being away,' Victor told her – and they enjoyed the change. But they both wanted a life with less separateness in it and the next time he had to work abroad they went together.

9

The Together

Early in 1962 the Pritchetts travelled to southern California, where Victor spent a semester teaching at Berkeley. It was their first experience of California and hers of any kind of campus life, but after some days of jet-lagged insomnia and homesickness, compounded by storms and 'two or three dullish dinner parties with heavy-handed Profs',[1] they began to enjoy themselves. Victor liked his students, and anyway his teaching responsibilities were light. He bought an open-topped car and, after Dorothy had taken a few lessons to get her used to American highways ('frightful . . . a sort of motor race, with cars shooting about one by the score. . . . It would suit Al. . . .'), she successfully passed her local driving test. They went to the Hungry I to see the satirical comedian Mort Sahl and attended a lunch ('at 11.15!!!') for President Kennedy, who was on a visit to the university. Kennedy 'looked young, energetic and delightful', Dorothy wrote to Oliver, 'and spoke far better than the local academic Ponderosities'.[2]

Before long, they were being entertained in Hollywood. Alfred Hitchcock – Victor's contemporary and, like him, from a lower-middle-class background on the fringe of London – was filming *The Birds* in Bodega Bay and sent a chauffeur-driven Cadillac to collect the couple for dinner. It was a vivid evening. Pritchett wrote afterwards that Hitchcock 'looks, I always think, like a ripe Victoria plum endowed with the gift of speech'.[3] In between signing autographs, 'Hitch' asked 'Vic', as he insisted on calling him, if he would give him an opinion on the screenplay of Daphne du Maurier's story. He added that he was interested in turning Pritchett's 'The Wheelbarrow' into a movie. A week's holiday at the Hitchcocks' house in Santa Cruz soon followed, the Pritchetts sleeping, as a star-struck Dorothy told her son-in-law, 'where Cary Grant, Ingrid Bergman, James Stewart and Grace Kelly had slept before us'. Later, after Victor had given a lecture at Pomona

College, to the east of Los Angeles, their new friend arranged a studio tour for them.[4]

Pritchett had done some film making during the war, not only in documentaries but with a lightly propagandist short drama scripted by him called *Two Fathers*, released shortly before the Normandy invasion. (It's about a Frenchman and an Englishman forced to share a hotel room. After their initial suspicions, they discover various links and grounds for mutual respect – each of them has lost a child to the war – but the focus is on a more bathetic kind of ordinariness which they have in common: their unprepossessing underclothes, the care with which the Englishman, played by Bernard Miles, brushes his hair.)[5] Still, some of his reactions to *The Birds* were more literary than filmic.[6] Not allowing for the effects of casting and performance on the script, he tended to assume that where there were problems with characterisation the solutions would inevitably require more writing. He also found the love story and the thriller insufficiently tied together: the narrative, he said, 'tends to split dangerously in two'. While he wasn't bothered by the improbability of some aspects – especially the women's making the panic-stricken children leave the school building, where they seem safe enough, and run home through the attacking crows and gulls – he did point out that the end was unsatisfactorily abrupt.

Various changes were made to Evan Hunter's script on the basis of Pritchett's five-page critique. The character of Mitch's former girl-friend, the schoolteacher Annie, whom Pritchett found 'goody-goody' and too 'obligingly good-natured' in the original version, was given more edge, and the film's ending, though still somewhat perfunctory, was filled out so as to answer at least some of his questions. (The fact that we see no one except the surviving main characters fleeing the town was explained, for example, by the addition of a radio news bulletin which mentions that most of the inhabitants have already got out.) Pritchett also suggested that the hold Mitch's mother has over him might be balanced by filling out Melanie's background, so as to explain, and also add to, a sense of her waywardness. In the original he thought Melanie 'insipid': 'I know that it is a convention that the characters in a thriller must not be so strongly characterised that they divert the audience from the thrills of fear and suspense that are the overwhelming interesting [*sic*] of the story,' he hurriedly wrote,

> and that the very mildness of the people accentuates the effect of the horror they will undergo. But if the people are under-characterised

the story will fall apart when the terror strikes; one will get the impression that they are in two different stories – in this case a light comedy and a terror tale – that do not weld together . . . We gather . . . that Melanie has had real wild potentialities. It is true that she is mischievous and that her love affair amuses because it is an affair between a mischievous girl and a prig; but I think a lot might [be] gained . . . by making her wildness more evident.

Hitchcock worked on this in directorial ways – putting a lot of screeching tyres, for example, into Melanie's drive from San Francisco to Bodega Bay – but he also asked Pritchett to add some new dialogue. The result was the scene in the sand dunes during the children's party, when Melanie tells Mitch she has been teaching 'four letter words' to a mina bird that she's going to give to a straitlaced aunt, and ('Very pained and with sudden violence') reveals that her mother 'ditched us when I was eleven, went off with some hotel man in the East'.

Pritchett's name doesn't appear in the credits of *The Birds* and the film doesn't escape his initial criticisms, several of which were to be made independently by reviewers. Stanley Kauffmann, for example, wrote, 'The dialogue is stupid, the characters insufficiently developed to rank as clichés, the story incohesive.'[7] But the improvements Pritchett was at least partly responsible for were significant and contributed to the film's popular success. Meanwhile, there was the question of 'The Wheelbarrow'.

The problem with it for Hitchcock was: not enough sex, not enough action. Where William Shawn had baulked at Evans's admiring Miss Freshwater's niece's legs, Alfred Hitchcock wanted rape and murder. Evans might – might he not? – make sexual advances and, in the ensuing struggle, either kill or be killed by his employer. Privately aghast at, while not unamused by, the suggestion, Pritchett nonetheless did his best with it.[8] Where, in the published story, Miss Freshwater's niece indulges Evans's longing for the wheelbarrow, Pritchett now tried a new turn in the plot. She decides to put the wheelbarrow up for auction, together with her aunt's other effects. Evans pursues both it and his employer. There's a scuffle among the piled-up odds and ends, and she defends herself with an old ice skate. Bleeding, Evans rushes at Miss Freshwater's niece and she falls backwards into a big trunk, whereupon he shuts her into it. She rapidly suffocates. After some moments of panic, Evans calms himself and uses the wheelbarrow to take the trunk out to the bonfire, where he burns it and his victim, before setting off, as at the end of the original story, to preach hellfire at the local mission. In a second version the death is reversed. Miss Freshwater's niece survives the tussle and it's Evans who falls into the trunk and is trapped. His son turns up to look for him and, before the woman can stop him, helpfully tips the trunk on to the bonfire with the other rubbish. Hitchcock didn't take either attempt any further, but the possibility that he might have done added some excitement to the Pritchetts' lives.

In May, the Berkeley semester ended and the couple set off on a slow journey back to England, travelling along the west coast from San Francisco to Seattle, up the Sound to Vancouver and then on across Canada. The trip was again organised and paid for by *Holiday*, with sponsorship from Pan-Am. Pritchett later wrote well about it,[9] his British perceptions about what was involved in being Canadian sharpened both by his earlier brief experience of the country, in his twenties, and by his having arrived there this time by way of California. He quickly saw that the American idea of a social melting pot didn't apply in Canada – perhaps didn't really apply anywhere. In the medium term, at least, the situation seemed to him a matter of the peaceful coexistence of almost entirely separate cultures, rather than of full assimilation. The Poles, Dutch, Germans and Italians whom he met remained Poles, Dutch, Germans and Italians. 'Canada does not easily melt. . . . Canadianization does not exist as a principle or practice.'[10]

Pritchett had become more than usually sensitive to the impulse to hang on to one's cultural identity, partly as a result of his feelings about his return to London, partly because of his always strong but, as he grew older, increasing resistance to change, and partly through the effects of living abroad with Dorothy for the first time. She was fascinated by North America: by the mixture of resemblances with and differences from what she was accustomed to. And meanwhile both were getting more used to the advantages of the special relationship between Victor's work and its American audience. 'In Europe, the proper medicine for artists is felt to be acid, ironical discouragement,' he wrote in a draft for what was to become *Midnight Oil*. 'I have had, all my life, a regard for American positiveness and warmth.'[11] He had, of course, been heavily dependent on his US market ever since he started writing for the *Christian Science Monitor* and now once again made significantly more of his income in the USA than in Britain. But he wasn't always conscious of how far the literary-economic balance of power in general had shifted and, despite the evidence of his own situation, it struck him as odd that many Canadian writers 'cannot earn a living in their own country'.[12] In the coming twenty years, what with commissions involving US travel and a number of visiting academic appointments, the USA was in practice to be his and Dorothy's second home. No sooner had they returned to England in time for the publication of *London Perceived*,[13] than they were planning a return to New York, where Pritchett prepared the second of his city books with Evelyn Hofer.

The Pritchetts stayed at first with Mary McCarthy's ex-husband Bowden Broadwater, at his apartment on East 94th Street: directly above Roger Angell and his wife Carol – and very close to Barbara Kerr, who now lived on East 92nd. In June 1963 Victor wrote to Norah Smallwood saying Dorothy was enjoying New York and that they were both 'very hot, very happy. . . .'[14] He was doing what he had always loved: 'tramping the streets and gradually . . . filling up my notebook'.[15] They spent talkative evenings with various friends at Sardi's, the Century, the Algonquin. Pritchett had always responded to the city's luxuries ('one becomes *un corrompu*,' he wrote, to explain why he had never lived in Greenwich Village),[16] as well as to its traditional historic aspects. As in his London book, he became absorbed in the relation of Manhattan to its surrounding water. He saw more, too, of the hybridity which he had described earlier in Canada, noticing that poorer immigrants hang on to the cultural habits which those who get rich discard, so that in the lives of the poor – in this instance, particularly of respectable people in Harlem – you can see the past of a place surviving.[17]

As ever, he brought a fantastical imaginative response to the most familiar sights. On the glazed floor of the concourse in Grand Central Station, 'your footsteps whisper and voices are remote like a distant liturgy. The doors of the elevators silently open and dumb-struck people come out mysteriously from somewhere above, as if New Yorkers were being born every minute, fully grown, in the sky.'[18] That awkward juxtaposition of 'remote' and 'distant' is an example of some occasional slacknesses in the writing, but the main impact, as in all of Pritchett's best travel books – even *Marching Spain* – comes from his reacting as if newly to what he has long loved and pondered. It was almost forty years since he had first written about the miracle of the elevator. For readers in the twenty-first century, of course, *New York Proclaimed* has an extra dimension in being prelapsarian – or, rather, preconstructionist: the World Trade Center had not only not yet fallen, it was still to be built.

Coming as Pritchett did from what was to him the still vivid experience of the Blitz, he tended to exaggerate the peacefulness of Manhattan's history. But the contrast also heightened his awareness of the city's vulnerability, especially at a time of widespread fears about nuclear war. Like everyone else, he mistook the danger, but he was ominously clear that there *was* one: 'New Yorkers understand that at any moment it could be destroyed as easily as any other place in the world. It is linked to the common lot of the smashable.'[19]

Prophecy apart, there may be an echo of how narrowly his own life escaped a smash just now. Dorothy returned to London before Victor and, in her absence, he had one last fling with Barbara. The affair had rekindled the previous year when, on one of her trips to London, Barbara had got in touch again. He had failed to resist that time, though the reunion had at first depressed him: 'after the first glow of seeing you, I faced the reality that 9 years has gone clean out of our knowledge of each other.' But it had also revived his feeling for her: 'It's so painful and extraordinary that nevertheless you inhabit my mind.'[20] He sent flowers to her hotel and gave her a copy of *London Perceived*, drawing her attention to the picture of Cyril in the Red Lion. The pub had associations for them: it was 'where I once took you for a rapid glass of sherry before we went to Kew. . . . Oh, I wish tonight it could happen all over again!'[21] Now, in the Hotel Elysée on East 54th Street, he was thrilled to find Barbara 'printed on my body again, every delicious inch of you. . . . that devastating vision of a seventeen year old girl marvellously unspoiled by the years'.[22]

The cumulative intensity of their times together in the city over the years seems to be hinted at near the end of *New York Proclaimed*, in a shift of tense and in the ambiguous use of the second person:

> You slide away in your taxi, turning your head sadly at side streets . . . you smell the smell of New York – for me, sweet. . . . In winter you had seen the skaters at Rockefeller Center and in the park; they were, it seemed, skating on champagne. In the spring or autumn, you had walked feeling your veins and arteries were alight. The traffic seemed to have carpets under its wheels.

'I live for the moment,' the briefly re-infatuated sixty-two-year-old wrote to Barbara, 'especially the dangerous emotional moment, in spite of my solid (?) qualities.' On his return to London, writing from the safety of the Savile Club, he sent her a love poem in the manner of John

Donne, which he had written in the Elysée.[23] But those 'solid qualities' gradually reasserted themselves, the question mark disappeared and, although he and Barbara continued to correspond for a while, they never saw each other again.

At Regent's Park Terrace in 1963, life was resumed much as before. Oliver – who, with his father's help, was starting to find his way into journalism – had kept an eye on the house while he and his mother were away. Josephine and Brian had returned to England in 1961, when their family had grown again with the birth of a daughter, Olivia. A third child, Caspar, came in September 1963. Victor and Dorothy never fully adjusted to having a spy as a son-in-law but, given Victor's anti-Soviet sympathies, he could scarcely complain about the nature of Brian's work. Brian left the army in 1964 and the young family moved to London, so Victor and Dorothy were able to see more of the grandchildren. Victor embarked on a series of comic cartoons for them, depicting crocodiles and mythical bird-beasts called kobulas, and figuring in them himself as 'Granpa Kokokobula'.

He still worked unflaggingly, though his role at the *New Statesman* seemed to him to have diminished slightly since the arrival of Karl Miller as literary editor in 1961. Pritchett had for a long time been the *éminence grise* of the paper's back half. Under Miller's predecessor, Janet Adam Smith, he had taken his pick of the books, while being consulted about who should review those he didn't choose for himself. Miller was his own man and wanted to widen the cast of reviewers, bringing in versatile young critics including (a change which was affecting all literary pages) more people with university connections: Anita Brookner, D. J. Enright, John Gross, Frank Kermode, Christopher Ricks. The policy caused some resentment among older readers and contributors accustomed to the belletristic approach which Miller wanted to get away from.[24] All the same, Miller was conscious of what he later described as Pritchett's 'unparalleled access to the public' and continued to get him to write for the paper. While Pritchett was at Berkeley, for example, he had contributed a 'Books in General' essay on Sainte-Beuve and an enthusiastic review of Gerald Brenan's *A Life of One's Own*, as well as pieces on biography, on the literature of the American West, on Italo Svevo, Maxim Gorky and Max Beerbohm. It didn't seem quite enough. 'No books. Nothing to graze on,' he complained to Miller, on the back of a picture postcard of some cows.[25] But gradually the new editor–reviewer relationship settled down and, when

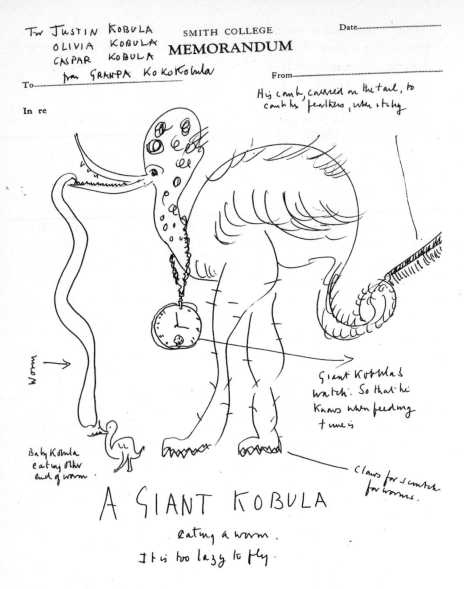

To JUSTIN KOBULA
OLIVIA KOBULA
CASPAR KOBULA

from GRANPA KoKoKobula

SMITH COLLEGE
MEMORANDUM

Date............

To............

From............

In re

His comb, carried on the tail, to comb his feathers, when itchy

Worm →

Giant Kobulas watch. So that he knows when feeding time is

Baby Kobula eating other end of worm.

Claws for scratch for worms.

A GIANT KOBULA

eating a worm.
It is too lazy to fly.

new changes at the *Statesman* were to push Miller into a corner, Pritchett was among his supporters.[26]

There was no reduction in the demands *Holiday* magazine made on his time. A book of pieces done for them, mainly about central Europe but also including Turkey and Iran, was due to appear in 1964. Some rivalrous grumbles came from Roger Angell on this score. Part of *The New Yorker*'s understanding about a first-reading agreement (now worth $700 a year to Pritchett), Angell pointed out to the writer's US agent, Peter Matson, was that its editors got something to read.[27] After the 1959–60 flurry, Pritchett published just one short story in the magazine in 1961, another in 1962, then nothing until November 1964. It was a shame, Angell said, because 'he is certainly one of the top two or three short story writers in the world today'. Before long, Angell was putting direct pressure on Pritchett himself: 'please, *please* write some stories for us. We need you in the magazine not just as a critic (the recent review was very fine) but as a fiction writer. Surely, you must need us for *some* purpose – perhaps only as a barnacle-scraper after another long prose voyage for Holiday.'[28]

Pritchett was anyway worried, as he often had been before, about some of the directions his work seemed to be taking. In a piece about the literary profession, published in the *New Statesman* late in 1964, he wrote, 'The fewer novels or plays you write – because of other, parasitic interests – the fewer you will have the ability to write. The law ruling the arts is that they must be pursued to excess. Excess is not favoured by our conditions: a book which has taken two years to write dies in a few weeks. . . .'[29]

He wasn't unused to the problem, of course, and defended himself pointedly to Angell by reminding him that the advantage of writing for *Holiday* was that he did so on commission, whereas a first-reading agreement guaranteed nothing except itself. (He didn't mention that some of these *Holiday* pieces – which were often sold on to other magazines – by now brought in considerably more money than even *The New Yorker* paid.)[30] He admitted to some domestic distractions. Soon after she was fifty, Dorothy underwent a hysterectomy at the Elizabeth Garrett Anderson Hospital and, though he didn't tell Angell, Victor, too, had been unwell lately.[31] Besides, he was of an age at which most men would have been about to retire. He managed in these years to write a few stories which found favour at *The New Yorker* and elsewhere, but by Pritchett's high standards of connection with daily truth they often seem contrived, literary: 'The Liars', for example, which is about an old woman who has a regular Thursday visit from a man whose task it is to make up stories for her, or 'The Nest Builder', about an interior decorator who brings catastrophe to the personal life of anyone who hires him, until he meets his match – in both senses – in a woman who, by the end, 'had redecorated him'.[32]

At its best, his short fiction avoids this kind of *cherchez la fin* dapperness. As Edmund Wilson wrote to Pritchett, his stories 'don't have the kind of ending one expects . . . the point is that in your masterly use of detail, you so exactly hit the nail on the head that the reader expects a more usual kind of point at the end, & I haven't always grasped that the final details, though they may seem as much at random . . . are equally significant in their accuracy'.[33] The work Pritchett did in the early to mid 1960s is never without confidence or panache (details like the steel measure of the emotionally destructive decorator, which 'whizzed up the jamb of the door and lashed there for a second or two'),[34] but not until 1968–9, with 'Blind Love', 'Our Oldest Friend' and 'Our Wife' (published as 'The Captain's Daughter' in *The New Yorker*, amid a long series of rejections),[35] did his fiction begin to return to form.

His travels, too, had lost some of their zest. While his writing about cities familiar to him – including new essays on Madrid and Seville for *Holiday* magazine – was as sharp as ever, he seemed less eager to encounter new places, especially when he had to leave Dorothy behind. From Turkey, as from India, his Wodehousean letters to her must have amused, but their jokiness lacks his usual subtlety: 'the blue mosque was rather beautiful, but the floor totally covered with a hundred Turkey carpets gave a sort of Maples effect,' he wrote. 'I was staggered to see a genuine A-rab come in and prostrate himself before the tablet door that faces Mecca and howl a bit.'[36] If he had been unaware of the falling off, he was alerted to it by some of the more bracing reviews, not least in the *New Statesman*. Writing there in 1963, the novelist Brigid Brophy dismissed the cast of Pritchett's *The Key to My Heart* as suffering from 'the quaintness of people in Happy Family cards'. The social comedy, she said, 'is of an Ealing Studios kind'.[37] When Pritchett's latest travel compilation, *Foreign Faces*, appeared in September 1964, it was reviewed in the *Statesman* by another good fiction writer, Dan Jacobson who, though more circumspect, was alert to the wearier aspects of these magazine commissions, especially their national stereotypes ('The Bulgars are a heavy people "with heavy eyebrows and strong proud faces" . . . The people of Seville are incurable actors . . . "At heart every Persian is a mystic"'). Jacobson also not unjustly described the articles on Soviet satellite countries as 'dutiful in tone'.[38] He wasn't alone in his opinion. Reviewing *Foreign Faces* in the *Sunday Times*, Cyril Connolly more pungently accused Pritchett of 'dollarophoria' ('from dollar (unit of currency) and "euphoria"[,] sense of fictitious well-being. . . . Symptoms: Jocularity, a quickly evaporating sense of urgency and enthusiasm about nothing'). Connolly said he wished *Holiday* would send Pritchett for a year to a country where he knew the language.[39]

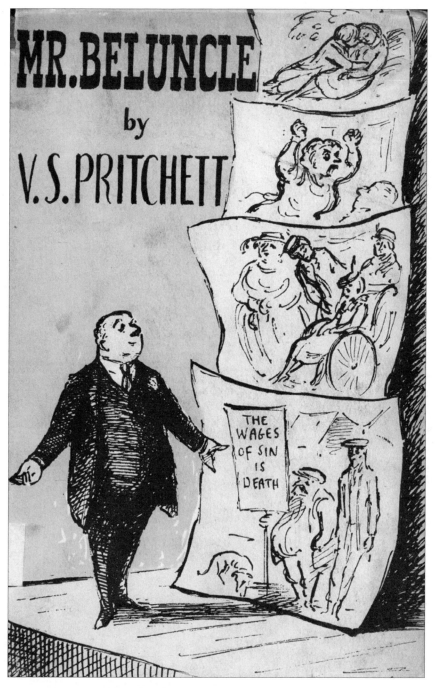

17. Edward Ardizzone's cover for *Mr Beluncle*, 1951

18. Gerald Brenan

19. Al Alvarez

20. Frances and Ralph Partridge

21. Barbara Wendell Kerr,
c. 1953

22. The pipe smoker

23, 24, 25. At 12 Regent's Park Terrace,
late 1950s and 60s

26. Cyril Pritchett in the Red Lion, Duke of York Street, one of Evelyn Hofer's
photographs for *London Perceived*

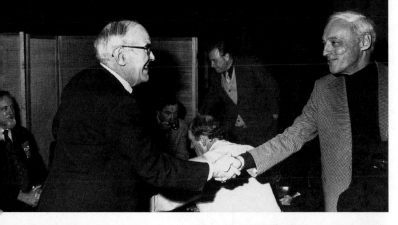

27. With Saul Bellow

28. With Eudora Welty

29. With Angus Wilson

30. Receiving an Hon. D.Litt, Leeds, 1971

31. Sir Victor and
Lady Pritchett at
Buckingham Palace, 1975

32. On a PEN tour, mid 1970s,
Dorothy leading the way

33. Portrait by Clara Vulliamy
commissioned by the Society
of Authors

34. Celebrating his 90th
birthday at Chatto & Windus

35. 'What else is there to do but write?'

36. With his grandson Matthew Pritchett and Matthew's daughter Edith, 1994

Penguin, which had been offered the paperback rights, subsequently turned the book down.[40] There were other setbacks. An attempt by Pritchett's London agency – prompted, perhaps, by his flurry with Alfred Hitchcock – to interest Paramount and Columbia in film rights to some of his stories was unproductive.[41]

Pritchett was as sensitive to criticism and to failure as most writers. But he wasn't short of admirers, and apart from his native energy and resilience – not to speak of the sheer need to keep earning his living – there was still plenty to encourage him. A new literary paper, the *New York Review of Books*, began in 1963, and Pritchett was among its first and most regular contributors. In May 1964 Penguin bought the rights in a new *Collected Stories* and he took Dorothy on holiday in Spain on the proceeds.[42] His recent fan mail included a letter from the Prime Minister's wife, Mary Wilson, prompted by Pritchett's *New Statesman* article on the funeral of Winston Churchill.[43]

Pritchett himself was on his way to becoming a grand old man, and, for that reason as well as others, it's understandable that, like many other former sceptics, he had set aside his original reservations about Churchill. Early in the Second World War he had written, 'We've been hypnotised by an orator and I don't think Winston is really all that good as an orator. Every phrase is second hand. . . . Tell me who is more dangerous than a brilliant man in old age.'[44] A quarter of a century on, he was more in tune with popular opinion about Churchill and the funeral article is a powerful piece of writing which embodies its own claim that 'state occasions are London's poetry'. It also interweaves a meditation on lost national greatness with some half-concealed personal notes: Pritchett continuing his adjustment – prolonged by absences abroad – to being back in London. 'Undistracted by empire now,' he wrote, 'we felt intimately that we were at home, that we were seeing our own lives, that we were inhabitants. . . .' The article is full of vivid and immediately recognisable detail (the 'astonishingly individual and natural' faces of the sailors leading the gun carriage) and of reflections on how the occasion revealed in the London crowds aspects of Englishness which had been reflected back by Churchill: 'What a race of born actors, in the mass!'; 'There is always a wink of self-indulgence in the London face'. Pritchett intimately conveys what it was like to be there on that winter's day ('It was important to put on two pairs of socks'), and assesses Churchill's place in history without allowing his readers to forget that notions of uniqueness and irreplaceability can be exaggerated. He doesn't deny the common comparison with Wellington and makes good use of Tennyson's ode on Wellington's death. But, as he points out in his last words, the precedent has something reassuring to say: 'the last of the great men? In 1852 it was feared that Wellington was the last.'

Any discouragement or flagging energy Pritchett may have briefly suffered was dispelled, around now, by the interest of all his publishers in a possible book of memoirs.[45] The idea came at a good moment. *New York Proclaimed* had led to a third joint commission with Evelyn Hofer, about Dublin, where the Pritchetts installed themselves in the autumn of 1965. They spent a couple of months in a handsome Georgian flat at 23 Pembroke Road, just south of the centre. Irish weather brought on colds and bronchitis, but Pritchett was stimulated all the same by being back in the surroundings of his early twenties and wrote a new story.[46] Dublin was still a relatively small town, and Pembroke Road is just round the corner both from where Victor had married Evelyn and from the flat they lived in on their return from America in 1926.[47] 'If I were to write an account of my education,' he only half hypothesised, 'the city of Dublin would have to appear as one of my schoolmasters.'[48] By the time *Dublin: A Portrait* appeared in 1967, *A Cab at the Door* – the first volume of the *Bildungsroman* for which much of his work had in a sense been a set of early drafts – was almost complete. 'This is obviously the most important book yet to come from Victor's pen,' A. D. Peters wrote to Norah Smallwood, with more than his usual commercial confidence.[49]

As he drafted and redrafted the opening of *A Cab at the Door*, trying to decide how to write about himself, Pritchett was often making judgements about what that self consisted of. However difficult the process, though, it had the advantage of being undertaken from a position of revived emotional security. Karl Miller was quick to spot this. 'I think you must be a happy writer,' he said to Pritchett in the course of a radio interview in 1967. 'Do you accept that designation?' Seeming a little startled, Pritchett answered, 'Oh yes – indeed. I like writing and, er, the *together*.'[50] Decades later, 'together' was the word that came naturally to Matthew Pritchett in describing how he thought of his grandfather. 'I can never think of Grandpa as distinct from Granny. I thought of them together.'

How to describe happiness? When Tolstoy wrote the famous opening of *Anna Karenina*, it was already conventional to believe that unhappiness is more distinctive, more interesting. 'Happiness writes white,' the saying goes. The poets of Augustan Rome thought differently: meditations on what makes a happy life are common in Latin poetry. And despite the counter-emphasis in European Romanticism and, increasingly, in nineteenth-century prose fiction, there were writers among those admired by Pritchett who continued the theme. Robert Louis Stevenson – himself, like Pritchett, in reaction against a puritan inheritance – claimed, 'There is no duty we so much underrate as the duty of being happy.' Duty or not, it's surely a gift: one which all those who knew Pritchett in his later years recognised in him and loved. Jason Epstein, one of the founders of the *New York Review of Books* and the American publisher of Pritchett's books from the 1960s on, spoke about it with particular vividness: 'He was so enthusiastic about everything. I never saw him in a bad mood. He never had a bad word to say about anyone, that I knew of. The marriage seemed to me ideal. Dorothy was devoted to him in a way that women would not be devoted to their husbands today.' Epstein had no sense that this devotion was in any way oppressive to Dorothy. 'Oh, *no*! That was her work. They were a partnership. They were in business together.' Pritchett, he concluded, was that rarity among authors, 'a totally sensible man'. Epstein thought that if everyone were like him, we'd have a much better world to live in. 'I mean, imagine.'

Everyone who knew him best after Dorothy had stopped drinking says much the same. Arthur Crook's partner Juliet Wrightson says, 'When I think of them I just think of laughing. We were always laughing.' To Peter Vansittart, Victor 'seemed the only person I've known of distinction who was happy. Happy in his children and his wife, in his career, in his work – in his life.' One of the Pritchetts' neighbours, Claire Tomalin, for a time literary editor of the *New Statesman*, has a vivid memory of dropping in at Regent's Park Terrace to deliver a book or collect a review, and seeing Dorothy meticulously laying an elegant table for two. 'It was my first view of how an old couple can have a good life together in which things are rather carefully thought out. I was impressed by it.' To their grandchildren, too, the most remarkable thing about them was the pleasure they took in each other. As Georgia Pritchett was to recall, 'when one of them was speaking, the other would have a lovely look of expectation.' The novelist Elizabeth Jane Howard, who saw a lot of them when she lived in Camden after breaking up with her husband Kingsley Amis, says simply that Victor adored Dorothy, 'absolutely adored her, and she had that sort of sparkle and glow of somebody who knows that they're tremendously loved and that nothing can go wrong and that they're the best person in the world. They hardly needed other people, really, although they would enjoy them when they came along. They were astonishingly self-sufficient.'

Since Pritchett wrote about everything he knew, it isn't surprising that he himself wrote about happiness. As early as 1938, a features editor at the *News Chronicle* had commissioned him to do a piece on the subject. Pritchett acknowledged how subjective the state was – the most wretched-seeming lives have been experienced as happy (he instanced Hazlitt) – and also that it 'does not lend itself to description', perhaps because it is 'without history' and doesn't seem to rule how people behave.[51] He made a brave claim that, faced with the world's poverty, injustice and cruelty, happiness was impossible and in the course of this argument explicitly criticised the Bloomsbury code of the pursuit of personal happiness which, as he said, could only benefit 'the leisured, the secure and the instructed'. Ostensibly, then, his conclusion is that happiness has a lot to do with being in harmony with social good. But the most original and convincing parts of the piece are at odds with this. Nazism, he pointed out, was proof that 'people find strength, meaning and happiness in bad beliefs, as well as good ones'. In the end, he knew that happiness is as arbitrary and gratuitous as a sense of humour – which he also had.

Still, the subject continued to absorb him and to affect his work. Though Pritchett had known his share of misery and had always been drawn to romanticism, he early on, in his published persona, discarded any absorption in the melancholy ego. He was not, as he had told Brenan, one of those who 'prefer jealousy to love, unhappiness to happiness, power over others to pleasure for themselves, unkindness to kindness. . . .'[52] Clearly at some level his preferences were inherited. While *A Cab at the Door* gives grounds for scepticism both about Victor's father's irrepressibility and about his mother's readiness to laugh through her frequent tears, the sheer survival of the marriage is an indication of the couple's psychological resilience. Victor himself saw more happiness in the marriage of his Yorkshire great-aunt Sarah and her husband Arthur who, he wrote, 'were notorious (in the family) for the incredible folly of adoring each other'.[53] But of course there were factors other than heredity. Pritchett's memoirs pay tribute to the strength and depth of his own experience of married love with Dorothy. And it mattered to him that he was successful in his career – albeit not so much so, either in critical or material terms, that he could afford to relax in it for long enough to become bored. As he writes at the end of *Midnight Oil*, 'I have done, given my circumstances and my character, what I have been able to do and I have enjoyed it.'

This essential modesty – the idea that the only way to make anything of one's gifts is through a combination of being realistic about them and very hard work – shouldn't be taken entirely at its own valuation. His intelligence, memory, observation, sympathy, wit were, of course, exceptional qualities. What can make them seem familiar, even 'ordinary', is not only Pritchett's self-deprecation, but his frank London zest. Few autobiographers since Pepys have been so enthusiastic about their pleasures. Pepys, Pritchett wrote in a phrase which also described himself, is 'an eager careerist, struck by the wonder of it all'.[54] To be sure, the 'all' of Pritchett's memoirs is less confessional than Pepys's. Even when one has allowed for the crucial difference that Pritchett, unlike Pepys, wrote for an immediate audience (and one which included, not least, his wife), he was a less badly behaved man. But the vitality, curiosity and industry which he admired in Pepys are all characteristic of himself. *A Cab at the Door* is a phrasebook of happiness: 'So began my love of change, journeys and new places'; 'The discovery of foreign languages had an intoxicating effect on me'; 'The pleasure of my life as an office boy lay in being one of the London crowd and I actually enjoyed standing in a compartment packed with fifteen people on my way to Bromley North. . . . The thing I liked best was being sent on errands in Bermondsey'; 'The sight of skill and of traditional expertness is irresistible to me'; 'I was happy. I was excited. I was setting myself free.'[55]

A few of the book's first reviewers saw that this is one of its distinctive qualities. Graham Hough, comparing Pritchett's years working in the docklands leather trade with Dickens's in the blacking factory, appreciated the lack of 'the sense of being cheated and deprived that stayed with Dickens all his life'.[56] Philip Toynbee, too, wrote about what he called the 'not-unhappiness' of the book, while admitting that he had had to overcome a 'faint resistance to [its] almost irresistible charm and energy'.[57] More often, though, critics were sidetracked by the obvious-seeming comparison with Edmund Gosse's *Father and Son*, without noticing the crucial differences of which Pritchett himself was very conscious. True, Gosse's upbringing, like his own, involved what Pritchett, in an essay on the earlier writer, described as the 'extreme peculiarity' in religion which can be 'exciting, even enlarging' to a child.[58] And the puritanism of Gosse's world corresponded to something in Pritchett's. Here, though, the difference of intensity is more important than any superficial resemblances. In the case of Gosse, puritanism brought deprivations of a kind which Pritchett had not suffered: the young Edmund was not allowed to read fiction, for example. And Edmund ailed, where the young Victor was robustly healthy.

Whatever the emphases of the reviews, they were generally very enthusiastic and several called for a sequel.[59] A Cab at the Door was a hit in more tangible ways, too. Within a week of publication it had sold over 5000 copies in hardback. Penguin bought the paperback rights. The Readers Union book club negotiated an issue of 13,000–15,000 copies to its members. BBC radio serialised extracts in ten instalments.

Pritchett was in the USA at the time and the response there was similarly enthusiastic. The New Yorker and the New York Review of Books competed to serialise the book. Roger Angell was incensed with Pritchett's US agent, Peter Matson, for selling the rights to the NYRB, on the basis that The New Yorker's first-reading agreement with his client only covered fiction.[60] The New York Times, meanwhile, hailed A Cab at the Door as 'a supremely good memoir, enchantingly readable in style and beyond that, almost unique in content'.[61] Harper's called it 'as honest and tough a piece of reporting and self-appraisal as you are likely to find', adding, in case this sounded a shade arduous, 'Happily it's fun too.'[62] Pritchett felt that he had arrived at last[63] and boasted that he had been invited ('again') to be interviewed on 'their top T.V. show, which has caused a good deal of awe in the sacred glades of Harvard and Brandeis'.[64]

However separate he felt from his academic colleagues, teaching was by now crucial to his life as a writer. He had finished the book at Smith College, the very good small private university in Northampton, Massachusetts where he was fast becoming a fixture.[65] It was 'a wonderfully quiet place to write in', he told Smallwood: 'Gallons of pure air.' He found local society 'rather humdrum' and worried that it was dull for Dorothy ('no Victor's or Garrick to slip out to').[66] But there were 'one or two gay people about',[67] including two sociable and eminent literary scholars, Daniel Aaron and Frank Ellis, and their wives.[68] (The Ellises had a house in Spain not far from Gerald Brenan, where the Pritchetts sometimes stayed.) It was easy to escape to Boston or New York, and they saw a lot of Lillian Hellman. Dorothy, encouraged by Roger Angell, tried to get as involved in the baseball World Series on TV as she had been in the football World Cup: 'From *that* game', Pritchett told Angell, 'she used to stagger to bed with dislocated shoulders and peculiar limps.'[69] On campus, American academic idioms continued to amuse him. When a beautiful girl described herself to him as an 'English major', he told his friend James Stern that he 'decorated her with moustaches & gave her gout'.[70]

If Smith was conducive to steady work, one of the unspoken but obvious reasons was that it meant steady income. On average, through the 1960s, Pritchett published more than one book a year. Yet for all his productivity and the critical success of *A Cab at the Door*, he couldn't have lived on his books alone for long, or particularly well. In Britain, *A Cab at the Door* was the most popular one he had written. But in 1966 Chatto had advanced £2000 on the thirty-shilling hardback, against royalties of fifteen per cent, so he had to sell almost 9000 copies before he started to see any more money. Penguin's advance on the paperback was £1000, but against a tight royalty of seven and a half per cent. And though the Readers Union deal sounded big, it in fact brought him precisely five (old) pence per copy: about £300 in total. The book's American earnings were comparable: sound, but far from life-changing.

For now, the necessary combination of journalism and teaching continued to work well. His reputation was at a new high. In 1968 he was made a Commander of the Order of the British Empire: one step down from a knighthood and an honour which – like all forms of public recognition – delighted him: 'I am shamelessly pleased,' he told Roger Angell.[71] He was made Zisskind Professor at Brandeis and was invited to give the Clark Lectures at King's College, Cambridge: one of the most prestigious series of its kind. *A Cab at the Door* won him a Heinemann award in 1969. That autumn, he was back at Smith, living at 58 Paradise Road. 'Here we are in Paradise,' he unavoidably joked to Norah Smallwood, 'and really, in the autumn blaze of vermillion [*sic*] and gold, it is rather like it in this pretty and peaceful New England place which is all dragon flies and sunbathing and docile girls and cream cakes and soft Profs.'[72]

Among the stories he was working on around this time was one narrated by a student who falls for her teacher. At first, it's his marriage that she's attracted to, but the unreciprocating, pipe-smoking professor soon becomes the main focus. To escape her obsession, the girl eventually gets her father to take her home, but not before – in a scene which guaranteed rejection by *The New Yorker*[73] – she puts the professor's pipe in her mouth. 'The taste was sour and I thought how dirty men are. I was afraid I was going to be sick.'[74] There's nothing to suggest, though, that the piece was any more than what its title calls it, 'Creative Writing', and everything to suggest that Pritchett's main idea of Paradise was in fact less to do with 'docile girls', or even cream cakes, than with very hard work. He turned his Clark lectures on 'George Meredith and English Comedy' into a book. He wrote a lot of reviews. He published a new collection of stories under the title *Blind Love*, and he was writing many more. *The New Yorker* published 'The Captain's Daughter' in its Christmas issue in 1969 and around the same time accepted 'The Diver', though not without objections of a now familiar sort.[75]

'The Diver' is the first-person narrative of a Pritchett-like Englishman who, as an aspiring young writer, works in an office in Paris. From a distance, he admires a woman in her thirties, Mme Chamson, who runs a nearby mending and cleaning business. The young man is accidentally knocked into the river and Mme Chamson takes him home to get dry. The ensuing sexual encounter, predictable in essence but not in detail, is described with a comic mix of delicacy and recklessness. Roger Angell told Pritchett that everyone at *The New Yorker* admired the story 'extravagantly', but confessed – while implying some distance in this between himself and William Shawn – that Pritchett's 'fears about the "naughtiness" of the tale and our old tight-lipped reactions to the sexual realities have been somewhat justified'. He added that the story had 'occasioned still another major discussion of this issue here – an issue on which we are, as you know, divided'.[76] One of the worries was the potential double entendre in the word 'diver'. The title was eventually changed in the magazine to 'The Fall' (though, as Pritchett pointed out, he had used this earlier, without any pun, for his story about the man obsessed with stage falls).[77] He was also asked to cut Mme Chamson's flirtatious double entendre, 'The diver's come up again.' These and other alterations took some time, and it was more than six months before the story finally appeared. As with 'The Wheelbarrow', most of the original version is restored in the book.[78]

Pritchett had rediscovered his fictional form. But he still had to fight for his work, and not only with *The New Yorker*. In November 1968 he delivered to Chatto the typescript of the collection of stories which was to become *Blind Love*. Having had no response, he wrote to the poet C. Day-Lewis, then an editor at Chatto, asking what was happening. Day-Lewis replied some weeks later, but with qualified enthusiasm.[79] Yet *Blind Love* contains some of Pritchett's best and most widely admired work. The title story was turned into a successful TV film at Sam Wanamaker's instigation in 1977.[80] And among the other contents, 'Our Oldest Friend' in particular, published in *Encounter* in July 1969, is funny, touching and technically absorbing – *A Dance to the Music of Time* in miniature.

A group of men and their wives are at the men's school reunion. The narrative uses one of Pritchett's favourite devices: setting up what seems to be one kind of character and situation, introducing a series of unexpected turns, and ending with a person, and in a tone, quite different from the outset. It's also a feat of ventriloquism, uttering with sympathetic but not uncritical precision the formulas of a world which its author had come to know well, but to which he could never fully belong. The cue, as so often, was a person who had long preoccupied him: his former editor, first at the *Christian Science Monitor*, then at the *Fortnightly Review*, W. Horsfall Carter. In life and in fiction, Horsfall Carter was Pritchett's Widmerpool. Pritchett wrote about him in more than one letter to Gerald Brenan and with a satirical intensity unusual even for that unbuttoned correspondence. One autumn in the early 1950s, for example, the Pritchetts, on their way to Rome, had bumped into him on the cross-Channel ferry:

> Always when I'm about to go on a continental journey I meet my oldest friend – Fall off Carthorse or – as we now call him – Hot & Cold Carter. Plumper, pink and prosperous, he has at last struck fortune. He has migrated to Strasbourg, belongs to the Council of Europe, pays no income tax, has a large income and is delighted 'because now I can speak French all the time . . .' What a dream of dullness he is. And sure enough, before I got home, there was a letter giving me 'contacts' in Spain. He is the world's friend, the insatiable orphan, the forget-me-not in the button hole.[81]

Pritchett was determined to put him into a story[82] and eventually did so more than once. Chaucer in 'The Snag' – the man who goes halfway up Snowdon – has many of his characteristics, as does Bertie in 'The Accompanist'. But Saxon, in 'Our Oldest Friend', is a fuller and, in the end, more troubling version. In the flawless opening paragraphs, it seems unlikely – and unnecessary – that he will be more than a brilliantly observed comic cameo:

> 'Look out!' someone said. 'Here comes Saxon.'

It was too late. Moving off the dance floor and pausing at the door with the blatant long sight of the stalker, Saxon saw us all in our quiet corner of the lounge and came over. He stopped and stood with his hand on his hips and his legs apart, like a goalkeeper. Then he came forward.

'Ah! This *is* nice!' he crowed, in the cockerel voice that took us back to the Oxford years. He pulled up a chair and placed it so that none of us could easily get out. It passed through our heads that we had seen that dinner-jacket of his before. He must have had it since the last term at school. It was short, eager and juvenile in the sleeves and now his chest had bolstered it, he seemed to be bursting with buns and toffee. A piece of stiff fair hair stuck up boyishly at the back. He crossed his short legs and squeezed them with satisfaction as his sharp blue eyes looked around our circle over his strong glasses.

'How awfully nice.' For niceness was everything for him. 'Everyone is here,' he said. . . .[83]

The picture grows complicated in various ways. The story's 'us' is filled out into its constituent identities, not only individual personalities within the deceptively cohesive-seeming group, but their different pasts and embattled presents. There is everyone's increasing interest in an absent character, the unmarried Tessa Lattersmith, who seems to connect all the men (like a daisy chain, as one of their wives sardonically says), and who in the present situation also threatens to disconnect them. It gradually becomes clear that if anyone is more perturbed than the others by Tessa, it's Saxon, and this realisation brings various memories and oblique admissions with it, especially of how Saxon was bullied by the rest of the men when they were all at school together. The immediate effects of all this on Saxon and the others, not to speak of Tessa herself when she arrives and on the story as a whole, are quietly radical. Dexterously, Pritchett shifts the focus away from Saxon, in his ludicrousness and then his pathos and finally his sheer innocence, to Tessa. Certain phrases – 'In principle yes, in practice no', and particularly 'our oldest friend' – are moved around in different contexts like words in a sestina. The title is not only applied to different individuals, but scrutinised as a social formula: a badge of authenticity, a term of deprecation, a piece of conversational leverage. This is a world in which to 'go back a long way together', as Tessa goes back a long way with everyone – especially the man known by his school nickname, 'the

Dustman' – can be an ordeal as well as a reassurance. The story ends with a dance and by this time any one of at least three people can be seen as the main character:

> Soon all of us were on the floor, the Dustman shoving Mrs Selby along as if to her doom, and Tessa following him with her eyes all the time, as Saxon leapt into his passionate, dreadful and unavailing antics all round her. Once in a while she would note where he was, open her mouth to say something pleasant, and then coldly change her mind.[84]

Eudora Welty wrote to Pritchett, 'Those multiple point of view stories are marvels. It's somehow like watching the story without losing a moment or a step put *itself* together into its whole, become its own achievement – that's an illusion, I think! Their energy is everywhere and no other writer can touch it.'[85]

In the late 1960s and early 1970s, Pritchett not only packed his notebooks with ideas for more fiction,[86] but was also working on what was to become *Midnight Oil*. Unpublished passages from the drafts that poured from him – page after page in his tight, scratchy hand – give many hints about his feelings at the time, not least about the intense relation between himself and his work: the sensation he always had after coming to the end of a piece of writing, for example, 'that I have burned out the self that wrote it, and must now find another', or the mixture of curiosity and restlessness which afflicted him as he wandered through familiar places, on the one hand 'a curious disgust of knowing', a longing to be somewhere new but, on the other, a sense that to be on home territory was to be both imaginatively free and alert to every nuance of what might be happening behind every window he passes.[87] He talks, too, about the almost tangible impact of words on him since his youngest days – words like *quincaillerie*, *voies urinaires*, *cinquième*, the sound and appearance of which had besotted him in Paris. (His hotel room was on the fifth floor, so *cinquième* spelt freedom.) Although he was unduly severe on his early writing, he had a vivid recall of what he now saw as the youthful fanaticism behind it, and of the most trivial impulses and encouragements involved. He made several funny attempts at describing his memory of the paperclip which held the first cheque he ever received from the *Christian Science Monitor* ('From that time I trace a feeling for paperclips'; 'to that time I trace a feeling for paperclips which develops into one of the strong passions of a writer's life. They are his private hoard. One has the sensation one could cash them' . . .).

While memories of the remote past came to Pritchett as freshly as ever, he was conscious that the new book was drawing him on to more intimate ground. Everything he wrote, of course, was read, typed and commented on by Dorothy. It was inevitable in these circumstances that he should have played down his first marriage, but less so – at least in the view of his otherwise delighted US editor, Jason Epstein – that the book says very little about his children. 'In view of your interest in your own parents,' Epstein wrote, 'this seems odd.'[88]

Is it strange that Pritchett has less to say about himself as a father than as a son? He was, as Epstein knew, a proud, devoted and encouraging parent and grandparent. When Oliver wrote a short story, around now, Victor didn't hesitate to pass it on to Roger Angell, and his letters to his son in the early stages in his career were full of good advice and offers of practical help.[89] To both children, he was confiding and amusing, treating them with solicitude but on equal terms with himself. In 1967, for example, when Karl Miller fell out with the then editor of the *New Statesman*, Paul Johnson, Victor's typically fair-minded account of the situation to Oliver, by then in his late twenties, could have been written to an old friend:

Yes, Karl Miller has resigned. He has never got on with Paul Johnson – they both accuse each other of arrogance and treachery – and although I've done my best to stop it coming to this, Karl resigned in a rage and Paul was obviously delighted. I think it is a tragedy. It is always fatal to let a political editor override the literary side. . . . What pugnacious Karl will do, I don't know. Even talks of starting another paper which, I would say, under present conditions is impossible. I'm very depressed about the whole business. I don't know what you think – but did *you* find the paper too academic. I know it was occasionally dry; and the sexiness was getting a bit of a bore. And there was too much in-group writing. Still, in general, the paper could stand it. Obviously, there is intense feeling among Karl's large following. . . . Karl feels ill-used & that he was the victim of a plot. He stood by his principles but I think was self-betrayed by his edgy temper. Still I'm on his side about it.[90]

There's a similar ease in Victor's letters to Josephine, which were often full of literary gossip (earlier, in 1959: 'there was the *Lolita* excitement and I had lunch with the old lepidopterist himself, a very intelligent man who cant bear *Dr Zhivago*. I reproached him for that; he reproached me back. We saw Bill Sansom whose horse got struck by lightning which was quite fitting because he believes in omens and felt it coming'),[91] as well as of more domestic news. In Northampton, Victor wrote to her, satirising his and Dorothy's surroundings in Paradise Road: 'I write this seated in a shocking-pink, pseudo-Regency armchair with my feet on a deep-pile, Hoover-filling, pale Apricot, nylon-enriched and, probably, peach-fed carpet, with sofas to match. . . . When anything amusing happens here we will send you a cable.'[92] Meanwhile, the fond paterfamilias continued to send cartoons to his grandchildren: squirrels, an American lorry, himself and Dorothy dressed in furs against the New England winter.

So the absence from *Midnight Oil* of any account of what was involved in being a parent, rather than just the child of his own parents, had nothing to do with a lack of interest in or affection for his offspring. One element, perhaps, was sheer un-American reticence: a wish – like that shown in his giving pseudonyms to many of the people he includes – not to involve others in his disclosures, however undamaging they were. Another lay in the book's essential nature. Its main effort is to capture the past and, even where a relatively recent episode is involved, the point – as in Pritchett's description of the disappearing selves embodied in his writing – is that until the narrative revives it, it has gone. The children, by contrast, like Dorothy herself (who also figures relatively little in the book, except as the almost abstract source of his married happiness), were very much of the present and future. Still, the gap remarked on by Jason Epstein is consistent with Pritchett's continuing tendency to communicate himself, one way or another, as having been more solitary than he really was. He tried to make amends in fiction: to Dorothy in 'The Marvellous Girl', written soon after *Midnight Oil* appeared; and to the children in his story about their lives at Maidencourt and Ham Spray, 'Cocky Olly', which was one of the last that he published.[93]

Midnight Oil appeared in October 1971. Graham Hough again got it right, praising the 'rare alliance of skilful composition with transparent candour and truth', and commenting on how unusual it is as an account 'of non-literary life in areas that remain quite uncelebrated'.[94] Hough also drew attention to the new light the book shed on the 1930s, despite the number of memoirs that had already come from that time: 'His story is quite different, and reminds us how false and partial the conventional picture of a literary period can become.'

These were celebratory times for Pritchett. His memoirs brought a new audience to his fiction. One element in this was BBC radio which, apart from serialising the books themselves, produced a number of readings from and dramatisations of his stories: 'The Fly in the Ointment' and 'The Saint' in 1970; 'The Key to My Heart' in 1971; and, in 1974 – when his seventh original collection, *The Camberwell Beauty*, was published – no fewer than four items from earlier books: 'The Ape', 'Double Divan', 'Eleven O'Clock' and 'The Sailor'. There were other rewards of various kinds. The Garrick gave him a seventieth birthday dinner 'with the Poet Laureate [C. Day-Lewis] at the head of the table: it was an evening of wild exaggeration and, at the end, as old Priestley said on a similar occasion, "Anyone who would like to come down to the Thames Embankment and watch me walk on the water is welcome." '95

He was invited to teach at Columbia University. In 1971, Leeds University made him an Honorary Doctor of Letters – the first of several such honours to be bestowed on him[96] – and he became an Honorary Member of the American Academy of Arts and Letters.

In October that year, *Playboy* magazine became a less likely patron of intellectual gravitas by putting on a writers' conference (Pritchett called it a gymkhana) on a range of current political and social issues. Pritchett was one of the luminaries who gathered in Chicago, along with J. K. Galbraith, Arthur Schlesinger Jr and Kenneth Tynan. The humorist Art Buchwald was also there (he addressed Hugh Hefner as 'Your Holiness').[97] 'The bunnies did not appear,' Pritchett commented, but in their absence a television reporter 'said on the air that Dorothy was the most amusing woman he had met in Chicago: so we are waiting . . . for her to get a TV contract'.[98] Around this time, too, Pritchett's manuscripts were becoming sought after in the USA. In 1973, acting on his behalf, the bookseller Bertram Rota sold a batch of his papers to the Harry Ransom Humanities Research Center at the University of Texas at Austin – the biggest of several important American archives of twentieth-century British literature – for £1750. Not long before, he had been paid $1000 for a short talk sponsored by the American Academy and Institute. It began to seem as if, for now at least, he was bankable.

Another result of Pritchett's fame was the number of people connected with him and his family who suddenly got in touch: among them a Canadian niece, granddaughter of his father's brother Edward. And then there were people whose own relations figured in the books, and who wanted to give their side of the story. Pritchett had hardly suspected, when he was recalling his old boss in the Bermondsey leather trade fifty years earlier, that the family business was still flourishing and that the boss's son would feel that the memory of his long-dead father had been slighted. *A Cab at the Door* was serialised in the *Observer* and the paper soon received a letter from Donald K. Beale, of W. Beale & Co., Fancy Leather Manufacturers, 'Established 1907', Bermondsey. Donald Beale confirmed some of Pritchett's memories of Walter Beale, such as his fondness for Shakespeare, but sternly denied Pritchett's claim that he was financially incompetent. Pritchett was wrong, too, to have said that the business had been inherited. Not so: Walter Beale started it himself in 1907. 'Like many others before and after him,' his son wrote, 'he certainly found it an uphill task before he became established and he was always very grateful to his suppliers for their support and encouragement. These suppliers . . . have since mentioned many times to me how they respected my father. . . .' Here, as in other respects, Pritchett's memories of his struggles to find his own path had involved imputing an easier one to others. He wrote an apology and there the matter ended.

Meanwhile, family life took up an increasing amount of his and Dorothy's time. They were able to give their grandchildren steady, untroubled attention of a kind which they were conscious their own children had lacked. The Brenans stayed at Regent's Park Terrace in the summer of 1972, and praised their 'kindness and happy marriage' to Frances Partridge. Frances herself spent 'a very jolly evening' with them all not long afterwards. 'The Pritchetts delighted me by seeming so flourishing,' she wrote in her diary, 'and at the same time warmly welcoming. I do hope we can keep the dialogue going. V.S.P. was in high spirits and brilliance. . . .' It was one of many such parties: evenings full of anecdotes and comic fantasies. Dorothy, as well as Victor, was on good form. She had a joke which began as a serious-seeming story. She was in her late fifties by now and Victor was over seventy. She said she had read something that recommended the middle-aged and elderly not to wait to have sex until they were in bed at night: 'You must keep your marriage alive,' she summarised, 'and if you feel like having sex at lunchtime, you should have sex at lunchtime.' She went on, 'So the other day, we decided at lunch just to have sex. And it was fantastic. But we'll never go to *that* restaurant again.' (She was to repeat this to her grandchildren later. 'No adult had ever told me a rude joke before in my life,' Matthew recalls. 'And it was exactly how I think of them. I always feel that my life is so much duller than theirs.')

The following year, Frances Partridge recorded a similar party:

A high-powered dinner at the Pritchetts' last night – the widow of Vaughan-Williams . . . A writer called Francis King . . . Far the most high-powered was Philip Hope-Wallace, tall, hostile to women I would say, and very funny, I think I'll have to say witty. There was a delicious dinner, a lot of laughter, and much euphoria on the Pritchetts' part. It was the sort of dinner-party where ghost stories are told. I talked mostly to V.S.P. and drove the two male guests home. Woke in the night realizing I'd drunk too much.[99]

Dorothy, of course, drank no alcohol that night, or ever, these days. If anyone gave her a glass of wine, she simply passed it to the nearest man, saying it was always lucky to be next to her at a party. She and Victor were at last as much together, again, as they had been thirty-five years earlier. A couple of months before that 'high-powered' dinner, Victor wrote what Roger Angell rightly called his 'beautiful and memorable' new story about that first meeting, 'The Marvellous Girl'.[100]

10

Novels without Dialogue

The many pictures of him done in those years – by painters[1] as well as photographers – tend to show a conventionally dressed man, almost always wearing a jacket and colourful tie, pulling sagaciously on his briar pipe. He looks directly at us through his large spectacles, keen-eyed, shrewd, good-humouredly jowled, self-confident. He might be a popular physician, or the chairman of an old-established family business: a wine merchant, perhaps, or a land agent.

This is Pritchett in repose. In ordinary life he was animated, less respectable. When he talked, you would see the nicotine stains on his teeth. His lips moved lopsidedly, one side held tight as if to hold an absent pipe in place but giving an impression, too, of trying to keep the expressiveness of the other side in check. He was still an actor. Talking on a TV programme about a moment in a novel by Knut Hamsun where hunger gnaws at the hero's chest, Pritchett pulled at his jersey with his hands while his spectacles slipped awry, magnifying and distorting his leaping eyes.

The sheer responsive energy was unmistakable. In his seventies and early eighties, while increasingly often speaking at the memorial services of his contemporaries (becoming so weary of them that he left instructions that there should be no such event for himself), he began what were in effect three new stages in his career: as a biographer, as a literary statesman, and as the reviewer and mentor of the latest generation of gifted writers. All this while he continued to write short stories: three new collections between 1974 and 1980.

The biographies are more of a departure than they might seem, though Pritchett had always, of course, used the genre in his criticism. He knew perfectly well that the tradition represented by Samuel Johnson's *Lives of the Poets* or Sainte-Beuve's *Portraits littéraires* had come to be thought intellectually disreputable, especially in the academy, and he enjoyed teasing the purists.[2] His Clark Lectures were given at Cambridge University – the *fons et origo* of Practical Criticism, with its pre-deconstructionist focus on 'the words on the page' and its disdain for the distractions of external information. No one was more alert to words than Pritchett, but he knew that they didn't arrive on the page from nowhere, or from no one. 'There is something in criticism called the biographical fallacy which we are told the critic ought to avoid,' he told his Cambridge audience. 'I am not going to avoid it.'[3] Not only did he not avoid biography; there was, as always, something distinctly *auto*biographical about his approach to his subject, George Meredith: man of letters, friend of the Pre-Raphaelites and author of *The Egoist*, among many other novels. In relating aspects of Meredith's style to his personal background – to the grandfather who was a tailor with aristocratic pretensions, to the father who went bankrupt, to Meredith's sense of himself as a foreigner in England – Pritchett finds a way into his subject which is all the more vivid and personal for its links to his own upbringing and self-image.

Pritchett's main point, though, was not only to hint at the extent to which all writers draw on their experiences in their work, but to make literary-historical short cuts of the kind which helped dynamise his journalistic criticism. It's no distance from tailors to Carlyle's *Sartor Resartus* and, having made that link in Meredith's case, Pritchett is quick to find others, deftly showing what Meredith took from earlier writers, what he gave to later ones and, by comparison, exactly what is individual about him. In the process he continually throws out stimulating, aphoristic asides: for example, that we have to read Victorian fiction 'with a translator's effort', so different is the world it originates in from our own; or that nineteenth-century architecture, with its cathedral-like railway stations and its monastic commercial buildings, is 'an attempt, by an exuberant looting of history, to distract the city from what its life is really like and what it is doing'.[4]

As a book-length critical meditation on a writer about whom he had already published more than one essay,[5] *George Meredith and English Comedy* is a trial run for Pritchett's biographies of Balzac (1973), Turgenev (1977) and Chekhov (1988). In retrospect, each seems a perfect subject for him – what Eudora Welty, writing to him about the Chekhov study, called a 'Harmonic Convergence of planets'.[6] But so would many others have been, and others were indeed mooted: Shelley, Dumas *père et fils*, George Sand (about whom he got as far as writing a proposal which he didn't in the end pursue), Byron, Maupassant (another idea which he took some distance), Kipling, Tolstoy. . . .[7] It's clear from his notebooks that he also at various times thought of writing a third volume of autobiography, one in which he would concentrate on writers he had known personally.

Balzac, though, offered particular scope for a continuation of Pritchett's recent thoughts about his own early years in France, as well as about the psychology of compulsive debt. His pages on the novelist's wild accountancy – in itself a kind of serial fiction, as Pritchett points out – are vivid, comic, appalled. Balzac enabled him, too, to pursue his explicit belief that 'the work of all novelists' is 'diffused autobiography'.[8] In a personality totally different from his own yet at some points quite similar (Balzac's industriousness, for example, or the fact that in characterisation he 'likes a strong outline'), Pritchett found the subject for an absorbing narrative of psychological criticism.

Psychological speculation, too. Pritchett was too imaginative a writer to be afraid of touching in the gaps in knowledge. 'Perhaps he was too sudden,' he writes of Balzac's being unexpectedly and mortifyingly repulsed by the Marquise de Castries. 'Remember that . . . she had a mysteriously injured body.'[9] This is where his main interest lies: in Balzac's interactions with other people, and in the interactions between *those* interactions and his fiction. For all the colourfulness of the subject, there is – as in Pritchett's novels – no sustained narrative drive or suspense. What holds the reader is the compression and reanimation of a lifetime's intense critical and imaginative thought, traditional in form and style, to be sure, but densely, almost telegraphically, laden:

> In his prose and as a psychologist Balzac is far less accomplished and sensitive than Stendhal. He is rudimentary, but Proust, who admired him, went to him as a master. Balzac is no poet; his lyrical writing is conventional and sentimental; and he can be too journalistically knowing. But . . . his power of documentation, his ubiquity as a novelist are extraordinary. . . . We are constantly aware of his person for he writes as one seriously possessed.[10]

'rudimentary', 'journalistically knowing', 'ubiquity': the terms are both impressionistic and exact.

The fact that Pritchett was writing not just biography but his own uniquely accessible and absorbing form of literary criticism wasn't understood by all his reviewers. And if *Balzac* was daring in its fresh use of an old critical mode, so, too, its publishers took a risk in dressing it up in a four-square format with pictures on every page, turning it into a coffee-table book. The biographer Richard Holmes called the result 'a haphazard album', and the French scholar John Weightman grumbled that it lacked evaluation.[11] It was left to Harold Beaver, writing anonymously in the *TLS*, to make the intelligent connection that in being 'Decked out with portraits and prints' the book appropriately resembled 'the laden walls of a nineteenth-century salon'. The critical vocabulary itself was not missing, Beaver showed, but simply half concealed behind 'Something of a French epigrammatic tone – a touch of La Rochefoucauld'.[12] Pritchett's *Balzac*, as he wrote, is 'a vintage essay by an English writer whose own command of irony and comedy is akin to his subject'.

There's a comparable affinity in *The Gentle Barbarian*, Pritchett's book on Turgenev, though here he could easily have felt more constrained. He knew no Russian. He was personally friendly with some true experts: April FitzLyon, on whose life of Pauline Viardot he drew heavily; her Russian husband, Kyril (whom he enlisted to read him a few pages in the original, 'to get the sound') and Isaiah Berlin.[13] Yet Pritchett, as Berlin warmly acknowledged, had an authority of his own: that of an imaginative writer and critic who had returned to Turgenev again and again, both as a creative touchstone and as the subject of several substantial essays written over forty years.[14] Berlin – no more fearful of current intellectual fashion than Pritchett – thought he had acquired a kind of moral authority, too. 'Not only are you the best living English critic of literature (and life too – my Russian roots make me think them indissoluble),' the philosopher wrote to him, 'but you are also a very good man.'[15]

In *The Gentle Barbarian*, Pritchett writes with unmistakable originality at various points, particularly on the importance of Spanish literature to Turgenev. And even where the book's ideas didn't begin with him, Pritchett gives them his own decisive stamp, for example, in 'reminding' us that 'Turgenev is a founder and innovator: the great novels of the nineteenth century were in the future'.[16] (Part of Pritchett's conjuring trick is to make our ignorance seem less than it is: we don't know how this coloured handkerchief of knowledge got into our pocket, but he seems to have found it there.) As Isaiah Berlin recognised, his friend had insider status. Turgenev, Pritchett says, 'does not allow one character to obscure another; he lets each . . . do what it is his nature to do. And each one delights because of the gentle but firm manner in which he makes them add unsuspected traits to themselves. All is movement.'[17] Or:

> He had little power of invention but, as many writers of talent do, he got round this by turning his defects to advantage and discovered the hidden logic and drama of mood. A trivial word spoken when the company are for a moment silent will have the grace effect of a bell-like echo later on in the story. At once the structure of the story is sonata-like, one is left with the reverberations of a note hanging in the air . . .[18]

Literary biography as alive as this doesn't, as the form's detractors claim, draw attention away from the work, but takes the reader to it, and into it. There was no hypocrisy in Pritchett's opening assertion: 'My chief concern has been to enlarge the understanding of [Turgenev's] superb short stories.'[19]

Yet, at the same time, there are signs that in his labours on this book and on *Balzac* Pritchett missed the freedoms of fiction. 'Biography has the fundamental weakness that it can rarely tell us what was said or unsaid between the parties,' he writes in *The Gentle Barbarian*, 'it is a novel without dialogue.'[20] Between 1974, when *The Camberwell Beauty* appeared, and early 1978, when *The New Yorker* published 'On the Edge of the Cliff', he published only one short story.[21]

He was busy on several fronts other than biography. From 1971 he was President of the English branch of PEN (Poets, Essayists and Novelists), the organisation founded in Britain after the First World War with the aim of developing contacts between writers worldwide and protecting their interests. The work was not arduous and was mainly organised by the secretary – in those days, Josephine Pullein-Thompson, who looked on her presidents as amiable but slightly incompetent figureheads mainly to be judged by their willingness, or otherwise, to stack chairs after meetings. Pritchett, like his predecessor L. P. Hartley, made efforts with the chairs but, as with typing and driving, he never really got the knack: 'He kept *advancing* with them,' Pullein-Thompson recalled, 'he tried it in every possible way.'

This disability was not the main obstacle when it came to electing Heinrich Böll's successor as President of International PEN. At international level, the organisation had become split between members who wanted to concentrate on more or less purely literary, intellectual and social activities, and those who – partly under the influence of the Cold War – thought the focus should be on authors' freedom: helping anyone whose writing was threatened by censorship, imprisonment or other forms of political repression. To members in the second camp, Pritchett seemed too apolitical and also not young enough. The Swedish writer Per Wästberg, who had been Director of Amnesty International and was in his early forties, stood against him, but – thanks in part to support from cultures more respectful of seniority – Pritchett won by twenty-nine votes to fifteen.[22]

The sceptical were soon surprised and impressed by how much Pritchett knew of their countries' literatures. Although, from an Anglo-American point of view, he was an immensely visible and busy vehicle in the international literary traffic, he was in fact one which mainly moved in a single direction: westwards. Very little of his journalism and surprisingly few of his books appeared in languages other than English. German was an exception: his fiction and travel writing had begun to develop a profitable readership in Germany from the late 1950s on. A number of articles and theses were written about him in Continental Europe.[23] He also had some success in Japan. But his collections of literary essays weren't translated, and of the in all more than forty books of various kinds which he published in his lifetime, only two appeared in French and one each in any other European language: Bulgarian, Hungarian, Italian, Polish, Russian, Swedish – even Spanish (and in that case only in South America).[24]

Beyond the question of reputation, in terms of bureaucratic skills Pritchett was, as PEN's then Administrative Secretary later fondly recalled, 'absolutely hopeless'.[25] But because he won delegates' affection, not least through his unforced interest in them and their work, he was able to manage better than a more obviously efficient chairman might have done. Management was often needed. At the 1975 PEN Congress in Vienna, later described by the secretary as 'a cockpit for the contestants in PEN's own Cold War', the Communist East German delegation kept walking out. One source of grievance was PEN's acceptance of a donation from the West German Krupp Foundation, the money for which had originally come from arms manufacture. Pritchett pointed out that many useful charities had been set up as an act of restitution by people who had made their fortunes in questionable ways: he instanced the Carnegie Foundation. Did the East German delegation really want PEN to give the money back? Wouldn't this be seen as PEN's reliving two world wars 'for its own moral sustenance', and in the process bankrupting itself (the organisation was already chronically in debt) – rather than using such funds as it occasionally obtained towards the unselfish ends for which it had been set up? Some of those ends were, of course, the underlying cause of the fracas: totalitarian regimes were tired of being criticised for their treatment of dissident writers, and criticisms of this sort were frequent at the Vienna congress, where there was long and acrimonious debate over a motion supporting Czech writers against official harassment. (The East Germans waffled that this issue needed to be 'placed in a wider context', one which would accord with PEN's 'non-partisan principles . . . universality and international image'.) Pritchett, guided by his colourful and adroit International Secretary, Peter Elstob, only narrowly kept the meeting from dissolving into chaos.

From his own point of view, the main interest of the role was literary: he simply enjoyed and was absorbed by any contact with other writers. There were also, of course, some gossip-providing moments. In their suite at the Vienna Hilton, Victor and Dorothy were kept awake by violent quarrels in the adjacent bedroom between the playwright Eugène Ionesco and his wife. And at literary conferences, as in other contexts, Pritchett had always been amused by the persistence of cultural differences despite every pressure towards homogenisation. As early as 1956 he had written about the predicament of the English contingent at a typical PEN meeting:

> And then we shall be asked, where are literary circles? At which cafés do the coteries meet? What is the present state of manifesto writing? Where does Thought go on? What priests, which cabinet ministers, which ravening hostesses or intellectual *dames sans merci*, are feeding off which groups of poets and novelists; which publishers are in prison; where the points of conspiracy are; who has broken with whom? . . . We shall be obliged to explain away the ugly fact that nearly all English writers and editors are on speaking terms.[26]

The more ceremonial aspects of the presidency could be pleasant enough and Dorothy, in her early sixties, visibly took to them more than he did, striding out alongside any welcoming party while her husband followed on behind with the luggage. She was now Lady Pritchett, and both relished the status she was accorded as the President's consort and took care that sufficient respect was shown to Sir Victor himself. More than once, she ticked off the secretariat for not having secured a prominent enough place for him at this ceremony or that dinner and, when he was invited alone to a private meeting with the President of Israel, she caused a diplomatic flurry when she insisted on accompanying him. It was clear that Dorothy felt she was protecting Victor but clear, too, that she took an independent pleasure in these encounters – one which was usually reciprocated. She was handsome, intelligent, forthright and very good fun. Weary politicians and diplomats dragged to official functions which might otherwise, from their perspective, have seemed of little relevance cheered up when they found her sitting next to them.

The knighthood had come in 1975. Among the others honoured at the same time were Jocelyn Herbert's ex-husband Anthony Lousada, as well as Vera Lynn, who was made a Dame. 'Yes,' Pritchett wrote happily to Roger Angell, 'in a totally un-English fit – perhaps a sign of decadence – they decided to dub a writer – I believe John Betjeman is the only other – instead of the usual actors, publishers, footballers, scientists and musicians.'[27] He added that it didn't seem to make any practical difference: 'Shops, taxi-drivers etc. still warmly stick to Pritchard, "guv", "chief", "ducks", or "darling."'

In private, the couple took a lot of innocent pleasure in their new titles. 'Dorothy & I aren't quite sure who we are at the moment,' he told Al Alvarez. 'It's as though we are four people who've just met and we are very polite to each other in the house. Outside, too.'[28] The following Valentine's Day, he wrote to Dorothy, 'My dear Lady Pritchett, May I

My dear Lady Pritchelt

May I presume on

this happy day to offer to

your ladyship my entire

HEART

Sir Victor.

presume on this happy day to offer your ladyship my entire HEART,'
and drew a heart around the word, signing himself with a flourish, 'Sir
Victor'.[29] There was some gentle teasing among the family and friends.
'Don't trip over the carpet when you rise Sir Victor,' his sister Kathleen
warned him, and the writer Julia O'Faolain, daughter of his old friend
Sean, told him, ' "Sir Victor" sounds like someone who is about to do
something wicked in an old novel.'[30]

Not all the reactions were so good-natured. At a *TLS* Christmas
party where a famous poet, not yet knighted, was holding court among
young writers and critics, Pritchett was wedged in a corner. With sly
politesse, the poet asked the others, 'Do you know "Sir" Victor
Pritchett?' The English upper middle class have always excelled at such
put-downs: envy or malice disownable as teasing. Pritchett had met it
thousands of times. The only sign he gave of having noticed was that
his eyes darted amusedly from the poet to the others. What interested
him, it was clear, was not his own reaction, but theirs.

International PEN's meetings seemed to be becoming ever more
frequent. There were three that year alone, in Hong Kong, at The
Hague and in London, and much of the business was both quarrelsome
and purely internal: long debates about who should pay the accommodation costs of delegates at the meetings, or about whether the
organisation's business could be conducted in languages other than the
customary English and French. Pritchett had a new tussle with the East
German contingent in 1976, when they objected to the anti-
Communist Arthur Koestler's having been invited to give a keynote
speech. 'I hate conferences and all their petty acrimonies,' Pritchett
told Daniel Aaron.[31] Even without Roger Angell's frequent nudges
about the length of time that had passed since he had seen any fiction
from Pritchett, he would have been conscious that he needed to ration
his energies, not to speak of his earning power. With lucky timing, the
historian Veronica Wedgwood decided to stand down as President of
the Society of Authors. Like the presidency of PEN, it was an unpaid
role, but the Society was purely British in scope, so Pritchett could fit in
the meetings much more easily than PEN's. Besides, his links with the
organisation went back a long way.[32] He had been involved in its initial
setting up of the Somerset Maugham prize, had been consulted about
several of the Society's campaigns – for example, on behalf of writers
working freelance for the BBC – and had been a member of its Council
in the early 1960s. In 1977 he resigned as head of PEN with a speech
whose vein of light ironic teasing must have mystified the East Germans

(the minutes record: 'He thanked the Committee for putting up with him. He said that he was normally a very gentle man, but when he really let himself go there was no holding him, and he thanked the Committee for . . . not provoking him to those lengths').[33] Immediately, he became President of the Society of Authors. Meanwhile, the Turgenev book was finished and he began to focus once again on a combination of reviewing – particularly, these days, for the *New York Review of Books* (he wrote eleven long pieces for the fortnightly journal in 1977)[34] – and short fiction.

Pritchett had been thinking a good deal about old age: his own and that of his late father.* The theme naturally found its way into his writing. 'The Worshippers', for example, written in the late 1970s, is about a pair of old men – one of them, Lavender, in part based on Victor's brother Cyril – and their relationships with, and memories of, other old men in their own lives: memories which in Lavender's case, it emerges, are also fantasies. Pritchett beautifully entwines the unreliability of Lavender's stories about his background with the physical unreliability of his ageing body. The symbolic centre is a portrait of a man whom Lavender claims as an ancestor, but who in fact has no connection with him. There's a moment when Lavender reflects, 'It was disturbing when you thought about it . . . that an old man who must have weighed two hundred and fifty pounds in life should weigh so little in a portrait, even allowing for the frame.'[35] It comes soon after we've seen Lavender, once a seaman, strip down to his underpants to scrub out his office, and much of the story's poignancy comes from this sheer corporeality. The characters are comically irritating, Lavender with his naval slang and his other petty vanities; the predatory Mrs Baum with her stock reactions ('Oh dear. . . . Look at that. Another bomb in Belfast'),[36] both of them desperately trying not to lose what's left of their grip. Yet Pritchett's fiction, as unyielding as a picture by Lucian Freud, forces us to care about them.

---

* In addition to 'Just a Little More' (see above, p. 186), he wrote another account of bereavement, based on his father's widowerhood, in 'The Spree'. The old man in the story 'seemed, because of his loneliness, to be dragging an increasing load of unsaid things behind him, things he had no one to tell. With his son and daughter-in-law and their young friends he sat with his mouth open ready to speak, but he could never get a word out. . . . What he needed was not friends, for since so many friends had died he had become a stranger: he needed another stranger. . . . He lowered his eyes and became shy. Grief – what was it? A craving. Yet not for a face or even a voice or even for love, but for a body. But dressed. Say, in a flowered dress.' CS, p. 922.

'The Spanish Bed', also written in the late 1970s, similarly explores ageing alongside questions of veracity, in this case in the Jamesian scenario of a man obsessed with a dead writer, whose books he collects and whose house he inhabits, but who finds himself in a psychological maze when he tries to track down the writer's former wife. (It may have occurred to Pritchett that anyone who became interested in his own life would face a problem like this.) Here, too, is a painting which turns out to be inauthentic,[37] and a no less questionable living person: does Dr Billiter meet two Miss Wards, or is there really only one? The uncertainty is philosophical, but it is also physical: the faces of the old, Pritchett notices, mutate unpredictably between a younger self and one that seems impossibly decrepit.

The most vivid and moving of this group of stories, though, is based on Gerald Brenan. Whatever Brenan was interested in became an obsession, and mortality was no exception: his letters and conversation were increasingly dominated by the subject. In the late 1960s, when he was well into his seventies, Brenan had been introduced to a clever and beautiful young woman called Lynda Price. She had recently left Chelsea Art School and her ambition was to be a poet. She fell in love with the widower's vivacious intellect, his inexhaustible appetite to teach, his library. According to his biographer, the relationship was never physical, though Gerald liked to give the impression that it was. Lynda moved in with him in Málaga and stayed for sixteen years, while marrying a man closer to her own age with whom she had children. When they were first together, Brenan wrote about her to everyone he knew. 'I want to . . . eat her, vocation and all. Or else jump over a cliff for her sake,' he said in one letter.[38] Pritchett took the setting of his story 'On the Edge of the Cliff' from a recent holiday in Cornwall, but he was so fascinated by his friend's situation that the setting may also have been influenced by Brenan's reckless words.[39]

In certain obvious ways, the story is a direct transcription. Rowena is a twenty-five-year-old poet, Harry a septuagenarian 'like a general with a literary turn'.[40] But what gives the narrative much of its power is, again, its intimate physicality ('His glasses were off and he had finished shaving and he turned a face savaged to the point of saintliness by age, but with a heavy underlip that made him look helplessly brutal. She laughed at the soap in his ears').[41] Along with this, once more, goes an intense atmosphere of psychological vulnerability mixed with protectiveness – not least, Harry's for Rowena. All is underpinned by the obvious yet never clichéd symbolism of the terrain, especially on the couple's walk to Withy Hole, a place where the sea tunnels cruelly in under the cliffs:

> The wind did not move the old man's tough thatch of hair but made his big ears stick out. Rowena bound her loose hair with a scarf. From low cliff to high cliff, over the cropped turf . . . where the millions of sea pinks and daisies were scattered, mile after mile in their colonies, the old man led the way, digging his knees into the air, gesticulating, talking. . . .
>
> Now, once more, they were looking at the great meaningless wound. As he stood at the edge he seemed to her to be at one with it. It reminded her of his mouth when she had once seen it (with a horror she tried to wipe from her mind) before he had put his dentures in. Of her father's too.
>
> . . . They found a bank on the seaward side out of the wind where the sun burned and they rested.
>
> 'Heaven,' she said and closed her eyes. . . .
>
> 'What are you thinking about?' she asked without opening her eyes.
>
> He was going to say 'At my age one is always thinking about death,' but he said 'You.'[42]

The writing is densely packed, from the vivid unexpectedness of 'digging his knees into the air' to the eliding associations of love, death and heaven. Earlier in the story, Harry met a former mistress accompanied by a young man whom he mistook for her son. There's a subtle interplay with how the relationship between Harry and Rowena simultaneously develops and, like the cliff edge, is undermined. Soon after Rowena goes to bed with Harry for the first time, we learn that he hasn't been telling her the whole truth about his earlier affair.

Amid this mixed colouring, much of what preoccupied Pritchett, not only in these particular stories but in others he wrote in his late seventies, was truth-telling and its opposites: the adulterous deception of one old friend by another in his acid sketch, 'The Accompanist', or the kinder but no less hypocritical stratagems by which the deceived mistress in 'A Family Man' both outwits and protects her lover's wife. The latter story is striking, too, for its insight into the situation of a voluntarily single, emancipated woman, a continuous theme of Pritchett's, put down here in a few spare, ironic strokes. The more Berenice imagined her rival, Mrs Cork, the more she felt for her, the more she saw eye to eye with her in the pleasant busy middle ground of womanish feelings and moods, for as a woman living alone she felt a firm loyalty to her sex. During this last summer when the family were on holiday she had seen them glued together again as they sat with dozens of other families in the aeroplane that was taking them abroad, so that it seemed to her that the London sky was rumbling day after day, night after night, with matrimony thirty thousand feet above the city. . . . Among families she felt herself to be strange and necessary – a necessary secret.[43]

These pieces are not without accidental signs of the author's ageing. The young people in 'The Accompanist' come across as middle aged, and the idiom of 'A Family Man' is similarly dated (when did English-women last address each other in private as 'Mrs' whatever?). But they are fluid, bold, full of sharp insights and surprises, and leave their readers in a place quite different from where they thought they were being taken.

If Pritchett wasn't always sure how the young spoke, or thought, he more often than not got them right, as in the case of Rowena in 'On the Edge of the Cliff'. As a reviewer, he was exceptionally sympathetic to the work of young writers. He was among the first to praise *Midnight's Children*: Salman Rushdie was, he announced, 'a great novelist – one with startling imaginative and intellectual resources, a master of perpetual story-telling'.[44] He wrote discriminatingly about Ian McEwan, 'the most arresting talent in the youngest generation of English short story writers'.[45] To Paul Theroux, his enthusiastic review of *Railway Bazaar* 'mattered to me more than any review I have ever got'[46] and was the start of a friendship. At the *New Statesman*, Pritchett was a valued mentor to young members of the editorial staff, Martin Amis among them.[47] To Oliver Pritchett, meanwhile, who was also making a literary career, he was 'fantastically supportive'. Oliver, like his father before him, was by now married with a young son and daughter, paying the bills through journalism and getting some short stories published, as well as a novel, *A Prize Paradise*.[48] 'All these were generously praised by my father,' he later wrote, 'over-praised, I'm afraid.' But while Pritchett was a generous critic, he was not, in fact, an overgenerous one. He knew how to praise – a harder skill than it might seem – but what made his good opinion worth having was precisely the stringency of his taste. Even with Oliver's work, his judgements could be practical to the point of bluntness: 'The first paragraph of your tale can be cut to the two first lines; in fact a general shredding throughout would be worthwhile. . . . At present it is rather flat and dispersed.'[49]

He relaxed his standards for just one author, in the earliest stages of her career. Oliver's and Joan's daughter Georgia began to tell stories before she could write, buttonholing members of her family with them and recording them on tape. She was the only person allowed to sit in Pritchett's study while he worked. She would sit there as quietly as she could, making models out of his wire-and-cotton pipe cleaners, waiting for the moment when he would go to his bookcase and she might get him to talk. When she was ten or twelve, the publication of collections of his stories prompted her to give him exercise books containing some of her own, and also to send him comments on his work, writer to writer. Victor gravely returned these compliments but Georgia, to her later regret, didn't keep his letters. She was soon preoccupied with another book, her autobiography, and with the difficulty of having too much material – especially about 'the dreadful cruelty of my parents' – to keep to the two-volume exemplar set by her grandfather. He told her not to worry and just to write it all down.

Georgia's enthusiasm for reading, as well as writing, along with her brother Matthew's for painting, helped to make up for some disappointments of their grandfather's. His Turgenev book sold poorly – less than a thousand copies in the UK.[50] Norah Smallwood confidently urged a promotional drive by Chatto, but enthusiasm for a proposed new collected edition of his stories had to overcome the fact that large numbers of copies of his recent books remained in the warehouse. When Carmen Callil took over as Managing Director of Chatto in the early 1980s, Pritchett suspected her of neglecting him. In fact, she exerted a lot of pressure to get his earlier books reprinted, but met strong resistance from her more budget-conscious colleagues.[51]

One perception gaining ground in the climate of the time was that Pritchett's fiction gave short shrift to women. When *Dead Man Leading* was suggested for a possible reissue, an internal report at Chatto commented,

> There seems to be another VSP staple idea here, also found in *Mr B[eluncle]*, that women, however strong they are as individuals, simply cannot comprehend the driving ambitions of men and that their sexual or emotional demands, especially when amplified by marriage or motherhood, inevitably threaten men's clarity of mind and power of achievement.[52]

It was true that Pritchett's views on sexual politics were essentially traditional and out of tune with the mood of the 1970s. He was too wide awake not to have noticed this and there was an element of obstinate mischief in his reaction. Just as in his books on Meredith and Balzac he challenged current academic orthodoxy about literary biography, so, though less comprehendingly, he set out to tease the generation of Kate Millett and Germaine Greer by insisting on a distinction between 'masculine' and 'feminine' traditions in fiction.[53] But he had always loved and needed women, and imagined them vividly in his fiction. As Val Cunningham was to say, 'He understands the love of sons and mothers as few other writers and critics do. His stories are notable for their deep inwardness with men among women, with mothers and wives as presences.'[54] Pritchett was no bigot. When, as a political gesture, the *Guardian*'s literary editor, W. L. Webb brought Angela Carter to the all-male literary lunch club at Bertorelli's, Pritchett, unlike some of his stuffier fellow members, went out of his way to talk to her and their conversation continued animatedly throughout most of the meal.[55] But he would not himself have broken the rules like Webb, and when it was proposed that another literary society to which he belonged should be opened to women, he surprised some members by making it clear that if it happened he would resign.[56]

What was this about? It may have been a straightforwardly domestic reaction. Dorothy had always been a jealous woman and, like many other wives, appreciated her husband's all-male social life as a pleasantly unthreatening break in marital proximity. But on Victor's own part, the weakening of status which anyone can feel in old age may have been compounded by the increasingly vocal feminism of women who had reached positions of cultural power which affected him. Carmen Callil was an example. Although she did her best for Pritchett, whom she adored, he didn't know this and, coming as she had from the feminist publishing house Virago, her reputation didn't reassure him.

Meanwhile, the atmosphere even at the distinctly male-dominated *New Statesman* was unsettled by a different and, it transpired for Pritchett – who, apart from writing regularly for the magazine, was still on the board – more direct kind of threat. The paper was struggling financially and, in 1977, the latest of its hard-pressed editors, the genial Anthony Howard, moved on. Three candidates emerged as front runners to succeed him. The process was democratic: every member of the magazine's staff, from deputy editor to cartoonist, had a vote. The shortlist consisted of Neil Ascherson, an acute liberal-left commentator mainly associated with the *Observer*, where he had recently been East European correspondent; the brilliant and multifaceted poet James Fenton, who had been a correspondent in Indo-China and was currently the *New Statesman's* political columnist, but who was not yet thirty; and Bruce Page, a no-nonsense Australian journalist who had spent much of his career on the *Sunday Times* and more recently had been working for the relatively downmarket and conservative *Daily Express*.

Older hands were divided between support for Page, whom they thought the most dynamic and hard-headed of the three, and Ascherson, with whom they had more political sympathy. Both men were in their forties. Pritchett favoured Ascherson, partly out of a shrewd sense that he would be more likely to safeguard the cultural standards of the 'back half'. But younger people on the staff, such as Christopher Hitchens and Martin Amis – who had taken over from Claire Tomalin as literary editor – favoured Fenton, who had been their contemporary at Oxford and was a close friend. Pritchett took Fenton seriously enough to have him to lunch at Regent's Park Terrace. But it was clear to him not only that, because of Fenton's relative inexperience, he couldn't win, but that he would let in Page by taking votes from Ascherson. Pritchett warned Amis of this but Fenton's supporters, to their later regret, persisted and Pritchett's fears were fulfilled.[57]

Page was robust but fundamentally out of sympathy with the magazine's style. Literally so: he rejected any premium on good writing.[58] When Amis gave up the literary editorship to concentrate on his own work, Page brought in the clever Marxist critic and novelist, David Caute, to succeed him. Loyal readers were dismayed by the ensuing influx of stodginess. Soon, many of them, along with several of the magazine's best writers, moved on to the new *London Review of Books*, whose founding editor was an earlier *Statesman* refugee, Karl Miller.[59] Pritchett, meanwhile, resigned from the board. Out of old loyalty to the magazine he said that his decision was unrelated to Page's appointment, but no one believed him, Page least of all.[60]

The sequel was unhappy. The deputy literary editor, Julian Barnes, stayed on for a time and did his best to keep channels of communication with Pritchett open. In May 1979 he accepted a new story by him, 'Tea with Mrs Bittell', but it kept being squeezed out, and at the end of November, after a succession of promises and postponements, David Caute wrote Pritchett a graceless letter saying 'we shall not, after all, publish your story. . . . For this magazine it's quite long and I must admit that, while admiring its qualities of tact and observation, I have only a limited enthusiasm for it.'[61]

This was half a century after a story by Pritchett first appeared in the *New Statesman* and about as clumsy an end to the association as could have been imagined. It said more about what was happening to the magazine than about Pritchett's current international standing. Although *The New Yorker*, too, had declined 'Tea with Mrs Bittell', it continued to publish other stories and articles by Pritchett into the early 1980s. And he remained a regular contributor to the *New York Review of Books*. Still, he was wounded, and Caute's behaviour, though attributed by Julian Barnes simply to failure of taste,[62] may also in part have reflected the fact that, in a culture increasingly swayed by academic trends, Pritchett's standing was newly in question. An American student of the time who found his essays helpful was firmly warned off by her professor on the ground that he was too impressionistic, too biographical: where was the theoretical under-pinning?[63] Karl Miller had encountered similar objections earlier, when he was Pritchett's editor at the *Statesman*, and memorably defended him in the *New York Review of Books*. 'He is said to guess and improvise too much,' Miller wrote, 'to be too elliptical and impressionistic'; but the best answer to such charges, he said, lay not only in Pritchett's criticism, but in *A Cab at the Door* and *Midnight Oil*: 'These very funny and very serious books are a rebuke to comedy as it is normally practised, and their precisions are a rebuke to the devotees of precision.'[64]

Pritchett himself, in turn, had rarely been hesitant about rebuking academia when he thought it necessary. Reviewing Victor Brombert's 1966 book on Flaubert, he had written: 'It is depressing to find so good a critic of Flaubert – of all people – scattering academic jargon and archaisms in his prose.' He criticised 'the present academic habit of turning literary criticism into technology' and concluded that criticism 'does not add to its status by opening an intellectual hardware store'.[65] The piece was quoted by Gore Vidal, in a flamboyant rebuttal of Pritchett's detractors published in 1979:

> We had fallen into the error of believing that [novels] were written for critics, for literary historians, for students or for leisured persons of academic tastes. . . . Our universities are positively humming with the sound of fools rushing in. The odd angel bleakly hovers; casts no

shadow . . . as McDonald's drives out good food, so these hacks of academe drive out good prose.[66]

Pritchett, by contrast, Vidal wrote, had continued for a third of a century

> to be the best English-language critic of . . . well, the *living* novel. . . . At work on a text, Pritchett is rather like one of those amorphic sea-creatures who float from bright complicated shell to shell. Once at home within the shell he is able to describe for us in precise detail the secrets of the shell's interior; and he is able to show us, from the maker's own angle, the world the maker saw.

'It would be nice', Vidal concluded, 'if Sir Victor lived forever.'

Parents and grandparents live on in their descendants. Like Oliver and his family, Josephine and hers now lived in south London, her husband Brian having left the army to work as a parliamentary lobbyist and part-time author.[67] Victor was an affectionate if, these days, a sometimes abstracted patriarch. In common with most people who have had their first children relatively late, he could be bewildered by the evidence of change which the young forced on him: what could have possessed Caspar Murphy, a grandson of whom he was very fond, to shave his head and get tattooed? The grandchildren were conscious of a gap between Victor's reputation and the quiet figure they encountered at Regent's Park Terrace. In retrospect, some of them are unsure whether this was a matter of writerly preoccupation – the observer keeping himself in the background – or of deference to their grandmother, whose forcefulness grew more apparent as Victor aged. 'Granny was such a powerful, dominant figure that she demanded all the attention,' Josephine's sons agreed later. 'Grandpa was much more passive, and sat back.' Oliver's artist-to-be son Matthew, who was particularly fascinated by his grandfather's links with the Paris of modernism and the Spain of the 1930s, saw this removedness in him, too, but understood from it that writing was hard work: 'You know, it wasn't just inspiration and "Oh my goodness here we go". It was like climbing a mountain.'

Georgia, meanwhile, always had a particularly close relationship with both of her father's parents. At sixteen, she went to Victor's old school, Alleyn's, going on to read English Literature at university.

Victor lent her some of the set books – Coleridge, Keats, Victorian novelists, Saul Bellow – but what pleased him most was that she was still writing. She was a frequent visitor to 12 Regent's Park Terrace – though, to save Victor's energies, Dorothy firmly organised his contacts with most members of the family, giving precise instructions about when they should arrive (or even, they joked, when they should phone) and sending them on their way soon after lunch was over. Victor needed this protection. He still believed in his own energy but in fact he tired easily and was becoming forgetful. Increasingly, Dorothy had to prompt him: 'She was the archivist,' Georgia recalls. 'She remembered everything, all the stories. She knew his work better than he did. What was lovely was that she always loved hearing him tell anecdotes that she'd obviously heard lots of times before.'

Often, those anecdotes were about their earlier life together. 'Cocky Olly', published in his last collection of stories, *A Careless Widow*, when he was eighty-eight, is about the game Josephine and Oliver had played with the Dunn girls and their friends at Stokke, and particularly about the Partridges and their unhappy long-dead son, Burgo. Victor continued to write stories about the old and their muddles, especially in relation to possessions – the 'Things' which gave a title to one of these pieces. The notebook dated 1986 in which he drafted 'Cocky Olly' includes grumbles about the geriatric atmosphere of the Garrick ('An old folks home'), and about people who suck up to their famous seniors, including an old friend whom he nicknamed 'Arse-licker', describing him harshly as 'The young man who attaches himself to an older man, with the idea of self-advancement.' Another note begins sadly, 'The Old Man – there is nothing to say for old age, vigorous though he is.'[68]

Memory apart – and a good memory had been one of his assets – Pritchett showed few public signs of flagging. He busied himself with the needs of other writers, both in his official role at the Society of Authors and more personally. On Pritchett's eightieth birthday, Gerald Brenan had written him one of the dramatic farewell letters to which Brenan's friends were becoming accustomed during his long decline:

> my mind has gone and only works in flashes . . . what on earth is to be done with me? No Basque E.T.A. man has appeared to give me a last shot. I long to die at once and get the famous passage over. . . . But before I say goodbye to you and Dorothy I would like to thank you for all the warmth & friendship you have shown me in the past.

Now I shall choose my private moment for doing my vanishing trick and not bother you again. . . .[69]

Another seven years were to pass before Brenan actually vanished and in the interim came other letters lamenting his continual – but, it was to transpire, much exaggerated – financial worries. Pritchett, who had not forgotten Brenan's early generosity, mobilised support in England, persuading the Royal Literary Fund (under the presidency of his friend Janet Adam Smith) to send the old man a grant of £4500 to tide him over and leading a successful campaign for a regular income to be made available to him out of the Civil List.[70]

Pritchett's own labours continued. He collected an *Oxford Book of Short Stories*, published in 1981 after difficult negotiations with his editors at OUP over what the best choices might be (the selection was anglophone but it included American, Irish and Commonwealth writers, as well as British ones), and also about copyright and availability. He still taught in the USA, mainly these days at Vanderbilt University in Nashville in Tennessee. He wrote about the story of *La Bohème* for the Metropolitan Opera in 1983. He published yet new books of essays and stories, and filled notebooks with ideas for more. 'The Wedding' was turned into a television drama.[71] Eventually, though, even Ptitchett had to slow down. He suffered an attack of bronchial pneumonia and began to have problems with his prostate gland. As a result, he took a break from reviewing, which was still one of his main sources of income. His last biography – of Chekhov – took him four years to write: not long by the standards of most authors half his age, but too long for him. The publishers' advance ran out halfway through. Dorothy managed their funds shrewdly, but it had always been a prerequisite of Victor's work that, to some degree, it should be driven by a sense of financial pressure. In real terms, his predicament in old age was no worse than Gerald Brenan's had been. To the old, though, financial anxiety isn't always measurable by the strictest accounting. The Royal Literary Fund understood this and, in May 1986, the Fund's new President, Arthur Crook, pushed through the letter box of his old friend and neighbour a cheque for £5000. Pritchett, in thanks, described the money rightly as 'a welcome token of the friendship of fellow writers'.

The Chekhov book eventually appeared in 1988. It was published by Hodder and Stoughton. 'God! & I've just written to him asking what he's doing,' Carmen Callil scribbled on a Chatto internal memo informing her of the Hodder deal. 'I don't think we're keeping in touch with him enough.' Only a few weeks before, yet another publisher had published a Pritchett miscellany. 'I think it's ridiculous that Quartet have brought out a V. S. Pritchett Reader,' Callil wrote on that occasion to her beleaguered staff, 'he is one of our most important backlist authors and it's we who should be reissuing his works.'[72]

Pritchett's fame was evident enough. He was often interviewed on television, not least about what it was like to grow old, a topic about which he could be very funny ('It excites me to go up and down stairs. I rather swank about it').[73] He admitted, though, that he found it hard to distinguish between his current sense of himself and how he had felt in the past. Having been born in 1900, he said, 'Makes me feel historic, you know. I used to feel historical when I was five.' It was mainly through other people that he sensed the difference: through local children, especially, who sometimes jeered at him: 'Yes, I mind that – I'd damn well hit them if I could reach them.'

Filmed and photographed, painted and interviewed, Pritchett was increasingly preoccupied with the gap between self and reputation, and explored it again in 'The Image Trade', the last story in the last of his books, about an ageing writer's dealings with a famous photographer. The latter is a man of unsettling certainty in his working methods (he moves a blue pot which the writer's wife gave him twenty-four years earlier; 'How dare you move my wife?' the writer confusedly thinks), and also one whose concentration on externals brings the writer's inner turmoil almost to the point of paranoia, while simultaneously to a point of cruel lucidity:

> My face is nothing. At my age I don't need it. It is no more than a servant I push around before me. Or a football I kick ahead of me, taking all the blows, in shops, in the streets. . . . I send it to smirk at parties, to give lectures. It has a mouth. I've no idea what it says. It calls people by the wrong names. It is an indiscriminate little grinner. It kisses people I've never met.

Fame, Pritchett knew well, is oddly localised. The writer in 'The Image Trade' sees a picture of himself at the crowded opening of the photographer's show; but when he goes home afterwards, no one notices him getting off the bus. Groups of book lovers taking guided tours of Hampstead and Camden would often crowd the pavement near his house, and Pritchett would hear his name mentioned among those of other famous local residents, while pushing his way through unrecognised, on his way to the shops.

Dorothy still sent him out to do the household shopping, but as his eighties turned into his nineties he sometimes used the same list twice on the same day, or got lost altogether, until the famous neighbours scattered in search and he was brought home, protesting violently. He could show a startlingly fiery side. His notebooks alternated between clarity and touching confusion: 'I live at 12 Rents. Many cars are parked there. Can I see my own writing.'[74] On walks in Regent's Park and Primrose Hill, he had to remind himself that it was thought best for old men not to talk to people they didn't know. As always, he put down exactly what he had found: 'There is a firm unwritten law of behaviour. You may stare at people but you must not talk to strangers. . . . You are there to walk not to talk to strangers . . . If you sit on a seat & merely say "Nice Day", there will be a shocked silence. There will be a firm silence. You are a walker not a talker.' A more cheerful note reads, 'Park. Best sight – children of course. They can run.' He told Oliver he badly wanted to write another story. Oliver advised him to rest on his laurels, but his father went on trying. It wasn't for nothing that one of Walter's favourite phrases, 'just a little more', had stuck in his mind. However reluctantly, Victor was still his father's son.

One last book of new stories, A Careless Widow, appeared in 1989 and won the £10,000 W. H. Smith award. For several years, Jason Epstein had been urging the idea of publishing major collections of the stories and essays. They appeared in 1990 and 1992 respectively: despite their titles, far from complete, yet containing more than 2500 pages between them. Frank Kermode, speaking for almost all reviewers, called the project 'an irrefutable testimony' to Pritchett's stature.[75]

The author himself, by now, had at last put down his pen, at least as far as work for publication was concerned. In his early nineties there were various ailments. Dorothy looked after him well and was reluctant to ask for help. It was unclear whether he understood everything that was going on in his family: the tragedies that struck when first Josephine's husband, Brian, then her only daughter, Livvy, died; Justin's successes in a shipping company, Matthew's as a newspaper cartoonist, Caspar's finding his way into social work like his mother, the beginnings of Georgia's career – initially in BBC radio – as a professional writer. There was no doubt, though, about his pleasure in the first of his great-grandchildren.[76]

In April 1995 he had a stroke and spent a couple of weeks in

University College Hospital, where he impressed the nurses by speaking, and sometimes singing, in foreign tongues: was Sir Victor French? Spanish? At home, Dorothy had their bed moved into the ground-floor dining room at the front of the house, where they awkwardly camped. He enjoyed being taken out by his children and grandchildren, especially to Queen Mary's Rose Garden in Regent's Park, but on one occasion he mistook a grandson for his bank manager and in general he inclined to fret that Dorothy might not know where he was. Things became increasingly difficult. Mark Le Fanu, Secretary of the Society of Authors, wrote early in 1996 to condole with Dorothy and to offer whatever help the Society could give to its President, and she replied frankly,

> Things are very sad here. Victor's leg . . . gives a lot of pain and his memory of recent events and times has quite gone. He talks, eats and drinks quite happily, and though exasperated when he talks and thinks of writing and can't, is cheerful. Highlight of week is Thursday, when Oliver comes to stay the night or Josephine takes him for a drive. About money: I am taking a lot of private help but managing, but since you raise the matter I'll tell if our funds run out. Much love to you all from both of us. . . . [77]

Still, almost a year passed before, in December 1996, she could be persuaded to let him be moved into a nursing home: the Goldsborough, in Hornsey Lane. There, the following month, he had a second major stroke. He died at the Whittington Hospital on 20 March 1997.

The younger Dorothy, bereft and – as far as friends but not family were concerned – increasingly reclusive, developed a cancer and followed him only four years later. She had told Georgia that, after Victor's death, she dreamed about him every night: 'romantic, loving dreams in which they were reunited'. Because of this, she always looked forward to sleep.

Pritchett's obituaries were full and laudatory, but some years earlier he himself had said most of what was needed in one of the wobbly entries in the last of his many notebooks: 'A walker. . . . Cheered by the beauty of my wife. Angered by high taxes. . . . I like travel. I like books. I do not care much for television. I fear death.'[78] The final words, on a separate page and twice underlined, are:

Three Cheers, standing ovation.

Further Acknowledgements

A lot of people who knew Pritchett, in addition to those mentioned in the earlier Acknowledgements, gave assistance of various kinds. I particularly thank Daniel Aaron, Mark Amory, Martin Amis, Nicholas Ayer, Ann Baer, Julian Barnes, George Core, Barbara Epstein, James Fenton, Dean Flower, Paul Freedman, Margaret Gardiner, Wynne and Kitty Godley, Joy Law, Mark Le Fanu, Ved Mehta, Karl Miller, Janetta Parladé, William Pritchard, Josephine Pullein-Thompson, Andrew Roberts, Natasha Spender, Dee Wells and Kyril Zinoviev. I am also grateful to David and June Rabbitts for showing me Maidencourt, where they now live, and for Mr Rabbitts's memories of the Pritchetts; to Josette Loder, of Stokke Manor; and to John Allsopp, of Wadwick House.

Archivists often know more about the contents of their collections than do researchers and I've been fortunate in this respect in the archives I have consulted. My special debts to the Ransom Center at Austin Texas and to the New York Public Library have already been mentioned. Among the staff at Austin I thank in particular the Director, Tom Staley and his colleagues Pat Fox, John Kirkpatrick and Tara Wenger. At the Berg, I was lucky to have the assistance and friendship of Diana Burnham and Stephen Crook. I am also grateful to the President of the New York Public Library, Paul LeClerc, to the curator of the Berg Collection, Isaac Gewirtz, and in particular to Philip Milito for checking references to Berg materials.

In alphabetical order of other collections, I thank the Archives of Alleyn's School and their Honorary Archivist, Peter Rodway; the Library of the Athenaeum and its Librarian, Sarah Dodgson; the BBC Written Archives and their former researcher, Haven Lutaaya; the archive of Bedales School; the Biblioteca Municipal de San Juan, Ibiza, and its librarian Antonia Ferrer; the Manuscripts Division of the British

Further Acknowledgements

Library and one of its curators, Chris Fletcher; the British Library's Newspaper Library at Colindale; the archive of the First Church of Christ Scientist; the London Library; the Office of the Registrar General, Dublin; the Rare Books and Special Collections Department at Firestone Library, Princeton University; the Public Record Office; the Special Collections at Reading University and their archivist, Michael Bott; the Society of Authors; and the University of Sussex Library Special Collections. I am also grateful to the secretary of the Beefsteak Club, the Librarian of the Garrick Club and Bertram Rota Ltd.

Suggestions, advice, answers to enquiries and help and support of other kinds came from Maria Aitken, Donald Antrim, Amy Azzarito, Martin Beagles, Thomas Bender, Andrew Biswell, Emily Braun, Tom Buk-Swienty, Elisabeth Cameron, Martha Campbell, Elisheva Carlebach, Anne Chisholm, Stefan Collini, Caleb Crain, Iliana Cranston, Katherine Del Tufo, Helen Dunmore, John Fairleigh, Giles Fitzherbert, Colin Fox, Jonathan Gathorne-Hardy, Ian Gibson, Bei Ling Huang, Jenny Hughes, Samuel and Liz Hynes, Ann Kelly, Roger Keyes, Franziska Kirchner, Pamela Leo, Peter Martin, Caroline Moorehead, Tom Paulin, Antonia Phillips, Caryl Phillips, Alain Raitt, Stacy Schiff, Helen Simpson, Susan Sontag, John Sutherland, Colm Toibin, Beryl Treglown and the late Geoffrey Treglown, Sam Treglown, the late Sir Stephen Tumim, Clare Vigors, Caroline Walsh, Maurice Walsh, James Wood and Sofka Zinoviev.

One of Dorothy Pritchett's last wishes was that English Heritage should put up a blue plaque to her husband. The relevant committee has baffled everyone by its resistance to this widely supported idea. Among those who have helped press the case – though so far without success – are the secretary of the Royal Society of Literature, Maggie Fergusson, and James Campbell of the *Times Literary Supplement*.

Permissions

The authorship of copyright materials from which extracts have been quoted is made clear in the text or in the notes, or both. The claims in copyright of the authors of those materials or their heirs and assigns are acknowledged by the author and publisher of this book. Every attempt has been made to contact the literary estates concerned. The author and publisher are particularly grateful to the following copyright holders and/or their agents: Gordon Pritchett; Oliver Pritchett (quotations from V. S. Pritchett and Lady Pritchett): A. Alvarez; Margaret Hanbury,

27 Walcot Square, London SE11 4UP (Estate of Gerald Brenan); Pollinger Ltd (the Richard Church Estate); Richard Garnett (David Garnett); Luke Gertler (Mark Gertler); Gill Coleridge (Frances Partridge); Elena Wilson and Farrar, Straus and Giroux, LCC (Edmund Wilson). Thanks are due, too, to the following for permission to quote from materials in their possession: the BBC Written Archives; the Berg Collection of English and American Literature at the New York Public Library, Astor, Lenox and Tilden Foundations; the Harry Ransom Humanities Research Center at the University of Texas at Austin, Gerald Brenan Collection, John Lehmann Papers and V. S. Pritchett Collection. Materials from the *New Yorker* Archives in the New York Public Library are reproduced courtesy of *The New Yorker*/The Condé Nast Publications Inc., www.newyorker.com.

References and Abbreviations

This is a book for the general reader, but it makes use of unpublished and uncollected materials which scholars may want to refer to. I have tried to make the footnotes detailed enough to enable anyone to find the source without too much difficulty, but for simplicity's sake, in the case of references to manuscript materials and to newspapers and magazines, where a date is available, I have generally used that alone rather than fuller bibliographical details. Failing a date, in the case of material in public archives I give the file reference.

1 *Short titles of books by VSP*
Unless otherwise stated, the text referred to is the first UK edition.

AHA	*At Home and Abroad*	1989
BL	*Blind Love*	1969
BG	*Books in General*	1953
CD	*A Cab at the Door*	1968
CB	*The Camberwell Beauty*	1974
CE	*Complete Essays*	1992
CS	*Complete Short Stories*	1990
CW	*A Careless Widow*	1989
Chekhov	*Chekhov: A Spirit Set Free*	1988
Clare D	*Clare Drummer*	1929
DML	*Dead Man Leading*	1937
Dublin	*Dublin: A Portrait*	1967
FO	*The Fly in the Ointment*	1978
Foreign Faces	*Foreign Faces*	1964 (US *The Offensive Traveller*)
IMGB	*In My Good Books*	1942
IMNH	*It May Never Happen and other stories*	1945

KMH	The Key to My Heart	1963
Living Novel	The Living Novel	1946
LP	London Perceived	1962
MS	Marching Spain	1928
Meredith	George Meredith and English Comedy	1970
MO	Midnight Oil	1971
Mr B	Mr Beluncle	1951
NYP	New York Proclaimed	1965
NLL	Nothing Like Leather	1935
OEC	On the Edge of the Cliff	1980
ST	The Spanish Temper	1954
SV	The Spanish Virgin and other stories	1930
Turgenev	The Gentle Barbarian: The Life and Work of Turgenev	1977
YMYOL	You Make Your Own Life	1938
WMGCH	When My Girl Comes Home	1961

2   Newspapers and magazines

CSM	Christian Science Monitor
FR	Fortnightly Review
LM	London Mercury
MG	Manchester Guardian
NS	New Statesman and Nation
NY	The New Yorker
NYRB	New York Review of Books
NYT	New York Times
ST	Sunday Times
T&T	Time and Tide
TLS	Times Literary Supplement

3   Collections

In each case, the description obviously refers to the collection's Pritchett holdings, unless otherwise indicated.

Two large collections of correspondence are used so extensively that, except where the dates of the letters are unknown, I have not given their sources in the notes: the letters between Victor Pritchett and his second wife, Dorothy which, unless otherwise cited, are in the Berg; and those between him and Gerald Brenan which, again unless otherwise cited, are in HRC.

BBC	BBC Written Archives, Caversham
Berg	Berg Collection, New York Public Library
BK Coll	Private collection of Barbara Kerr
BL	British Library
C&W	Archives of Chatto and Windus, Reading University Library
HRC	Harry Ransom Humanities Research Center, University of Texas at Austin
JB Coll	Private collection of Josephine Bryant
NS Archive	*New Statesman* Archive, Sussex University Library Special Collections
NY Archive	*New Yorker* Archive, New York Public Library
OP Coll	Private collection of Oliver Pritchett
Princeton	Princeton University Library, Department of Rare Books and Special Collections

4	*Other abbreviations used in the notes*
BK	Barbara Kerr
DP	Dorothy Pritchett
DR	Dorothy Roberts (maiden name of DP)
GB	Gerald Brenan
nd	no date
OP	Oliver Pritchett
pm	postmark date
VSP	V. S. Pritchett

5   *Interview sources*

Where an interview is referred to, it was planned in advance, tape-recorded, and in many cases followed up with letters, telephone conversations and/or e-mails. ('Conversation' implies a more impromptu exchange.) The dates on which the interviews were done are as follows:

A. Alvarez	4.1.02
Josephine Bryant (née Pritchett)	8.8.01, 14.12.01, 30.8.02
Arthur Cook and Juliet Wrightson	4.9.01
Jean Davies (née Roberts)	20.10.01
Nell Dunn	31.9.01
Jason Epstein	21.3.02
Margaret Gardiner	11.12.01
Wynne and Kitty Godley	28.8.01
Jocelyn Herbert	4.4.02

Evelyn Hofer	17.5.03
Elizabeth Jane Howard	31.1.02
Paul Johnson	4.3.04
Barbara Kerr	2.3.02
Francis King	29.8.02
Mark Le Fanu	5.7.02
Naomi Lewis	6.2.02, 3.7.02
Peter Matson	20.5.03
Nicholas Maxwell	9.1.03
Venetia Kay (née Maxwell)	3.1.03
Derwent May	17.1.02
Caspar and Justin Murphy	2.10.03
Janetta Parladé	24.7.01
Elizabeth Paterson	22.8.02
Frances Partridge	13.7.01
Georgia Pritchett	29.10.03
Gordon Pritchett	11.5.01, 28.8.01
Matthew Pritchett	15.9.03
Oliver Pritchett	7.8.01, 18.12.01, 2.9.02
Serena Rothschild	24.10.01
Claire Tomalin	15.2.02
Peter Vansittart	31.1.02
Edith Webb (née Roberts)	20.10.01
Dee Wells and Nicholas Ayer	2.7.02
David Willison	31.10.01

Notes

Chapter 1

1. VSP to GB, nd from Parkhill Road (therefore *c.* 1946)
2. VSP to GB, nd [*c.* 1953]. (HRC, file 1, folder 19).
3. John Haffenden, *Novelists in Interview*, 1985, p. 227.
4. Peter Vansittart, *In the Fifties*, 1995, p. 146.
5. *VSP*, BBC, Radio 3, 24.12.97.
6. VSP to GB, 4.5.53.
7. Dorothy called this 'money for jam'. Undated letter to Josephine from Northampton, Mass., 1972 (JB Coll).
8. The quotations are from drafts of an article on 'Autobiography' (HRC).
9. The interview was conducted by Karl Miller. BBC, Third Programme, *The Lively Arts*, 16.6.67 (BBC).
10. When John Haffenden mentioned the inconsistency to him, he gave no sign of thinking it needed explaining (*Novelists in Interview*, 1985, p. 213).
11. VSP to GB, 30.9.50.
12. Gordon was sure, for example, that a friend of his brother's, named Coote, was a member of the differently spelt banking family.
13. First draft of *A Cab at the Door* (HRC, p. 11).
14. He had eight children. His first son, Bill, was strikingly like Victor in appearance, according to his niece, Joy Sheridan (née Pritchett) (Letter from Joy Sheridan to VSP, prompted by the publication of his memoirs, Berg, Box 49, file 1).
15. This must have been the place in Yorkshire which Pritchett remembered as 'Repton'.
16. VSP to GB, 19.12.40.
17. Kathleen's married name was Dale.
18. 'All his shoes were handmade specially for him by a man in Glasgow and he would have I suppose ten pairs of black and on the other side of his dressing room ten pairs of brown' (interview with Gordon Pritchett).
19. In *Midnight Oil*, he dated it from when he was in Ireland, but it began earlier (*MO*, p. 117). This was, of course, the heyday of initials. Stevenson was always known as RLS, Shaw as GBS. One of VSP's sisters-in-law spoke to me of 'RPT': she meant Regent's Park Terrace.
20. See below, p. 104.

21. His essay of the following year, 'On Leaning Over Walls' (CSM, 7.10.26), is another act of homage, with its echoes of Stevenson's 'An Apology for Idlers'.
22. MG, 9.2.28 and in book form in SV.
23. Adrian Alington and others, *Beginnings*, 1935, pp. 104–5.
24. *Beginnings*, p. 109.
25. In the year of publication, 1900, it had gone into three English editions plus a Tauchnitz European edition.
26. *Beginnings*, p. 112.
27. Interview with Gordon Pritchett.
28. *Beginnings*, p. 118.
29. *NLL*, p. 3.
30. Octavo notebook dated 'Stokke June 1949', entry for April 1951 (HRC).
31. *The Spanish Temper*, 1954; *London Perceived*, 1962; *New York Proclaimed*, 1965; *Dublin: A Portrait*, 1967.
32. OP Coll.
33. VSP to Gordon Pritchett, Paris, 19.6.21 (OP Coll).
34. VSP to Gordon Pritchett, 'Paris Ye 23rd Feb 1922' (OP Coll).
35. VSP to Gordon Pritchett, 'The Seventh Heaven of August 1921' (OP Coll).
36. VSP to Gordon Pritchett, 16.4.22. (OP Coll).
37. VSP to Gordon Pritchett from 142 W. 73rd St, New York, 11.9.25 (OP Coll).
38. Pritchett tell us that it was his father, again, who insisted on his taking modern rather than ancient languages, but without drawing the conclusion that in this as well as the other matters, he was actually more right than wrong (CD, p. 146.)
39. These statistics are taken from A. H. Halsey (ed.), *British Social Trends since 1900*, 1972, revised edn 1988, chapters 6 and 7.
40. CD, p. 128.
41. OP Coll.
42. VSP to Gordon Pritchett, 11.9.25 (OP Coll).
43. CD, pp. 133–4. Letter to VSP from Allan Turpin, 4.1.72 (Berg).
44. CD, p. 196.
45. Bryan R. Wilson, *Sects and Society: A Sociological Study of Three Religious Groups in Britain*, 1961, p. 125.
46. See Robert Currie, Alan Gilbert and Lee Horsley, *Churches and Churchgoers: Patterns of Church Growth in the British Isles since 1700*, 1977.
47. Abbot, an experienced journalist, was taken on in 1922 in succession to Frederick Dixon. The new head of his European Bureau was John Sidney Braithwaite. Other British writers hired under Abbot's editorship included Hugh Spender (uncle of Stephen) and Harold Hobson. See the useful, if partisan, history of the *Monitor* by Erwin D. Canham, *Commitment to Freedom: The Story of the 'Christian Science Monitor'*, Boston, Mass., 1958.
48. *Sects and Society*, p. 179.
49. VSP to James Stern, 1.11.66 (BL). See CD, p. 220.

50. CD, p. 121.
51. CD, p. 220.
52. MO, p. 77. The ignorance was, of course, reciprocal. Pritchett doesn't appear in accounts of the literary Paris of those years, such as Noel Riley's *Sylvia Beach and the Lost Generation: A History of Literary Paris in the Twenties and Thirties*, 1983. In old age, though, Pritchett told his granddaughter Georgia that he was 'proud to remember a scene in Paris when *Ulysses* was published. Scores of people in Montparnasse were walking up the street carrying that famous bright blue fat paperback under their arms and were reading it aloud in cafés' (undated pc, *c.* 1986, in the possession of Georgia Pritchett).
53. See D. W. Brogan, *The Development of Modern France*, 1940, revised end, 1967, pp. 571ff.
54. Tom Paulin has persuasively argued that Keynes's descriptions influenced T. S. Eliot in *The Waste Land*: 'Many cunning passages: How Maynard Keynes made his mark on *The Waste Land*', *TLS*, 29.11.02, pp. 14–15.
55. 'Crossing the Loire', CSM, 20. 12. 22; 'Night on the Normandy Coast', CSM, 9.10.22.
56. MO, p. 80.
57. VSP to GP, 5.5.22 (OP Coll).
58. MO, p. 10. As VSP admits on the next page, 'The bid for freedom was not as bold as I needed to think it.'
59. MO, p. 105.
60. All the early versions of both books are in HRC.
61. MO, p. 49.
62. MO, pp. 52–3.
63. It doesn't appear until the third of the three main drafts of MO in HRC.
64. MO, p. 60.
65. MO, p. 79
66. MO, p. 81
67. MO, p. 10

Chapter 2

1. At number 13. It first appears in *Thom's Official Directory of Great Britain and Ireland* for 1924. There were already two Christian Science Reading Rooms in Dublin, one at 35 Molesworth Street, off Kildare Street; the other close by at 85 Grafton Street.
2. My main sources for Evelyn Vigors's history have been interviews with her son, Nicholas Maxwell, one of her daughters, Venetia Kay, and her nephew, Sir David Willison. I was also much helped by Clare Vigors (Mrs Nicholas Vigors). Genealogical details come from various volumes of *Burke's Landed Gentry* and *Burke's Irish Family Records*. I am very grateful to John Fairleigh, who first put me in touch with Venetia Kay in response to a letter I had written to the *Irish Times*.
3. See Kathleen Villiers-Tuthill, *History of Clifden 1810–1860*, privately printed, 1981.
4. He is Lieutenant-General Sir David Willison KCB, OBE, MC.

5. Her son believes the illness was cancer but others in the family sardonically reduce it to appendicitis.
6. Evelyn was born on 31 October 1898. According to MO, Victor travelled to Ireland on 1 February 1923.
7. 'Beloved Vagabonds', CSM, 10.9.23; 'In Childlike Ireland', 5.10.23; 'About Ennis', 31.10.23.
8. CSM, 7.2.23, 26.3.23, 5.6.23, 23.7.23, 5.1.24.
9. CSM, 26.2.23, 'From Dublin to Cork'.
10. CSM, 27.2.23, 'Saturday Morning in Cork'.
11. See, for example, MO, p. 132.
12. CSM, 17.8.23.
13. CSM, 6.3.23, 'A Glimpse at a Southern Irish Town'.
14. *Dublin*, 6; 29.6.23, 'Northward Bound'.
15. Peter Vansittart, *Survival Tactics: A Literary Life*, 1999, p. 58.
16. Notebook kept by VSP on his first stay in Ireland (HRC).
17. CSM, 26.9.23.
18. CSM, 5.10.23, 'In Childlike Ireland', 10.9.23, 'Beloved Vagabonds', 31.10.23, 'About Ennis'.
19. CSM, 9.3.23, 'Mr Mulcahy of Blarney'.
20. Cf. *The Macdermots of Ballycloran*. Roy Foster writes about the dealings of earlier English writers such as Trollope and Thackeray with Ireland in *Paddy and Mr Punch: Connections in Irish and English History*, 1993, pp. 291–5.
21. 'Fishy' first appeared in the *Manchester Guardian*, 9.2.28 and was reprinted in *SV*.
22. In terms of its immediate human situation, 'The Two Brothers' was based on a couple of men whom Pritchett encountered during his second spell in Ireland, in 1926–7 (MO, p. 121).
23. MO, p. 122.
24. 'To America', CSM, 24.9.26.
25. *Clare D*, p. 8.
26. 'The snobberies of the Ascendancy were very Colonial – as I now see. . . . I was slow to see that I was meeting an upper class in decay . . .' (MO, p. 119).
27. *Clare D*, p. 243.
28. On the manuscript of *Clare Drummer*, now in HRC, Pritchett later wrote, 'I was writing this in 1927 at a cottage in Berkshire.' The cottage was Lower Woodend, in Marlow – see a letter from VSP to Gordon Pritchett, nd (OP Coll).
29. Pages 153–4 of the final typescript (Berg).
30. Notebook begun 1936 (HRC).
31. CE, p. 383.
32. CE, p. 265.
33. *Dublin*, p. 4.
34. 'Creating an Atmosphere', CSM, 28.8.26.
35. NLL, p. 98.
36. MO, p. 126.
37. In the later 1910s and early 1920s Evelyn and Hyacinth stayed at least once a year with their uncle (Philip Vigors's elder brother), aunt and

cousins at Burgage, Leighlinbridge, Co. Carlow, and Hyacinth was still an occasional visitor as late as 1934. After her marriage to Victor, Evelyn doesn't reappear in the visitors' book.

38. His journal for 1927 records that the relations 'more or less dropped us . . . after our marriage'. Entry for 11.12.27 (HRC).

39. Interviewed in 1975 by Douglas A. Hughes, a professor at Washington State University, Pritchett mentioned that although he didn't read *Ulysses* until years after it first appeared, he had read *Dubliners* 'very early' (Berg, box 17, folder 6). In its context, the implication seems to be that he read it before going to Paris, though in MO, p. 126, he puts the event in his Dublin days.

40. 13.11.23, 'James Stephens and the Legends'; 23.6.23, 'A Chat with W. B. Yeats'; 8.12.23, 'An Interview with W. B. Yeats'. (From the point of view of the fictional element in Pritchett's autobiographies, it is salutary to compare these pieces with how he described his first meeting with Yeats in MO, pp. 127–9, almost half a century later.) Other information about Pritchett's Irish reading at this time comes from his *Monitor* piece, 'The Celtic Twilight', published as early as 19.3.23, as well as from MO.

41. *Dublin*, p. 14.

42. See CSM, 19.12.23, 'The Third Floor Front'. To listen to Reid, Pritchett wrote, 'was to discover that beauty is simple and natural, requiring not the throbs of emphasis, but quiet in which to be heard'.

43. For the artists see, for example, CSM, 9.7.23, 'Gossip with an Irish Artist'; 17.9.23, 'The Royal Hibernian Academy'. Pritchett later wrote about the people he knew in Ireland in the first chapter of *Dublin: A Portrait*, as well as in MO. Stephen Bone and his wife Mary became particularly close friends and correspondents of Victor and Evelyn (OP Coll).

44. Copy of wedding certificate supplied by the office of the Registrar General, Dublin 2.

45. Unpublished passages from final draft for MO, p. 154 (Berg).

46. 'There was nothing of the "deeply interfused"; there was something that could be known, and which it was necessary to know. . . . The transcendentalist dream in which I had lived up to then came to an end' (MO, p. 138).

47. 'Impressions: Irun to Madrid', published CSM, 8.2.24. Submission dates are taken from the list he kept, see illustration and p. 104.

48. On Morocco, the first of his many articles. 'Press In Madrid Urges Withdrawal of Spanish Troops', was published on the *Monitor*'s front page on 13.3.34. Examples of the other topics include 'The Road to El Pardo', 17.3.24; 'A New Spain Emerging Through Door of Education', 20.3.24; 'A Spanish "First Night"', 2.5.24; 'Spanish Dictator To Continue Rule – Pledges Reforms', 7.5.24; 'The Activities and Status of Spanish Women', 25.11.24.

49. See, for example, CSM, 13.3.24, 17.10.24.

50. 28.3.24.

51. 8.7.24. The *Monitor* informed readers, 'It is becoming more and more apparent that General Ludendorff and not Herr Hitler is now the real leader of the German Fascisti.'

52. 'The indications are that civil government will be a long time coming, and that if it does come . . . it will be ultra-conservative' ('Primo de Rivera Directorate Said to Be Near Disintegration', 12.5.24).
53. 'Maps and Men and Mountains', CSM, 16.8.24.
54. 'The Opinions of Ahmed El Suki', 17.4.25.
55. 'Catalonia – The Contrast', CSM, 25.4.25.
56. MO, p. 153.
57. Interviews with Venetia Kay and Nicholas Maxwell.
58. See, for example, CSM, 22.10.26: 'The writer [VSP] took a small French two seater round the whole of Spain in January and February and also into some of the remoter regions.'
59. Her daughter Venetia Kay has the driving licence now (see plate section). Evelyn was a good driver and made what she could of the gift. Her son Nicholas Maxwell has two pictures of her sent to the Winter Gardens Theatre in Waterlow, Cheshire, on the back of which she briefly lists her qualifications as: 'Character comedy. Screen and stage experience. Ride. Swim. Drive a car.'
60. 'The Road to Cape Cod', 7.7.25; 'Provincetown', 4.3.25; 'Over the Border into Quebec', 14.8.25; 'With the Lumbermen of French Canada', 22.8.25, 27.8.25 and 31.8.25.
61. 'Three Ladies', CSM, 15.9.25.
62. 'New York and the Higher Mathematics', CSM, 8.9.25. Orlando, in his/her 'present moment' incarnation, recovers a belief in miracles in the lift in Marshall & Snelgrove: 'The very fabric of life now, she thought as she rose, is magic' (Brenda Lyons (ed.), Virginia Woolf, *Orlando: A Biography*, 1993, pp. 207–8).
63. 'Broadway Lights', CSM, 18.9.25; 'The Arctic in Greenwich Village', 5.10.25; 'Crossing the Hudson', 13.10.25. The suspension bridge at Bear Mountain opened in November 1924.
64. 'A Capital in Capitals', CSM, 27.11.25; 'Theories About American Football', 22.12.25.
65. Interview with Nicholas Maxwell. Evelyn was particularly clear that he should go to university.
66. The trip for Pritchett's piece on motoring in Spain, CSM, 22.10.26, was undertaken earlier that year. The visit to North Africa and southern Italy evidently came later: 'Into the Benni Yeni', CSM, 22.6.26; 'Nezar Said Silent at the Door', 7.7.26; 'Toward the Desert', 16.7.26; 'A Balcony in the Sahara', 24.7.26; 'In the Light of the Lemons', 31.7.26 (about Palermo); 'Unmysterious Land', 21.8.26 (an episode in Corsica). More pieces based on the latter tour appeared in the *Monitor*'s 'Winter Sunshine Supplement', 23.10.26: 'The Sun in Sicily', 'Naples and the Riviera', 'South of Tunisia', 'Workaday Algeria', 'Beauty of Island of Capri', etc.
67. 'The Fort in the Clouds of Northern Algeria', 16.6.26.
68. 'In the Light of the Lemons', 31.7.26.
69. 'Tragedy in a Greek Theatre' was first submitted in June 1926 to the *London Mercury* and other journals. It was taken by *Cornhill*, which paid him twelve guineas for the story, published in January 1927 (List of Articles, HRC).

70. The contents are listed in his ledger for 5.4.27. Apart from his novella 'The Spanish Virgin', which he had not yet written, they essentially comprise the collection published under that title in 1930.
71. First mooted in August 1925 and between then and October 1926 rejected by Jonathan Cape, Martin Secker, Chatto and Windus, John Murray and Constable.
72. VSP to GP, 17.11.26 (OP Coll).
73. VSP to GP, 19.2.27 (OP Coll).
74. HRC.
75. VSP to GP, nd (OP Coll).
76. Interview with Venetia Kay.
77. Journal dated '1940 Maidencourt', entry for 16 December 1940 (Berg).
78. Final ms draft of *MO*, p. 235a (HRC).
79. VSP to GB. Nd but evidently late 1940s: the letter was written from Stokke and is about Gerald's somewhat overenthusiastic experiments in educating his daughter, Miranda, about sex.
80. Ernest Benn, 1932.
81. See below pp. 54–55. For their divorce, see pp. 85, 89.
82. 14 April 1927.
83. MS, pp. 3–4. Warren Street is a guess; it is the nearest station to 117 Charlotte Street.
84. In CSM, beginning with 'To Spain and the World's Side', 17.5.27 and continuing throughout the year. The *Manchester Guardian* published part of what was eventually chapter 9 as 'The Inn', 20.8.27; another section as 'The Hills Pursue', 29.12.27; and part of chapter 13 as 'In Plasencia', 31.1.28. *Outlook* published 'The Spanish Wedding' – eventually another part of chapter 13–19.10.27. Soon, Pritchett was also writing about Spain for *Travel* magazine, where his articles appeared with lavish photographs: 'Main Street in Provincial Spain', March 1928, pp. 7–56; 'A Wayfarer in Medieval Zamorra', April 1928, pp. 21–50.
85. The ledger entry for 18.7.27 records that he had sent Peters 'Spanish Bk 1st ten chapters'.
86. MS, p. 95.
87. MS, pp. 130–1.
88. MS, p. 163.
89. MS, p. 178
90. Diary (HRC).
91. *Clare D*, p. 249.
92. 'Coming to London' (Berg).
93. The plays were as follows (the date given is the first night; Evelyn's part is given in brackets): *The Sport of Kings* by Ian Hay, 13.8.27 (Tweeney); *The Fake* by Frederick Lonsdale, 20.8.27 (Waitress); *Hawley's of the High Street* by Walter Ellis, 24.9.27 (Edith); *The Rat: the Story of an Apache Era* by David Lestrange, 22.10.27 (Thérèse); *Tod the Tailor* by W. Griffin, 29.12.27 (Clem). The reference to Mr Vigors's acting was in *Era*, 4.1.28. See J. P. Wearing, *The London Stage 1920–1929: A Calendar of Plays and Players*, 1984.
94. Diary, 21.11.27 (HRC).

95. 'Rain in the Sierra' in 1927; 'The Sack of Lights', 'Fishy' and 'In the Haunted Room' in 1928; 'The Cuckoo Clock' in 1930; 'Agranti for Lisbon', 'Slooter's Vengeance' and 'A Serious Question' in 1931; 'The Upright Man' and 'In Autumn Quietly' in 1933.

96. Diary, 9.12.27.

97. Diary, 17.12. 27.

98. Diary for 1928–9, entry for 2.6.[28] (HRC).

99. Diary, 22.10.[28].

100. Diary, 31.12.[28].

101. Berg, box 42, folder 1.

102. OP Coll.

103. Sussex University, Kingsley Martin papers, SxMs11, box 6: Olga Martin papers.

104. Richard Church to VSP, 29.8.30 (Berg).

105. Richard Church to VSP, 27.3.31 (Berg).

106. Richard Church to VSP, 14.7.32 (Berg).

107. Richard Church to VSP, 14.10.32, 13.2.33, 30.5.33.

108. There are other rather contradictory hints in some notes evidently written much later, in HRC. He implies that his (undated) 'Ultimate breakup with E.' happened while they were at 8 Fitzroy Street, and that subsequently he moved, first to the other side of the street, where he lived above an Italian pasta merchant, and then to Doughty Street. But he also says that 'E & I had a terrible, non house-trained cat' at Doughty Street, where they spent 'A bad winter, very poor'.

109. Both of them in *NS*: 'X-Ray', 30.7.32; 'The Upright Man', 31.12.32.

110. *Collected Stories*, 1982, p. ix.

111. That is, into collections under Pritchett's sole name. Some earlier stories were anthologised in *Best Stories of . . .*

112. *FR*, August 1930, p. 235.

113. *FR*, February 1931, p. 209–17.

114. Diary, 9.12.27.

115. There is a related element in 'The Spanish Virgin', where Crystal comes to think that 'I ought to have married someone and had a lot of babies. But I wasted all my time' (SV, p. 164).

116. SV, p. 80.

117. Eight-page reader's report on 'The Listening Years' (= *Nothing Like Leather*), to Victor Gollancz from Mr [G.] Gould, 1.1.34 (Berg, box 51, folder 1).

118. Ts page numbered 102 (HRC).

119. It first appeared in *Outlook*, 10.3.28.

120. SV, pp. 260–5. As so often in his fiction, this character seems to have been based on a real encounter of Pritchett's. It is described later in *London Perceived* (1962).

121. CE, p. 1052.

Chapter 3
1. He later deferred to Gerald Brenan, but the first of Brenan's books about Spain did not appear until 1943.
2. Among Pritchett's English contemporaries, J. B. Trend, later Professor of Spanish at Cambridge, was a frequent visitor there after he became Spanish correspondent of the *Athenaeum* in 1919.
3. 'A New Spain Emerging Through Door of Education', CSM, 20.3.24.
4. J. E. Crawford Flitch's translation, *Tragic Sense of Life*, 1921. The word he renders as 'wills', *quiere*, also means 'desires' and 'loves'.
5. 'The Crisis', BBC Radio, Third Programme, 19.1.47.
6. MS, p. 224
7. MS, pp. 44, 62.
8. MS, p. 103.
9. MS, pp. 103–4.
10. MS, pp. 101–2, 148. The Malagueno's civic loyalty went into the character of the Marques, in 'The Spanish Virgin'.
11. In his dream the night before his departure, Evelyn (unnamed) shouts something about Don Quixote at him, 'and I began to remember with embarrassment that I had not read all of the book, but it was impossible to explain that to her and to tell her one is never so heroic as one dreams' (MS, p. 1).
12. MS, p. 2.
13. MS, p. 5.
14. MS, p. 100.
15. Eudora Welty to VSP, nd (OP Coll).
16. MS, p. 179.
17. MS, p. 79.
18. NS, 7.12.35.
19. The BBC Written Archives have correspondence from VSP in Madrid, dating from this time, about plans for protests on May Day and about the latest reshuffle of the Spanish government.
20. ST, p. 210. He argues here that Europe-orientated Barcelona is an exception to the rule.
21. 'Tendencies of the Modern Novel: V. Spain', FR, February 1934, p. 207.
22. NS, 30.4.38. Despite this piece, Pritchett is seen by Jeffrey Meyers as having been, through his other reviews and essays on Orwell, a key contributor to the myth of him as a kind of secular saint (*George Orwell: The Critical Heritage*, 1975).
23. In Valentine Cunningham (ed.), *Spanish Front: Writers on the Civil War*, 1986.
24. Hemingway: FR, December 1932; Maugham: FR, August 1935; Belmonte: FR, July 1937 and NS, 31.7.37; fifteenth-century Spain: NS, 7.3.36.
25. Interview with Gordon Pritchett, who, with his wife Susan, was staying with Victor and Evelyn in Bloomsbury at the time. With the kind of detail that could have come from one of Victor's stories, Gordon later remembered that his brother's frock coat had been hung badly on a hook on the back of a door, and had developed a hump below the collar. They all took turns to iron it with a damp cloth.

26. NS, 6.8.32.
27. NS, 28.4.34.
28. NS, 24.8.35.
29. 'Spain the Ancient Struggle', CSM, 30.12.36.
30. 'Spain and the Future', *Spectator*, 4.9.36.
31. I am grateful to Martin Beagles for his views on this question. Beagles holds Pritchett 'about as responsible as anyone else for propagating a certain idea of Spain as "the old and necessary enemy of the West"' but, against that, acknowledges that 'at least he went to the trouble of meeting and speaking to Spanish thinkers, writers, etc; in this he was unlike most other British Hispanists and travel writers of the 20th century, the prime example being VSP's friend Gerald Brenan, who had really no contact with any Spanish people who were not servants, cleaners, etc.' (private communication).
32. 'Spain the Ancient Struggle', CSM, 30.12.36.
33. 'Days in Castile', *FR*, December 1934, p. 720.
34. Zuloaga in Zumaya to VSP, 12.10.34 (OP Coll). He added a message for Evelyn: 'I hope that Mrs Pritchett is painting hard. I send her my best regards.'
35. 'Interlude in Spain', *FR*, July 1935, pp. 68–75.
36. NS, 24.8.35.
37. 'Tendencies of the Modern Novel: V. Spain', *FR*, February 1934, pp. 203–11.
38. 'A Hero of our Time?', *London Mercury*, 36, 1937, pp. 359–64.
39. Journal begun June 1936 (HRC). The undated entry is headed '*Originality*.' Pritchett returned to the theme in *Why Do I Write?* (see below, p. 148): 'When the inner history of any writer's mind is written . . . we find (I believe) that there is a break at some point in his life. At some point he splits off from the people who surround him and he discovers the necessity of talking to himself and not to them' (V. S. Pritchett, Elizabeth Bowen and Graham Greene, *Why Do I Write?*, 1948, p. 18).
40. NS, 16.10.37.
41. Journal begun June 1936 (HRC).
42. 'The Passing of Spanish Liberalism', *Spectator*, 11.12.36.
43. Ralph Bates to VSP from Gerona, 20.7. ny (c. 1935) (OP Coll).
44. NS, 4.9.37 and 16.10.37.
45. Apart from those mentioned separately, see for example 'Miguel de Unamuno', *Spectator*, 28.2.36; 'Spain and the Future', *Spectator*, 4.9.36; 'The Passing of Spanish Liberalism', *Spectator*, 11.12.36; 'Ebb and Flow in Spain', *Spectator*, 21.5.37.
46. Notebook (HRC).
47. Jonathan Gathorne-Hardy, *The Interior Castle: A Life of Gerald Brenan*, 1992.
48. *Interior Castle*, p. 316.
49. ST, p. 7.
50. ST, pp. 214–16.
51. Robert Louis Stevenson, *Novels and Stories*, ed. V. S. Pritchett, 1945, p. xiv. Writing about *The Amateur Emigrant* in his introduction, Pritchett

commented 'he travelled steerage, as the romantic spectator, with one of the many shiploads of working-class emigrants who were leaving Scotland at this time in despair; and that was social violence' (p. viii).

52. ST, p. 13.
53. ST, p. 15.
54. ST, p. 82.
55. ST, p. 94.
56. ST, p. 140.
57. VSP journal 1.9.68 (HRC); GB to DP, nd (HRC).
58. ST, pp. 144f.
59. ST, p. 173.
60. ST, p. 180.
61. ST, p. 186. Cf MS, pp. 208–9.
62. Frances Partridge to VSP, 24.4.[54] (Berg).
63. Robert Lowell to VSP, 12.4.67 (Berg).
64. Luis Araquistáin to VSP, 5.10.55 (Berg).
65. This point was made at the time by Erik de Mauny, writing anonymously in *The Times Literary Supplement* ('The Art of V. S. Pritchett', *TLS*, 6.8.54).

Chapter 4

1. CS, p. 897. First published in *The New Yorker* in 1973.
2. DP to VSP [pm 23.2.43]; interview with OP.
3. VSP to DP 6.11. ny from Maidencourt, so during the Second World War.
4. VSP to GB, 5.11.44.
5. Berg, box 46, folder 6, nd.
6. DR to VSP, nd [pm 5.5.35].
7. DR to VSP, nd [pm 7.5.35].
8. Interview with Jean Davies.
9. According to Edith, her mother won a medal for a horse she bred for the Duke of Westminster.
10. Interview with Edith Webb.
11. Berg, box 46, folder 4, nd.
12. Berg, box 46, folder 4, nd.
13. DR to VSP, nd [pm 22.12.34].
14. Interviews with Venetia Kay and Nicholas Maxwell. Donald had been brought up in Canada and at the time they met was working as an assistant editor on *Shipping World*. His father, a doctor, came from Scotland, where his family had a big house in Dumfriesshire. There was some family opposition to the relationship on the ground of Evelyn's age.
15. It's certain that she became pregnant by him in the autumn of 1936. Their first child, Nicholas, was born on 3 July 1937. Donald was not yet twenty-one (so unable to marry without his parents' consent) and the couple did not marry until 1938.
16. E.g. Naomi Royde-Smith to VSP 7.9.35 and 2.10.35 (OP). ('As I have not heard from you in answer to my invitation to tea I conclude that in the business of letting your studio you have lost track of our correspondence.')

17. VSP to DR, undated letters (Berg, box 44, folder 2).
18. DR to VSP, nd (Berg, box 46, folder 6).
19. DR to VSP, 9.5.35.
20. Edith V. Rintoul to VSP, 6.3.36, 24.6.36, 29.6.36, 11.3.37 (OP Coll).
21. For example, *Towards a National Policy*, 1911; *Constructive Conservatism*, 1913.
22. Introduction by VSP to Winifred Stamp, *'Doctor Himself'*: *an Unorthodox Biography of Harry Roberts 1871–1946*, 1949.
23. See below p. 133.
24. DR to VSP, nd [pm 13.5.35].
25. VSP to Ian Parsons, 6.1.35 (C&W).
26. DR to VSP, nd (Berg, box 46, folder 6).
27. It was awarded to Evelyn at the High Court of Justice Probate Divorce and Admiralty Division on 28.2.36, on the ground of Victor's adultery (Berg).
28. VSP to DR, nd (Berg, box 44, folder 3).
29. See above, pp. 74.
30. See below, p. 99f.
31. VSP to DR, nd [pm 28.1.36].
32. *Mr Beluncle*, p. 196; for his essay on the Carlyles, first published in *NS*, 16.2.52, see *CE*, pp. 403–13.
33. One of his letters to her begins, 'My darling, Here's an account of my moods and meanderings' (Berg, box 44, folder 2).
34. DR to VSP, nd (Berg, box 46, folder 7).
35. VSP to DR, nd (Berg, box 44, folder 3).
36. See for example, p. 129 below.
37. Nd but from 3 Penn House, so *c*. 1934–5 (Berg, box 44, folder 2).
38. VSP to DP, 16.11.36.
39. Interview with Edith Webb.
40. 9.9.36 before the Hon. Sir Wilfred Hubert Poyer Lewis in the High Court of Justice Probate Divorce and Admiralty Division (Berg).
41. Copy of letter from VSP to Evelyn Pritchett (Berg, box 42, folder 1).
42. Mark Gertler to VSP, 'Coronation Day' [1937] (so 12.5.37, when George VI was crowned) (OP Coll). Gertler's son Luke was later at school with the Pritchett children.
43. VSP to DR, nd. 'I'm so *thrilled* you're anxious to have babies,' Dorothy wrote to him in a letter postmarked 1.5.35.
44. DR to VSP [pm 3.5.35]. Some time in the same year she wrote, 'I'm thinking you've gone out to dinner with Janet Adam-Smith or Barbara-Something-Else-Smith or Margaret Gardiner or to a party at Kingsley [Martin]'s. I'm not in favour of Kingsley's party. Don't trust women' (Berg, box 45, folder 2).
45. Unpublished in his lifetime, as far as I know. The typescript, with the address of Maidencourt (see below, p. 114f) is in the Berg, box 24, folder 6.
46. It can be seen as Pritchett's part-comic cockney version of the episode in Thomas Mann's *The Magic Mountain*, where Hans Castorp feels a kind of social scruple about looking at his friend Joachim's X-ray, as if it were a private letter.

47. 'X-ray', 30.7.32; 'Upright Man', 31.12.32.
48. Another influence on the change may have been Gollancz's rejection of *Nothing Like Leather* – see above, p. 58.
49. See Paul Theroux's introduction to the 1984 reissue by Oxford Twentieth Century Classics.
50. 'An accursed profession, journalism drives its members to think in headlines, interviews, quotable words and melodrama. Every thought they have is printed and on the front page the moment they think it' (*DML*, p. 20).
51. Nd (Berg, box 49, folder 3).
52. *DML*, p. 3.
53. See below p. 105.
54. *DML*, p. 5.
55. *DML*, p. 69.
56. *DML*, p. 109. These evocations of *Hamlet* in Brazil, together with Gilbert Phillips's later hallucinatory memories of *Pickwick Papers*, as he sits in a storm, lost in the jungle, may echo the ending of Evelyn Waugh's recent *A Handful of Dust*, 1934, where Tony Last is forced to read Dickens to his jungle captor.
57. *DML*, p. 314.
58. See especially *DML*, pp. 61ff., on the considerations which 'prevent travellers from writing true histories of their expeditions'.
59. *DML*, p. 147.
60. It appeared in the *New Statesman* on 4.9.37. *DML* had appeared the previous spring.
61. *NS*, 26.12.36 and 18.12.37.
62. The Old Mill, Langstone Harbour, Havant, Hampshire. They were there for some months from August 1937, while Pritchett was putting the finishing touches to the contents of *You Make Your Own Life* (C&W).
63. See below, p. 101. 'Sense of Humour' was immediately and widely anthologised, for example in Everyman's *Modern Short Stories* (1938) and the first volume of *Penguin New Writing* (1940) (C&W).
64. VSP to JL, 14.5.36 (HRC, Lehmann Papers). Six weeks later Pritchett wrote, 'I'm very glad you liked *The Commercial Traveller* and that you are going to put it into New Writing. The fee is all right – that is to say, its damn little for weeks of hard work, but the people who pay me 15 and 20 guineas for stories would certainly not publish this one.' VSP to JL, 27.6.36 (HRC, Lehmann Papers).
65. JL to VSP, 22.6.36 (OP Coll).
66. VSP to GB, 26.3.38.
67. VSP to John Lehmann, 29.1.38 (HRC).
68. VSP to John Lehmann, 26.6.39 (HRC).
69. JB Coll.

Chapter 5
1. See illustration, p. 42. The ledger is now among the Pritchett papers in HRC.
2. *Spectator*, 15.3.30.
3. *FR*, 1.10.35, 1.9.35; Malcolm Cowley's *Exile's Return*, *NS*, 14.9.35;

T&T, 18.5.35; Somerset Maugham's *Don Fernando*, *FR*, 1.8.35; *NS*, 12.10.35.

4. *NS*, 30.3.35, 24.8.35.
5. See for example 'The Scapegoat' (*CCS*, pp. 105–19), first published in the *London Mercury* in November 1937. For examples of reviews by Pritchett sympathetic to the predicament of Jews in the 1930s, see *T&T*, 27.7.35, *NS*, 30.11.35. The latter is a review of two books on anti-semitism.
6. *NS*, 27.2.32.
7. His first appearance in the MG was with 'The Family of Carmen', 30.12.24.
8. Kingsley Martin, *Editor: A Second Volume of Autobiography 1931–45*.
9. David Garnett to VSP, nd (Berg, box 47, folder 6).
10. For example in a letter to Mortimer, saying how much he owed to him for commissioning his essays, and that 'without your guidance, suggestions, praise and criticism I would never have learned to make anything of them'. VSP to Raymond Mortimer, 3.2.[53], from Wadwick (Princeton).
11. The *Statesman*'s circulation rose from 14,000 to 30,000 during the 1930s. (By 1945, it had reached 70,000.) C. H. Rolph, *Kingsley: The Life, Letters and Diaries of Kingsley Martin*, 1973, Penguin edn 1978.
12. *NS*, 18.2.33, 29.4.33, 24.6.35.
13. *Genji*: *FR*, August 1932, August 1933; Montaigne: October 1931; Hazlitt: February 1932, February 1933; Shaw: January 1932; Lawrence: April and October 1932, March 1933.
14. *FR*, April 1932.
15. *Spectator*, 14.6.30.
16. Rose Macaulay, 'The Return to Horridness in Literature', *Spectator*, 10.3.33; VSP, 'On Calling a Spade . . .', *Spectator*, 17.3.33.
17. *FR*, February 1934.
18. He wrote nothing more for the weekly *T&T* in these years. In 1936 he wrote eight pieces for *FR*, four for *LM* and three for the *Spectator*. In 1937 the scores were: *FR* five, *LM* five, *Spectator* one; in 1938–9: *FR* four, *LM* six, *Spectator* none. Even in the later 1930s, though, he continued to publish not only reviews but long essays outside the *New Statesman*: for example, an essay entitled 'Ebb and Flow in Spain' in the *Spectator*, 21.5.37 and one on 'Politics and the English Novel' in *FR*, June 1938.
19. *CSM*, 9.12.25, unsigned (attribution from 'List of Articles').
20. *CSM*, 23.11.27.
21. *NS*, 9.12.33.
22. Submitted 30.1.28 (List of Articles, HRC).
23. Interview with Al Alvarez.
24. *NS*, 7.6.74.
25. *T&T*, 12.10.35.
26. See above, p. 6of.
27. Conversation with Ved Mehta.
28. *LM*, 36, 1937, pp. 359–64.
29. *CE*, p. 114.
30. *CE*, p. 194.

31. CE, p. 325.
32. 'Robbing Peter to pay Paul', 'Between Scylla and Charybdis', 'Killing the goose that lays the golden egg', 'To cross the Rubicon', 'To cut the Gordian knot', 'To cleanse the Augean stables' and 'To pour oil on troubled waters' (NS, 12.1.35). Among the solutions Pritchett liked were 'Cut the Freudian knot', 'Steer carefully between Belloc and Chesterton', 'Killing our pigs to save our bacon' and 'To bleach the Blackshirts' (NS, 26.1.36). Other setters of NS competitions at this time included Richard Church, Cyril Connolly, Winifred Holtby and Raymond Mortimer.
33. LM, 31.3.35.
34. NS, 7.12.35.
35. NS competition no. 277.
36. DR to VSP, pm 3.5.35.
37. Undated letter (Berg, box 46, folder 7.)
38. DR to VSP, nd (Berg, box 46, folder 1).
39. Lloyd Williams to VSP, 21.2.35 (BBC).
40. VSP to GB, 12.39.
41. VSP to John Lehmann, nd (Princeton).
42. VSP to John Lehmann, 30.5.39 (HRC).
43. VSP to GB, 8.2.[40].
44. David Rabbitts later remembered thinking that this was two-thirds of a farm worker's wage.
45. Journal, 21.1.40 (Berg).
46. Maydencot, as it was originally known, had been granted to Wyatt's father by Henry VIII. Sir Thomas Wyatt sold it in 1542 (Research undertaken for David Rabbitts by Debrett Ancestry Research).
47. 'What We Lost' (Berg, box 37, folder 11).
48. Undated entry in notebook journal begun June 1936 (HRC).
49. VSP to Harold Raymond, 10.12.42 (C&W). As the needs of the armed forces grew more pressing, Pritchett's employers at the *New Statesman* and the Ministry of Information had to make more than one intervention to protect him from conscription. He was officially registered in September 1942 (Registration No. HVK 1366, Reading), but his military service was deferred through the Periodical & Trade Press Deferment Advisory Committee, initially for six months from 14 December 1942 and then for a further three, until 7 September 1943. The original application was made by the *New Statesman*. In July 1943 the Ministry of Information contacted the BBC for evidence in support of its own application for further deferment on Pritchett's behalf (BBC correspondence beginning 29.7.43).
50. VSP to GB, 26.10.40.
51. Journal begun 1936 (HRC).
52. Journal begun 1940, 16.4.41 (Berg).
53. Journal begun 1936 (HRC).
54. Journal begun 1940 (Berg).
55. For example, in September 1940 and March 1941. Journal begun 1940, 24.9.40, 4.3.41 (Berg). 'They bomb every night around these parts,' Pritchett told John Lehmann (VSP to John Lehmann, 6.9.40, Princeton).

56. Journal begun 1940 (Berg).
57. VSP to GB, 19.12.40. Pritchett may have been half remembering Gorky's 1909 description of the buildings of New York as a jaw full of rotting teeth and mere stumps, which he quoted later in *New York Proclaimed*, p. 81.
58. Journal begun 1940 (Berg).
59. VSP to John Lehmann, 30.8.[40] (HRC).
60. The ambience is described vividly by Robert Hewison in *Under Siege: Literary Life in London 1939–45*, 1977.
61. VSP to GB, 4.6. ny.
62. VSP to GB, nd (HRC, file 2, folder 6).
63. VSP to GB, 11.9.41.
64. VSP to DP, nd (Berg, box 42, folder 5).
65. Journal 1942–45 (HRC).
66. *Build the Ships. The Official Story of the Shipyards in Wartime*, 1946, p. 16.
67. Ibid., p. 41.
68. Ibid., p. 34.
69. VSP to DP [pm 24.2.43].
70. Ibid.
71. VSP to Harold Raymond, nd [received 30.8.43] (C&W).
72. VSP to GB, 4.6. ny.
73. 'George Orwell', *NS*, 28.1.50.
74. 'The Crystal Spirit', *CE*, pp. 1180–3.
75. Christopher Salmon to Tony Rendall, 14.5.41 (BBC).
76. Lloyd Williams to VSP, 21.2.35 and 11.3.35 (BBC).
77. BBC Written Archives, VSP Copyright folder, 1942.
78. BBC talk on 'The Theatre I Want', reprinted in *Listener*, 6.4.44.
79. Frances Partridge, *Everything to Lose: Diaries 1945–1960*, 1985, p. 19.
80. BBC discussion on 'What is the Point of Arguing?', reprinted in *Listener*, 9.10.41.
81. 'The Art of Conversation' (Berg, box 27, folder 5). The original title of 'The Evils of Spain' was 'Conversation Piece'.
82. Henry Moore: BBC discussion on 'The Living Image', reprinted in *Listener*, 13.11.41; 'The Capacity to Think', *Listener*, 23.10.41.
83. 'The Writer and his Public', *Listener*, 17.10.[40.
84. VSP to Gerald Bullett, 11.11.[40] (BBC).
85. VSP to GB [pm 4.5.46].
86. Broadcast 11.2.43 (BBC).
87. 'Temperament of Genius', *CE*, p. 1299.
88. VSP to GB, 30.6.48.
89. VSP to DP [pm 16.10.42].
90. Conversation with David Rabbitts.
91. VSP to John Lehmann, 28.4.41 (HRC). Oliver Pritchett later recalled, 'My mother's story was called "Blind Man's Bluff", I believe. She never allowed us to see it although we asked several times. She was very protective of it.' It seems that there was more than one story. In an undated wartime letter to her, Victor wrote, 'I am so proud of your story and you must promise to show me the others' (Berg).

92. Or *The Times Literary Supplement*: see 'The *TLS* in the Second World War, and how to fill some gaps in modern British cultural history', in *Grub Street and the Ivory Tower*, ed. Jeremy Treglown and Bridget Bennett, 1998, pp. 135–50.

93. For example, in the radio drama documentary, *Heart of Britain*, which he wrote (transmitted 2.10.43) (BBC).

94. Pritchett mentioned this in a radio programme, *Return Journey* (BBC, Home Service, 13.10.46), quoting Fox: 'there was a great fair at Sedbergh at which servants used to be hired; and I declared the Day of the Lord through the fair.'

95. *NS*, 11.1.41.

96. *NS*, 26.2.44, reprinted in *CE*, p. 205.

97. *NS*, 22.1.44, reprinted in *CE*, p. 268.

98. Journal for 1942–5, entries dated 25 and 26 January 1943 (HRC). John Lehmann wrote that Colefax 'pursued lions, I think, more assiduously and more single-mindedly than Emerald [Cunard]. About this time she noted that Victor Pritchett's star was rising. . . . She persuaded me to engage him to accompany me one evening to sherry at the exquisite little house in Lord North Street, where the guests sat round in an arrangement that was continually being shuffled by Sybil, who dashed about, perching on a footstool at one's feet for a few moments' conversation, inevitable prelude to a removal of oneself to another part of the room and a fresh conversation. She pounced on Victor with lion-worshipping ardour, and he very soon became one of her most frequent and most doted-on guests' (*I Am My Brother: Autobiography*, 2, 1960, pp. 187–8). Ruth was probably Ruth Lewinsky, a well-off patron of the arts who lived in a large house near the Brenans in Aldbourne (information from Oliver Pritchett).

99. Journal begun 1940, 28.1.41 (Berg).

100. Journal begun June 1936, 15.12.39 (HRC).

101. VSP to Harold Raymond, 30.1.40 (C&W).

102. Journal begun 1940, entry for 3.2.41 (Berg).

103. Ibid., 17.1.[41].

104. Journal 1942–5, miscellaneous entries for 1943 (HRC).

105. VSP to DP, 17.6.42.

106. DP to VSP, nd [pm 4.6.42].

107. VSP to DP, 21.12.[40].

108. VSP to DP, 24.2.43.

109. For example, to a party in October 1941, where H. G. Wells flirted with her. Journal begun 1940, 16.10.41 (Berg).

110. VSP to GB, nd (HRC, file 1, folder 12).

111. Pritchett wrote about invasion fears in this same journal (now in the Berg). The notebook ends at the foot of its final page, with the words dated February 1942 quoted above. Pritchett began another (now at HRC) the following 26 November, when he was about to go on a trip to Shropshire with Dorothy and the children.

112. Nd (Berg, box 42, folder 5).

113. The letter is resolutely pragmatic and 'modern': 'now I have done what I long wanted to do: I've broken off with her. I have done this because

she no longer attracts me and I have told her this. I have also told her that I want only you in my life' (VSP to DP, nd, Berg, box 44, folder 3).

114. DP to VSP [pm 11.6.42].
115. VSP to DP, 25.9.42.
116. VSP to DP, 6.11. ny from Maidencourt.
117. See, for example, VSP to GB c. 1944: 'I've done 2 weeks at the Staggers. I live above the office on Monday & Tuesday & get a lot of work done at night. . . . In spite of all I get on with my novel. And I eat Greek lunches and drink more beer than I used. Dorothy gets in despair on Mondays & Tuesdays, but has been chained to the house because one of the children is ill' (HRC, file 1, folder 7).
118. VSP to GB, 22.2.44.
119. VSP to GB, nd (HRC, file 1, folder 13).
120. NS, 7.4.45.
121. NS, 12.5.45.
122. NS, 6.6.53, 5.2.65. See below, p. 213–4.
123. NY archive, box 521.
124. His first piece for the *NYRB* appeared on 31.10.63. His contributions can be accessed through the *NYRB*'s invaluable online archive at www.nybooks.com/authors/3374.
125. Interview with Naomi Lewis.
126. Edith Sitwell to VSP, 3.10.48 (Berg, © Francis Sitwell 2004). Edith Sitwell had imagined 'mash': Romilly wrote 'blanched uniformity'.
127. VSP to GB, 31.12.48.
128. VSP to GB, nd (HRC, file 1, folder 5).

Chapter 6

1. VSP to GB, 18.4.40.
2. For example, he recommended Brenan to Blanche Knopf (VSP to GB, 4.5.53) and helped get *The Face of Spain* published by the *New Statesman*'s book-publishing arm, the Turnstile Press, in May 1955 (VSP to GB, 26.5. [pm 55]). Earlier, he encouraged him to join the Society of Authors and gave him advice about paying Gamel as a secretary and charging this against income tax (VSP to GB, 16.10.48).
3. VSP to GB, 13.3.41.
4. CS, pp. 364–80. Similarly, the nucleus of the Noisy Brackett stories is to be found in a letter to Brenan of 4.5.53. There are many other examples of this kind of rehearsal in the correspondence: see for example discussion of 'The Fall' and 'Our Oldest Friend', pp. 190–1, 221–3, below.
5. VSP to GB, 27.5.38.
6. VSP to GB [pm 31.5.49].
7. GB to VSP, nd [July 1937]. Later, Brenan was to write, 'Those who have some means think that the most important thing in the world is love. The poor know that it is money' (*Thoughts in a Dry Season*, 1978, 'Love').
8. Journal 1942–5, entry for 2.8.[45]: 'In May I was given £500 (or rather it was advanced to me) by Peters, so that I might drop sundry journalism and write a novel. Peters said it was a gamble on his part; if I failed I was not to worry. . . . I have now written 35 pages i.e. about 8000 words. . . . Appalling' (HRC).

9. Jonathan Gathorne-Hardy dates the loan 12 June 1951 (*The Interior Castle*, p. 391), but Pritchett's lengthy letters agonising about his decision are clearly dated 15 and 30 June 1948, while Brenan's original letter to him about it has no date. Gathorne-Hardy also refers to the fact that Pritchett was at the time 'living in London', but the family had moved back to the country by 1949.

10. In 2003 David Rabbitts was still living at Maidencourt with his wife June, having farmed there for more than sixty years and trebled its original acreage.

11. VSP to GB, 28.1.46.

12. See below, pp. 194–196.

13. Among the neighbours whom they saw most of were the painter Lawrence Gowing and Julia Strachey, the Baths of Longleat, the Brenans and the Partridges, as well as Raymond Mortimer and his gay friends Edward Sackville-West, Eardley Knollys and Patrick Trevor-Roper, who shared a country house nearby.

14. They went to Salkey, near Dublin, with the children and enjoyed themselves. Any painful associations for Victor and, by association, for Dorothy, were cancelled out by the many changes that had taken place since he was last in Ireland. He wrote to Brenan, 'nice men with good minds like Sean O'Faolain are in despair and have renounced all their romanticism about the race & the language etc.' (VSP to GB, 8.5.47).

15. Pritchett told Brenan, 'There is even a refrigerator' (VSP to GB, nd, HRC, file 4, folder 5).

16. VSP to John Lehmann, 6.2.52 (Princeton).

17. This particular drama occurred while they were still at Maidencourt (BBC, 18.6.45).

18. The *NS* anthology was *Turnstile One: A Literary Miscellany from 'The New Statesman and Nation'*, 1948. Pritchett inscribed her copy 'with love for all your research and work on this book' (OP Coll). Pritchett almost included a composition by a twelve-year-old schoolgirl, Jacqueline Stiven, sent to the *New Statesman* by her aunt, which David Garnett had published without realising that it had been copied out more or less word for word from Virginia Woolf's *A Room of One's Own*. He was saved from the mistake by an editor at Turnstile Press, Ann Baer, who happened to have been at school with the girl and remembered the story (private communication from Ann Baer).

19. Conversations with Frances Partridge, Nell Dunn, Jonathan Gathorne-Hardy.

20. Told that Dorothy came from a horsy background, Serena Rothschild (*née* Dunn), said, 'That absolutely amazes me.'

21. The copy was sold by Ulysses bookshop, 40 Museum Street, WC1 at the end of 2002. The quotation is taken from its catalogue 91, entry 553.

22. *Personal Record 1920–72*, 1974, pp. 337–8.

23. VSP to GB, nd (HRC, file 1, folder 19) (for date see VSP to GB from Maidencourt [pm 12.6.44], HRC).

24. This was in 1947, when the book appeared in the USA (*New Yorker*, 1.11.47). When Pritchett opened a book, Wilson wrote, 'something in it may come to life that we did not suspect was there'.

25. C&W 1951 folder and May 1959, correspondence with Raleigh Trevelyan. Arrow Books paid a further £125 for a reprint, which appeared in 1959.
26. Letter from Halifax Building Society to *New Statesman*, 13.4.46 (*NS* Archive).
27. Society of Authors Archive.
28. Greene referred to this in several letters to Pritchett, especially in their old age. Pritchett's review, he said, was 'an *accolade* from a much older & better writer' (21.12.81); it 'gave me such encouragement in a period of despair' (7.9.84). 'Since that first encouragement you gave me when I was really thinking of giving up you have been my mentor. How proud I was when we became friends. There is no other writer alive whose opinion I value so much' (27.1.87) (Berg).
29. Because of Greene's negligence, the project was eventually dropped (BBC).
30. VSP to GB, *c.* 1939–40.
31. VSP to GB from Seville [1951] (HRC).
32. VSP to GB, nd (HRC, file 1, folder 1).
33. VSP to GB, 13.2.50.
34. Interview with Nell Dunn.
35. VSP to GB, nd (HRC, file 4, folder 8). Frances Partridge records the same 'dancing-bottle-party': 'Everyone was rather drunk when we arrived, particularly Philip Toynbee (lachrymose) and Robin Mount (comic). Others present were the Pritchetts and Julia [Strachey] (neither of them at their ease), Virginia Tennant, Lord Bath . . . the Kees. . . .' (*Everything to Lose: Diaries 1945–1960*, 1985, 1.8.49).
36. VSP to GB, 13.2.50.
37. See below, p. 156.
38. Notebook begun 1945 (Berg).
39. VSP to Raymond Mortimer, 3.2.[53] and 15.2.53 (Princeton).
40. VSP to GB, 27.5.[pm 52]. The writer Edward Sackville-West, later Lord Sackville, belonged to the literary-and-big-house-and-garden family made famous by his cousin Vita.
41. VSP to GB, 27.5.[52] and 9.11.[52].
42. *Why Do I Write? An exchange of views between Elizabeth Bowen, Graham Greene, V. S. Pritchett*, 1948, pp. 7–8.
43. VSP to GB, 26.5.48.
44. Journal begun 1940, 16.12.40 (Berg).
45. VSP to Gordon Pritchett, 7.11.26 (OP Coll).
46. VSP to John Lehmann, nd [1939] (HRC).
47. VSP to GB, [pm 1.3.49].
48. VSP to GB, 21.1.51.
49. VSP to GB, 1.8.51. Pritchett had told John Lehmann of his doubts about 'the Auden-Spender business', warning him in 1943 not to let *New Writing and Daylight* become dominated by it (VSP to John Lehmann, 28.7.43) (Princeton).
50. Ian Parsons to VSP, 10.5.37. In 1942, Harold Raymond agreed to pay an advance on another prospective book of short stories, 'provided that we can't hit on a better way of facilitating the production of that next

novel of yours'. He added, 'There are a number of your short stories which make me feel that you could produce a novel with a very big sale indeed' (2.7.42, C&W).

51. *Spectator*, 20.7.29; *TLS*, 22.8.29.
52. *The Weekend Review*, 9.8.30. Hartley called it 'an exceedingly attractive story, amusing, pathetic, ironic, dramatic, brimming with vitality.'
53. For example by L. A. G. Strong in the *Spectator*, 6.2.32, and by Marjorie Grant Cook, writing anonymously in the *TLS*, 7.4.32.
54. Peter Quennell made this comparison in *NS*, 26.1.35. The *Spectator* described Mathew Burkle as 'one of the few really memorable creations in modern fiction', 18.1.35.
55. Derek Verschoyle in the *Spectator*, 9.4.37.
56. This after refusing a 1945 request from Eyre and Spottiswode to print it in its new Century Library series: Graham Greene to Harold Raymond, 24.1.45 (C&W). Much later, *Dead Man Leading* was reissued in paperback by OUP with an introduction by Paul Theroux, 1984.
57. *T&T*, 3.11.51.
58. The advance paid on *Mr Beluncle* in 1950 was £100. This was on top of £293.17s.9d. outstanding on previous books (C&W, 12.9.50, 7.1.52).
59. *NS*, 20.10.51.
60. VSP to GB [pm 18.10.51].
61. Raymond Mortimer to VSP, 6.9.51 (Berg).
62. Kingsley Martin to VSP, 23.10.51 (*NS* Archive).
63. 'Mr. Pritchett's Novels', *TLS*, 19.10.51.
64. VSP to GB, 20.10.51.
65. This and other attributions of anonymous *TLS* reviews can be found in *The 'TLS' Centenary Archive*, ed. Deborah McVea and Jeremy Treglown, www.tls.psmedia.com.
66. *TLS*, 6.8.54.
67. *Mr B*, p. 81.
68. Connolly's house-buying mania is funnily described in Jeremy Lewis's *Cyril Connolly: A Life* (1997). One of the many houses he fell for was Wadwick. Pritchett told Brenan, 'He covetted [*sic*] our house at once; wanted the trees as if they were the first asparagus of the season' (VSP to GB, 14.6[pm 53]).
69. *Mr B*, p. 51.
70. 'I read it with avidity especially as in this chronicle of the family I seem to have the (inverted) distinction of being left out. It is magnificently written & I was very amused & depressed by turns' (Kathleen to VSP, 25.11.51, Berg).
71. *CE*, p. 321.
72. *Mr B*, p. 14.
73. *Mr B*, p. 36.
74. Specifically in relation to Shchedrin's *The Golovlyov Family* (*CE*, p. 329).
75. The term comes to Mrs Dykes's mind, for example, in her thoughts about Lady Roads: 'the woman victim abused . . . by a husband. . . .' (*Mr B*, p. 190).

76. Especially in George, whom Mr Beluncle has promised that he will 'see about' a job for him, but who is crushingly dismissed when he reminds him about it:

    'Now, George,' said Mr Beluncle sharply, 'don't irritate me. At your age I found my own job. I didn't go to my father; in any case my father couldn't help me, he was a poor man. . . . Now go and turn my bath on.'

    'You said yesterday, ask today,' said George.

    George turned away. His eyes shone with tears that did not fall and he walked slowly away, bewildered, carrying his love for his father away with him, like someone . . . with an unwanted load (*Mr B*, p. 56).

77. *Mr B*, p. 206.

78. Apart from the claustrophobic Beluncle household, and its inmates' various attempts to escape from it – especially poor Ethel Beluncle's brief dash around the lake, intent on drowning herself – there is a lighter glance at Henry's uxorious colleague Mr Cook, 'who would invite Miss Vanner to his house at Ilford, where she could see his modest work of art: five daughters and their mother, all sitting round a table and making fun of him' (*Mr B*, p. 149).

79. For example, at one stage there was a scene in which, when Henry is courting Lady Roads's daughter, he answers the inevitable English question about where he went to school by saying 'Boyston'. Like the Dulwich of Pritchett's upbringing, it is the name of a smart college, as well as of a town: 'Lady Roads nodded with new approval and her daughter, too. . . . It was impossible for Henry Beluncle to lose this advantage. Anything that would get him out of his past life and which would annul it, he decided to use' (Folder of discarded segments for *Mr Beluncle*, ts pages numbered 32–3, HRC).

80. The cure is not only implausible and melodramatic but over-symmetrical, chiming as it does with her sister's resolve to break with Beluncle and Henry's break with his religion. As far as the novel's losing track of seemingly important details is concerned, another is the boys' discovery of Mrs Truslove's glove at the house their father plans to buy. (And why does Beluncle travel to work by train, when he keeps a car at the office?)

81. Not for want of trying by publishers. There were reissues by Chatto in 1972 and again in 1981, and by OUP in 1986.

Chapter 7

1. Cyril Pritchett to VSP, 17.1.52 (Berg).
2. Gordon Pritchett to VSP, 17.11.51, 24.1.52 (Berg).
3. He mentioned such plans – though in very general terms – in letters to Gerald (2.4.52) and to Norah Smallwood at Chatto. In the latter case he was declining a commission from *Geographical Magazine* 'because I'm so deeply involved at last in short stories and what I hope will prove to be what I ought to be doing: a novel' (10.5.55, C&W).
4. DP to VSP [autumn 1955] (Berg, box 46, folder 2).
5. CE, p. 227.
6. Apparently unpublished. The script is in HRC.
7. HRC has several drafts of an essay on 'Boredom'. Pritchett points out

that boredom was a kind of fashion statement in the work of Byron and Lermontov. He reveals that it was an issue for himself personally and that one of his remedies was 'doodling'.

8. VSP to GB, [pm 14.3.50].
9. VSP to GB, 28.6.52.
10. MO, p. 202.
11. Interview with Josephine Bryant.
12. VSP to GB nd [pm 24.9.53]. Pritchett elsewhere described Janet Stone as 'That rather nice but bazaar opening girl, like royalty'.
13. VSP to GB, 18.2.48.
14. VSP to GB, nd.
15. VSP to Norah Smallwood, 4.1.53 (C&W).
16. VSP to GB, [pm 28.8.49].
17. VSP to GB, 8.5.47.
18. See below, pp. 177.
19. VSP to GB, 28.3.50.
20. VSP to GB, 18.11.49. He was back in Italy the following autumn, lecturing in Rome, Naples, Bologna, Milan, Turin.
21. A. Alvarez, *Where Did It All Go Right?*, 1999, pp. 155–64.
22. VSP to GB, 20.7.[53].
23. VSP to Harold Raymond, 1.2.47 (C&W). The invitation came from Bonamy Dobrée and F. P. Wilson.
24. VSP to GB, 16.10.[53].
25. Ibid.
26. VSP to DP, 14.10.[53].
27. VSP to DP, 22.10.[53]. To Gerald Brenan, Pritchett also described Blackmur as 'unhappy, garrullous [*sic*] & autobiographical'. (VSP to GB, 25.4.[54]). See also VSP to a Mr Fraser, 27.2.77 (Princeton).
28. VSP to GB, 16.10.[53].
29. *Where Did It All Go Right?*, p. 13.
30. VSP to DP, 22.10.[53].
31. VSP to GB, 25.4.[54].
32. VSP to DP, 28.10.[53].
33. VSP to DP, 19.11.[53].
34. VSP to GB, 20.4.[54].
35. A. D. Peters to Chatto & Windus, 13.11.52 (C&W). As a result, Knopf wanted to be able to sell the book in Europe, which Chatto agreed to, under protest. Similarly, the idea for *London Perceived* originally emanated from the American publisher William Jovanovich, as part of a series which appeared in the UK under the Heinemann imprint (see below, p. 198). The publishing history of Pritchett's books provides many other illustrations of transatlantic disputes over territory and other aspects of cultural ownership.
36. Conversation with Susan Sontag.
37. VSP to DP, 16.11.53.
38. Blanche Knopf to Ian Parsons, 4.12.53 (C&W).
39. VSP to DP, 28.10.[53].
40. VSP to DP, 31.10.[53].
41. VSP to DP, nd (Berg, box 42, folder 13).

42. Nd (Berg, box 42, folder 13); DP to Norah Smallwood, nd (C&W).
43. VSP to DP 4[or 9?].12.[53].
44. VSP to DP, nd (Berg, box 42, folder 13).
45. VSP to DP, nd (Berg, box 42, folder 13).
46. VSP to DP, nd (Berg, box 42, folder 13).
47. VSP to DP, nd (Berg, box 42, folder 13).
48. VSP to DP, nd (Berg, box 42, folder 13).
49. *Where Did It All Go Right?*, p. 164.
50. VSP to BK, 26.1.[63] (BK Coll).
51. Interview with Barbara Kerr.
52. VSP to GB, 20.4.[54].
53. He wrote to her with it at Christmas 1962, saying 'I have always used it since for all my writing' (VSP to BK, 20.12.62, BK Coll).
54. VSP to BK, nd but from the context written when he was in Manhattan in 1962, preparing *New York Proclaimed* (BK Coll).
55. VSP to DP, nd (Berg, box 42, folder 13).
56. Interview with Jocelyn Herbert.
57. Frances Partridge, *Everything to Lose: Diaries 1945–1960*, 1985, p. 206.
58. *Everything to Lose*, 27.8.54.
59. He reminded her of this outing in a later letter (VSP to BK, 26.1.[63], BK Coll).
60. Berg, box 40.
61. VSP to R. P. Blackmur, 30.9.54 (Princeton).
62. VSP to Al Alvarez, 7.6.[54] (BL).
63. Ibid.
64. VSP to GB, 7.12.[54].
65. Gamel Woolsey, tr., *The Spendthrifts*, 1953.
66. VSP to GB, 7.12.[pm 54].
67. Conversation with Robert Kee.
68. VSP to Blackmur, 3.1.55 (Princeton).
69. Wyndham Lewis's satirical novel *Tarr* was first published in 1918.
70. VSP to GB, 26.5.[pm 55].
71. 12.5% to 5000, then 15% (C&W, 5.1.55).
72. C&W, 6.1.55.
73. BBC, 16.2.[55].
74. BBC. The recordings were made on 30.3.55 and 31.5.55.
75. BBC, 22.6.55.
76. Notebook (Berg, box 40).
77. NS, 20.8.55.
78. 'The Paris Season', NS, 2.7.55.
79. In a letter to GB immediately after his return from South America in December 1955, VSP said that she had 'drunk no alcohol since June' (28.12.55).
80. VSP to GB, 20.9.55.
81. Crossman was an assistant editor of the NS from 1938 to 1955. He was 'very disappointed in me', Victor later told Barbara (VSP to BK, 26.1.[63], BK Coll).
82. VSP to GB, 1.7.[pm 55].
83. VSP to GB, 25.7.55.

84. Ibid.
85. VSP to GB, 12.8.55.
86. Nd (Berg, box 43, folder 1).
87. VSP to DP, 6.11.[55].
88. VSP to DP, 8.1.[55].
89. VSP to DP, from Hotel Carrera, Santiago de Chile [pm 2.11.55]. Princess Margaret's wish to marry Peter Townshend caused a constitutional crisis because her sister, as Queen, was – and is – head of the Church of England and the Church forbade divorce. The Princess gave in to pressure exerted in part by the then Archbishop of Canterbury, Geoffrey Fisher.
90. DP to VSP, nd (Berg, box 46, folder 2).
91. VSP to DP [pm 8.11.55].
92. VSP to GB, 28.12.[55].

Chapter 8

1. 'Signing the Pledge', NS, 9.7.71.
2. *Encounter*, October 1956; CS, pp. 516–37.
3. CS, p. 537.
4. CS, pp. 351–63. It first appeared in NY, 5.11.49.
5. CS, pp. 391–400. First published in *Harper's Magazine*, February 1948.
6. *Observer*, 29.4.56.
7. 'Two Roast Beefs', NY, 12.7.52; 'Passing the Ball', NY, 5.9.53.
8. He told Norah Smallwood that seeing the volume in the bookshops was 'a comfort to me' (15.6.[56]), C&W). For sales see Norah Smallwood to VSP, 18.6.56 (C&W).
9. Collection of the author.
10. VSP to BK, 17.12.62 (BK Coll).
11. VSP to DP, 13.12.[56].
12. VSP to DP, 12.8.57. There is more than one reference to affairs of Dorothy's in their letters from around this time, but whatever these relationships amounted to, they were well concealed from the children and the details are not known.
13. VSP to A. Alvarez, 23.4.56 (BL).
14. His own description was 'general nervous illness'.
15. VSP to GB, 12.3.[56].
16. VSP to A. Alvarez, 23.4.[56] (BL).
17. VSP to A. Alvarez, 4.6.[56] (BL).
18. NS Archive, 25.7.56.
19. VSP to GB, 4.5.53.
20. VSP to DP, 12.8.57. Early research into alcoholism had suggested that people were more likely to deal seriously with their addiction when they had 'hit the bottom' and that one of the signs of this was their having been left by spouse and children. It was a common assumption that people still living with their families were 'not desperate enough to be helped'. From this, it was a short step to the doctors' advising the spouses of alcoholics to make a temporary separation (Nan Robertson, *Getting Better: Inside Alcoholics Anonymous*, 1988, p. 62).

21. Both book and film appeared on both sides of the Atlantic in 1955. Susan Hayward won an Academy award for her film portrayal of Roth. Another influential film in which AA played a leading role was *Days of Wine and Roses*, which appeared in two versions, first in 1958, then, with Jack Lemmon and Lee Remick, in 1962.
22. Dorothy told her sister Edith these details about her recovery.
23. VSP to GB, 22.12.56.
24. VSP to BK, nd (BK Coll).
25. VSP to GB, 22.12.56.
26. Interview with Claire Tomalin, who in 1963 moved with her family into 57 Gloucester Crescent, which backed on to the Pritchetts' house.
27. Interview with Claire Tomalin.
28. Woolf had been among other things literary editor of the *Nation*, 1923–30, before its merger with the *New Statesman*.
29. 'The Necklace', NY, 15.2.58.
30. VSP to GB [pm 16.4.57]. VSP to Josephine [pm 10.2.57] (JB). There may have been a deeper element in the argument. Of the countries whose literature he most valued, Russia was the only one Victor had never been to.
31. Interview with Nicholas Maxwell.
32. VSP to GB, 18.12.[57]. Pritchett's in fact very interesting essay, the various versions of which are in the *New Yorker* archives along with extensive editorial correspondence about it, convincingly found fault with the translation, especially in its rendering of slang and dialect. The translator, Francis Steegmuller, was an established *New Yorker* contributor and one whom the magazine was at this time wooing particularly keenly but in the face of certain hitches. Katherine White wrote to Steegmuller in April 1957 expressing her 'delight' in his *Madame Bovary* and asking for new stories, but when he promptly sent one, it was declined (13.5.57). This was the situation when Pritchett's review arrived. On 18.6.57, William Shawn sent him a cheque with a diplomatically phrased letter: 'Because of reviews of books that were more pressing, journalistically, we have been forced, sorry to say, to hold out your piece. I wonder whether it would be agreeable to you for us to compress what you have written into one of our briefer, anonymous reviews, so that we can take notice of the Steegmuller book soon.' The piece was duly pared down in successive stages from a long essay to a short unsigned note, but with the unintended consequence that in this form its criticisms were even more prominent.
33. Notebook begun 28.1.57 (HRC).
34. 'The Necklace' appeared in NY, 15.2.58. Pritchett mentions the formulaic aspect of the device in his book on Chekhov, p. 39. Other writers who have used it include Maupassant and James.
35. Interview with Gordon Pritchett.
36. CS, p. 512.
37. Katherine White to Pritchett's US agent, 3.4.56 (NY Archive).
38. NY Archive, box 763.
39. The two writers' friendship went back to 1936. After the lunch party at which they first met, Bates told Pritchett, 'For years I've thought that if

I could win *you* finally over I should be O.K. as a writer' (H. E. Bates to VSP, 11.2.36, OP Coll).

40. They were collected as *The Key to My Heart*, 1963.
41. Edmund Wilson to VSP, 19.4.65 (Berg).
42. Roger Angell to VSP, 27.2.59 (NY Archive).
43. In *When My Girl Comes Home*, 1961.
44. Angell described it in a vivid tribute to Pritchett after his death: NY, 22–9.12.97. The two men's professional dealings are related in detail in an absorbing chapter of Jonathan Bloom's Oxford D. Phil. thesis, *Revision and Vision: The Short Stories of V. S. Pritchett and William Trevor*, 2002, pp. 101–43.
45. See n. 38.
46. Peter Matson to Roger Angell, 8.7.59 (NY Archive).
47. VSP to Roger Angell, 29.5.60 (NY Archive).
48. WMGCH, pp. 9–36.
49. *Listener*, 19.10.61.
50. *Blind Love*, 1969; *The Camberwell Beauty*, 1974; *On the Edge of the Cliff*, 1980; *Collected Stories*, 1982. Nine stories are included in *The Other Side of a Frontier: A V. S. Pritchett Reader*, 1984, which also represents most of the other aspects of his writing.
51. *The War Against Cliché*, 2001, p. 71.
52. CS, 429–40. First published as 'Stage Fall' in *Argosy*, September 1960 (and not to be confused with 'The Diver', which appeared as 'The Fall' when it was published by *The New Yorker* in June 1970).
53. VSP to GB, 14.2.53.
54. CS, p. 432.
55. CS, p. 436.
56. CS, p. 440.
57. LP, pp. 33, 26.
58. VSP to GB, 2.4.52.
59. LP, p. 8.
60. Interview with Gordon Pritchett.
61. 'Marching Life', NY, 22–9.12.97.
62. VSP to GB, 23.1.48.
63. Roger Angell to VSP, 14.10.60 (NY Archive).
64. VSP to DP, nd. 'I've got on a good way with my revision [of 'When my Girl Comes Home'] – I've done about 24 pages – sometimes it seems brilliant, sometimes rather dispersed. I had a stroke of luck at the N.S. when I found a book on Japanese sculpture and when I got it home I discovered in it a good Japanese name for Hilda's husband – Shinji Nishi Kawa who is an art historian in Tokio. I don't know whether you see the beauty of it – Hilda's Indian was called Mr Singh, and Mr Fulmino, in his propensity for error, has supposed Singh and Shingi are the same name. That becomes very funny and I spent yesterday giggling over it. . . .' (Berg, box 43, folder 8).
65. CS, p. 442.
66. See the article on Pritchett by John S. Stimpson in *Dictionary of Literary Biography*, vol. 139, *British Short-Fiction Writers, 1945–1980*, ed. Dean Baldwin, 1994, p. 190.

67. VSP to A. Alvarez, 22.10.74 (BL).
68. CS, p. 456.
69. CS, p. 449. James Wood has written interestingly about the way that 'Pritchett's characters colonize at a time when their country was withdrawing from Empire. They are children of diminishment. . . . [A]s their country once expanded, so they now expand. Each is a pocket imperialist, in a colony of one.' He shows vividly how this works in several other stories. 'There is Peacock [in "The Fall"], anachronistically offering himself, as it were, to Queen Victoria; or the couple in "Sense of Humour", riding in a hearse and imagining themselves royalty. And there is a wonderful moment in . . . "The Wheelbarrow", in which a Welsh taxi-driver . . . suddenly . . . picks up a volume of verse from an old box in the house, glances at it and then throws it down: '"Everyone knows', he said scornfully, 'that the Welsh are the founders of all the poetry in Europe'"' ('An English Chekhov', TLS, 4.1.02).
70. CS, p. 443.
71. VSP to DP, nd (Berg, box 43, folders 4, 5, 6).
72. VSP to John Lehmann, 4.7.46 (HRC).
73. VSP to GB, 2.4.52.
74. William Jovanovich to Ian Parsons, 10.10.60 and IP's reply, 15.11.60 (C&W).
75. In the UK it ran into three editions in two years, the third of them a lavish 'collector's edition' by the Reprint Society, and was reissued by Chatto in 1974. There have been paperback reissues on both sides of the Atlantic, the most recent of them in 1986 by the Hogarth Press.
76. LP, pp. 103–6.
77. Interview with Evelyn Hofer. VSP in conversation with Karl Miller about *Dublin: A Portrait*, 16.6.67 (BBC).
78. LP, p. 46.
79. LP, p. 96.
80. LP, pp. 11–15.
81. He had recently been put up for the Garrick, where he was proposed by Ian Parsons and seconded by John Lehmann. Among the members who signed their names in his support were Osbert Lancaster, Michael Redgrave and Stephen Spender. The process was completed on 7 November 1963 (information provided by Enid Foster, Librarian of the Garrick Club).
82. VSP to BK, 9.12.[60] (BK Coll).
83. VSP to GB, 31.12.[60].
84. VSP to DP, nd (Berg, box 43, folder 8).

Chapter 9
1. VSP to OP, 16.2.62 (OP Coll).
2. DP to OP, 19.3.62 (OP Coll).
3. VSP to OP, 23.3.62 (OP Coll).
4. DP to Brian Murphy, 27.4.[62] (JB Coll).
5. *Two Fathers* was a Crown Film Unit Production, directed by Anthony Asquith.

6. Hitchcock's letters to Pritchett about *The Birds*, and Dorothy's carbon copies of Pritchett's replies and of the passages of extra dialogue he wrote for the film in March and April 1962, are still in the possession of Pritchett's son.
7. Lelie Halliwell, *Film Guide*, 7th edition, 1989, p. 108.
8. VSP to OP, 23.3.62 (OP Coll).
9. 'Across the Vast Land', 1964, reprinted in *At Home and Abroad*, 1989, pp. 218–45.
10. *AHA*, p. 230.
11. MO, 3rd draft ts pp. 84–5 (HRC).
12. *AHA*, p. 233.
13. *London Perceived* appeared in November 1962.
14. VSP to Norah Smallwood, 28.6.63 (C&W).
15. VSP to Norah Smallwood, 11.7.[63] (C&W).
16. *NYP*, p. 86.
17. *NYP*, pp. 95–6.
18. *NYP*, p. 56.
19. *NYP*, p. 58.
20. VSP to BK, nd (BK Coll).
21. Ibid.
22. Ibid.
23. 'I'm no poet,' Pritchett wrote, 'but when I got back from you that night I wrote an obscure poem, a draft which I'll never complete, about our bodies, as discovered ten thousand years hence:
    A bracelet clipped in bones of gilt
    In this embrace – a trinket of the tomb;
    Dead for ten thousand years the silly lovers clip,
    By lust perfected in a hieroglyph.
    Once in this jewel, where sting and wound conjoin
    There smoked a perfume and a choke of cries
    – But who felt what's the secret of closed eyes.
    Written, badly, written I know, under intoxication, in that chilly N.Y. hotel with the wind in the plastic pseudo-Venetian blinds. But with emotion' (VSP to BK, nd). (The letter mentions the death of Hugh Gaitskell, which happened in 1963.) (BK Coll).
24. Miller had been a pupil of Leavis and people suspicious of the Leavisite tendency (among them the *New Statesman*'s historian, Edward Hyams) were particularly suspicious of Miller: see Edward Hyams, *The New Statesman: The History of the First Fifty Years, 1913–63*, 1963, p. 165.
25. Sent to the author by Karl Miller.
26. See below, p. 224.
27. Roger Angell to Peter Matson (*NY Archive*, box 802, 1963). Pritchett responded, uneasily, 'I'm really like Fords at Dagenham (Eng) where they are always going slow or are on unofficial strike' (VSP to Angell, 28.4.63, *NY Archive*).
28. Roger Angell to VSP, 25.2.65 (*NY Archive*).
29. *NS*, 27.11.64.
30. Interview with Peter Matson.
31. Letter to his GP, 18.3.65 (Berg, box 42, folder 1).

32. 'The Liars', *NY*, 21.11.64, CS, pp. 752–62; 'The Nest Builders', *NY*, 11.12.65, CS, pp. 667–77.
33. Edmund Wilson to VSP, 17.3.70 (Berg).
34. CS, p. 669.
35. *NY*, 27.12.69. 'Blind Love' (originally titled 'The Swimming Pool'), which had been rejected by the magazine on 17.10.68, led off the eponymous collection published in 1969. *The New Yorker*'s other apologetic rejections included 'The Cage Birds', 16.9.68 and 'Our Oldest Friend', 30.9.68.
36. VSP to DP, nd [1960] (Berg, box 43, folder 5).
37. *NS*, 25.10.63. Something similar was said in *NYT*, 15.11.64.
38. *NS*, 25.9.64.
39. *ST*, 27.9.64.
40. C&W, 29.12.64.
41. There are various items about this in the C&W files for 1963–4.
42. C&W, 8.5.64.
43. Mary Wilson to VSP, 6.2.65 (Berg).
44. VSP to GB, 4.6.[?40].
45. See, for example, Alfred Knopf to VSP, 30.9.65 (C&W).
46. VSP to Roger Angell, 21.10.65 (NY Archive). The story was 'The Skeleton', published in *NY*, 5.3.66.
47. In Waterloo Road. See above, p. 47.
48. *Dublin*, p. 3.
49. A. D. Peters to Norah Smallwood, 9.8.66 (C&W). Peters secured an advance of £2000 against royalties which began at a generous 15%.
50. *The Lively Arts*, BBC Radio, Third Programme, transmitted 28.6.67 (BBC).
51. *News Chronicle*, 17.3.38.
52. VSP to GB, 1.7.[55].
53. CD, pp. 45–6.
54. 'The Great Snail', CE, pp. 1057–61.
55. CD, pp. 31, 147, 184, 193, 236.
56. *NS*, 23.2.68. A similar point was made later by Francis King, who commented on the lack of rancour in Pritchett's memoirs. 'In spite of his difficult childhood he was a man totally secure, I think,' BBC, Radio 3, *VSP*, 14.12.97 (BBC).
57. *Observer*, 25.2.68.
58. See 'A Plymouth Brother', CE, pp. 234–9.
59. Apart from the reviews mentioned, see also, for example, D. A. N. Jones in the *Listener*, 14.3.68; Janet Adam Smith in *The Times*, 24.2.68.
60. Interview with Peter Matson; NY Archive, box 831.
61. *NYT*, 28.4.68.
62. *Harper's*, May 1968.
63. VSP to Norah Smallwood, 2.3.68 (C&W).
64. VSP to Norah Smallwood, 24.6.68 (C&W).
65. He first went to Smith in 1966–7 as writer in residence and held a series of appointments there, especially as Elizabeth Drew Visiting Professor of English in 1971–2.

66. VSP to Josephine Murphy, nd (JB Coll).
67. VSP to Norah Smallwood, 6.4.67 (C&W).
68. Congratulating Aaron on his forthcoming move to Harvard, VSP told Aaron, 'You really *made* Smith for us' (11.3.72, Daniel Aaron to the author).
69. VSP to Roger Angell, 12.10.66 (*NY* Archive).
70. VSP to James Stern, 1.11.66 (BL).
71. VSP to Roger Angell, 27.1.68 (*NY* Archive).
72. VSP to Norah Smallwood, 13.10.69 (C&W).
73. NY Archive, box 838.
74. Berg, box 12, folder 6.
75. 'The Captain's Daughter', *NY*, 27.12.69; 'The Diver' appeared as 'The Fall', *NY*, 20.6.70.
76. Roger Angell to VSP, 11.11.69 (*NY* Archive).
77. See above, pp. 190–1.
78. In *The Camberwell Beauty*. See CS, pp. 858–70. Documentation concerning the changes to the story is divided between Angell's letters to VSP in Berg, box 49, folder 4, Pritchett's replies in box 851 of the NY Archive and a carbon copy of the ts in various states of correction in Berg, box 12, folder 11.
79. C. Day-Lewis to VSP, 17.12.68 (C&W).
80. Produced by Michael Dunlop for Granada TV and directed by Waris Hussein. Wanamaker played the blind Armitage and Mary Peach his assistant, Mrs Johnson. The adaptation was by James Saunders.
81. VSP to GB, nd but from context *c*. 1950.
82. VSP to GB, 7.11.ny [?50]. The title 'My Oldest Friend' appears in a list of fifteen possible fictional subjects, dated April 1951 (Notebook begun Stokke 1949, HRC).
83. CS, p. 763.
84. CS, p. 773.
85. The letter, written many years later, was prompted by the re-publication of 'Our Oldest Friend' in *More Collected Stories* (Eudora Welty to VSP, 18.12.83, Berg).
86. Pritchett's fiction notebooks for 1969 and 1970 are among those in the Berg (box 40, items 7 and 8). There are also nine notebooks from the later 1970s (box 41).
87. These drafts are in HRC.
88. Jason Epstein to VSP, 5.4.71 (Berg).
89. NY Archive, box 851.
90. VSP to OP, nd (OP Coll).
91. VSP to Josephine Murphy, 13.11.59 (JB Coll).
92. VSP to Josephine Murphy, 30.9.69 (JB Coll).
93. For 'The Marvellous Girl' see above pp. 79–80. The story about the children is 'Cocky Olly', CS, p. 1127.
94. *NS*, 22.10.71.
95. VSP to Daniel Aaron, 30.12.70 (Daniel Aaron to the author).
96. The others were at Columbia, 1978, Sussex, 1980 and Harvard, 1985.
97. John Lahr (ed.), *The Diaries of Kenneth Tynan*, 2001, p. 71.
98. VSP to Norah Smallwood, 26.9.71 (C&W).

99. Frances Partridge, *Ups and Downs: Diaries 1972–75*, 2001, 26.8.72, 1.9.72, 16.8.73.
100. Roger Angell to VSP, 19.6.73 (NY Archive).

Chapter 10

1. For example, Clara Vulliamy, a commission for the Society of Authors.
2. He was also teasing F. R. Leavis, who had written Meredith off. See John Haffenden, *Novelists in Interview*, 1985, p. 226.
3. *Meredith*, p. 33.
4. *Meredith*, pp. 121, 37.
5. 'Meredith', CE, pp. 517–26; 'Meredith's Brainstuff', CE, pp. 711–20.
6. Eudora Welty to VSP, nd [c. 1988] (OP Coll).
7. C&W correspondence, 1973–4.
8. *Balzac*, p. 108.
9. *Balzac*, p. 135.
10. *Balzac*, p. 162.
11. Holmes, *The Times*, 6.9.73; Weightman, *Observer*, 9.7.73.
12. TLS, 14.9.73. The book's illustrations were chosen by Joy Law.
13. Berlin wrote about Turgenev in *Russian Thinkers*.
14. 'A Hero of Our Time' (CE, 44–9) first appeared exactly forty years before *The Gentle Barbarian*, in 1937 (*London Mercury*, 36, 1937, pp. 359–64). See also 'The Russian Day', CE, pp. 319–24, 'Turgenev in Baden', CE, pp. 752–60, 'Spectators', CE, pp. 1133–7.
15. Isaiah Berlin to VSP, 3.2.81 (Berg).
16. *Turgenev*, p. 86.
17. *Turgenev*, p. 202.
18. *Turgenev*, p. 88.
19. *Turgenev*, Acknowledgements.
20. *Turgenev*, p. 175.
21. 'The Vice-Consul', *NS*, 24 & 31.12.76.
22. These paragraphs draw on an interview with Elizabeth Paterson, former Administrative Secretary of PEN; on copies of minutes of PEN meetings supplied by her; and on her book, *Postcards from Abroad: Memories of PEN*, 2001.
23. Notably a special issue of the journal *Les Cahiers de la Nouvelle* (Presses de l'Université d'Angers) in 1986.
24. *Suelos forestales*. Details of these translations are given in the *Index Translationum* and in an interview with Pritchett in 1985 (*Les Cahiers de la Nouvelle*, no. 6, Spring 1986, p. 36).
25. Interview with Elizabeth Paterson.
26. 'Conducted Tour', *NS*, 7.7.56.
27. VSP to Roger Angell, nd (NY Archive, box 882).
28. VSP to A. Alvarez, 3.7.75 (BL).
29. VSP to DP, nd (Berg, box 43, folder 5).
30. Kathleen Dale to VSP, nd (Berg, box 50, folder 1); Julia O'Faolain to VSP, 3.5.76 (Berg).
31. VSP to Daniel Aaron, 12.12.74 (Daniel Aaron to the author).
32. The first relevant item in the Society's archive is from 1940, when VSP contributed to its symposium on 'Authors and War'.

33. Minutes of meeting of International Executive Committee of PEN, 1977.
34. As compared with two in 1975, and three in 1976. In later years the figures are 1978: 6; 1979: 9; 1980: 8; 1981: 4; 1982: 4; 1983: 4; 1984: 5; and thereafter one or two a year until 1987.
35. CS, p. 1024.
36. CS, p. 1032.
37. CS, p. 990.
38. Gathorne-Hardy, *The Interior Castle*, p. 513.
39. According to Pritchett's journal, Gerald first told him and Dorothy about Lynda on 1.9.68. Brenan's cliff metaphor is quoted by Gathorne-Hardy from a letter to David Garnett, 1.5.68, but Brenan tended to repeat himself, and also to be widely quoted among his friends. It seems unlikely that Pritchett's choice of scene was coincidental, though in immediate terms it was certainly prompted by the Cornish holiday in June 1977, to which Pritchett's response was, in his own fashion, no less zestful than that of Harry in his story. He wrote afterwards to Norah Smallwood, 'We've just returned from marvellous blistering sunshine among the spring flowers in Cornwall. Those gallons of Cornish cream and air are stupefying' (6.6.77, C&W).
40. CS, p. 958,
41. CS, p. 957.
42. CS, pp. 964–5.
43. CS, p. 977.
44. CE, p. 1200.
45. Berg, box 30, 'McEwan' – a review of *In Between the Sheets*.
46. Paul Theroux to VSP, 20.2.76 (Berg).
47. As he had been to earlier members of the staff. When Nicholas Tomalin gave up his brief tenure as literary editor of the *Statesman* in 1968, he told Pritchett, 'I would have been lost here without you. I sometimes felt you were editing me rather than I you; certainly your kindness gave me a confidence I lacked' (Nicholas Tomalin to VSP, 7.3.68, NS Archive). Pritchett was particularly taken with Amis. He told Claire Tomalin, 'I think Martin is brilliant and I like him very much indeed' and, when Amis in turn left the magazine, he wrote to him, 'I hope you're going to be doing something that you'll like and that will be good for your great talents' (22.6.77, 19.1.79, NS Archive).
48. Among the differences between their situations was that Oliver's wife, Joan, is a professional writer, the author (as Josephine Haworth) of books about country life and riding.
49. VSP to OP, nd (OP Coll).
50. Norah Smallwood sent an internal memo on 24.6.77 saying that sales of *The Gentle Barbarian* were only 744: 'I don't remember a book by V. S. Pritchett being as low' (C&W).
51. *The Spanish Temper* was reissued by the Hogarth Press, but Jeremy Lewis, Andrew Motion and Jenny Uglow – all of them on Callil's staff – were resistant to *Mr Beluncle* and *Dead Man Leading* (C&W internal correspondence, 21.10.82, 8.12.82, 30.5.83).
52. C&W, 30.5.83. In a 1993 BBC radio discussion about Pritchett's

criticism, Michèle Roberts argued that he wrote too little about women and about gender issues.

53. *Meredith*, pp. 14–18.
54. VSP, BBC, Radio 3, 14.12.97.
55. Interview with Peter Vansittart.
56. Conversation with Mark Amory about the Literary Society.
57. Conversations with Martin Amis and James Fenton, correspondence with Julian Barnes.
58. One of Page's first actions was to scrap the magazine's regular *sottisier*, 'This English'.
59. Miller was by then 'grumping away quite happily' at University College London, VSP told their mutual friend Daniel Aaron, 12.12.74 (Daniel Aaron to the author). (Miller succeeded Frank Kermode as Lord Northcliffe Professor of Modern English Literature at UCL in 1974. While at UCL, he began the *London Review of Books* in 1979.)
60. See, for example, *Observer*, 21.5.78. Among other directors who resigned were Paul Johnson and the paper's manager, John Campbell.
61. Julian Barnes to VSP, 11.5.79, 11.9.79; David Caute to VSP, 27.11.79 (*NS* Archive).
62. Julian Barnes to the author, 19.2.04.
63. Esther Harriott, 'Remembering V. S. Pritchett', *Newsday*, 11.5.97.
64. *NYRB*, 20.7.72.
65. See *The Myth Makers*, 1979, p. 135.
66. *NYRB*, 28.6.79.
67. Brian Murphy was the author of a number of popular non-fiction titles, including *Computers in your Life* (1966), *The Business of Spying* (1973) and *The Angler's Companion* (1978).
68. Notebook, 1986 (HRC).
69. GB to VSP, 15.12.80 (OP Coll).
70. Gathorne-Hardy, *The Interior Castle*, pp. 581–2.
71. By Tyne Tees TV, screenplay by Thomas Ellice, producer Keith Richardson, director Gordon Flemyng.
72. Callil added, 'Note that the T.L.S. of 22nd June 1984, reviewing "The Spanish Temper" said that we shouldn't have done that book but "Marching Spain" (1928) instead. Can we start with a consideration of that book?' (C&W, 4.7.84).
73. Thames TV, *Afternoon Plus 4*, an interview by Mavis Nicholson with VSP on the publication of *Man of Letters: Selected Essays* (1985).
74. Notebook (HRC).
75. *NYT*, 24.3.91.
76. Matthew Pritchett and his wife Pascale had two children while VSP was alive: Edith, born in 1994, and May, in 1996.
77. DP to Mark Le Fanu, 10.2.96.
78. Notebook (HRC).

Index